Empire and the Bomb

EMPIRE AND THE BOMB

How the U.S. Uses Nuclear Weapons to Dominate the World

Joseph Gerson

LONDON • ANN ARBOR, MI

Published in association with

American Friends Service Committee
New England Regional Office

First published 2007 by Pluto Press
345 Archway Road, London N6 5AA
and 839 Greene Street, Ann Arbor, MI 48106

In association with American Friends Service Committee, New England Regional Office,
2161 Massachusetts Ave., Cambridge, Massachusetts 02140, USA.
www.afsc.org/pes
E-mail: afscnero@afsc.org

www.plutobooks.com

British Library Cataloguing in Publication Data
A catalogue record for this book is available from the British Library

Hardback
ISNB-13 978 0 7453 2495 1
ISBN-10 0 7453 2495 9

Paperback
ISBN-13 978 0 7453 2494 4
ISBN-10 0 7453 2494 0

Library of Congress Cataloging in Publication Data applied for

10 9 8 7 6 5 4 3 2 1

Designed and produced for Pluto Press by
Chase Publishing Services Ltd, Fortescue, Sidmouth, EX10 9QG, England
Typeset from disk by Newgen Imaging Systems (P) Ltd, Chennai, India
Printed and bound in the United States of America

Dedicated to the memories of Leon and Evelyn Gerson, my parents, and to Hiroshima, Nagasaki, and "Global" *Hibakusha*.

For my son and daughter, Leon and Hannah, and for the rising generation.

Contents

All I ask is that, in the midst of a murderous world, we agree to reflect on murder and to make a choice.

Albert Camus, *Neither Victims nor Executioners*

Power and force are indeed decisive realities in the human world, but they are not the only ones. To make them absolute is to remove all reliable links between men [and women].

Karl Jaspers, *The Question of German Guilt*

In the foreign-policy world, history is power. Who is right or wrong in the past either gives or withholds power today.

Leslie Gelb, Council on Foreign Relations

Acknowledgements

First thanks must go to Lani Gerson, my friend and partner in life, without whose love, patience, and support this book and so much else would not be. In many ways this is Roger van Zwanenberg's book. He encouraged me to go beyond my initial desire to revise and update my earlier book, *With Hiroshima Eyes: Atomic War, Nuclear Extortion, and Moral Imagination*. The following pages draw on that work, but, to my surprise a new and more ambitious book has emerged. Roger was also graciously patient and extended deadlines to help ensure that that this would become "the book." Thank you, Roger. Melanie Patrick, Helen Griffith and Robert Webb of Pluto Press have also been patient and supportive as we have brought *Empire and the Bomb* into the world. Thanks also go to Ruth Willats for her careful copyediting and for helping me keep my endnotes straight.

The American Friends Service Committee has provided me with a rare privilege. Working with the AFSC for three decades has enabled me to explore and live my values to their fullest as an organizer, scholar, and something of a peace movement diplomat. The support provided and tolerance displayed by staff and committee members of the AFSC in New England, many of whom are dear friends, have been essential to this and many other projects and are deeply appreciated. Special thanks go to Joseph Gainza who provided feedback on several of the chapters, who chimed in with the sub-title, and who led the campaign described in Chapter 9, which led Vermont to become the first US state to officially call for nuclear weapons abolition.

Similarly important have been the support extended to me, the lessons shared, and the friendships of many in the Japanese peace and nuclear weapons abolition movements. Foremost among them are Hiroshi Takakusaki and Rieko Asato of *Gensuikyo*; Junko Kayashige, Senji Yamaguchi, Shoji Sawada, Terumi Tanaka, and Satoru Konishi of *Nihon Hidankyo*; and Muto Ichiyo of PP21, AMPO, and *Japanesia*.

"No man is an island," and few ideas are truly original. While they bear no responsibility for my mistakes, friends, colleagues, and teachers on three continents who have encouraged, taught, and struggled with me along the way, must be thanked or acknowledged. Among them are: Walden Bello, Jules Davids, Wilfred Desan, Peggy Duff, Daniel Ellsberg, Cora Fabros, Lawrence J. Friedman, David McReynolds, Zia Mian, Elizabeth Minnich, Kinshide Mushakoji, Chandra Muzzafar, Tony Palomba, Carroll Quigley, Mark Reader, Daniel Boone Schirmer, Hashim

Shirabi, Achin Vanaik, and three generations of nuclear abolitionists who have prepared the way.

The careful reader will note that in this book I am particularly indebted to the work of scholars who have preceded me on this path. Among them are Gar Alperovitz, Barry Blechman, Noam Chomsky, Bruce Cumings, Irene Gendzier, Tsuyoshi Hasegawa, Nguyen Tien Hung, Michio Kaku, Don Oberdorfer, Michael B. Oren, Gareth Porter, Joseph Rotblat, Jerrold L. Schecter, Martin J. Sherwin, William Appleman Williams, and Howard Zinn. Additional thanks go to those who helped with this work in so many ways: Ray Addicott, John Burroughs, Leslie Cohen, Phyllis Cohen, Sam Diener, Jerry Elmer, Joseph Gainza, Hugh Hosman, Oliver Howard, Melinda Knowles, John McAuliffe, Reiko Maeda, Monika Parikh, Suzanne Pearce, Pat Rabby, Luc Schuster, and Wilbert van der Zeijden. Thanks, too, to Eunjung Katsiaficas who helped with the last-minute formatting of the notes.

This book is a publication of the Peace and Economic Security Program of the New England Regional Office of the American Friends Service Committee.

Foreword

By Walden Bello*

This book focuses the reader on the source of global destabilization: not Iran or North Korea but the United States. If countries such as North Korea have moved to acquire nuclear weapons, it is partly—some would say greatly—out of fear that the US nuclear (and conventional) arsenal might eventually be used against them.

And who can blame them? Joseph Gerson shows that ever since the bombing of Hiroshima and Nagasaki, the US has deployed nuclear weapons as the centerpiece of its strategy of achieving and maintaining global hegemony. He documents with admirable scholarship the way that American leaders have not been sparing of the threat to use nuclear weapons to achieve US foreign policy objectives. He shows that whatever may be the differences between the "grand strategies" of the administrations of Bill Clinton and George W. Bush, nuclear weapons have been a centerpiece of their approaches, as it was in previous post-war presidencies. He reminds us that the doctrine of "full spectrum dominance," the cornerstone of which is nuclear arms, did not come into being with George W. Bush. Bush simply took over a doctrine developed under Clinton and pushed its logic to the doctrine of unsurpassable power, the cornerstone of which is the threat of preemptive attack via nuclear and other weapons, resumption of anti-missile defense research and deployment, and development of new nuclear weapons such as the "bunker buster" bomb.

In this illuminating study, Gerson also takes apart the conventional establishment wisdom that "mutually assured destruction" (MAD) or the balance of nuclear terror has had stabilizing effects. Underpinning US hegemony, whether in the Cold War era or in the unipolar era, US nuclear weapons have been profoundly destabilizing in that they provoked resistance to hegemony, part of which was a defensive drive to acquire nuclear weapons capability. Even the efforts of so-called non-state actors to acquire nuclear weapons technology cannot be separated from a desire to achieve "parity" with a nuclear-armed US in order to resist the latter's hegemonic power.

* Recipient of Right Livelihood Award (Alternative Nobel Prize) for 2003 and Professor of Sociology at the University of the Philippines, Walden Bello is also executive director of the Bangkok-based research and advocacy institute Focus on the Global South.

Both the Clinton and Bush administrations framed the key challenge of the times as the prevention of nuclear proliferation. Yet notice is hardly taken of the fact that a great part of the problem stems from the fact that the nuclear powers did not fulfill their side of the bargain. Under the terms of the Nuclear Non-Proliferation Treaty that entered into force in 1970, signatories agreed not to develop nuclear weapons in exchange for the promise of the five nuclear armed states that they would initiate steps toward nuclear disarmament. That side of the bargain was never kept—was perhaps never intended to be kept—and this remains a great disincentive for compliance by many non-nuclear governments. Gerson's book reminds us that the world will not tolerate double standards, whether in human rights, democracy, or in the matter of nuclear weapons.

The perspective provided by this book is valuable because Joseph Gerson is not just an expert in the nuclear question. He is a campaigner who has dedicated the greater part of his life to the abolition of nuclear arms and the achievement of global peace. One of his great merits has been to keep his eye on the central problem and to never waver or be distracted: there may be changes in great power politics and administrations may come and go but the grand destabilizer remains the same: the nuclear strategy and weaponry by which the US maintains its global hegemony. Unless the peoples of the United States and the world are able to push the US to get rid of its nuclear arsenal, there will be no real peace. This book is a forceful reminder of this truth and challenge.

Introduction

In recent years our daily press has again been preoccupied with dangers posed by nuclear weapons. As Cold War fears of an omnicidal US–Soviet thermonuclear exchange faded, the specters of "rogue" nuclear states and non-state terrorists with atomic bombs haunted the world. During the 2002 build-up to the US invasion of Iraq, Vice-President Dick Cheney informed the world that Baghdad had resumed its nuclear weapons program, and Secretary of State Condoleezza Rice insisted that it would be foolhardy to wait for a mushroom cloud to take the Iraqi nuclear threat seriously. Although US intelligence sources reportedly believe that it could be a decade before the clerical regime in Iran has the capability to produce nuclear weapons, the secrecy that long shrouded Teheran's nuclear industry (begun with US assistance) and the Iranian government's insistence that it has a "right to enrich uranium" for power generation are frequently described as posing a mortal threat to regional and global peace. On the other side of Asia, North Korea's communist monarch, Kim Jong Il, is now known to possess nuclear weapons and is believed to have the ability to assemble two additional nuclear weapons a year.[1] China, with its estimated 360 tactical and strategic nuclear weapons, has been identified as the United States' most serious "strategic competitor."[2] And, since the September 11, 2001 attacks on the World Trade Center and the Pentagon, US Republican and Democratic leaders have agreed that potential nuclear attacks by non-state terrorists like al-Qaeda are the greatest security threat facing the country.[3]

Only on the rarest of occasions are deeper questions raised, let alone answered: What drives nuclear weapons proliferation? How and when has the US used its genocidal and omnicidal nuclear arsenal? Has the US honored and implemented its Nuclear Nonproliferation Treaty obligations? Does any nation have the right—legally or morally—to possess and threaten the use of nuclear weapons?

These are the questions addressed in this study, and the answers are profoundly disturbing. As many who have been on the receiving end of US "Full Spectrum Dominance" know, Washington's use and threatened use of first-strike nuclear attacks to expand, consolidate, and maintain its empire have been the principal force driving nuclear weapons proliferation. On at least 30 occasions since the atomic bombings of Hiroshima and Nagasaki, every US president has prepared and/or threatened to initiate nuclear war during international crises, confrontations, and wars—primarily in the Third World. And, while insisting that nearly all other nations fulfill their Nuclear Nonproliferation Treaty (NPT) obligations (India being one exception, and Israel, which has not signed the NPT, falling into a category of its own), the US government has never been serious about its Article VI obligation to engage in "good faith" negotiations for the complete elimination of nuclear weapons. As former CIA Director John Deutch reported, the US never intended to honor its obligation—that was just something it had to say to get what it wanted from other nations.[4]

Over the past six decades the US has used its nuclear arsenal in five, often interrelated ways. These are described in the case studies and histories that follow. First, obviously, is battlefield use, with the "battlefield" writ large to include the people of Hiroshima and Nagasaki. The long-held consensus among scholars has been that these first atomic bombings were not necessary to end the war against Japan, but rather were designed to serve a second function of the US nuclear arsenal: dictating the parameters of the global (dis)order by implicitly terrorizing US enemies and allies ("vassal states" in the words of former National Security Advisor Zbigniew Brzezinski[5]). The third function, first practiced by Harry Truman during the 1946 crisis over Azerbaijan in northern Iran and relied on repeatedly in wars in Asia and the Middle East, as well as during the crises over Berlin and during the Cuban Missile Crisis, has been to threaten opponents with first-strike nuclear attacks to terrorize them into negotiating on terms acceptable to the US or, as in the Bush I and II wars against Iraq, to ensure that desperate governments do not defend themselves with chemical or biological weapons. Once the Soviet Union joined the nuclear club, the US arsenal began to play a fourth role—making US "conventional forces," in the words of former Secretary of Defense Harold Brown, "meaningful instruments of military and political power."[6] As Noam Chomsky explained, Brown was saying that implicit and explicit US nuclear threats were repeatedly used to intimidate those who might consider intervening militarily to assist those the US is determined to attack. The final role of the US nuclear arsenal, deterrence, came into play only when the Soviet Union began to achieve nuclear parity in the closing years of the Vietnam War. This is popularly understood to mean preventing a surprise first-strike attack against the US by guaranteeing "mutual assured destruction" (MAD). Any nation foolish enough to attack the US with nuclear weapons would itself be annihilated. However, Pentagon leaders have testified that deterrence has never been their policy, and they have defined "deterrence" as preventing other nations from taking "courses of action" that are inimical to US interests.[7]

This could include decisions related to allocation of scarce resources like oil and water, defending access to markets, or preventing "conventional" non-nuclear attacks against US allies and clients, i.e. role No. 2, using genocidal nuclear weapons to define and enforce the parameters and rules of the US-dominated global (dis)order.

It is not the thesis of this book that US use and threatened use of nuclear weapons have always succeeded. Instead, the book documents how successive presidents, their most senior advisors, and many in the Pentagon have believed that the use of nuclear weapons has achieved US goals in the past. Furthermore, it illustrates how they have repeatedly replicated what they thought were successful models. In fact, even the atomic bombings of Hiroshima and Nagasaki achieved only one of their two purposes. These first bombs of the Cold War did communicate a terrorizing message to Stalin and the Soviet elite about the capabilities of the new weapons and about the US will to use them. Yet within weeks of the bombings Washington was sharing influence in Korea with Moscow. Four years later, northern China and Manchuria, which US leaders thought they had won with the Hiroshima and Nagasaki bombs, fell into what was seen as the Soviet sphere. In 1954 France declined the offer of two A-bombs to break the Vietnamese siege at Dien Bien Phu, and in 1969 North Vietnam refused to be intimidated by Nixon's "November ultimatum." The US commitment to nuclear dominance and its practice of threatening nuclear attacks have been counterproductive, increasing the dangers of nuclear war in yet another way: spurring nuclear weapons proliferation. No nation will long tolerate what it experiences as an unjust imbalance of power. It was primarily for this reason that the Soviet Union (now Russia), China, North Korea, and quite probably Iran opted for nuclear weapons.

ROAD MAP

A road map can be helpful to readers. Before describing this book's origins, where it came from, let's look forward to where it is going.

The book is organized in what are essentially four parts: 1) framing in the overview chapter, "Deadly Connections: Empire and Nuclear Weapons"; 2) Cold War uses of US atomic and hydrogen bombs from the devastations of Hiroshima and Nagasaki, through repeated preparations and threats of US nuclear first strikes growing out of conflicts, crises, and wars in Asia, the Middle East, and Europe; 3) US post-Cold War use of nuclear weapons; and 4) a concluding chapter about the imperative and possibilities of nuclear weapons abolition.

Chapter 1 provides the analysis for understanding the histories that follow. It begins by examining the taboo against seeing US history as an imperial project, explaining how the country's Founding Fathers modeled their endeavor after Europe's most successful empires. The chapter then outlines the expansion of the US Empire, its structure and functions until the first years of the G. W. Bush presidency. Finally, it documents how the empire was expanded, consolidated, and enforced through nuclear war and threats of first-strike nuclear attacks.

Chapter 1 also contains three elements that challenge conventional wisdom, which is often based more on propaganda, deceptions, and socialization than on phenomenological reality. The author explores the development and use of nuclear weapons—the "cornerstone of US policies"—within the context of "total war." This "revolution in military affairs" first manifested itself during the American Civil War and became the dominant paradigm for so-called "advanced" nations throughout much of the twentieth century. The destructive power of new weapons technologies grew with the industrial revolution and new capabilities which became available with the burgeoning information age. Central to this chapter and to its analysis is the unmasking of the deceptive discourse of "deterrence": the claims and belief that deterring nuclear attacks by the Soviet Union and other nations has been the primary purpose of the US nuclear arsenal and its nuclear doctrines. Detailed here and in Chapter 2 are the lies, propaganda, and censorship related to US nuclear policy which began with the Manhattan Project, and, with the Hiroshima and Nagasaki A-bombings, became essential to maintaining the illusion of legitimacy as US global power came to rely on preparations for and threats of nuclear attack. Drawing on Pentagon testimonies and doctrines, as well as the history of nuclear threats against the Soviet Union and non-nuclear nations, short shrift is made of the shibboleth of "deterrence." Finally, and perhaps most controversially, this book joins *Hibakusha*, leading US scientists who opposed the development of the hydrogen bomb, Hannah Arendt, and others in naming the inconvenient truth that US nuclear weapons and war policies are evil. What else is one to conclude when successive governments have prepared and threatened genocide, even omnicide, to preserve the careers, power, prestige, and profits of a few?

The Hiroshima–Nagasaki chapter explains why these two cities and their people were laid waste by the world's first nuclear weapons, focusing on the determinative factor: gaining strategic advantage and a "hammer" over the Soviet Union for the Cold War that had already begun. The many additional factors contributing to Truman's decision to use the A-bombs against cities with "densely packed workers' homes" are reviewed. Also included is a detailed explanation of why the A-bombings were not essential to end the war on terms acceptable to the US. Most damning is the irrefutable evidence that Truman and his advisors were well aware of this.

This chapter also frames the moral and analytical foundations of this work by providing detailed descriptions of the atomic "hell" inflicted by US leaders to gain short-term strategic and political advantages. Abstractions and clichés have occluded our understandings of what nuclear weapons—even comparatively small ones—mean to human beings and the communities in which we live. To overcome this the deeply disturbing testimonies of *Hibakusha* and reports by the first foreign journalists who made their way to Hiroshima and Nagasaki are quoted at length. These personal testimonies make painful reading, but they are essential to understanding the fundamental evil of nuclear weapons and the deepest meanings of US foreign and military policies, as well as those of other nuclear weapons states. Ironically, the atomic bombings achieved only a pyrrhic victory.

Chapters 3–6 review the evolving Cold War doctrines adopted to reinforce the US global empire, from Dwight Eisenhower's "massive retaliation" through Ronald Reagan's "discriminate deterrence," and delve deeply into the histories of US Cold War nuclear threats. This is done for three reasons: 1) to prove that preserving empire—not deterrence—has been the primary purpose of the US nuclear arsenal; 2) to help readers, especially those in the US, understand how others have experienced the US and its nuclear threats—this should also help readers grasp more completely the forces driving nuclear weapons proliferation and why the US is increasingly seen as a pariah state; 3) finally, by providing a detailed history, the hope is that readers—including scholars—will discern other and similar patterns, some of which may have eluded this author.

This part of the book presents detailed histories of US threats and preparations to launch first-strike nuclear attacks during the Cold War. Contrary to popular conceptions, these histories illuminate that not only did the US enjoy "commanding" nuclear superiority through the first 30 years of the Cold War, but also repeatedly used this to impose its will. Three of these four chapters focus on nuclear threats made during wars and crises in Asia and the Middle East, with the fourth devoted to the Cuban Missile Crisis, during which US leaders believed that there was a 30–50 percent probability that the US would initiate a nuclear war to preserve its prestige and influence (and to protect President Kennedy's political career). Among the lessons to be learned are how Washington's "commanding" nuclear superiority made it possible to exercise global dominance, and that it was when US precincts in the Third World were threatened and attacked—not Washington's European allies—that the world faced the greatest danger of nuclear infernos. We learn that in order to hold "one of the greatest material prizes in the history of warfare"—Middle East oil, which serves as the "jugular vein" of the global economy and still fuels much of the US military machine—the US was repeatedly willing to risk a thermonuclear exchange with the Soviet Union. We also learn that US presidents and other foreign leaders do not fully control their militaries, including their ability to threaten and initiate nuclear wars.

Chapters 7 and 8 examine the ways in which the US has used its nuclear arsenal to extend the "unipolar moment" to permit US elites to continue enjoying the privileges of continued twentieth-century patterns of empire. Included is a brief history of the immediate aftermath of the Cold War, when the US moved to secure and reinforce its control of Middle East oil and its nuclear dominance. Rather than delivering a peace dividend, George H. W. Bush fought a war—backed by preparations for and threats of nuclear war—to demonstrate that "what we say goes," and put forward a strategic doctrine that gave priority to preventing the emergence of any regional or global rivals. Clinton's Pentagon insisted on "full spectrum dominance"—maintaining the ability to dominate any potential enemy anywhere in the world at any level of power. And George W. Bush embraced nuclear weapons with a zeal not seen since the early Reagan years in his administration's campaign to impose what Vice-President Cheney termed "the arrangement for the twenty-first century"—the colonization of time as well as the planet. Along the way, as an expression of "counter-proliferation" policies, Iraq and North Korea were repeatedly threatened with nuclear attack, with additional preparations or threats being made against Iran and Libya.

Common to these three presidencies was their insistence on maintaining the hierarchy of nuclear terror. In addition to pressing funding, development, and deployment for new and more usable nuclear weapons and related systems, the three administrations undermined the NPT by refusing to honor or implement their Article VI obligation to negotiate in "good faith" to achieve the total elimination of nuclear weapons, while insisting that the NPT be made more stringent to prevent the emergence of more nuclear powers.

One of the challenges faced by the author was how to write authoritatively about the US–Iran confrontation in the midst of US-backed European negotiations with Iran, US military and nuclear threats directed against Teheran, and the proxy war being fought between Washington and Teheran in Lebanon and northern Israel as the book was being completed in summer 2006. Facing uncertainties about where the proxy war and wider confrontation would lead, it seemed that little more could be done than to join protests calling for a ceasefire in the Israeli–Hezbollah war and to touch all too briefly on the doctrinal foundation, the specific threats, and the preparations for possible US nuclear attacks against Iran. To that end, readers are reminded that the corollary to the Bush II administration's National Security Statement warned that "We may face no greater challenge from a single country than from Iran." Soon thereafter, the Pulitzer prize-winning journalist Seymour Hersh reported that the Pentagon had presented the White House with plans "for the use of bunker-buster tactical nuclear weapons . . . against underground nuclear sites," and that a target list had been drawn up. Hersh also reported that "American Naval tactical aircraft, operating from carriers in the Arabian Sea, have been flying simulated nuclear weapons delivery missions—rapid ascending maneuvers known as 'over the shoulder' bombing"—for nearly a year. While the Bush administration responded to the resulting uproar by stating that its "preferred path is diplomatic," it also warned that it had "not ruled out military attacks if negotiations should fail."[8] To underline the seriousness of its threat, the Pentagon announced plans to simulate a "low-yield nuclear weapon strike against a hardened tunnel" at the Nevada test site on behalf of the Defense Threat Reduction Agency.[9]

The final chapter honors warnings by *Hibakusha*, scientists, government leaders, and popular movements that "nuclear weapons and human beings cannot coexist." These often courageous figures have taught that another—nuclear weapons-free—world is possible. To reverse humanity's headlong race to nuclear annihilation, they have circulated petitions, marched in the streets, hammered missile nose cones, testified before Congress and the United Nations, developed model nuclear weapons abolition treaties, and struggled at the heights of state power to reach the Promised Land. To understand these efforts and the movement, the chapter opens with a review of the history of appeals for nuclear weapons abolition that began even before the Hiroshima and Nagasaki A-bombs wrought their deadly destruction, and describes UN resolutions, treaty commitments, and the International Court of Justice advisory decision on the illegality of the use and threatened use of nuclear weapons, which have taken popular demands into the realms of state power. The chapter also provides a summary history of popular demands for arms control and the treaties that resulted from both these popular movements and *realpolitik* considerations. Arms control agreements imposed limits, but they also served to identify where and how the nuclear powers would continue their arms races.

Rarely in the "game of nations" does reality change simply because someone has a better idea. As the anti-slavery abolitionist Frederick Douglass remarked, power concedes nothing without a struggle, to which must be added that struggles take place at the ballot box, through art and the realm of ideas, as well as in the streets and halls of power. With the hope that readers will join popular movements for nuclear weapons abolition or build on their noble efforts, an impressionistic introduction to these movements in Europe, North America, and Asia and to the inspired efforts of Nobel laureates and visionary statesmen is provided.

AUTOBIOGRAPHY AND NON-FICTION

There are autobiographical elements in all non-fiction, and these should be identified. As I have sat wedded to my laptop writing this deeply disturbing history, I have frequently been reminded of the lesson taught by Professor Ello in 1965 as he welcomed his charges to Georgetown University's School of Foreign Service at a time when future presidents of the United States, El Salvador, and the Philippines attended the institution. "The study of international relations," he told us, "is analogous to studying the rules of the game among Mafia families."[10] This, of course, was an oversimplification, and while it certainly grabbed our attention, it is not universally applicable. Life-affirming dynamics, not Mafia rules, were at play when the Beatles first performed on American television, when cellist YoYo Ma recorded tangos in Buenos Aires, and when peace activists from across the world meet to share information and coordinate actions. But, in researching and writing the pages that follow, I was repeatedly struck by a deepening awareness that successive US power cliques have seized imperial state power, legally and otherwise. Some who got in the way of US imperial power were assassinated (President Diem in South Vietnam; Salvador Allende in Chile) or threatened with assassination (Fidel Castro in Cuba; Nguyen Van Thieu in Vietnam). Others were toppled through subversion (Mosadeq in Iraq; Sukarno in Indonesia; Jacobo Arbenz in Guatemala). Still others' turf has been invaded (Cuba, Philippines, Vietnam, Iraq, and many more), while the countries of some who refused to play by Washington's rules have been threatened with nuclear annihilation.

Theodore Roosevelt's "big stick" was not for play in the garden, and Richard Nixon was not the only leader to speak like a thug. George Kennan, who conceived the Cold War containment doctrine, advised that the country's "real task" was to maintain "this position of disparity" whereby 6 percent of the world's population enjoyed 50 percent of its wealth. Kennan was clear that "we are going to have to deal in straight power concepts." Dean Acheson, another primary author of US Cold War strategy, believed that "So long as we had the thumbscrew on Khrushchev, we should have given it another turn every day." And the first President Bush, widely thought to have been more refined than his son, repeatedly threatened Iraq with nuclear attacks and bombed the country "into the pre-industrial age" in order to demonstrate that "what we say goes."[11]

A second autobiographical element in this book is the seed that germinated into my research about the relationship between US nuclear war policy and the maintenance of empire. This compelling interest began in the final days of the 1973 Middle East war in the form of an Armed Forces radio broadcast. I was living in Europe at the time, and as I traveled to meet colleagues in Copenhagen, I did my best to keep abreast of news reports about the final stages of the "October War." By the night of October 24, we knew that the war was essentially over. Israel had prevailed and agreed to a ceasefire. Imagine, then, waking to the news that the US military had been placed on a global nuclear alert. As I later learned, and describe in Chapter 6, Moscow had announced its acceptance of an Egyptian proposal that US and Soviet military forces intervene to halt Israeli ceasefire violations and to break the Israeli blockade of Egypt's encircled Third Army, which was in danger of perishing for want of water and food. Henry Kissinger's nuclear mobilization was designed to force the Russians to back off. Having marginalized Soviet influence in the oil-rich "geostrategic center of the struggle for world power," Kissinger was willing to risk nuclear war to preserve this strategic advantage. The linkage between empire and nuclear war, and its implications for the future, thus became undeniable to me.

In December 1981, while in Lebanon, I learned that the country would soon be invaded by Israel. When the invasion came in June 1982, even as 1 million people marched in New York City to secure a halt to the nuclear arms race, the US peace movement remained silent about the possibility that the Middle East war could escalate into nuclear confrontation. The US stood behind Israel, while Moscow backed Syria, and Israel had already threatened to use its nuclear weapons during the 1973 war. This prompted me to have conversations with Daniel Ellsberg who had helped design US nuclear war policies for Presidents Kennedy and Johnson, to read what he and others had written on the subject, and to organize a "Deadly Connections" conference at the Massachusetts Institute of Technology in December 1982. There Ellsberg, joined by Randall Forsberg and others, helped leading figures in the US peace movement understand the linkages between US military interventions and nuclear war.

Amidst a welter of history and details, and drawing on his experiences at the Pentagon and the RAND Corporation, Ellsberg made two particularly cogent points. Like a thief who points his gun at a victim's head during an armed robbery, whether or not the trigger is pulled, US presidents had repeatedly pointed and used their nuclear "guns" during international crises, conflicts, and wars. Citing another gun analogy first used by Franklin Roosevelt's and Truman's Secretary of War, Henry Stimson, Ellsberg taught that in the same way that a gunslinger used his six guns by ostentatiously displaying them as he sauntered down Main Street, US presidents and the Pentagon have repeatedly strutted their nuclear stuff on the world stage. Worse, Ellsberg described in detail how "every US president, with the possible exception of Gerald Ford," had prepared and threatened to initiate nuclear war.[12]

The final autobiographical reference comes from the French writer François Mauriac, who wrote: "No love, no friendship, can cross the path of our destiny without leaving some mark on it forever." The mark of the *Hibakusha*—the witnesses/survivors of the first atomic bombings—pervades what the reader will find here. In 1984, I was privileged to participate for the first time in the annual World Conference against Atomic and Hydrogen Bombs in Hiroshima and Nagasaki. There, at midnight, I first confronted the hypocenter of the nuclear age and Hiroshima's haunting A-bomb Dome. In the cities' museums, I was immersed in history and surrounded by the artifacts of nuclear hell. Still more compelling were the painful memories and powerful testimonies of the *Hibakusha*, some of whom have become dear friends. In addition to their descriptions of what they had endured and witnessed, their words "Never again" echoed the lesson of Auschwitz.

July 27, 2006

1
Deadly Connections: Empire and Nuclear Weapons

> American factories are making more than the American people can use; American soil is producing more than they can consume. Fate has written our policy for us: the trade of the world must and shall be ours.
>
> Senator Albert J. Beveridge, 1897[1]

> If someone holds a classroom full of children hostage with a machine gun, threatening to kill them unless his demands are met, we consider him a dangerous, crazy terrorist. But if a head of state holds millions of civilians hostage with nuclear weapons, many consider this as perfectly normal. We must end that double standard and recognize nuclear weapons for what they are: instruments of terror.
>
> Johan Galtung and Dietrich Fischer[2]

In Hiroshima, as the first anniversary of the notorious September 11 terrorist attacks against the US approached, Senji Yamaguchi addressed the World Conference against Atomic and Hydrogen Bombs in Nagasaki. He is a small disfigured man whose body and mind were seared by the Nagasaki A-bomb almost 60 years earlier. He was blessed with a friendly spirit, clear moral vision, and exceptional courage. At the height of what has been termed the "Second Cold War" in the 1980s, he addressed the UN General Assembly. Over the course of his life, he survived excruciating burns, radiation sickness, more than 20 surgical procedures, countless hospitalizations, and two suicide attempts, resulting from the Nagasaki nuclear holocaust. After beginning his talk slowly, almost quietly, his voice rose to a cry: "I firmly believe that the atomic bombing was the worst act of terrorism in history . . . Nuclear weapons must be completely abolished."

Four decades earlier, in 1965, with the Japanese press reporting that the US had sited hydrogen bombs at its air base in Danang, South Vietnam, Chieko Watanabe had spoken from essentially the same platform as Senji Yamaguchi. As an adolescent in Nagasaki, she was sent to work in an electrical machinery factory and was there on August 9, 1945. The force of the atomic blast crumpled the building, pinning Watanabe's small body, legs akimbo, beneath twisted steel beams, and breaking her back. She never walked again and suffered debilitating radiation sickness. As she addressed the World Conference, Watanabe-san condemned US use of toxic gas and napalm which were "incinerating . . . Vietnam and murdering its people." She also warned that if people did not act, the US would use nuclear weapons against Vietnam, creating still more *Hibakusha*—A-bomb witness/survivors.

This was not hyperbole. Eighteen months later, when US forces were surrounded and besieged at Khe Sanh by at least 40,000 North Vietnamese and National Liberation Force troops, US generals and President Johnson publicly threatened to respond with nuclear weapons. Lyndon Johnson was not the first president to threaten Vietnam with nuclear attack, nor would he be the last. Since the first nuclear holocausts were inflicted on Hiroshima and Nagasaki, there has been a deadly connection between US nuclear terrorism and the maintenance of the US empire.

It is widely understood that the first nuclear bombings were used to bring the war with Japan to an immediate end. Less well known is that the A-bombings were not militarily necessary. Many factors led to the decision to use the bombs, but one was determinative: their roles in winning strategic advantages for the US in the Cold War that had already begun. It is also widely believed that the Nagasaki A-bombing was the last time nuclear weapons were used. This is a fallacy. Secretary of War Stimson understood that having an atomic bomb is like having a "gun on your hip." Its ostentatious display would be terrorizing, whether US leaders chose to pull the trigger or not.[3] Having learned this lesson, and believing that previous US nuclear threats have succeeded, every president since Truman has prepared or threatened nuclear war during crises, confrontations, and wars to preserve Washington's global "sphere of influence." For six decades the US has used nuclear weapons to dominate the world. Washington's genocidal and potentially omnicidal nuclear arsenal and its first-strike doctrines continue to serve as ultimate enforcers of what Vice-President Cheney described as "the arrangement for the twenty-first century."

This chapter begins by introducing Truman's annihilation of Hiroshima and much of Nagasaki in order to gain strategic advantage in northeast Asia and to intimidate Joseph Stalin and other Soviet leaders. Drawing on the work of leading mainstream and revisionist scholars, as well as statements of senior US policymakers, it describes the growth of the US Empire and how it was structured and has functioned throughout most of the twentieth century. The chapter then turns to explore how, with the end of the Cold War, and with Chairman of the Joint Chiefs of Staff Colin Powell complaining that the Pentagon was running out of enemies, post-Cold War US governments aggressively labored to adjust to these new realities: revising strategic doctrines, reconfiguring the US nuclear arsenal and the policies determining when and how it would be used, launching wars to consolidate US control over oil-rich regions, and reorganizing and reinforcing the military alliances that serve as the empire's coercive infrastructure.

The chapter then provides an overview of the history of the more than 30 occasions—the majority in Asia and the Middle East—when US presidents prepared and threatened to initiate genocidal or omnicidal nuclear war. To help readers understand why US leaders have so frequently found it necessary to reinforce "conventional" military operations with nuclear threats, I have drawn heavily on the analyses of US presidents and the testimonies of military leaders, as well as on published military doctrines. The chapter concludes with meditations on the origins of nuclear weapons and nuclear war-fighting doctrines in the modern Western tradition of "total war." In doing so I have moved beyond traditional analysis by confronting the deeply disturbing existential reality that "the cornerstone of US policies" is rooted in evil, threatening human survival and subverting democratic values and practice. I argue that nuclear weapons abolition and the concept of "common security," which played a major role in ending the Cold War, offer humanity the most realistic alternatives to security and survival.

AN IMPERIAL HAMMER

Although it is not widely known beyond academia, the consensus today among informed scholars is that the atomic bombings of Hiroshima and Nagasaki were unnecessary. As Gar Alperovitz wrote on the 50th anniversary of the atomic bombings, "[A]lternatives to the bomb existed and . . . Truman and his advisors knew it."[4] As the decoded intercepts of Japanese diplomatic correspondence informed Truman and his senior advisors, Emperor Hirohito was seeking to end the war on terms they would eventually accept. In fact, senior US military leaders advised against using the new weapon for a host of reasons, including hallowed precepts of the laws of war.[5] Nonetheless, Secretary of State Byrnes and Secretary of War Stimson pressed the use of the A-bomb for its "salutary effect on relations with the Soviet Union."[6]

Stimson was more conflicted than Byrnes. He confided to Truman that with the US fire bombings that had razed nearly every major Japanese city to the ground, and with the atomic bombings that were to come, the US could "get the reputation of outdoing Hitler in atrocities."[7] But he also calculated that if the atomic bombs ended the war against Japan before the Soviets launched their East Asian offensive, Russian influence in Asia could be limited to the concessions made by Roosevelt at Yalta.

Byrnes' arguments were more primitive and parochial. Like Stimson, he was "anxious to get the Japanese affair over with before the Russians got in." He also anticipated that "after [the] atomic bomb Japan will surrender and Russia will not get in so much on the kill, thereby being in a position to press claims against China."[8] Like Truman, he spoke in terms of revenge, justifying the atomic bombings as appropriate vengeance for the bombing of Pearl Harbor and the loss of US lives. Byrnes was also anxious to reinforce his protégé's political future, warning Truman that he could lose the 1948 election if the electorate learned that the US had spent $2 billion to build the bomb and then had not used it.[9]

Thus, to impose an immediate end to the war before the Soviet Union could seize northern China, Manchuria, Korea, the Kurile Islands, and Hokkaido in northern Japan; to terrorize the Soviet leadership for the coming Cold War; and to insulate Truman's political ambitions, the people and cities of Hiroshima and Nagasaki were sacrificed on the altar of nuclear imperialism.[10]

As Robert Oppenheimer and other Manhattan Project scientists anticipated, the Hiroshima and Nagasaki bombs set off a second chain-reaction: the proliferation of nuclear weapons. Other nations followed suit, seeking to counter or to emulate Washington's ability to practice nuclear terrorism. First came the Soviet Union and Britain, then France and China. They, in turn, were followed by Israel, India, Pakistan, and North Korea.

EMPIRE AND TABOO

In the last years of the Cold War, the historian Howard Zinn paid homage to George Orwell's insight that governments work to control the past in order to control the present and the future. He explained that "[I]f the American people are . . . not given the information about the history of American intervention in the world, it is as if we were all born yesterday . . . the president's speech on TV becomes the only fresh bit of information we have, and . . . if he says 'Ah, we're in danger in the Caribbean, the Russians are threatening us here and there' without a sense of history you believe that."[11]

Without an understanding of US history, especially the growth and development of its empire, the atomic bombings of Hiroshima and Nagasaki and Washington's subsequent practice of nuclear terrorism are incomprehensible. In fact, the US nuclear arsenal has been the "big stick" used by three generations of leaders to enforce US global dominance. Although many US Americans are subconsciously aware of the empire, which reached its zenith in the last years of the twentieth century, few acknowledge its existence.

While most US Americans are ignorant of their nation's imperial history, it is widely understood in capitals and *barrios* around the world. Chandra Muzzafar, the renowned Malaysian political and religious scholar, described the US Empire and how it works in an open letter addressed to the heads of state gathered in Indonesia to celebrate the 50th anniversary of the Bandung Conference. The 1955 Conference which launched the Non-Aligned Movement flailed colonialism and neocolonialism, and Muzaffar's 2005 letter chastised contemporary leaders' complicity with the US Empire, which he described in the following terms:

> global hegemony of the powerful is, perhaps, even more real today than it was in the past. The starkest manifestation of this is . . . Washington's military hegemony. With 800 military bases that gird the globe and a military dominance that stretches from the inner depths of the ocean to the outer reaches of space, how many other nations on earth argue that [they are] truly independent and sovereign in the face of such formidable fire power? While its military might is the fulcrum of its global hegemony, Washington also seeks to maintain its dominance in other spheres. In international politics . . . a government that challenges, even obliquely, a decision which is at the heart of Washington's foreign policy is bound to incur the wrath of the world's sole superpower. . . . Washington is not adverse to subverting any economic move at the regional or international level which it perceives as inimical to the neo-liberal capitalist global structure that it helms. Through the information it provides and the entertainment it promotes, the US has also popularized a global culture which threatens to marginalize other value systems and worldviews . . . .
>
> While Washington is at the apex of this hegemonic global power structure, other capitals from London and Tel Aviv and Tokyo and Canberra are integral to it . . . [12]

Although Professor Muzaffar's analysis is consistent with thinking in the elite Council on Foreign Relations and with many neoconservatives who populated the second Bush presidency, it is not what most US Americans have in mind when they pledge allegiance to the flag or sing the national anthem at the beginning of the school day or at the start of sporting events.

Why this disjunction? The sophisticated system of US censorship, self-deception, conscious and unconscious national chauvinism, and insecurities within the media and academia have combined with the dishonesty of many politicians to make it difficult for US Americans to think freely or to see reality as it is experienced by others. Few are aware that the US today is more empire than democracy, or that since 1945 successive governments have prepared and threatened nuclear attacks to expand and maintain the empire.[13]

For nearly a century, until US neoconservatives began using the words "imperialism" and "empire" to describe the US project, these terms were taboo in scholarly and political discourse, and in "polite circles." To use them resulted in marginalization and in many cases the loss of livelihood. This national self-deception, from the invasions of Cuba and the Philippines in 1898, through World War II, Vietnam, and the invasions of Iraq, has made it difficult for most US Americans to understand their country's role in the world or the terrorism on which US global power and privilege are based.

An intriguing aspect of elite and popular imperial denial is the fact that for years, in schools across the country, young people have been taught, implicitly and explicitly, that as Rome was to Athens, so the US is to the British Empire. Left unstated is the reality that, as Zinn has written, "[w]hat the experience of Athens suggests is that a nation may be relatively liberal at home and yet totally ruthless abroad . . . An entire nation is made into mercenaries, being paid with a bit of democracy at home for participating in the destruction of life abroad."[14] Recall that it was "democratic" Athens' insistence on maintaining its empire that resulted in the Peloponnesian War and Athens' subsequent decline.[15]

For a century, many euphemisms were used to enforce this dual thinking and to cope with the taboo. As World War II drew to a close, the Council on Foreign Relations planned for the management of "The Grand Area."[16] Throughout the Cold War, the terms "the free world" and "US sphere of influence" were used to refer to the US dominion. Late in the Cold War, when he found it necessary to refocus the thinking of the US foreign policy establishment, Zbigniew Brzezinski, the founding Director of the Trilateral Commission and President Jimmy Carter's national security advisor, was among the few in the US establishment to ignore the proscription. He began his article "America's New Geostrategy," in the journal *Foreign Affairs*, with the words: "The rumors of America's imminent imperial decline are somewhat premature."[17]

Scholars, including Noam Chomsky, William Appleman Williams, Howard Zinn and others who named and analyzed the history of US Empire, have been recognized for their unique courage as well as for their exceptional scholarship. Not until the second Bush presidency, when Washington adopted the language of unilateralism and dispatched its legions to invade Afghanistan and Iraq to consolidate US control over the world's oil supplies, did influential neoconservatives and liberals acknowledge their endorsement of the US imperial project.[18] Doing so earlier would have impeded popular mobilization in the first decades of the post-colonial era, and it would have undermined support for US foreign and military policies throughout the Third World and in Europe. However, as Niall Ferguson and others have argued, in the post-Cold War era, to preserve the empire it became necessary to affirm its existence and to draw explicitly on the lessons and precedents of previous empires. In one of the first forays into normalizing the post-Cold War imperial discourse, Walter Russell Mead, of the Council on Foreign Relations, taught that the US was simply one of a long line of great nations and empires that "have been shining and stinking since the start of recorded history."[19]

From Iraq to Singapore and from the Bahamas to Diego Garcia, much of *Pax Americana* has been built on the ruins of *Pax Britannica*. Like the British, US governments "have excelled in discovering reasons that obligated them to conquer the world."[20] This exceptional US destiny has been articulated across two centuries in the Monroe, Truman, Eisenhower, Nixon, Carter, and Bush Doctrines. It has been manifested through repeated wars and in more than 200 military "interventions," from Tangiers to Tokyo.[21]

Unlike the English, who were taught to value empire and were inspired to fight to maintain the *imperium* because, among other things, it kept down the price of tea,[22] the US public was long insulated from the reality that the US Empire exists to serve the elite. In addition to ensuring profits by means of securing privileged access to other nations' raw materials, labor, markets, and technologies, empire has been seen as a way to maintain "social peace" within the country by providing jobs and thus ensuring economic security.[23] The few who are still aware of the Lend-Lease Agreement with Britain or the wartime Anglo-American alliance, usually fail to note that Britain was saved from Nazi Germany by the US at the expense of its global empire. Similarly, few in the US know that the 1941–45 war against Japan grew out of two centuries of imperial competition for influence and control in China. That Chinese political culture continues to be profoundly influenced by the sufferings wrought in the course of this imperial history is shocking information for most US Americans.

Amidst the denial, the US "national security" elite has presided over and led a complex imperial system, the broad outlines of which most literate US Americans have unconsciously internalized. As Mead explained in his seminal work *Mortal Splendor*, a first tier of nations has long shared the benefits and costs of *Pax Americana*. These "junior partners" included Japan, the other G-7 nations, and Western European liberal democracies whose "opinions on important issues [were] usually solicited—if not always deferred to." A second tier of nations have been those "whose economic and political situations hover[ed] between first- and third-tier conditions": for example, Saudi Arabia, Singapore, Korea, Greece, and Brazil. They have "enjoy[ed] much less freedom from external intervention in their domestic affairs" and were "more vulnerable to economic coercion" by Washington and by first-tier nations. At the bottom of the imperial pyramid are the Third and Fourth World nations of the Global South, countries such as El Salvador,

East Timor, Mozambique, Afghanistan, Haiti, Egypt, and Kuwait. They have had "minimal representation in the councils of empire," and their "national governments in many cases are solely the representatives of foreign powers."[24] In addition to functioning on state-to-state levels, the system has been reinforced by complex international institutions including the United Nations, the World Bank, and International Monetary Fund, and more recently by the World Trade Organization. One of the central questions of the twenty-first century is what capitalist China's relationship to this system will be.

While British imperial cultural influences and political models predominated in shaping the US imperial state and culture, it has been influenced by other forces. Though twice defeated in world wars, Prussian military culture found a host on the western shore of the Atlantic Ocean. To defeat Germany, US political culture, its military, and its society were transformed in ways that mimicked German models, including the creation of the military-industrial complex. Even in the early years of the Cold War, outgoing President Eisenhower found the forces of this complex so subversive of democracy that he warned the country about its "total influence . . . in every city, every statehouse, every office of the Federal Government."[25]

The assumption of US superiority, righteousness, and munificence which are essential to a culture of dominance and empire are deeply ingrained. For decades, World War II was incessantly relived and mythologized on television and cinema screens in documentaries, dramas, and comedies. For baby-boomers, Sunday television began and ended with lessons and propaganda about US military prowess. The Army's *The Big Picture* greeted children at sunrise and the Navy's *Victory at Sea* was screened before bedtime. Recasting the war in the then still strong colonial settler mentality, the image of the US as the reluctant but always successful warrior-nation came to movie theaters as *Shane* and *High Noon*, and was omnipresent as televised cowboy westerns. The message was clear: use of deadly force was as American as apple pie.

Trend-setting Broadway musicals also provided archetypes through which US Americans came to understand themselves and their places in the world. Like the English and Germans before them, "Americans" were to see themselves as a superior people, with the responsibility to refashion the world in their image, and when necessary to serve as the "world's policeman." Thus, in *The King and I*, our white English cousins introduced an Asian monarch to modernity. In *South Pacific*, US Americans were an anti-racist and civilizing force in a land where "Bloody Mary's chewing beetlenuts." And in *Camelot*, the play appropriated by the Kennedys to market themselves, US Americans were encouraged to dream what it would be like "If I Ruled the World." This megalomaniacal fantasy, later institutionalized as the post-Cold War doctrines of the "New World Order," "full spectrum dominance," and "unilateralism" was so consistent with the times that it was recorded by many of the nation's leading crooners.[26]

The course of empire has its costs, or as Mead reminded readers, its stench. People are killed, often brutally, and in great numbers. Racism is reinforced, and hatreds—sometimes enduring for generations or centuries—are created. Even the most powerful economies can be devastated and distorted in the course of preparing for and fighting endless wars. Democratic values, truth, and individual freedoms are the inevitable first casualties of war and empire. The war in Vietnam and secret bombing of Cambodia led inevitably to the constitutional crisis called "Watergate."[27] A generation later, the shame of systematic torture in the "gulag" extending from Guantánamo to Abu Ghraib and Afghanistan was an unavoidable consequence of wars waged in alliances with warlords, monarchs, and dictators.

Despite its rhetoric of freedom, US wars of intervention, its subversion of foreign governments, and its support for military, dictatorial, and authoritarian regimes have been a function of US policy decisions. Two years after the atomic bombings of Hiroshima and Nagasaki, George Kennan, author of the Cold War "containment doctrine," described the framework and goals of the US Empire in a 1948 TOP SECRET memorandum while serving as the head of the State Department's Policy Planning Department:

> We have about 50 percent of the world's wealth, but only 6.3 percent of its population .... In this situation, we cannot fail to be the object of envy and resentment. Our real task in the coming period is to devise a pattern of relationships which will permit us to maintain this position of disparity .... We need not deceive ourselves that we can afford today the luxury of altruism and world-benefaction .... We should cease to talk about vague and ... unreal objectives such as human rights, the raising of the living standards and democratization. The day is not far off when we are going to have to deal in straight power concepts. The less we are then hampered by idealistic slogans, the better.[28]

Half a century later, after Western Europe and Japan had recovered from wartime devastation, President Clinton echoed Kennan when he stated that "We have four percent of the world's population, and we want to keep 22 percent of the world's wealth."[29] This helps to explain why the first major commitment Clinton made on assuming the presidency was his promise not to cut the military's budget, despite the end of the Cold War.

As demonstrated in Clinton's "divide-and-rule" approach to Europe and the publicly announced inspiration taken by senior figures in the second Bush administration from late nineteenth-century founders of the US Empire,[30] the end of the Cold War marked a return to earlier imperial patterns. From Cuba to China, US presidents again explained foreign and military policies in terms of access to markets, human rights, and the advance of civilization—much as their predecessors had done a century earlier. Once again, as the poet Edna St. Vincent Millay wrote early in the twentieth century, there was "fighting in the Balkans."[31] US Marines returned to Haiti in the name of "democracy," while the CIA connived to restore oil-rich Venezuela to its "proper" role as a prize US estate. While turning a blind eye to client dictators and warlords, so-called "humanitarian" military interventions in Haiti, Kosovo, and East Timor served to expand or maintain US influence and to provide political legitimacy for the military establishment and its budget. Oil, however, remained "the prize." As oil-rich nations approached peak production and global demands for oil soared, the rhetoric of democracy was again used to mobilize the US American people for war and to mismanage generational political transitions in strategically important Middle East nations.

In the midst of this complex set of diplomacy and wars, Washington's ultimate enforcer remained "the bomb."

A SUCCESSION OF IMPERIAL DOCTRINES

As the end of the Cold War began to be anticipated, the Reagan administration prepared the way for the new era with a report and doctrine titled *Discriminate Deterrence*. Developed by the Pentagon's bipartisan Commission on Integrated Long-Term Strategy, whose members included leading figures in the establishment—Henry Kissinger, Zbigniew Brzezinski, General Andrew Goodpaster, General John Vessey, Samuel Huntington, and others—the report called for a global strategy to ensure that the US remained the dominant global power for "the long term."[32]

The Commission's diagnosis and prescriptions were clear: Japan and Western Europe were beginning to challenge US global hegemony.[33] The power of US "conventional" weapons was declining relative to several increasingly well-armed Third World nations, and as many as 40 countries could become nuclear weapons powers by the year 2010. To remain the world's dominant power, the US should no longer attempt to control developments in every part of the world. Instead, it recommended that US power and resources focus on three regions: the Persian Gulf (to control the world's oil supplies and the national economies dependent on that oil), the Mediterranean (to control Europe and the Middle East), and the Pacific Ocean (to control Japan and other emerging Asian-Pacific economies). As Washington faced difficult budget choices, the Commission recommended that the Pentagon give priority to modernizing its nuclear arsenal, to increasing air- and sea-lift capabilities for rapid military intervention, and to investing in high-tech weaponry.[34]

The "vision" for the 1990–91 "Desert Storm" war fought to oust Iraqi forces from Kuwait and to create what Bush called a "New World Order" for the post-Cold War era was rooted in *Discriminate Deterrence*, but it also reflected a new doctrine that was not articulated until after the war. Preparations for the war and the US assault were designed to achieve multiple goals: to reassert US control over Middle East oil reserves (the "jugular vein" of global capitalism), to discipline US allies and reaffirm US military alliances, and to terrorize the world's nations in a "demonstration war." These objectives went well beyond *Discriminate Deterrence*'s prescriptions.

Under the leadership of Secretary of Defense Cheney and his assistant Paul Wolfowitz, a new doctrine was developed, the initial draft of which was leaked to the press shortly after the "Desert Storm" war. This "Defense Policy Guidance" bluntly described the Pentagon's dangerous and ambitious commitments: "Our first objective," it read, "is to prevent the reemergence of a new rival." Although the doctrine named North Korea as the focus of concerns in Asia, this was a euphemism for containing China's rising power. In the Asia-Pacific region, the report read, "we must maintain our status as a military power of the first magnitude."[35] China was not explicitly named as a strategic competitor because doing so could have crystallized the emerging US–Chinese competition before Washington was prepared to do so.

The Clinton years were less "a bridge to the twenty-first century" than the span between the two Bush presidencies. Although the Cheney–Wolfowitz strategy document was ostensibly withdrawn after being leaked, it was never officially rescinded. In Asia, the Clinton administration worked to integrate China into the US–Japanese-dominated system through often conflicting commitments to diplomatic and economic engagement and military threats. To preserve US influence in Europe, Clinton and his senior advisors focused on providing new rationales for NATO to legitimize the continued presence of US forces—including nuclear weapons—across the continent. By working to expand both NATO and the European Union, it laid the foundation for playing what Donald Rumsfeld would later call "New Europe" against the "Old."

In its final year, the Clinton Pentagon came up with a new slogan for an old ambition: "full spectrum dominance." In the traditions of Alexander the Great, Julius Caesar, and Genghis Khan, the new doctrine of escalation dominance spelled out the commitment to achieve and maintain the ability to dominate any nation, at any time, at any level of power—including first-strike nuclear attack.

The Bush II–Cheney administration that followed brought new intensity to "full spectrum dominance." It also introduced a radically different, and disastrous, vision of how to run the empire. Its National Security

Statement echoed Francis Fukuyama's boast that the end of the Cold War marked the "end of history." The Statement declared that the US political and economic systems were the single model for prosperity. US military power so far exceeded that of any potential rival that the administration believed it could impose what Cheney termed "the arrangement for the twenty-first century."[36] Instead of soliciting the opinions and support of "second-tier" nations, the Bush Doctrine stated that nations were "either for us or against us." Those who were "against us" would have to anticipate the consequences of US-enforced diplomatic and economic isolation and the devastations of US unilateral "shock and awe" military attacks and extended occupations. Going beyond Bush I's "New World Order," the Strategy Statement implicitly threatened both China and the European Union. Preemptive attacks, the doctrine stated, were warranted to prevent the *emergence* of potential regional or global rivals. Such rivals need not attack or threaten the US with attack to be destroyed. This openly articulated commitment to aggression was unprecedented in US history.

Following the collapse of the Soviet Union, most people in the US and elsewhere believed that the danger of nuclear war had been contained, if not completely eliminated. Unfortunately, US leaders continued to honor Roosevelt's admonition about the importance of carrying a "big stick." Despite the loss of the Soviet enemy and the International Court of Justice's ruling on the illegality of nuclear war, not to mention nuclear weapons abolition campaigns launched by retired senior US military officers and traditional peace movements, post-Cold War US governments continued to rely on implicit and explicit threats of nuclear attack to reinforce US power and ambitions.

True, Bush Sr.'s 1991 decision to reduce the dangers of nuclear war by ordering redeployment of most tactical nuclear weapons to bases in the US, to which President Mikhail Gorbachev responded with reciprocal orders, did decrease the danger of nuclear war. And those who were led to believe that he supported a fissile material cut-off treaty also found it a source of hope.[37]

These initiatives, however, were not the full picture. The "Desert Storm" victory over Iraq was made possible in part by the US nuclear terrorism that preceded it. A series of nuclear threats were communicated, orally and in writing, to Saddam Hussein and his foreign minister by President Bush, Vice-President Dan Quayle, Secretary of Defense Dick Cheney and UK Prime Minister John Major,[38] and an estimated 700–1,000 nuclear weapons were deployed to the countries and seas surrounding Iraq. In a chilling example of how deeply nuclear war-fighting has been integrated into day-to-day military planning, General Norman Schwarzkopf forwarded a proposal for the use of tactical nuclear weapons against Iraqi targets to the Pentagon for approval.[39]

With the deterioration of the Russian nuclear arsenal and its related infrastructure, President Clinton pressed the US nuclear advantage. In response to the International Court of Justice's consideration of the legality of the use and threatened use of nuclear weapons and calls by retired generals and admirals to abolish nuclear weapons, Clinton informed the world that nuclear weapons would remain "the cornerstone" of US policy. With this commitment, reinforced by his political insecurities, the Clinton administration backed away from efforts to negotiate a fissile material cut-off treaty, and the administration initiated no significant arms reduction negotiations. Throughout the Clinton era, 15,000 strategic and tactical nuclear weapons remained on alert or were stockpiled for possible use.[40]

More dangerous was the Clinton administration's initial approach to North Korea, which was widely believed to have developed an undeclared arsenal of between two and four atomic bombs. Although North Korean missiles could not reach the US, South Korea and Japan were within range. Not comprehending that an impoverished but proud nation might not jump immediately to the US tune, Clinton, in 1994, continued the tradition of threatening North Korea with nuclear attack, and in doing so strayed perilously close to a nuclear cataclysm.

Despite the apparently radical differences between Bush I's and Clinton's multilateralist approaches and Bush II's arrogant unilateralism, there was considerable continuity in nuclear doctrines. Counter-proliferation policy was inaugurated as US policy in the Clinton Nuclear Posture Review, laying the foundation for Bush II's Strategic Proliferation Security Initiative, for the Bush–Cheney assault on the Nuclear Nonproliferation Treaty, and for Bush II era nuclear threats against Iraq, Iran, and North Korea. The Clinton administration's and Congressional Democrats' support for "missile defense" research and development made possible Bush II's deployments of what Chinese officials warned was a shield to complement the Pentagon's first-strike nuclear swords.

The Bush–Cheney administration's passion for and commitment to preparing and threatening first-strike nuclear wars were different and reminiscent of the first years of the Reagan presidency a generation earlier. To reinforce the imposition of Vice-President Cheney's "arrangement for the twenty-first century," the pre-inaugural recommendations of the neo-conservative Project for the Twenty-First Century were rapidly transformed into national policy. In its 2002 Nuclear Posture Review, the Bush II administration reiterated its commitment to first-strike nuclear war-fighting, named seven nations as primary nuclear targets, and urged funding for the development of new and more usable nuclear weapons. It mandated accelerated preparations at the Nevada test site to ensure that new weapons and stockpiled warheads could reliably inflict nuclear holocausts in the future.

It also pressed expansion of the nuclear weapons laboratories to design and develop a new generation of nuclear weapons to reinforce US nuclear dominance through most of the twenty-first century. Although there were major differences between father and son, Bush Jr. followed in his father's tradition in at least one regard. During the run-up to the 2003 invasion, Iraq was again threatened with nuclear attack.[41] As in the past, these post-Cold War nuclear policies, preparations, and threats went largely unnoticed and unremarked. Instead, US nuclear consciousness was molded by alarms about "loose nukes" and the nuclear ambitions of "rogue" regimes.

Some of these fears were legitimate. In the immediate aftermath of the Soviet Union's collapse, a major concern was that Ukraine's nuclear arsenal, inherited from the USSR, made it the world's third most powerful nuclear power. This, it was feared, would "force" Germany to become a nuclear state. India and Pakistan gate-crashed the nuclear club, and were briefly declared outlaw nations for refusing to surrender their newly demonstrated nuclear arsenals. On Russia's southern flanks, Ukraine and Kazakhstan *each* had more nuclear weapons than France, Britain, China, Pakistan, India, and Israel *combined*. North Korea did indeed have a nuclear weapons program, and it was widely feared that if Pyongyang demonstrated its nuclear capabilities, Japan, South Korea, and possibly Taiwan would follow.

As is now well known, other fears were manufactured and manipulated to provide political cover and to mobilize US Americans for "regime change" wars in oil-rich nations. In a disinformation campaign that will undermine US credibility for decades to come, Bush II and his senior advisors mobilized the US and its allies for the invasion of Iraq with a series of lies about what proved to be Baghdad's nonexistent nuclear weapons program and an illusory stockpile of chemical and biological weapons of mass destruction. Cheney announced that he was "convinced that Saddam will acquire nuclear weapons fairly soon," and that "[t]he risks of inaction are far greater than the risks of action." Condoleezza Rice warned that "we don't want the smoking gun to be a mushroom cloud." Secretary of Defense Rumsfeld testified that Saddam Hussein's "regime is determined to acquire the means to strike the U.S., its friends and allies with weapons of mass destruction." Iraq, he said, was "seeking nuclear weapons" and had "designs for at least two different nuclear devices." Bush repeated the British disinformation that Saddam Hussein could order an attack with weapons of mass destruction "within as few as forty-five minutes."[42]

With additional fears that weapons-grade plutonium was being smuggled from Russia through Germany and other countries, and with al-Qaeda seeking nuclear capabilities, leading Republicans and Democrats agreed that the greatest danger facing the US was the possibility of "terrorists . . . gaining weapons of mass murder."[43]

Obscured by this hysteria and misinformation was the fact that the US had become, as the *New York Times* editorialized, the "nuclear rogue" driving nuclear weapons proliferation, and that, as the Natural Resources Defense Council reported, the US was "faking nuclear restraint."[44] Missing from all but a few reports and editorials was the understanding that the Bush administration was "clear that nuclear weapons will remain the cornerstone of U.S. military power for the next fifty years."[45]

MYTHS OF NUCLEAR INNOCENCE AND THE PRACTICE OF NUCLEAR TERRORISM

For the vast majority of US Americans, nuclear weapons and nuclear war are distant abstractions, last used, we are repeatedly told, far away and long ago to win the war against Japan. Nuclear weapons are widely believed to have contained the Soviet Union. And, although most US Americans believe that the world would be more secure if no nation possessed nuclear weapons,[46] the common belief is that as long as the "good guys" have the biggest, best, and most nuclear weapons, there is little in the nuclear realm to worry about.

The "Mandarins of Power,"[47] leading scholars who implicitly or explicitly serve the empire, have learned which questions *not* to ask and bear considerable responsibility for this innocence and ignorance. With few notable exceptions,[48] US nuclear weapons scholarship is marked by a fascination with the scientists who won the race to build the first atomic and hydrogen bombs; with so-called "deterrence" theory and the dynamics of the US–Soviet nuclear arms race; and in recent years with the dangers of "loose nukes."

Most of the histories of the Manhattan Project and biographies of its Promethean priesthood (J. Robert Oppenheimer, Ernest O. Lawrence, Leo Szilard, Enrico Fermi, Edward Teller, and others) are framed in unconscious patriotism, influenced by wartime propaganda, by assumptions about the legitimacy of revenge, and by the lies spun by those most closely associated with the decision to eliminate Hiroshima and Nagasaki. The continuing debates about Oppenheimer's early flirtations with Depression-era Marxism and other scientists' collaborations with Senator Joe McCarthy often mask continuing and often covert debates about arms control, nuclear dominance, and abolition. Similarly, accounts of scientists' debates over whether the Japanese should have been warned before the bombings were ordered, whether a demonstration A-bombing of an atoll would have sufficed to win Japan's surrender, and how to control the bomb after the war reflect contention over the moral rectitude of the US.

The most disturbing information about the dawn of the nuclear age has been consigned to an Orwellian memory hole. Absent are Truman's lies to himself and to others that the A-bombs would be used "so that military objectives and soldiers and sailors are the target and not women and children,"[49] that the A-bombs were dropped "to save as many American lives as possible,"[50] and that they were inflicted to "spare the Japanese people from utter destruction."[51] Missing are the accounts of Japanese elite and governmental efforts to negotiate surrender prior to the A-bombings on the terms accepted by Truman *after the atomic bombings*. Finally, political histories of the Manhattan Project and of subsequent US nuclear war policies written within a US frame of reference devote scant attention to the human consequences of the Project's bombs: what actually happened to individuals and their families represented in the abstracted numbers: 40,000, 70,000, 100,000, 210,000—and the survivors scarred physically and mentally for life.

Presented as necessary to "end the war," the mythology about the heroism of the scientists and the necessity of the Hiroshima and Nagasaki A-bombings serve to legitimize continued preparations for nuclear war and thus to preserve US global dominance. A serious political motive lay behind the Air Force's campaign to sterilize the Smithsonian Museum's 50th anniversary commemoration of the Hiroshima and Nagasaki A-bombings and the subsequent "Enola Gay exhibit" at the Air and Space Museum in 2003. Had the museum included information about Admiral Leahy's and General Eisenhower's charges that "it wasn't necessary to hit them with that awful thing,"[52] about Japanese efforts to surrender, and photographs of the ravaged bodies of Sumiteru Taniguchi and other *Hibakusha*, the legitimacy of the first atomic bombings would have been seriously undermined. This in turn would have raised yet more probing questions about the legitimacy of the "cornerstone" of subsequent US foreign and military policies.

Einstein wrote that "Few people are capable of expressing with equanimity opinions which differ from the prejudices of their social environment. Most people are even incapable of forming such opinions." This certainly describes what has passed for mainstream "scholarship" on post-Nagasaki US use of its nuclear arsenal.

Until the post-Cold War era's focus on "loose nukes" and the Korean and Iranian nuclear weapons programs, most US nuclear weapons-related literature concentrated on the US–Soviet confrontation across divided Europe. For decades, the vast asymmetries of US and Soviet power were ignored.[53] Instead, we were urged to "think the unthinkable" with Herman Kahn; to be educated about nuclear weapons and foreign policy by Henry Kissinger; to learn to live with nuclear weapons along with Albert Carnesale and Samuel Huntington; to stem the tide with Glenn Seaborg; to decide with Joseph Nye whether we were nuclear hawks, doves, or owls; and to reduce—but not remove—the nuclear danger with McGeorge Bundy and Admiral Crowe.

This literature vastly exaggerated the deterrent roles of the US nuclear arsenal while understating its offensive first-strike *raison d'être*. As a result, most students and many scholars remain ignorant about the imperial purposes and functions of Washington's nuclear arsenals.[54]

Kept in the dark about the history of US preparations and threats to initiate nuclear wars, US citizens cannot fully engage in constitutional democracy or fulfill their unique role in preventing nuclear war, thus helping to ensure humanity's survival.

TERRORISM NOT DETERRENCE

It has long been commonly believed that deterrence is the primary role of the US nuclear arsenal. The truth is that the US nuclear arsenal has been at least as essential to maintaining the US Empire as it has been to popular conceptions of "deterrence." Most people properly understand deterrence as preventing nuclear attack by threatening a cataclysmic, nation-destroying, second-strike attack against the source of a nuclear attack on the US. But, in 2005, the Pentagon informed the world that this was *not* its understanding. Its unofficial *Doctrine for Joint Nuclear Operations* dictated that "the central focus of deterrence is for one nation to exert such influence over a potential adversary's decision process that the potential adversary makes a deliberate choice to refrain from a COA [course of action]."[55] In the 1950s and early 1960s this meant dictating the parameters of Soviet and Chinese support for Vietnam. Four decades later, consistent with the Bush Doctrine, it included preventing the emergence of rivals to US regional and global dominance. With the exception of the relative US–Soviet nuclear parity from the mid-1970s to the late 1980s, the US has enjoyed a "dramatic imbalance of [nuclear] power,"[56] which it has used to expand and to maintain its "Grand Area."

Much of the historical record remains hidden in classified government files, but the memoirs of presidents and their aides, the public record, and scholarly research reveal the damning and little explored history of US nuclear terrorism and extortion. The low points of this history are many: Truman's 1946 threat to annihilate Moscow if the Soviet Union failed to withdraw immediately from Azerbaijan province in northern Iran; Eisenhower's repeated nuclear threats during crises in Asia, the Middle East, and Latin America; the Cuban Missile Crisis; Johnson's and Nixon's preparations and threats to use nuclear weapons in Vietnam and during Middle East wars; and the "Carter Doctrine," which threatened the use of "any means necessary" to retain control of the oil-rich Persian Gulf.

This history reveals that post-Cold War nuclear threats by the two Presidents Bush and Clinton reflected more continuity than change. Military doctrines changed from Eisenhower's "massive retaliation" to Kennedy's "flexible response," and from the Nixon and Carter Doctrines to "full spectrum dominance" and the Clinton and Bush Nuclear Posture Reviews, but the willingness to practice nuclear terrorism remained a constant.

Before the *Doctrine for Joint Nuclear Operations* illuminated the arsenal's roles in enforcing dominance rather than deterrence, scholars documented that the Pentagon and its political allies had long exaggerated the Soviet nuclear threat to justify increased military spending and the acquisition of new weapons systems. They also demonstrated that Cold War presidents often joined in the charade to cover their anti-communist political flanks or to reduce the pressures they faced to launch disastrous foreign military interventions. Contrary to what the public was led to believe, Eisenhower knew that "If we were to release our nuclear stockpile on the Soviet Union, the main danger would arise not from retaliation but from fallout in the earth's atmosphere." Later, when the US had tens of thousands of nuclear weapons, General David C. Jones, chairman of the Joint Chiefs of Staff, testified that mutual assured destruction (MAD) was not US policy, saying, "I think it is a very dangerous strategy. It is not the strategy that we are implementing today within the military . . . I do not subscribe to the idea that we ever had it as our basic strategy."[57]

The US nuclear arsenal has, of course, served "deterrent" functions since the first Soviet nuclear explosion in 1949, including nuclear threats to ensure that Moscow respected the post-World War II division of Europe. Deterrence has been a greater concern for lesser powers which have seen obtaining nuclear arsenals as a means of preventing possible attacks by greater nuclear powers. The Soviet Union built its nuclear arsenal to deter possible nuclear attacks by the US and Britain. China developed its arsenal to deter both the US and the Soviet Union (now Russia). While threatening Pakistan, India's nuclear program was primarily designed to counter the potential threat from China. And Pakistan's arsenal, developed with Chinese assistance, was built to deter India. France and Israel had slightly different motivations. The *force de frappe* reasserted the French claim to be a major power in the postcolonial era and provided the ultimate coin of postmodern sovereignty. Israel joined the club to augment its conventional military strength. And, in the late 1990s and in the first years of the twenty-first century, both North Korea and Iran pursued their nuclear programs to insulate their nations from US (and in the case of Iran, Israeli) threats.

The 1961 "Berlin Crisis" was long understood to be a textbook case of Cold War deterrence. The confrontation met the criteria of a US–Soviet clash in the heart of Europe. In fact, the resolution of the crisis was not a function of MAD, but a reflection of the radical asymmetry of nuclear power. It was illustrated by the readiness of the US to use nuclear threats to reinforce its power and influence by trumping what was a *conventional* Soviet military threat. Responding to growing West German economic vitality and political strength and to US nuclear weapons deployments in Germany, Soviet premier Nikita Khrushchev demanded that a separate peace treaty be negotiated with East Germany. This implicitly threatened West Berlin's status as a divided city and Western access to the city which was, functionally, an island within East Germany. Kennedy countered with an uncompromising speech to communicate his "unalterable determination . . . to maintain its position and rights in West Berlin."[58]

While not a function of classical "nuclear deterrence," Khrushchev was deterred from following through on his demands. Like Kennedy, Khrushchev was well aware that the US could launch a "disarming first strike" against Soviet nuclear forces, and that the Pentagon knew where to find the Soviet Union's missile sites and could "catch them all on the ground." As Roger Hilsman, Director of the State Department's Bureau of Intelligence and Research, later reported, "the whole Soviet ICBM [inter continental ballistic missile] system was . . . obsolescent,"[59] and its slow bomber fleet was no competition for the US Air Force. Being "rational actors," the Kremlin knew its limits and backed down in the face of Washington's overwhelming military power.

Both the Kremlin and the Washington establishment took the wrong lessons from the debacle. A year later they faced off again in the Cuban Missile Crisis. It was sparked in part by the US effort to overthrow Fidel Castro, but more by Khrushchev's desperate effort to equalize the imbalance of terror. With only four unreliable ICBMs and antiquated fleets of bombers and submarines, Khrushchev was in pursuit of a shortcut to nuclear parity and a deterrent force by secretly attempting to deploy intermediate range missiles in Cuba, well within striking range of the US.

To preserve its nuclear dominance, to reinforce the Monroe Doctrine principle that Latin America lies within the US "sphere of interest," and to demonstrate that the US had the right to deploy missiles on the Soviet border, while the Soviet Union could not reciprocate, Kennedy and most senior advisors were willing to gamble with nuclear catastrophe. As Noam Chomsky has since reflected, there may not have been such another "moment of madness and lunacy in human history" as when Kennedy and his most senior advisors escalated the crisis, which they believed carried the probability of between a third and a half that the US would initiate nuclear war.[60]

By the mid-1970s, with the growth of the Soviet economy and after two decades devoted to building missile, submarine, and bomber forces needed to ensure the ability to launch devastating second-strike retaliatory attack, the Soviets achieved relative nuclear parity and the ability to inflict MAD. Yet, as General Jones testified, MAD was not US policy. The Nixon administration pressed development of Trident, MX, cruise, and Pershing II missile systems to restore US nuclear superiority.[61]

Almost 20 years after the end of the Cold War, despite Washington's vast nuclear superiority, MAD still defines the parameters of US–Russian relations. China possesses a "minimum deterrent force" capable of annihilating Japan and of threatening death and destruction in the western US. Worse, with an estimated 4,000 strategic nuclear weapons on alert at any given moment,[62] miscalculations by political leaders or simple accidents could eliminate life on earth.

With the end of the Cold War, new rationales have been needed to maintain and modernize the US nuclear arsenal. With the demise of the "Soviet threat," deterrence lost what little legitimizing power it had. Socialized to understand the dangers of nuclear war exclusively in terms of US–Soviet confrontation, US political leaders, arms control advocates, and many in traditional nuclear disarmament movements were disoriented. Anxious to address a real but less immediate danger, Congressional Democrats and Republicans alike focused on so-called "loose nukes" in Russia's deteriorating arsenal that could be looted by the Russian Mafia or other non-state terrorists, including revolutionary Chechens or al-Qaeda. However, the genocidal US nuclear arsenal and the threat of MAD did not address these potential dangers. Threatening to savage the innocent people of Wajiristan in northwest Pakistan was unlikely to staunch whatever nuclear ambitions Osama Bin Laden might have had.

President Bush presented his rationale in his 2002 State of the Union address. Civilization, he asserted, was threatened by an "axis of evil": Iraq, Iran, and North Korea. His answer to these ostensible threats was counter-proliferation, including the threat of nuclear attacks. Although Bush's rhetoric bolstered popular support for the planned invasion of Iraq and served the neo-fascist stratagem of ruling through manipulation of fear and lies, there was no evidence that any of these nations posed a serious or immediate threat to US security.

OVERCOMING GEOPOLITICAL OBSTACLES

Why is Washington wedded to its practice of nuclear terrorism? The answer lies at the intersections of technology, empire, and geopolitics.

At the height of the Cold War, President Reagan enjoyed referring to the Soviet Union as the "Evil Empire," but nuclear terrorism has played a greater role in maintaining Washington's empire than Moscow's. The Russian Empire under tsars, commissars, and now presidents has been comparatively compact. Its furthest realms are relatively accessible to the intimidating power of Moscow's repressive apparatus and "conventional" military forces.

The US Empire is different. It extends from Mexico to the Middle East and from Berlin to Bangkok, thus posing greater challenges to deploying overwhelming US "conventional" military might to the furthest reaches of its empire.

In the years following World War II, President Eisenhower explained that "It would be impossible for the United States to maintain the military commitments which it now sustains around the world . . . did we not possess atomic weapons and the will to use them when necessary."[63] Two decades later, General Alexander Haig, Nixon's Chief of Staff and Reagan's Secretary of State, defended continued US reliance on nuclear terrorism by explaining that:

> Those in the West who advocate the adoption of a "no first use" policy seldom go on to propose that the United States reintroduce the draft, triple the size of its armed forces and put its economy on wartime footing. Yet in the absence of such steps, a pledge of no first use effectively leaves the West nothing with which to counterbalance the Soviet conventional advantages and geopolitical position . . .[64]

Chomsky framed it more critically:

> Our strategic nuclear weapons system provides us with a kind of umbrella within which we can carry out conventional actions, meaning aggression and subversion, without any concern that it will be impeded in any fashion . . . . Harold Brown, who was the Secretary of Defense under Carter . . . said that this is the core of our security system. He said that with this system in place, our conventional forces become "meaningful instruments of military and political power." That means that under this umbrella of strategic nuclear weapons . . . we have succeeded in sufficiently intimidating anyone who might help protect people who we are determined to attack. So . . . if we want to overthrow the government of Guatemala . . . or send a Rapid Deployment Force into the Middle East, or if we want to back a military coup in Indonesia . . . if we want to invade Vietnam . . . we can do this without too much concern that we'll be deterred because we have this intimidating power that will threaten anyone who might get in our way.[65]

This was the military, strategic, and technological environment that led Truman to threaten Moscow's destruction in 1946 and to rattle his nuclear saber against China and North Korea. This asymmetry of power gave Eisenhower the confidence to threaten nuclear attacks against China and Russia during Taiwan crises and Middle East wars. In other cases,

US presidents directed nuclear threats against "third-tier" nations in the South. As military doctrines changed from Eisenhower's "new look" massive retaliation to Kennedy's "flexible response" and Clinton's "full spectrum dominance," there was continuity in Washington's reliance on first-strike nuclear attacks to maintain the empire.

Thus, even as the danger of thermonuclear exchanges abated in the wake of the Cold War, the editors of the *Bulletin of the Atomic Scientists* found it necessary to move the hands of the publication's Doomsday clock closer to midnight.[66] While warning about the dangers of "loose nukes," al-Qaeda, and the "axis of evil," the first three post-Cold War presidents maintained and modernized the massive US nuclear arsenal. They pressed the development, and ultimately the deployment, of more "usable" first-strike nuclear weapons systems, and they prepared and threatened nuclear attacks against Iraq, Iran, North Korea, Libya, Syria, Russia, and China.[67]

TOTAL WAR AND THE "EVIL THING"

This history of the use of nuclear terrorism to enforce global empire raises deeper and more troubling questions which are intimated but not fully explored in the chapters that follow. As in any society, altruism and compassion have been essential to the US experience and its culture. Well into the late twentieth century, democratic seeds planted in the country's Declaration of Independence and Constitution grew to become more inclusive of society as a whole. But, as the continuing societal scars of the genocide of Native Americans, of slavery, of the nineteenth-century US colonial conquests, and as the continued exploitation of many workers and disregard for the poor testify, other forces have also long been active in US political life. Beliefs in US exceptionalism, superiority, and its "Manifest Destiny" to dominate were integral to political culture long before Albert Einstein signed Leo Szilard's fateful warning to President Roosevelt. The high point of US democracy, the post-World War II victories of the civil rights movement, came as President Kennedy recklessly risked hundreds of millions of lives during the Cuban Missile Crisis and as the Johnson administration crossed what it understood to be a nuclear Rubicon with its massive escalation of the US war against Vietnam.[68]

These dualities cannot be ignored, and they have been compounded by the embrace of nuclear terrorism as state and national policy. Near-absolute power has corrupted almost absolutely. The novelist E. L. Doctorow put it well when he wrote:

> We have had the bomb on our minds since 1945. It was first our weaponry and then our diplomacy, and now it's our economy. How can we suppose that something so monstrously powerful would not, after years, compose

> our identity? The great golem we have made against our enemies is our culture, our bomb culture—its logic, its faith, its vision.[69]

The US, as a state and as a society, was hardly innocent at the beginning of the twentieth century, but the mobilizations for and the fighting of two "world wars" transformed the nation in fundamental ways. Some were beneficial, such as Washington's contributions to the end of formal colonialism, hard-fought victories for racial and gender equality,[70] and the GI Bill, which permitted returning veterans to obtain higher educations. However, other forces were also at work.

Tragically, the decisions to fight Germany and Japan by means of "total" war—the industrialization of war-fighting and ultimately the race to build and use the atomic bomb—profoundly influenced US culture. They created a society which had more in common with the Kaiser's Germany and Fascist Italy than has generally been recognized. This transformation had still earlier roots. The American Civil War (1861–65) is seen by many as the beginning of "total war": the mobilization of the entire society and the targeting of the full range of the enemy's resources, including its industry, civilian population, and even its environment, in order to prevail. The Gatling gun, introduced during the Civil War, marked a revolution in murderous firepower. And Sherman's merciless march through Georgia included the destruction of Atlanta.

Internationally, "total war" began within weeks of Germany's 1914 invasion of the Low Countries when a Zeppelin bombed Antwerp and shattered the foundations of centuries of international law. Soon, Zeppelins were bombing London, instilling fear among the British.

Germans were not solely responsible for total war European-style. Shortly before assuming command of French forces, Marshal Foch implored: "You must henceforth go to the limits to find the aim of war. Since the vanquished party now never yields before it has been deprived of all means of reply, *what you have to aim at is the destruction of those very means of reply*."[71] The philosopher and novelist Hermann Hesse understood where this would lead, warning that "[i]f the war goes on," it would destroy Western civilization's Enlightenment foundations.[72]

President Franklin D. Roosevelt's dramatic wartime transformation was starkly illustrative of what US adoption of total war strategy did to the nation as a whole. In 1939, horrified by the air war that had begun in Europe, he urged Europeans to cease aerial bombardments of civilians, writing:

> The ruthless bombing from the air of civilians in unfortified centers of population during the course of hostilities . . . sickened the hearts of every civilized man and woman, and has profoundly shocked the conscience of humanity.

> If resort is had to this form of inhuman barbarism during the period of the tragic conflagration with which the world is now confronted, hundreds of thousands of innocent human beings . . . will lose their lives. I am therefore addressing this urgent appeal to every government which may be engaged in hostilities publicly to affirm its determination that its armed forces shall in no event, and under no circumstances, undertake the bombardment from the air of civilian populations or of unfortified cities.[73]

Within three years, General Doolittle's bombers rained death on Tokyo to raise US morale, and the president was fully committed to using nuclear weapons to win the war.[74]

Roosevelt was not a full partner in Churchill's fire bombings of German cities, and he protested the fire bombing of Dresden. But, at the cost of hundreds of thousands of lives, Roosevelt presided over the fire bombing of every major Japanese city except historic Kyoto and the four cities set aside as possible A-bomb targets. In the last months of World War II and the early years of the Cold War, German and Japanese scientists and engineers were recruited to help develop the US nuclear, missile, and germ warfare programs. Incendiary and chemical weapon attacks were soon used to obliterate much of Korea and Indochina, with the Vietnamese civilian death toll approaching 3 million.[75]

US research and development of hydrogen bombs, some 1,000 times more powerful than the Hiroshima and Nagasaki A-bombs, was begun because "the Germans were probably doing it."[76] And, for half a century, the US has deployed and repeatedly threatened attacks with its strategic nuclear weapons, each with the capacity to kill more people than were

annihilated in Auschwitz, Bergen-Belsen, and Treblinka. This, in turn, undermined the values, structure, and practice of US democracy.

Richard Falk has written that "The roots of first strike planning exist so deep as to suggest that even the posts of President and Secretary of Defense and Senator have become largely ornamental in relation to national security policy. Throwing 'the rascals' out, accordingly becomes a much more formidable task . . . " At a still deeper spiritual level, the embrace of total and nuclear war has institutionalized what Hannah Arendt described as the "banality of evil."[77]

Evil is "wickedness" and "moral depravity," uncompromising terms that describe the practice of nuclear terrorism. In 1945 many of the country's most senior military officials understood that the atomic bombings of Hiroshima and Nagasaki were unnecessary and violated the rules of war. Knowing that Truman was aware of Emperor Hirohito's efforts to surrender, it is difficult not to be shocked by his warning immediately following the Hiroshima bombing that "We are now prepared to obliterate more rapidly and completely every productive enterprise the Japanese have above ground in any city . . . If they do not now accept our terms they may expect a rain of ruin from the air, the like of which has never been seen on this earth."[78] Leo Szilard, who had started it all with "Einstein's" letter, understood that "had Germany used atomic bombs on two allied cities, those responsible would have been 'sentenced . . . to death at Nuremberg and hanged . . . ' "[79]

Then came the hydrogen bomb. The General Advisory Committee of senior scientists and officials assembled to advise Truman on whether or not to develop the H-bomb presented two reports. The majority report was clear that "a super-bomb should never be produced . . . we see a unique opportunity of providing . . . limitations on the totality of war and thus limiting the fear . . . of mankind." The minority report went further, advising that the "weapon cannot be justified on any ethical ground which gives a human being a certain individuality and dignity . . . The fact that no limits exist to the destructiveness of this weapon makes its very existence and the knowledge of its construction a danger to humanity as a whole. It is necessarily an evil thing considered in any light."[80]

When he left office, Eisenhower knew that US nuclear war plans included a Single Integrated Operational Plan (SIOP) that anticipated "the deaths of an estimated 360–525 million people." In the years that followed, Secretary of Defense Robert McNamara argued that a "reasonable goal" for nuclear war against the Soviet Union could be the destruction of 25 percent of its population (55 million people). At the beginning of the twenty-first century, only 51 US strategic warheads would be needed to inflict such damage, yet Washington's arsenal numbered more than 10,000 such weapons.[81]

Stating what should have been obvious, in 1996 the International Court of Justice (ICJ) ruled that the use and threatened use of nuclear weapons violate international law. Among the principles that the ICJ drew upon were that nuclear weapons are genocidal and potentially omnicidal; they cause indiscriminate harm to combatants and non-combatants alike and inflict unnecessary suffering; they violate the requirement that military responses be proportional; they destroy the ecosystem, thus endangering future generations; they violate international treaties outlawing the use of poison gas; and they inflict unacceptable damage to neutral nations.[82]

The Pentagon has, in fact, adopted a doctrine that it believes could lead to "ultimate doom"—the end of human life. Its Clinton era "The Essentials of Post-Cold War Deterrence" commits the US to maintaining "a capability to create a fear of national extinction" in the minds of those it seeks to intimidate. Chomsky has described this doctrine, which continues to shape

US policy and practice, as among "the most horrifying documents I've ever read." It asserts that "we have to rely primarily on nuclear weapons because unlike other weapons of mass destruction . . . the effects of nuclear weapons are immediate, devastating, overwhelming—not only destructive but terrifying. . . . We have to have a national persona of irrationality with forces 'out of control' so we really *terrify* everybody."[83]

"Evil" can be better understood in intimate personal terms. Hiroshima and Nagasaki *Hibakusha* have long accused the US of using them as "guinea pigs." Many tearfully and angrily describe what happened to them during the months and years following the A-bombings when US doctors examined them, but offered these tormented survivors no medical care or treatment.

In May 2000, Professor Shoji Sawada and Junko Kayashige, both Hiroshima *Hibakusha*, a Japanese Protestant minister, and their US hosts, met with Dr. Paul Seligman, then Deputy Assistant Secretary of the US Department of Energy. Dr. Seligman was responsible for overseeing all US studies on the health impacts of radiation. During the meeting, the *Hibakusha*'s charge of being used as guinea pigs was explained to him, and he was asked if he could put this damning charge to rest.

Seligman's response was immediate and unambiguous: "Oh no. We've used those studies for everything, including the design of new nuclear weapons."[84]

Hiroshima and Nagasaki *Hibakusha* are not the only ones to have been so abused. It has long been known that Japanese fishermen and the people of Rongelap Atoll in the Marshall Islands were intentionally exposed to fallout from the 1954 "Bravo" H-bomb test. More recently it has been learned that to prepare for possible future nuclear wars, the US and Japanese governments "withheld medical findings" from fishermen, and that a decades-long secret medical program, Project 4.1, was conducted to study the effects of radiation ingested from the environment. The study "included purposefully resettling people on lands highly contaminated by many of the 67 nuclear weapons tests conducted in the air, on land, and in the seas surrounding the Marshall Islands."[85] Down-winders concentrated in Utah and Idaho, uranium miners, soldiers and sailors, and other citizens were also knowingly exposed to deadly radiation across the US.

During the first three decades of the nuclear era, 23,000 US citizens were deliberately subjected to 1,400 radiation experiments, in most cases without their informed consent. These included mentally disabled children in institutional care who were fed plutonium with their breakfast cereal and soldiers ordered to march into the fallout of simulated battlefields to better prepare the Pentagon for war fighting in "nuclear environments." In 1993, when Clinton's newly appointed Secretary of the Department of Energy Hazel

O'Leary revealed what she had learned about these abuses, she confessed that "The only thing I could think of was Nazi Germany."[86] The former Soviet Union and other nuclear powers have committed similar crimes against their peoples and others.

This history, including repeated and secret preparations and threats to initiate genocidal nuclear war, explains why the US people's "conception of government may itself be too antiquated."[87] In this light, we need to ask if the US has truly been a "democracy" for the past 60 years. Decisions, even those that could have ended the country's national existence and extinguished human existence, were taken without the knowledge or involvement of its people. Since the beginning of the nuclear age, senior elected and military officials have systematically withheld essential information about the domestic consequences of the country's nuclear weapons production program and about the use and threatened use of these genocidal and omnicidal weapons. Even Vice-President Truman was kept ignorant of the Manhattan Project until after he assumed the presidency.

What, then, are the meanings and consequences of the existence of a secret and ultimately all-powerful state within a state? James Madison, US president from 1809 to 1817, had the answer: "A popular government without popular information or the means of acquiring it is but a prologue to a farce or a tragedy or perhaps both."[88] Two centuries later, Stewart Udall, former Secretary of the Interior, confirmed that "The atomic weapons race and the secrecy surrounding it crushed American democracy. It induced us to conduct government according to lies. It distorted justice. It undermined American morality . . . "[89]

Table 1.1 Partial Listing of Incidents of Nuclear Blackmail[90]

1946	Truman threatens the Soviets regarding northern Iran.
1946	Truman sends SAC bombers to intimidate Yugoslavia following the downing of a US aircraft over Yugoslavia.
1948	Truman threatens the Soviets in response to the Berlin blockade.
1950	Truman threatens the Chinese when US Marines are surrounded at Chosin Reservoir in Korea.
1951	Truman approves a military request to attack Manchuria with nuclear weapons if significant numbers of new Chinese forces enter the war.
1953	Eisenhower threatens China to force an end to the Korean War on terms acceptable to the US.
1954	Eisenhower's Secretary of State John Foster Dulles offers the French three tactical nuclear weapons to break the siege at Dien Bien Phu, Vietnam, supported by Nixon's public trial balloons.
1954	Eisenhower uses nuclear-armed SAC bombers to reinforce a CIA-backed coup in Guatemala.

Continued

Table 1.1 Continued

1956	Nikolai Bulganin threatens London and Paris with nuclear attacks, demanding withdrawal following their invasion of Egypt.
1956	Eisenhower counters by threatening the USSR while also demanding that the British and French withdraw from Egypt.
1958	Eisenhower orders the Joint Chiefs of Staff to prepare to use nuclear weapons against Iraq if necessary, to prevent extension of revolution into Kuwait.
1958	Eisenhower orders the Joint Chiefs of Staff to prepare to use nuclear weapons against China if they invade the island of Quemoy.
1961	Kennedy threatens Soviets during the Berlin Crisis.
1962	Cuban Missile Crisis.
1967	Johnson threatens the Soviets during the Middle East War.
1967	Johnson threatens nuclear attack to break the siege at Khe Sanh.
1969	Brezhnev threatens China during border war.
1969	Nixon's "November ultimatum" against Vietnam.
1970	Nixon signals US preparations to fight a nuclear war during the Black September War in Jordan.
1973	The Israeli government threatens to use nuclear weapons during the "October War."
1973	Kissinger threatens the Soviet Union during the last hours of the "October War" in the Middle East.
1973	Nixon pledges to South Vietnamese President Thieu that he will respond with nuclear attacks or the bombing of North Vietnam's dikes if it violates the provisions of the Paris Peace Accords.
1975	Secretary of Defense Schlesinger threatens North Korea with nuclear retaliation should it attack South Korea following the US defeat in Vietnam.
1980	The Carter Doctrine is announced.
1981	Reagan reaffirms the Carter Doctrine.
1982	British Prime Minister Margaret Thatcher threatens to eliminate Buenos Aires during the Falklands War.
1990	Pakistan threatens India during confrontation over Kashmir.
1990–91	Bush threatens Iraq during the Gulf War.
1993	Clinton threatens North Korea.
1994	Clinton's confrontation with North Korea.
1996	China threatens "Los Angeles" during confrontation over Taiwan.
1996	Clinton threatens Libya with nuclear attack to prevent completion of an underground chemical weapons production complex.
1998	Clinton threatens Iraq with nuclear attack.
1999	India and Pakistan threaten and prepare nuclear attacks during the Kargil War.
2001	US forces placed on a DEFCON alert in the immediate aftermath of the September 11 terrorist attacks.
2001	Secretary of Defense Donald Rumsfeld refuses to rule out using tactical nuclear weapons against Afghan caves believed to be sheltering Osama Bin Laden.
2002	Bush communicates an implied threat to counter any Iraqi use of chemical or biological weapons with a nuclear attack.
2003	US mobilization and implicit nuclear threats against North Korea.
2006	French President Jacques Chirac threatens first-strike nuclear attacks against nations that practice terrorism against France.
2006	Implicit US threats to bomb Iran's nuclear infrastructure with "bunker-buster" atomic bombs.

2
First Nuclear Terrorism—Hiroshima and Nagasaki

> In plain language 'strategic bombing' of civilians is an act of terrorism.[1]
>
> Yuki Tanaka

> I was not willing to let Russia reap the fruits of a long and bitter and gallant effort in which she had had no part.[2]
>
> President Harry Truman

On August 7, 1945, President Truman announced to the world that the first atomic bomb had been dropped on Hiroshima, a "military base." "We wished," he said, "*in this first attack* to avoid, insofar as possible, the killing of civilians."[3] The bombings, the US people and the world were told, were justifiable punishment for Japanese aggression and prevented a million US casualties.[4] In the months and decades that followed, these rationalizations were reinforced by an orchestrated media campaign augmented by censorship and secrecy. The campaign was designed to serve multiple goals: to convince the public of the necessity and legitimacy of the A-bombings; to obscure the true reasons for the A-bombings; to limit understanding of the death and destruction wrought by the A-bombs; and to maintain popular support for continuing preparations and threats to initiate future nuclear wars.[5]

Contrary to Truman's lies and the propaganda campaign, the bombings were terrorizing crimes against humanity. Hundreds of thousands of civilians, their wooden homes and their neighborhoods were purposely targeted. Hiroshima did have military installations, but the fact that the city was not seriously bombed after nearly every other Japanese city had been burned to the ground by US fire bombings reflected the port city's marginal military importance. In addition to being disproportionate and indiscriminate attacks, the atomic bombings were not needed to secure Japan's surrender. And, as those who gave the orders understood, the use of the atomic weapons marked the beginning of a new form of state terrorism and the practice of nuclear extortion.[6]

Hiroshima was destroyed within 10 seconds of the A-bomb's explosion, initially killing 70,000 people and leveling or burning all but a few of the city's buildings. Because "Fat Man," the Nagasaki A-bomb, exploded nearly 2 miles from its intended target, the destruction there was less than complete. The initial death toll was 40,000, annihilating the predominantly Christian Urakami district and exposing much of the city to deadly radioactive fallout carried by the wind and black rain. By year's end, the two bombs had claimed more than 210,000 lives. Hundreds of thousands more would suffer and die in the years to come from cancers, radiation sickness, and searing physical and emotional wounds. Many would commit suicide. Pregnant women delivered stillborn, mutant, or massively deformed offspring, many of whom lived just a few days, if at all.

President Truman and his senior advisors understood the "apocalyptic" power of the weapons used to destroy Hiroshima and Nagasaki and that there were alternatives to using them. As Truman confided in his memoirs and diary, the power of the atomic bombs was "great enough to destroy the whole world." He believed that the new weapons might be the "fire and destruction prophesied in the Euphrates Valley Era, after Noah and his fabulous ark."[7] He and his inner circle also knew that they were ordering the atomic bombings when the Japanese government, under orders from the Emperor, was desperately attempting to surrender on terms Truman accepted *after* Hiroshima and Nagasaki. Chairman of the Joint Chiefs of Staff Admiral Leahy, Army Chief of Staff General Marshall, Commander of US forces in Europe General Eisenhower, Commander of the US Army Air Forces General "Hap" Arnold, Commander of the Pacific Fleet Admiral Chester W. Nimitz, Army Air Force General Curtis LeMay, who organized the murderous fire bombing of nearly every Japanese city, and other senior military leaders either opposed or pressed alternatives to the atomic bombings.[8] In sometimes divergent ways, they understood that, as Leahy put it, "The use of this barbarous weapon at Hiroshima and Nagasaki was of no material assistance to our war against Japan."[9]

Four calculations drove Truman and his closest advisors to use the new weapon. They shared a profound concern that Roosevelt had conceded too much to Stalin at Yalta. By bringing the war to an immediate halt, before the Soviet Union "joined the kill," they hoped to limit the Soviets' postwar influence in northern China, Manchuria, Korea, and possibly even in Japan, a devastated but technologically advanced nation. With the destruction of Hiroshima and Nagasaki, US leaders sought to expand, consolidate, and preserve the East Asian domains of its "Grand Area."

Second, the people of Hiroshima and Nagasaki were sacrificed to ensure that "the Soviets would be more accommodating to the American point of view" in the Cold War era.[10] Truman believed that by demonstrating the terrorizing power of nuclear weapons and the US willingness to use them—even against civilians—he would have "a hammer over" Stalin.

The message was clear: we have the ability and the will to do this to human beings. Beware and behave.

There were also personal motives. Truman and Byrnes were concerned that if the US electorate learned that $2 billion (a staggering sum in those days) had been spent to build the super-bomb and that the new weapon had not been used, Truman would be voted out of office in the 1948 presidential election. Finally, there was simple vengeance fused with racism. As Truman wrote to Samuel McCrea Cavert of the Federal Council of Churches two days after the Nagasaki bombing, "When you have to deal with a beast you have to treat him as a beast."[11]

This chapter explains why the US and Japanese people were at war, the origins of the Manhattan Project which invented the A-bomb, and of myths that were created in a desperate effort to legitimize what were in fact massive crimes against humanity. Readers will find the paths not taken by Truman and his senior advisors, their knowledge of the emergence of a "peace camp" within the highest reaches of the Japanese government which sought open peace negotiations with the US, or to entice the Soviet Union into mediating an end to the war they knew they had lost. The chapter also describes what Tsuyoshi Hasegawa has termed "racing the enemy," the struggle between the US and the Soviet Union during the final weeks of the war to gain strategic advantages for the coming Cold War. Essential to this chapter are the descriptions of what the first atomic bombs inflicted on Hiroshima, Nagasaki, and their people. The compelling and terrifying *Hibakusha* testimonies are essential to understanding the ultimate nature and dangers of nuclear weapons. They thus illuminate the histories of US nuclear threats that are recounted in later chapters and the continuing threats of nuclear genocide and life-ending nuclear winter.

ORIGINS AND MYTHS

The US nuclear weapons program was launched on October 9, 1941, two months *before* the surprise Japanese attack on Pearl Harbor. A letter, written by the nuclear physicist Leo Szilard, signed by Albert Einstein, and sent to President Roosevelt in 1939 was the seed of what became the Manhattan Project. The letter warned Roosevelt that it was possible that in the course of the war that had already begun in Europe, Germany might be able to create a uranium bomb. A "single bomb of this type," Einstein and Szilard warned, "carried by boat and exploded in port, might very well destroy the whole port together with some of the surrounding territory."[12] Anticipating that the US would soon be at war with Germany and that a uranium bomb might determine its outcome, Roosevelt launched a one-sided nuclear arms race with Nazi Germany. General Leslie Groves was appointed as the project's senior administrator, and the theoretical physicist J. Robert Oppenheimer was pitted against Germany's Werner Heisenberg. Years later, Einstein would express profound remorse for his role in the invention and use of nuclear weapons.[13]

For reasons that are debated to this day, the German A-bomb project stalled.[14] By 1944, it was known in the highest circles of US power that Hitler would not have an atomic bomb in time to influence the war's outcome.[15] Yet, the pace within the Manhattan Project quickened.[16] Roosevelt and Stimson, Roosevelt's Secretary of War, planned to use the new weapon to force concessions from Moscow and use "the 'secret' of the atomic bomb as a means of obtaining a *quid pro quo* from the Soviet Union."[17] In March 1944, General Groves told a senior Manhattan Project scientist that "of course, the real purpose in making the bomb was to subdue the Soviets." Groves later confirmed this, writing that "there was never . . . from the time I took charge of this project any illusion on my part but that Russia was our enemy and that the project was conducted on that basis."[18]

Like the myth that Christopher Columbus discovered America, the fiction that Truman used atomic bombs against the people and cities of Hiroshima and Nagasaki to end the war and save US lives has become government-enforced common wisdom in the US and much of the world. A Gallup poll taken in 2005 for the 60th anniversary of the A-bombings revealed that 57 percent of US Americans believe the bombings were necessary and legitimate.[19] Yet, 40 years ago, the dean of US historians concluded that "The United States dropped the bomb to end the war against Japan and *thereby to stop the Russians in Asia, and to give them sober pause in eastern Europe*."[20] In the years that followed, the publication of wartime leaders' diaries and memoirs, the opening of official records in the US, the former Soviet Union, and Japan, and scholarly research created what the former official historian of the US Nuclear Regulatory Commission, J. Samuel Walker, described as a "consensus among scholars . . . that the bomb was not needed to avoid an invasion of Japan . . . . alternatives to the bomb existed and that Truman and his advisers knew it."[21]

President Eisenhower later recalled that he told Stimson that "Japan was already defeated and that dropping the bomb was completely unnecessary . . . our country should avoid shocking world opinion by the use of a weapon whose employment was, I thought, no longer mandatory as a measure to save American lives."[22] "The Japanese," Eisenhower advised, "were ready to surrender, and it wasn't necessary to hit them with that awful thing."[23] Admiral Leahy, then Chairman of the Joint Chiefs of Staff, agreed: "The use of this barbarous weapon at Hiroshima and Nagasaki," he later said, "was of no material assistance to our war against

Japan."[24] In mid-1945, General LeMay had calculated that the Japanese Imperial government would surrender by September 1 (three weeks after the atomic bombings) when his fire bombing campaign would have completed its destruction of "everything" in Japan.[25] That Japan was facing imminent defeat, and that the atomic bombings were not necessary to end the war, was well understood in Truman's inner circle. Secretary of State Byrnes, the president's most trusted advisor, later testified, "We wanted to get through with the Japanese phase of the war before the Russians came in."[26]

COMPETITION FOR ASIAN EMPIRE

Why were the US and Japan at war? More was involved than the Japanese attack on Pearl Harbor. Wartime propaganda, the postwar US–Japanese military alliance, and Cold War mythology have obscured the underlying continuity of twentieth- and twenty-first-century US foreign and military policy: expansion and maintenance of empire in the Pacific and Asia. A clash of imperial ambitions precipitated "The Day of Infamy" at Pearl Harbor.[27]

In the early decades of the twentieth century, Japan was a rising power, pressing at and beyond the limits and rules imposed by Britain and the US. Like Germany, Italy, and to a lesser extent the US, Tokyo came late to empire-building and to establishing colonies. After Admiral Perry and his gunboats forced Japan to "open" to the West in 1854, following 200 years of Tokugawa-imposed isolation, the Japanese elite believed they faced emulating the clear choice of being colonized like their neighbors or the Western nations that dominated the Asia/Pacific region. The leaders of Meiji and Taisho Japan opted for conquest and colonization.

As the Japanese historian Saburo Ienaga has written, "In China, Japan competed with the West for a place at the imperial table and a slice of the Chinese melon."[28] US support for Japanese conquest and expansion began with the 1895 Sino-Japanese War and the 1904–5 Russo-Japanese War. The 1905 Portsmouth Treaty, engineered by Theodore Roosevelt, provided for US recognition of Japanese hegemony in Korea in exchange for Japanese recognition of US colonization of the Philippines. It was when US and Japanese imperial ambitions collided in the 1930s that war began to appear unavoidable.

The US–Japanese clash grew out of the Great Depression, the Japanese chapter of which began in 1927. In Japan, the suffering and disorientation of the economic crisis compounded by the protectionist barriers that spread across the world undercut the international trade that was essential to the nation's economic security. This reinforced the drive to conquer and colonize China. In addition to providing new markets for Japanese goods, privileged access to resources and to cheap labor, colonial conquests offered Japanese the promise of jobs and opportunities for the island nation's people. As Ienaga observed, "The attitude was identical with the European and American conviction that control of colonies in Asia, the Pacific, and Africa was 'manifest destiny.' A national consensus approved of an imperialist policy toward China, but there were sharp disagreements and differing emphases over the implementation."[29] "Moderate" imperialists favored expansion, investments, and opening markets for Japan in China in cooperation with Britain and the US. The "militarists," who seized power through a series of contrived military "incidents" in China and assassinations and coups in Tokyo, preferred to launch a war to gain what they saw as "limitless" resources in China. These militarists believed the Japanese government would be "careless" to allow these resources to fall to Britain or the US, and they moved to suppress Chinese nationalism and to drive Britain and the US from the Asian continent.[30]

Like today, throughout the twentieth century access to and control of oil were essential to economic and military power, and it was the precipitating cause of the US–Japanese war. Few remember that the decision made by Japan's military government to attack the US resulted from its desperate need for oil. An oil embargo had been imposed on Japan as punishment for its 1940 conquest of French Indochina. With Japanese troops bogged down in fighting from Vietnam to Manchuria, and with an increasingly limited supply of oil to pursue its aggressions, the Japanese government faced a stark choice: it could end its Asian war with concessions and humiliating loss of face, or it could attempt to shatter the embargo through the conquest of oil-rich Indonesia and war against the US.

Many in the Japanese leadership knew that with a gross national product only one tenth that of the US, the island nation could not prevail. The military scenario for Japan's defeat in an island-hopping war and siege had already been published in the West, and it had been read in Japanese military circles.[31] Unable to halt the rush to war against the US, and knowing that "a tragic defeat" awaited them, Prime Minister Konoe resigned soon after the decision to attack the US and Britain was taken on September 6, 1941. Konoe's resignation delayed but could not prevent this disastrous phase of Japan's Fifteen-Year War. The hope of the doctrinaire and desperate men leading the Japanese government was that the destruction of the US Pacific Fleet at Pearl Harbor would buy them time. If Germany won the war in Europe, the US would not be in a position to reassert its hegemony in the Pacific. If Germany lost, Japan's emperor and the militarists who surrounded him gambled that Washington would prefer negotiating a new Asian/Pacific *modus vivendi* to fighting the bloody battles necessary to defeat Japan.[32]

RATIONALES AND PATHS NOT TAKEN

For six decades, the US people and much of the world have been subjected to a disinformation campaign designed to hide or obscure the rationales and human costs of the A-bombings. Beginning with the Manhattan Project's co-optation of *New York Times* journalist William Laurence and the censorship that accompanied the military occupation of Japan, through the controversies surrounding the Smithsonian Museum's 50th anniversary exhibit and 60th anniversary commemorations, powerful forces have worked to consign the historical record to Orwellian memory holes.

Most pernicious are the lies told to children. Written to pass knowledge from one generation to the next, children's books often reflect society's dominant beliefs and values. In this way, The American Heritage Junior Library provides an unvarnished expression of the prevailing US myth about the bombings of Hiroshima and Nagasaki:

> Even if the Russians invaded Manchuria and the British attacked Malaya in August as planned, no one expected the invasion of Japan to be anything but a slaughter. Before the Japanese mainland could be secured, American casualties would amount to as many as one million men; and the Japanese were expected to sacrifice twice that number in defense of their homeland. Then, on July 16, the bright glow of the Trinity test raised hopes that the war could be ended without an invasion . . . .[33]

This theme was repeated in Congress and the press during the surreal and politically charged debate over the Smithsonian Institution's proposed exhibit on the eve of the 50th anniversary of the Hiroshima and Nagasaki bombings. That exhibit was canceled even after museum officials subjected the exhibit's script to "historical cleansing" under intense pressure from right-wing members of Congress and veterans groups mobilized by Pentagon officials. The text and photographs which had been laboriously assembled and unanimously endorsed by the museum's advisory board of historians were eliminated. Statements by Admiral Leahy, Generals Eisenhower and Marshall, and other senior officials who opposed or had reservations about the atomic bombings were thought to be too subversive to be seen. So too was the description of the fire bombing of Tokyo as the "single most destructive non-nuclear attack in human history." Exhibit critics were not pacified by a revised script that repeated the mythology that the Japanese government was "not willing to surrender," that Truman ordered the atomic bombings primarily "to save lives," and that "if atomic bombs did not force Japan to surrender . . . [US] casualties could have risen to as many as a million."

There was little progress over the next decade. When the Smithsonian Museum finally placed the "Enola Gay" (the plane from which the Hiroshima A-bomb was dropped), on permanent exhibition in 2003, it was accompanied by a small plaque that simply reported that the atomic bomb dropped by the B-29 had brought the war to an end. *Time Magazine*'s 60th anniversary tribute to "America's World War II Triumph in the Pacific" repeated Truman-era propaganda that the Japanese government "rejected" Truman and Churchill's Potsdam Declaration, that Truman's "advisers estimated that casualties would run to the hundreds of thousands and perhaps exceed 1 million," and that "there is little question that in using the bombs he realized his military goal of bringing the war to a swift and far less deadly end."[34]

In fact, the military's estimates were that if they invaded Japan up to 46,000—not 1 million—US troops could be killed in the two-stage attack. Truman and his advisors were in fact cynical in their calculations. For them the atomic bomb had little to do with saving lives, but it was "the master card" that would trump the Soviets in anticipated postwar confrontations. Truman actually postponed the Potsdam summit with Stalin and Churchill to ensure that he had an atomic bomb in his negotiating hand, and he refused to accept Japan's efforts to mediate its surrender by diplomatic means.[35] Throughout the spring and early summer of 1945 Truman received reports from Admiral Leahy that "the Japanese were already defeated and ready to surrender."[36] Truman was informed about, discussed, and dismissed Emperor Hirohito's efforts to surrender before and during the Potsdam summit.

In the final months of the war, the Joint Chiefs of Staff's Joint Intelligence Committee also reported that "the increasing effects of air–sea blockade, the progressive and cumulative devastation wrought by strategic [fire] bombings, and the collapse of Germany" were leading the Japanese to understand that "absolute defeat is inevitable." The Committee also reported that an invasion of Honshu (politically and strategically the most important of Japan's four main islands) could take the lives of 40,000 US troops, and that the invasion of Kyushu, at a cost of 7,500 US lives, and might "well prove to be the decisive operation which would terminate the war."[37] The invasion of Kyushu was scheduled for November 1945 and the conquest of Honshu for early 1946. The interim would have provided months to negotiate the details of Japan's surrender, including the much discussed possibility of a demonstration A-bombing of an uninhabited atoll to impress Japan's rulers with the seriousness of the moment. US and British intelligence also projected that "When Russia came into the war . . . the Japanese would probably wish to get out on almost any terms short of the dethronement of the Emperor."[38]

It was Churchill who, soon after the Nagasaki A-bombing, announced that nuclear bombs had saved "well over 1,200,000 Allied lives," a number that even General Groves remarked was "a little high." Truman initially used the bogus figure of a quarter of a million US lives, but doubled it for his memoirs.[39]

On the basis of intelligence and military reports and related considerations, Assistant Secretary of War John McCloy, later Chairman of the Establishment, advised Secretary of War Stimson that "we should have our heads examined if we did not consider the possibility of bringing the war to a conclusion without further loss of life. I felt we could readily agree to let the Japanese retain the emperor as a constitutional monarch."[40]

As the end-game approached, and with Churchill's encouragement, senior State Department and military leaders raised the possibility of offering Japan better terms than the "unconditional surrender" that had been demanded. Former Ambassador Grew, McCloy, Navy Secretary Forrestal, and Stimson, who was not at ease about "competing with Hitler" in atrocities, advised Truman that "a carefully timed warning by the United States, Britain, China and the Soviet Union might provide the context for the Japanese to surrender."[41] "[T]he Japanese nation," Stimson reported, "has the mental intelligence and versatile capacity in such a crisis to recognize the folly of a fight to the finish and to accept the proffer of *what will amount to an unconditional surrender*."[42] Nonetheless Stimson, Byrnes, and Truman opted not to pursue diplomatic alternatives.

Political decisions, including those relating to war and peace, are rarely made for a single reason. The forces that shape major decisions are usually many and complex. Claims that the decision to bomb Hiroshima and Nagasaki reflected the momentum of the atom bomb project, the desire to bring the war to an early conclusion, and the demand of the collective unconscious for revenge, were certainly present.[43] So, too, were four assumptions that the historian Martin Sherwin explained were shared by President Truman and the Interim Committee that made the formal recommendation to use the A-bombs: 1) that the atomic bombs were legitimate weapons and would have been used by the Nazis if Germany won the race to build the bomb; 2) that the atomic bombings would have a "profound effect" on Japan's leaders; 3) that the public would want the bombs used; and 4) that the bombs would have "a salutary effect on relations with the Soviet Union."[44]

Other factors also contributed to the decision. Not the least of these was endemic racism against Asians in general and the Japanese in particular, an element of the "collective unconscious of the time," which had been deepened by wartime rhetoric. A week after the Pearl Harbor attacks, the popular weekly *LIFE Magazine* led the campaign of dehumanizing the enemy by addressing the US people's "distressing ignorance of the delicate question of how to tell a Chinese from a Jap." It explained that "The modern Japanese is the descendant of Mongoloids who invaded the Japanese archipelago back in the mists of prehistory, and of the native aborigines who possessed the islands before them." Describing a photograph of Premier Tojo that accompanied the article, *LIFE* taught that he "betrays aboriginal antecedents in a squat, long-torsoed build, broader, more massively boned head and face, flat, often pug nose . . . Japs like General Tojo show humorless intensity of ruthless mystics."[45] The Pentagon was less subtle. As one military publication put it, Japanese were lice, and that "[B]efore a complete cure may be effected . . . the breeding grounds around the Tokyo area, must be completely annihilated."[46] Encouraged by Washington, Hollywood depicted Japanese as "[d]egenerate, moral idiots . . . Stinking little savages," who should be "wipe[d] off the face of the earth."[47]

A more "humanitarian" rationale for the atom bombings was also put forward. James Conant, President of Harvard University who initially recommended that the bombs be targeted against civilians, and some of the Manhattan Project's senior scientists argued that using the atomic bomb would "awaken the world to the necessity of abolishing war altogether."[48]

It was, however, the bombs' terrorizing "salutatory effects on the Soviet Union," its terrorizing "diplomatic" dimensions, that dominated strategic thinking at the highest levels of government in Washington.

GEOSTRATEGY AND NUCLEAR TERROR

The intense secrecy surrounding "S-1" or the "Tube Alloy" effort, codewords for the Manhattan Project, allowed Roosevelt to monopolize decision-making about the atomic bomb and its uses. His scientific advisors and the Secretary of War and Secretary of State were allowed to give input when Roosevelt deemed it necessary. Roosevelt did turn to Vannevar Bush and Conant for advice, but he made his decisions about the development and use of nuclear weapons in consultation with Churchill. He "felt no obligation" to consult or to inform his scientific advisors about his decisions.[49]

As early as the Atlantic Conference in August 1941, in conversations with Churchill, Roosevelt began designing the postwar order to reinforce US privilege and power. Despite his later advocacy of the United Nations, from the beginning he refused to consider an international organization as the guarantor of global law and order. An American–British international police force, he believed, would be more effective. By 1942 Roosevelt recognized the political debt the US and Britain would owe Moscow for its sacrifices in defeating Nazi Germany. Roosevelt's concept of two "policemen" enforcing the new (dis)order, thus became four, with the Soviet

Union and France making it a quartet. Nations that violated the postwar order policed by the Big Four "would be quarantined . . . if they persisted . . . [they would be] bombed at the rate of a city a day until they agreed to behave."[50]

Roosevelt and Churchill's meeting in Quebec the following year is seen as the moment Roosevelt "began to deal with atomic energy as an *integral* part of his general diplomacy, linking and encompassing both the current wartime situation and the shape of affairs." Churchill too considered "the whole [atomic energy] affair on an after-the-war military basis." For him the atomic bomb was all that would lie "between the snows of Russia and the white cliffs of Dover . . . . It would never do to have Germany or Russia win the race for something which might be used for international blackmail."[51]

As the Manhattan Project approached "success," Roosevelt became clearer that the US would take "full advantage of the bomb's potential as a post-war instrument of Anglo-American diplomacy. There could still be four policemen, but only two of them would have the bomb."[52] If anyone other than Churchill influenced Roosevelt it was Stimson. He was deeply concerned about Soviet repression and its growing domination of Eastern Europe. At one point, he expressed the hope that after the atomic bombs were used to contain the Soviet Union's ambitions, they could be further used to discipline Moscow. Sharing secrets about the bombs' production, he thought, might be used to reward the Soviets for good behavior and "as a diplomatic instrument for shaping the peace."[53]

Roosevelt opted for Churchill's vision of an anti-Soviet US–British nuclear monopoly rather than Stimson's more nuanced approach. This was codified in the June 1943 Agreement and Declaration of Trust signed in Quebec, which specified "that the United States and Great Britain would cooperate in seeking to control available supplies of uranium and thorium ore both during and after the war." In Quebec, Roosevelt and Churchill also signed an *aide-mémoire* that stated, "When a bomb is finally available, it might perhaps, after mature consideration, be used against the Japanese, who should be warned that this bombardment will be repeated until they surrender." As Sherwin observed, at the time of Roosevelt's death in April 1945, "the question of the use of the bomb against Japan was more clearly settled than was general policy." Or, as Barton Bernstein later put it, "All of F.D.R.'s advisors who knew about the bomb always unquestioningly assumed that it would be used . . . By about mid-1944, most had comfortably concluded that the target would be Japan."[54]

Harry Truman should be classed with Richard Nixon, Ronald Reagan, George H., and George W. Bush in the brutal use of military power and the embrace of nuclear terrorism. Roosevelt died on April 12, and after serving just 82 days as Vice-President, Truman assumed office isolated, insecure, and relatively ignorant of foreign policy and military matters. Roosevelt had had little regard for the haberdasher from St. Louis. In a political coup at the 1944 Democratic Party's national convention, political bosses ousted Henry Wallace from the vice-presidency, replacing him with a machine politician who at the time of the convention had just 2 percent of the party's support. Roosevelt did not bother to inform Truman about the agreements made at Yalta or about the Manhattan Project. On becoming president, Truman thus found himself unusually dependent on old friends and Roosevelt's advisors.[55]

Truman's recollection of Secretary of War Stimson hanging back after the new president's first Cabinet meeting has passed into the lore of US political history. Sensitive to the politics of transition, Stimson informed the new president that while it was best to leave the details for another time, he should know that "a new explosive . . . with almost unbelievable destructive power" was under development. A fortnight later, Stimson explained how the atom bomb would be "decisive" in the postwar era,[56] and he suggested that the president create a "select committee" to consider the bomb's long-term implications. This was the origin of the Interim Committee, which soon recommended targets for the A-bombs.

Anti-communism and opposition to Russian dominance of Eastern Europe reinforced planning to use the new bombs. Although Roosevelt and Churchill had agreed at the Yalta summit that Poland's postwar government would be "friendly" to the Soviet Union, and despite repeated counsel from Stimson and Leahy that Moscow was consistently living up to its commitments, the newly installed president quickly fell under the influence of Averill Harriman, the Ambassador to Moscow, outgoing Secretary of State Edward R. Stettinius, and Churchill. They opposed Soviet domination of Poland, which to them symbolized the totality of East–West relations. They fed the president's fears with reports that Stalin had violated agreements and could not be trusted.[57]

Truman began his confrontation with Moscow on his second day as president. At Harriman's suggestion, Soviet Foreign Minister Molotov had traveled to Washington to express official Soviet condolences at Roosevelt's death and to meet the new president. In their first private meeting Truman was blunt, using uncompromising language that shocked Harriman as well as the Soviet Foreign Minister. Truman demanded that Moscow accept his understanding of the Yalta agreement and create a Polish government that represented all Polish people. Molotov's response that for the Soviet government "It [was] a matter of honor" to fulfill its Yalta commitments was met with derision. He later complained that he had "never been talked to like that in my life." Soviet Ambassador

Gromyko, who accompanied Molotov, reported that "Coldness was shown in [Truman's] every gesture. The new president rejected whatever was proposed to him and whatever topic the conversation touched on. It appeared at times he did not even hear the interlocutor." Truman behaved with "cock-like belligerency, contradicted almost every point raised by the Soviet side about the significance of the future world organization and about measures designed to prevent further aggression from Germany." Even Harriman was "taken aback" as he witnessed Truman abandon Roosevelt's approach and launch a campaign to eliminate Soviet influence from Europe.[58]

With Germany facing imminent defeat, Churchill and Stalin were anxious for a summit meeting with Truman to plan the last stages of the war against Japan and to resolve their differences over the postwar international "order." Truman, insecure about his diplomatic skills and with no guarantees that he would have a working atomic bomb in his negotiating hand, did not share his allies' sense of urgency. He thus appreciated and accepted Stimson's suggestion that the Potsdam summit be postponed until after the A-bomb test, code named "Trinity," was conducted in July. As Stimson noted at the time, the way to deal with the Russians was to "keep our mouths shut and let our actions speak for words . . . . The Russians will understand them better than anything else . . . . I call it a royal straight flush and we mustn't be a fool about the way we play it." Truman was less diplomatic: "If it explodes, as I think it will, I'll certainly have a hammer on those boys."[59]

GEOSTRATEGIC AMBITIONS

Additional factors informed planning for Potsdam and the decision to annihilate Hiroshima and Nagasaki. Of central importance was a debate that emerged in Washington over whether the Soviets would actually join the war against Japan, and whether doing so would serve US interests.

At the Teheran summit in October 1943, Stalin had agreed to join the war against Japan soon after Germany's defeat. Moscow would share the sacrifices needed to rout the Emperor's imperial forces. The Joint Chiefs' war plan called for the Soviets to keep the Japanese Army tied down in Manchuria and China, and to prevent redeployment of Japanese troops to their besieged home islands. In return for the Red Army's burden-sharing, Stalin was promised that Manchuria, Taiwan, and the Pescadores would be returned to China, that Korea would be placed under a 40-year trusteeship, and that the strategic port of Darien, the Manchurian railway, and southern Sakhalin would be returned to the Soviet Union.[60] Moscow would also be given the Kurile Islands, thereby opening strategic sea lanes to the Pacific. At Yalta the following year, the deal was sweetened in the tradition of colonial powers, with Moscow being promised the right to lease Port Arthur for use as a naval base.[61] By September 1944, Stalin was sharing some of his war plans with Ambassador Harriman. Between 20 and 30 Soviet divisions would be redeployed from Europe to fight the Japanese.[62]

However, six months later, with Germany on the verge of defeat and Japanese military power collapsing, the US Joint Chiefs became confident that Japan could be defeated without Soviet intervention. Given Stalin's commitment to join the war in August, pressure began to build in Washington to limit Soviet influence in Asia by preventing Soviet entry into the war. Truman's newly appointed Secretary of State James Byrnes believed that "somebody had made an awful mistake in bringing about a situation where Russia was permitted to come out of a war with the power she will have."[63] Harriman also advised that once Moscow joined the war against Japan, "Russian influence would move in quickly and toward ultimate domination . . . There could be no illusion about anything such as 'free China' once the Russians got in . . . [Russia] will in the end exercise control over whatever government may be established in Manchuria and Outer Mongolia."[64] Their arguments were reinforced by former Ambassador to Japan James Grew, who advised that Japan would be strategically important for the coming confrontation with the Soviet Union. It could serve, he understood, as the "keystone" of US power in Asia and the Pacific.

There was more to these concerns than Soviet behavior in Eastern and Central Europe. Since the early years of the Meiji Restoration, Japan and Russia had competed for influence in Manchuria, northern China, and Korea. With Japan facing defeat, Truman's advisors and US military leaders feared that a military and political vacuum would open in Asia which would be filled by the Kremlin. Rich and strategically important assets (and possibly a quarter of the world's population) would thus fall to the Soviet Union. Truman and his advisors were committed to holding them within the US imperial sphere.

The race for East Asia had, in fact, already begun. The Truman administration was unaware that almost a year earlier the Soviet Ambassador to Japan, Iakov Malik, had submitted a report to Stalin recommending priorities for Moscow's relations with Tokyo. Malik reported that Japan's defeat was "only a matter of time," and that its leaders would see closer ties with the Soviet Union as the only way out of its increasingly desperate war. If Moscow intervened before Japan's defeat and played Japan against the Anglo-Saxon allies, Stalin could have a major role in determining how the spoils of war were allocated. Malik advised that Stalin's priority should be gaining secure access to the Pacific, with the strategic and economic benefits that would follow. With this in mind he urged that Moscow draw out the war to gain time for its military intervention. He also urged that the Red Army seize Manchuria, Korea, Tsuchima, and the Kurile Islands. Stalin agreed, ordering that "the postwar territorial settlement should be dictated by the requirements of the Soviet state, not by its historical claim."[65]

Geography was also a priority for US war planners. Location was one of the two strategic assets that made Japan's inclusion in the "Grand Area" a preoccupation in Washington. US planners envisioned the Pacific as an "American lake" for the postwar period. With US forces occupying Japan and creating its postwar government, the island nation could become Grew's "keystone of the Pacific" and permit the US to complete its encirclement of the Soviet Union and to block Soviet naval access to the Pacific. To this day, the US maintains more than 100 military bases and installations across Japan.

Japan had other attractions. Although most of its industrial capacity was destroyed, the intellectual base upon which it had been built and its future industrial potential were strategic assets that US planners did not want to fall to Moscow. Japan was so central to US ambitions in Asia that five years after Tokyo's surrender the US again went to war in Asia, this time in Korea, primarily to protect Japan's strategic western flank. Later, in the 1960s and 1970s, one of Washington's primary war aims in Vietnam was to guarantee Japan's access to its "natural market" in Indochina, lest it become dependent on communist China.[66]

In May 1945, convinced that a future war with the Soviets was inevitable, former Ambassador Grew, in his role as Acting Secretary of State, raised four critical questions: 1) How much pressure should be exerted on the Kremlin to ensure that it honored its commitments to join the war? 2) Was Soviet involvement in the war so important to the US that Washington should avoid taking risks to limit Moscow's strategic gains in Asia? 3) Should the concessions in Asia, made to the Soviet Union at Yalta, be reconsidered? 4) If the Soviets demanded participation in the occupation of Japan, should the US acquiesce?[67]

These questions crystallized Stimson's understanding of the strategic potential of the atom bomb. "Once its power was demonstrated," he concluded, "the Soviets would be more accommodating to the American point of view. Territorial disputes could be settled amicably."[68]

JAPAN'S PEACE CAMP

US leaders knew that with Germany's surrender, Japan's rulers understood that time to negotiate an accommodation was running out. Those at the commanding heights in Washington had monitored the development of a secret peace camp that had been at work within the Japanese government for a year in an effort to avert what Emperor Hirohito later described as the "unbearable" conquest and occupation of Japan. The peace party's leading figures included the Emperor's most senior and trusted advisor, Chief Privy Council Kido, Foreign Minister Togo, and Navy Minister Yonai. In July 1944, after Japan's defeat at Saipan, Kido choreographed the collapse of General Tojo's government and arranged his replacement by Santaro Suzuki. Within a month, Yonai ordered a secret study about how the war could be ended, including how to overcome the power of uncompromising militarists in the Japanese Army. The study correctly predicted that to end the war the Emperor would have to intervene personally to impose his will on both the military and the government.[69]

Six months later, when Roosevelt, Stalin, and Churchill met at Yalta, Japan's former prime minister, Prince Konoe, informed the Emperor that "Japan's defeat is inevitable." To avoid a communist revolution following defeat, Konoe urged that the only way to ensure the survival of the Emperor and *kokutai* (the essence of the Meiji emperor system) was to "negotiate with the United States and Britain as soon as possible."[70]

Unfortunately, the "peace camp's" misreading of Soviet intentions, despite sobering reports from Ambassador Sato in Moscow, led it to invest its hopes in Soviet mediation. But, as Ambassador Malik had recommended, Soviet leaders and diplomats were doing their best to prolong the war, expressing support for Japan while deferring its diplomatic entreaties. Among the most important signals the Japanese peace camp missed was the true meaning of Moscow's understated April 5 announcement that it would not renew its Neutrality Pact with Tokyo. Although the announcement unsettled Japan's leaders, its implications—including the possibility that Russia could join the war in a year's time—were so great that the Japanese Supreme War Council could not move beyond cognitive dissonance. Unwilling to consider alternatives, it remained committed to winning Soviet mediation.

At the same time, with the death toll in Okinawa climbing to 150,000 civilians and 100,000 Japanese soldiers, it became increasingly clear that the Imperial Army's campaign to buy time for the Emperor and the home islands was doomed. By June, reports sent to the Emperor echoed those of General McArthur: "the Japanese fleet has been reduced to practical impotency. The Japanese Air Force has been reduced to . . . uncoordinated, suicidal attacks against our forces . . . Its attrition is heavy and its power for sustained action is diminishing rapidly." Japan "was running out of food, fuel, planes and raw materials of all kinds. Her major cities were in ruins, millions of her people were homeless and starving."[71]

Pressed by a growing sense of urgency, heightened by fears that Tokyo would be burned to the ground, Kido, Togo, Yanai, and their allies worked to build unity within the Japanese government to negotiate the war's end while ordering Japanese diplomats and intelligence officials in Europe to open discussions with the US. Thus Japan's minister in Switzerland began a dialogue with Allen Dulles, the OSS's (forerunner to the CIA) chief official in Europe, to "arrange for a cessation of hostilities." Similar explorations were launched at the Vatican and through Swedish diplomats. The Japanese ambassador in Portugal made it known "that actual peace terms were unimportant so long as the term 'unconditional surrender' was not employed." In Tokyo, proposals prepared for Prince Konoe called for sacrificing Okinawa, the Bonin Islands, and southern Sakhalin. The one imperative was to protect the Emperor and to preserve the *kokutai*.[72]

These offers came as no surprise to Allied leaders. In 1944, Churchill had observed that once Russia declared war, and Japan faced a three-part alliance, Tokyo would move to surrender. This, he suggested, might obviate the need for an invasion. By April 1945, planners for the Joint Chiefs of Staff had reached the same conclusion.[73]

As Ambassador Malik had anticipated, Japan's increasingly desperate leadership came to see "cultivation of good relations with the Soviet Union as . . . the only way for Japan to extricate itself from the war." In mid-April, Malik reported that "the new cabinet is pursuing its objective to create conditions for extricating Japan from the war." It "could not," he reported, "continue the war for more than eight months."[74] By mid-May, appreciating that Soviet "entry into the war will deal a death blow to the Empire," the Japanese Supreme War Council was preoccupied with the Soviet Union. The Council, still dominated by the military, adopted a policy calling for "immediate negotiations" to prevent the Soviets from entering the war and to seek its "mediation to terminate the war [o]n terms favorable to Japan." To entice the Kremlin the War Council proposed major concessions, but these fell short of what Roosevelt had promised Stalin at Yalta.[75]

It took Tokyo time to absorb Ambassador Sato's message that "Japan should do everything to terminate the war with the single aim of preserving the *kokutai*."[76] By mid-June, with defeat imminent in Okinawa and more than 30 Soviet divisions massing on the Manchurian border, nearly identical proposals were being developed by the "peace camps" in Tokyo and Washington. Unaware of the scale of Moscow's territorial ambitions and its intention to prolong and enter the war, Emperor Hirohito agreed to seek Soviet mediation on the basis of "peace with honor." He endorsed a plan calling for Japanese withdrawal from *all* occupied territories, partial disarmament, and preservation of the imperial system. Meanwhile, in Washington, former President Hoover urged Truman to win Japan's surrender "before the Soviets captured Manchuria, North China and Korea."

Surrender could be arranged, Hoover advised, "if Britain and America could persuade the Japanese they had no intention of eradicating them, eliminating their system of government, or interfering with their way of life." And, as it became increasingly clear to US planners that keeping Hirohito on the throne as a constitutional monarch would facilitate the US conquest and occupation of Japan, Stimson, Grew, Assistant Secretary of War McCloy and Secretary of the Navy Forrestal all reported that US strategic interests could be served with less than "unconditional surrender."[77]

POTSDAM

It was against this background and the Manhattan Project's final preparations for the "Trinity" A-bomb test that Truman set sail for Europe for the July 17–August 2, 1945 summit with Stalin and Churchill at Potsdam in occupied Germany. In addition to serving as the forum in which Truman would begin to play his "master card," both Stalin and the Japanese elite had critically important agendas for the summit. Prohibited by the Neutrality Pact from waging war against Japan until a year after its abrogation, Stalin sought legal cover to join the war by means of an allied invitation. Emperor Hirohito and the Japanese peace party hoped that the summit would open the way for Soviet mediation on their behalf with the US president.

On July 12, as Truman sailed to Europe, a message from Japanese Foreign Minister Togo to be delivered to Soviet Foreign Minister Molotov was intercepted by US intelligence and relayed to Truman. It read:

> His Majesty the Emperor, mindful of the fact that the present war daily brings greater evil and sacrifice on the peoples' of all the belligerent powers, desires from his heart that it may be quickly terminated. But so long as England and the United States insist upon unconditional surrender the Japanese Empire has no alternative to fight on . . . for the honor and existence of the Motherland. His Majesty is deeply reluctant to have any further blood lost among the people of both sides . . . It is the Emperor's private intention to send Prince Konoe to Moscow as a Special Envoy with a letter from him containing the statements given above. Please inform Molotov of this and get the Russians to consent to having the party enter the country.[78]

Truman and his advisors understood the Emperor's intention. As the president confided to his diary, "telegram from Jap Emperor asking for peace." He did nothing to exploit this opening.[79] Soviet ambitions similarly dictated stalling. Hirohito waited in vain for a reply.

Meanwhile preparations for the earliest possible use of the US nuclear weapons continued. The Interim Committee had met on May 31 and, without discussing whether using atomic bombs was necessary or appropriate, decided to use them as "terror weapon[s]" to produce a "profound psychological impression on as many Japanese as possible." The Committee took this decision despite serious reservations raised by Arthur H. Compton, who had brought the first Manhattan Project scientists together. He was concerned that the use of the bomb raised "profound and political questions." First among them was that it "introduces the question of mass slaughter, really for the first time in history . . . . the new weapon," he argued, "carries much more serious implications than the introduction of poison gas." The Army's General George Marshall concurred, and urged that the weapons "first be used against straight military objectives such as a large naval installation." Marshall feared "the opprobrium that might follow an ill-considered employment of such force," and he deeply opposed violating the military code of not killing civilians intentionally.[80]

Nonetheless, the Committee accepted Conant's recommendation that the best target would be a "vital war plant employing a large number of workers and closely surrounded by workers' homes." To demonstrate the atomic bombs' terrorizing power and to ensure that their power would not be wasted in less densely populated areas, they decided to target urban centers where civilians were concentrated, and not specific military or industrial sites on the cities' perimeters. Few Japanese cities met these criteria. General LeMay's fire bombings had destroyed 64 Japanese cities, and for lack of targets he had turned to incinerating larger towns. The secondary cities of Hiroshima, Kokura, Niigata, and Nagasaki were, however, placed off limits for LeMay's bombers to ensure that the new weapon would "have a fair background to show its strength."[81] The Committee also agreed that two weapons should be available for use in early August with more to follow if necessary. The bombings of Hiroshima and Nagasaki thus resulted from a *single* decision.

On their arrival in Potsdam, Truman and his advisors were informed that the Soviet Union would join the war on August 15. Truman's diary indicates that he understood the implications of Stalin's pledge: "He'll be in the Jap War on August 15th. Fini Japs when that comes about." He knew that the A-bombs would not be essential to ensure the near-immediate end to the war.

On July 16, with US leaders "anxious," in Byrnes' words, "to get the Japanese affair over with before the Russians got in,"[82] a relieved Stimson passed a note to Truman which read, "It's a Boy." This was code informing the president that the Trinity A-bomb test had been successful.

None of the US officials in Potsdam could understand the overwhelming sense of awe and fear, but also joy, felt by most who witnessed and experienced the first atomic explosion in the New Mexico desert. General Groves soon reported that "The test was successful beyond the most optimistic expectations of anyone . . . I estimate the energy generated to be in excess of 15,000 to 20,000 tons of TNT; and this is a conservative estimate." His report related that the blast was brighter than the sun, that it created a crater nearly a quarter of a mile in diameter, that its mushroom cloud climbed 8 miles into the sky, and that it had shattered a window 125 miles away![83] Oppenheimer was so shaken by what he had brought into the world that a sentence from the Hindu scriptures immediately occurred to him: "Now I am become Death, destroyer of worlds."[84]

In Potsdam news that the US arsenal now included Stimson's "royal straight flush" stiffened Truman's and Byrnes' determination to play their master card before Stalin could claim his spoils. As Churchill observed, "Truman was evidently much fortified . . . he stood up to the Russians in a most decisive manner . . . He told the Russians just where they got on and off and generally bossed the whole meeting." Churchill wrote to Anthony Eden, "It is quite clear that the United States does not at the present time desire Russian participation in the war against Japan."[85]

Stalin's only role in the Potsdam Declaration was to provide the venue for its promulgation by Truman and Churchill. The Soviet leader was taken by surprise and was not consulted about its content or advised about the timing of its release. Rejecting a draft prepared by the Joint Chiefs that would have protected Emperor Hirohito and preserved the imperial system, and anxious to *prevent* Japan's surrender before he could demonstrate the terrorizing power of the atomic bombs, Truman's Declaration insisted on Japan's "unconditional surrender." Truman and Churchill went out of their way to undermine the Japanese peace camp by using the Declaration to insist that there would be "no alternatives" to eliminating the authority and influence "of those who have deceived and misled the people into embarking on world conquest." They warned that "stern justice shall be meted out to all war criminals," including the Emperor. Understanding that "if we insisted on unconditional surrender, we could justify the dropping of the atomic bomb,"[86] Byrnes had also encouraged Truman to include the threat of Japan's "prompt and utter destruction." The Declaration was thus designed to prolong the war and to legitimate the atomic bombings, not to hasten its end.

Two brief exchanges at Potsdam were particularly revealing. The first came when Stalin, unaware of the US intelligence intercepts, briefed Truman about the Japanese request for Prince Konoe to travel to Moscow. The Soviet dictator indicated that there were three possible responses: "Ask the Japanese for more details, leading them to believe their plan had a chance; ignore the overture; or send back a definite refusal." Stalin indicated that his preference was "to lull the Japanese to sleep." Truman concurred. For competing reasons, each worked to prolong the war.[87]

The second exchange came when Truman "casually mentioned" to Stalin that the US had "a new weapon of unusual destructive force," implicitly threatening the Soviet Union. Stalin, who had been kept abreast of developments by Soviet spies at Los Alamos, was hardly surprised. His response that he hoped Truman would make "good use of it against the Japanese" disconcerted the president. The message, nonetheless, had been sent. Soviet Chief of Staff Marshal Georgi Zhukov, who met with Stalin shortly after the exchange, understood Truman's words as "political blackmail" and as a "psychological attack against . . . Stalin."[88]

Contrary to pronouncements by Truman and Stalin in the weeks that followed, the Japanese government did *not* reject the Potsdam Declaration. Having received no official notice of the ultimatum, it made no immediate formal response. The Declaration was not communicated through intermediaries in Switzerland, Sweden, or the Vatican, where diplomatic channels had been opened.[89] Tokyo's knowledge of the ultimatum came from reports picked up via shortwave radio as it was trumpeted by the Office of War Information as propaganda. Based on these broadcasts, Foreign Minister Togo reported to the Emperor that the Declaration was "a broad, general statement, and it leaves room for further study of the concrete terms . . . we plan to find out what these concrete terms are through the Soviet Union." As powerful Japanese industrialists learned about the Declaration, they encouraged its acceptance. And from Switzerland, the OSS reported that Japanese representatives had accepted the Proclamation.[90]

A "race" was now on between Washington and Moscow. The Truman administration seized on confused press reports that announced that Tokyo had "rejected" its demands. As Truman later explained, "I was not willing to let Russia reap the fruits of a long and bitter and gallant effort in which she had had no part."[91]

THE SIGNAL IS SENT

On July 25, less than ten days after the "Trinity" test turned desert sand into glass, the 509th Composite Group of the 20th Air Force, based on the recently conquered Tinian Island, received orders to deliver its "special bomb" as soon after August 3 as weather permitted. As additional bombs were delivered, the 509th was to work through its target list: Hiroshima, Kokura, Niigata, and Nagasaki. Foul weather slowed the race against the Soviets, but on the night of August 5 the "Enola Gay" and its "Little Boy" uranium bomb took off for Hiroshima.

At 8 a.m. on August 6, the people of Hiroshima felt relatively safe. Rumors had been circulating to explain why the city had not been bombed like other Japanese cities: Hiroshima was beautiful, and the Americans were saving it for their villas; there were important foreigners in the city, possibly including President Truman's mother; and the city was not on US maps. Less reassuring was the rumor that the Americans were preparing something "unusually big." Scientists even discussed the possibility that an atomic bomb might be used, but most thought it impossible.[92]

Another factor contributed to the false sense of security and to the number of casualties that followed. There were two air raid alerts during the night of August 5–6 and a third when the bombing mission's weather plane passed uneventfully over the city. At 7:32 a.m. the all-clear sounded. On a hot, bright, and beautiful morning people were at work or beginning their day. "Housewives were completing after-breakfast chores," and it was "early morning wartime routine."[93] Near the city center mobilized students labored in the sun, helping to demolish and carry away the rubble of small homes and shops to create fire breaks against the possibility that the city would be fire-bombed. For the same reason, many schoolchildren had been evacuated from the city to schools in rural districts.

"Little Boy" exploded on target, 1,800 feet above the Shima Hospital in the bustling Nakejima district. Within a second the heat of its massive fireball reached that of the sun, more than 1,000,000° C.[94] Within 10 seconds the bomb's explosive force and the resulting firestorm completely destroyed the city which lay across a flat plain, previously broken only by rivers. An estimated 100,000 people died that day and in the weeks immediately following. With nearly all of the city's buildings completely destroyed, its hospitals lay in ruins. More than half the city's doctors and nurses perished in the inferno.[95] Another 100,000 died in the following months from burns, injuries, and radiation sickness.[96]

Among the victims were up to 30,000 Koreans, most brought to Japan to serve as slave laborers in factories, mines, and work gangs. The dead also included several thousand Chinese, Manchurian, and Filipino slave laborers, more than 1,000 Japanese-Americans stranded in Japan by the war, and at least eleven US prisoners of war and other POWs from Australia, Holland, and Britain.[97]

Naomi Shohno, a *Hibakusha* who later became a physicist, described what happened on the ground:

> at the moment of the explosion a fireball with a temperature of *several million degrees centigrade* and an atmospheric pressure of several hundred thousand bars was formed at the burst point . . . . Buildings were smashed to pieces and incinerated by the blast and thermal rays, and it

> was the great quantities of dust from the destroyed buildings, carried by the winds, that cast the city into pitch-darkness just after the bombing. The violent winds also tossed people about . . . . As the fireball disappeared, the vacuum around the burst point pulled in dust, air, and the evaporated materials of the bomb, causing a mushroom cloud to rise . . . [B]ecause of the combined effects of the blast, thermal rays, fires, almost all buildings within about 2 kilometers of the hypocenter . . . were completely razed and consumed by fire *in an instant* . . . conflagrations occurred within about 3 kilometers of the hypocenter in Hiroshima and within about 3.5 kilometers in Nagasaki.[98]

By the time the mushroom cloud formed, the entire city was destroyed. People—including the mobilized students—within half a mile of the hypocenter were vaporized or reduced to lumps of charcoal. To this day, the trauma of survivors who were closest to the apocalyptic explosion is such that they are the least able to describe the enormity of what they saw and experienced.[99]

Japanese government statistics reported that 78,150 people were killed, 13,983 missing, and 37,425 injured; 62,000 of Hiroshima's 90,000 buildings destroyed, and 6,000 more were damaged beyond repair. The precise number of humans who perished will never be known because the number of troops and slave laborers deployed in the city was a state secret.

As John Dower has written, the people of Hiroshima experienced what they understand as hell—a Buddhist as well as a Western concept of a "fiery inferno peopled with monsters and naked, tormented bodies." "Hell," Dower explained, is "almost exactly what witnesses of Hiroshima and Nagasaki saw—a raging inferno; streets full of monstrously deformed creatures; excruciating pain, without medicine and without surcease . . . 'It was like Hell' is the most common refrain" of the survivors.

> Many other scenes also were imaginable only in hell. Outlines of bodies were permanently etched as white shadows in black nimbus on streets or walls, but the bodies themselves had disappeared . . . . there were innumerable corpses without apparent injury. Parts of bodies held their ground, like two legs severed below the knees, still standing. Many of the dead were turned into statues, some solid and others waiting to crumble at a touch.[100]

The traumas people experienced were unique and agonizing, but were shared by tens of thousands of their neighbors. The poet Sankichi Toge described a moment in the aftermath:

> Swirling yellow smoke lifts to reveal buildings split asunder, bridges collapsed, scorched wrecks that were trains and filled with commuters. Hiroshima a shoreless sea of rubble and smoldering embers. A figure with skin in pealing tatters wraps a scorched piece of cloth about its waist. Hands clasped to breast, sobbing, it steps over the former contents of someone's head to join a walking throng of naked fellow beings.[101]

Called away from the Hiroshima Military Hospital late on the night of August 5–6 to care for a farm girl, Dr Shuntaro Hida was a little more than 3 miles from the hypocenter. At 8:15 a.m., he spotted a B-29 bomber in the blue sky above Hiroshima. His description of what he experienced and witnessed is among the clearest and most comprehensive that have been written:

> A . . . tremendous flash struck my face and a penetrating light pierced my eyes. All of a sudden my face and arms were engulfed by an intense heat . . . Within an instant I was crawling on mats which lay on the floor and tried to flee outside by creeping along the surface . . . .
>
> MY WHOLE HEART TREMBLED AT WHAT I SAW. There was a great fire ring floating over the city. Within a moment, a massive deep white cloud grew out of the center of the ring. It grew quickly upward . . . . At the same time I could see a long black cloud as it spread over the entire width of the city. It spread along the side of the hill in our direction and began to surge over the Ohta Valley toward Hesaka village, enveloping in its path all the woods, groves, rice fields, farms and houses. What I saw was the beginning of an enormous storm created by the blast as it gathered up the mud and sand of the city and rolled it into a huge wave . . . .
>
> Suddenly I saw the roof of the primary school below the farmer's house easily stripped away by the cloud of dust. Before I could think about taking cover my whole body flew up in the air. The shutters and screens flew about me as if they were scraps of paper. The thatched roof of the farmer's house was blown away with the ceiling still attached . . . . Then I was lifted by the wave, carried ten meters across two rooms, and thrown against a large Buddhist altar. The huge roof and a large quantity of mud fell upon me with a crash. I felt some pain, but there was no time to think. I crept outside groping to find my way. My eyes, ears, nose and even my mouth were filled with mud. Fortunately, because the big pillars or walls were strong, the farmer's granddaughter was only pressed under the straw bed . . . With all my strength I pulled her out of the house . . .

> But I was a medical officer and my overwhelming sense of duty was driving me forward. Only this self-conceit compelled me to push forward on [a] bicycle and to overcome the fear . . . I sped down at top speed . . . when suddenly something came into my view. I quickly braked. . . . I . . . was surprised to see a figure which appeared from around the corner.
>
> It was anything but "a man." The strange figure came up to me little by little, unsteady on its feet. It surely seemed like the form of a man but it was completely naked, bloody, and covered with mud. The body was completely swollen. Rags hung from its bare breast and waist. The hands were held before the breasts with palms turned down. Water dripped from the tips of the rags . . . [W]hat I took to be rags were in fact pieces of human skin and the water drops were human blood. I could not distinguish between male and female, soldier or citizen. It had a curiously large head, swollen eyelids and big projected lips grew as if they formed half of its face. There was no hair on its burned head . . .
>
> . . . He found me with his burnt eyes and hastily tried to reach me. It must have been his last exertion for he took his final step and fell . . . . I looked at the road before me. Naked, burnt, and bloody, numberless survivors stood in my path. They were massed together, some crawling on their knees or on all fours, some stood with difficulty or leaned on another's shoulder. Not one showed any feature which forced me to recognize him or her as a human being.[102]

Junko Kayashige, an artist and teacher, was six years old on August 3, 1945 when her mother returned to Hiroshima with her and four of her sisters: the infant Toshiko, three-year-old Fumie, Michiko who was in the fourth grade, and Katsuko, who was in the sixth grade. Kayashige's two oldest sisters, Eiko, who worked in a steel factory, and Hiroko, who had been mobilized to help demolish buildings to make fire breaks, had stayed in the city, as had their father, who worked in a neighboring prefecture. An older brother was in the military in distant Yamaguchi prefecture.

Early on the morning of August 6, Kayashige's mother took the baby and left to visit an aunt in nearby Itsukaichi. Michiko rode off on a bicycle to buy ice for the icebox, while Kayashige and Fumie were sent to an uncle's nearby home. She and a cousin were sitting on the windowsill when they saw the "Enola Gay" fly over the city. She later testified:

> I do not know how much time passed. I found myself lying on the ground under the window, inside the house. The house escaped collapse, but the desk, chairs, bookshelves, *tatami* mats, and floorboards were gone. My sister, cousin, and aunt, having also been blown on the ground, were

> raising themselves when I saw them. We went outside. All our neighbors' houses were crushed to the ground. . . . an old woman in our neighborhood was crying for help, trapped under a stone wall. Her daughter-in-law strove to get her out, but the wall was too heavy. My aunt gave her a hand too . . . Houses around us were not on fire yet, but we became frightened when they started to catch fire. Trying to take three children with her, my aunt went back in the house to get some rope which she thought to use for tying them on her back. I waited outside for her to come back, but I could not bear to stay there any longer. I finally ran away by myself.

Kayashige was seriously burned on her face, arms, and legs, those parts of her body not protected by her white dress that had reflected the radiation:

> I went walking on the roofs of the houses which were smashed flat on the ground . . . there were people staggering . . . I could not tell men from women. The skin of their bodies and even their faces had peeled off and [was] dangling, looking like seaweed. Everyone was heading toward the mountain, so I followed . . . I came to the riverside after passing over the Nakahiro Bridge . . . When I looked back behind me, the bridge I had just walked across was in flames, burning terribly on both sides . . . .

Kayashige's sister Michiko disappeared in the explosion; her aunt died the next day. After days of searching among the dead and dying in the ruins of a school, Kayashige's father found Hiroko who had been demolishing buildings. She was severely burned and unable to move. He carried Hiroko home on boards strapped to a bicycle. As they traveled,

> [P]eople put their hands together and said the words of Buddhist prayer, thinking she was already dead. My sister said to my father "I am not dead yet." Even . . . hurt, she was able to say "I am home!" out loud when she arrived, which made all of us so glad and relieved. But whether she was sleeping or awake, maggots were very active. We kept picking them off her body, using tweezers, but they crawled into her flesh and caused her pain . . . .
>
> I can never forget the day my sister Hiroko died, that was the 17th of August, 1945. Those who had enough strength . . . were having a meal . . . . Then, "Mama, could you come for a second?" . . . My mother told her to wait for a moment. A little later she went to see my sister. With the voice of my mother crying "Hiroko! Hiroko!" we realized something was wrong. When we rushed to her bedside she was already dead. The sound of her voice, "I am home!" and "Mama, could you come for a second?" never leaves my ears. I feel I can still hear her voice.[103]

Those who made their way to the city to help with the relief effort were staggered by what they saw. Exposed to the deadly radiation, many soon fell victim to a mystifying disease that began with purple spots which appeared across their bodies, bleeding from their mouths and noses, and diarrhea. This was radiation sickness. Others fell ill months or even years later.

Like many *Hibakusha*, Professor Satoru Konishi still suffers from post-traumatic stress syndrome, partial amnesia, and survivor's guilt. In August 1945 he was a 16-year-old mobilized high school student, ostensibly working in a shipyard. Because there were no materials for shipbuilding, on the morning of August 6 he and other students were in a shack, their "so-called classroom." They felt the flash and heat wave of the blast before the windows and walls of their "classroom" were blown apart:

> After the blast passed, we crawled out. I found . . . one of my school-mates standing distracted. A drop of blood trickled down his cheek. About 500 meters in front of us, we saw a big pillar of white cloud rising fiercely into the sky; it looked like a dragon or tornado-monster. Here my memory fades . . .
>
> On the next morning, August 7, I went to the city with two of my school-mates. When I stood at the west end of the city, oh, the city had totally disappeared . . .
>
> All of a sudden, I heard a voice saying, "Give me water!" I looked and saw it. It was a face like a lump of tofu, so white, swollen, and soft, with its eyes, nose and mouth shapeless. It looked totally different from a human face. I cannot remember what I did and saw after that. One thing is sure, that I went away without giving him any water.

Decades later, after surviving debilitating bouts of radiation sickness, Professor Konishi asked one of the friends who had been with him what they had done that day: "We walked . . . all around the ruined city of Hiroshima that day. There were corpses lying here and there; bodies floating up and down on the rivers; scattered bones and debris." Trauma hides these images from Professor Konishi's consciousness, but he is still haunted by the memory of "that face like tofu."

Wilfred Burchett was the first foreign journalist to view Hiroshima, reaching the city a month after its annihilation. He reported:

> In Hiroshima, thirty days after the first atomic bomb destroyed the city . . . people are still dying, mysteriously and horribly . . . from an unknown something which I can only describe as the atomic plague.
>
> Hiroshima does not look like a bombed city. It looks as if a monster steamroller has passed over it and squashed it out of existence . . . The damage is far greater than photographs can show . . . you can look

> around for twenty-five and perhaps thirty square miles, you can see hardly a building . . . There is just nothing standing except for twenty factory chimneys—chimneys with no factories. A group of half a dozen gutted buildings. And then nothing . . . .
>
> In these hospitals I found people who, when the bomb fell, suffered absolutely no injuries, but now are dying from the uncanny after-effect . . . Their hair fell out. Bluish spots appeared on their bodies. And the bleeding began from the ears, nose, and mouth . . . They have been dying at the rate of 100 a day.[104]

It took time for the Imperial government in Tokyo to comprehend what had happened in Hiroshima and to formulate its response. With the A-bombed city's infrastructure destroyed and lines of communication between the city and the outside world shattered, fragmentary reports made their way to senior political and military leaders. The most substantive news came on August 7 in the form of a shortwave broadcast of Truman's public statement about the A-bombing. Uncertain how to respond, a Japanese Army team was sent to Hiroshima to report on what had happened, and the Cabinet sent a protest to the International Commission of the Red Cross condemning what it understood as the US "violation of international law prohibiting the use of poisonous gas."[105]

Truman's announcement was uncompromising and included lies to justify the atomic bombings. He reported that "A short time ago an American airplane dropped one bomb on Hiroshima and destroyed its usefulness to the enemy. That bomb has more power than 20,000 tons of T.N.T." He warned that "bombs are now in production and even more powerful forms are in development." His message concluded with a warning to the Japanese that is reminiscent of Genghis Khan:

> It was to spare the Japanese people from utter destruction that the ultimatum of July 26 was issued at Potsdam. Their leaders promptly rejected that ultimatum. If they do not now accept our terms they may expect a rain of ruin from the air, the like of which has never been seen on earth. Behind this air attack will follow sea and land forces in such numbers and power as they have not yet seen . . .[106]

Truman's "signal" was received in Moscow. Stalin is reported to have been so depressed by the news that he isolated himself for the rest of the day. He understood the atomic bombing as "an act of hostility directed against the Soviet Union" designed to end the war before the Soviets could join in the kill and claim their spoils. He also knew that the A-bombing was intended to "bully the Soviet Union."[107]

NAGASAKI

Stalin took heart late on August 7 when he learned that Ambassador Sato had requested a meeting with Foreign Minister Molotov. The request communicated that Japan had yet to surrender and that it still sought Soviet mediation. Seizing the opportunity, Stalin ordered the invasion of Manchuria to begin ahead of schedule on August 9.

By the morning of August 8, Emperor Hirohito understood and acted on the urgent need to end the war. Meeting with Foreign Minister Togo, he dictated that "Now that such a new weapon has appeared, it has become less and less possible to continue the war. We must not miss a chance to terminate the war by bargaining for more favorable conditions . . . my wish is to make such arrangements as to end the war as soon as possible."[108]

Later that day in Moscow (August 9, 2 a.m. Tokyo time), when Ambassador Sato finally met Molotov to press for Prince Konoe to travel to Moscow, the Ambassador was stunned to hear the Soviet Foreign Minister read him Moscow's declaration of war.

Sixty years later, debate continues about why Truman felt it necessary to inflict a second nuclear holocaust. The answer should be clear. The Japanese government had yet to formally surrender, and the Soviet Union was about to enter the war. Most importantly, the decision to use two A-bombs had been made earlier. New orders from the president would therefore have been necessary to prevent the Nagasaki bombing.

Nagasaki was, and remains, a very different city than Hiroshima. Located on the southwest coast of the Japanese archipelago, its long, narrow harbor extends between the mountains and hills which rise from the sea. Because of its distance from the capital, during Japan's two centuries of isolation from the world, Shoguns in Tokyo permitted the Dutch to maintain a small trading fortress there (which was more like a prison) on Dejima Island in the city's harbor. This provided a tiny opening through which technological and other developments in the rest of the world could be monitored. In August 1945, although spared the savaging of LeMay's fire bombings, like other Japanese cities its people were desperate. They were hungry; teenagers had been mobilized to work in the city's steel factories and other industries; and many feared their city would be targeted by bombing, but children had not yet been forced to evacuate to the countryside.

Nagasaki was not the primary target of "Bockscar," the B-29 armed with "Fat Man," the plutonium bomb named for Winston Churchill. As it approached its initial target, Kokura, "Bockscar" was challenged by heavy aircraft fire and fighter planes, and the city was shrouded by smoke. The bomber thus flew on to Nagasaki where the target area was obscured by clouds. With orders to bomb by sight rather than relying on the limited technology of the day, and with fuel running low, "Bockscar's" pilot released his atomic bomb on a target he could see: the industrial, and largely Christian, Urakami valley 2 miles north of the specified target. As in Hiroshima, air raid alerts had been frequent the previous night. At 11:02 a.m. when the plutonium bomb exploded, people were hard at work or beginning to prepare their midday meal.

"Fat Man" was more powerful than the Hiroshima bomb, but having been dropped off target, the devastation it wrought was less than anticipated. The Urakami district, home to the largest Catholic cathedral in Asia, was annihilated, but the city was buffered by a mountain between the Urakami district and the city center, sheltering much of Nagasaki from the heat, blast, and firestorm. The initial death toll was an estimated 40,000 people, with 75,000 injured and 155,000 exposed to deadly radiation; 66,000 homes were burned or damaged. By year's end, the estimated number killed had risen to 74,000 people. Wind patterns concentrated the radioactive black rain on the Nishiyama district, 2 miles from the epicenter.

As in Hiroshima, people who were not immediately killed were immersed in death.

On August 9, Sumiteru Taniguchi, a 16-year-old telegram boy, was riding his bicycle when:

> My eyes were blinded by a dazzling light and a burning wind . . . [It] threw me three meters forward, twisting my bicycle like a candy bar. Strangely, I was not bleeding, and there was no pain. I managed to drag myself into the basement of a munitions factory 300 meters ahead and suddenly an agonizing cramp started in my back and spread throughout my body.
>
> I lay groaning in that basement for three nights. Finally on the fourth day a rescue crew came and took me to the Isahaya Public School . . . Instead of medicine, our treatment consisted of having a mixture of newspaper ashes and grease applied to our burns.
>
> "Kill me!!" I must have yelled again and again. The pain from my burns and the despair all around me made me wish again and again that I were dead. Now when I look at this rotting blood and skin I seethe with these thoughts.[109]

A grotesque photograph of Taniguchi's tortured and bloody body was taken by the US Army. Decades later, when his wounds had yet to fully heal, the heart-rending and now subversive picture was banned from the Smithsonian Museum's 50th anniversary commemoration of the atomic bombings.

Senji Yamaguchi was also in Nagasaki on August 9. He was 14 and working in the Mitsubishi Arms Manufacturing Works, two-thirds of a mile from the hypocenter of the Nagasaki explosion:

> I was working outside with my shirt off. The heat rays from the explosion, about 3,300° Fahrenheit, scorched my upper body. The heat rays vaporized some people, while burning others into charcoal-like remains.
>
> I witnessed the shock wave from the explosion crush a pregnant woman against a wall and tear apart her abdomen. I could see her and her unborn baby dying. The blast instantly knocked down many homes and buildings as well. Mothers and children were trapped beneath the burning wreckage. They called out each other's names, and the mothers would cry out, pleading for someone to save their children. No one was able to help them, and they all burned alive. The people who came to rescue the immediate survivors or clear away the rotting corpses contracted radiation sickness. They died later, one after the other . . .
>
> People started suffering from illnesses caused by the atomic radiation shortly after the bombing. They developed various kinds of cancers, such as breast and liver cancers, and pregnant women gave birth to deformed babies.[110]

As in Hiroshima, the infrastructure of the city's services was obliterated. The Nagasaki University of Medicine had been the city's emergency medical center. Located several hundred yards from the hypocenter, it was instantly destroyed with many doctors and nurses consumed in the blast and fire. With no major hospital in the city and only 30 doctors able to respond, medical assistance was minimal. "[M]any of the patients accommodated at the emergency centers died retching, agonizing deaths before the night was over, without ever having been attended by a doctor. Of 3,500 people received at the Hiroshima Army Mutual Benefit Hospital, half died by the next day."[111]

On August 10, patients' bodies

> swelled like inflated balloons, with torsos like pigs, eyes no longer discernible from nose, arms and legs seemingly stretched to the point of bursting . . . . The injured were left to lie on the ground, without a roof to protect them from the scorching August sun. They lay there moaning, unable even to turn themselves over. Throughout the night the silence was frequently broken by the splashing sound of people casting themselves into the river, seeking to end their suffering by hastening death.[112]

George Weller was the first foreign correspondent to enter Nagasaki after the A-bombing. He wrote a series of articles about what he saw, but US Occupation authorities prevented their publication. They first finally appeared 60 years later:

> The atomic bomb's peculiar "disease" . . . is still snatching away lives here. Men, women and children with no outward marks of injury are dying daily in hospitals, some having walked around three or four weeks thinking they have escaped.
>
> The doctors here have every modern medicament, but candidly confessed . . . that the answer to the malady is beyond them . . .[113]

SURRENDER

On August 9, fearing that a third atomic bomb would be exploded over Tokyo, Emperor Hirohito asserted his authority and ended the political and procedural debates within the Supreme War Guidance Council. He informed the Council that "the time has come to bear the unbearable" and ordered the Council to accept the Potsdam Declaration.[114] Within hours a communiqué was sent to Washington, London, Moscow, and Chongqing. But, contrary to the Emperor's instructions, the Council accepted Potsdam's terms with the caveat that the "declaration does not comprise any demand which prejudices the prerogatives of His Majesty as a Sovereign Ruler."[115]

Truman and his advisors debated the conditional offer. Admiral Leahy argued that with the US having won the war, the Emperor's fate was a minor concern. Fearing that accepting anything less than unconditional surrender would mean Truman's political "crucifixion," Byrnes was opposed. It was Stimson who tipped the scales winning Truman's acceptance of the Japanese surrender offer by arguing that the imperative was to get Japan "into our hands before the Russians could put any substantial claim to occupy and help rule it."[116]

In drafting their response, Truman and his advisors chose not to consult Moscow. They feared, as Truman later recalled, that Stalin would delay his response to buy time for his offensive. "[I]t was in our interest," Truman later said, "that the Russians not push too far into Manchuria." Truman also believed that one of consequences of the atomic bombings would be that "Rumania, Bulgaria and Hungary" would no longer "be spheres of influence of any one power."[117]

The war did not come to an immediate end. While awaiting Japan's official response, more than 1,000 US bombers maintained pressure on

Japan, killing in excess of 15,000 people. On August 10, Truman ordered a temporary halt to the atomic bombings, but preparations continued for their resumption on August 19 when the third A-bomb would be ready for use. The War Department also continued planning A-bomb production on the assumption that more nuclear weapons would be used against Japan. Seven A-bombs were scheduled to be employed by the end of October.[118]

Japan's formal surrender announcement came on August 15 following the fiasco of a failed overnight coup by junior Army officers. The Emperor's radio broadcast did not accept culpability. It framed the capitulation in terms of Japanese and humanity's survival. In arcane Court language, the Emperor explained that "the enemy has begun to employ a new and most cruel bomb, the power of which to damage is indeed incalculable, taking the toll of many innocent lives. Should we continue to fight, it would result not only in an ultimate collapse and obliteration of the Japanese nation, but also in the total extinction of human civilization."

The Emperor's surrender did not induce Stalin to halt his offensive. Although the US had conceded Manchuria and southern Sakhalin to the Soviets, four strategic regions remained in contention, and Stalin's ambitions included Hokkaido, the northernmost of Japan's four main islands. By September 2, the date of Japan's formal and humiliating surrender on the battleship *Missouri* in Tokyo harbor, Soviet forces had occupied the Chinese ports at Darien and Port Arthur, as well as southern Sakhalin, North Korea, and the Kurile Islands. US threats of possible military confrontation proved necessary to prevent a Soviet invasion of Hokkaido.

The Cold War had begun. In October, President Truman used his Navy Day speech to mobilize the US people for the coming confrontation with the Soviet Union. With words that carried a perverse resonance during the second Bush presidency, Truman insisted that there could be "no compromise with the forces of evil," and that the "atomic bombs which fell on Hiroshima and Nagasaki must be a signal . . . "[119]

Secrecy became essential to sustain the myths of the A-bombings, to maintain popular support for US preparations for nuclear war, and to prevent vilification of those responsible for the A-bombings. MacArthur's Occupation imposed strict censorship to ensure "public tranquility," and it directed censors to concentrate on material about "atomic energy policy, atomic energy or atom bombs or . . . the effects of the Hiroshima and Nagasaki atomic bombs."[120] Press reports on these subjects were banned. Books were censored. Japanese doctors and scientists were forbidden to hold meetings or to publish research about the causes of their patients' afflictions. Censorship was so strict that ten years after the atomic bombings, Hiroshima's major newspaper had no typesetting materials for the words "atomic bomb" or "radioactivity."[121] Journalists' films and other photographic documentation were seized by Occupation forces, and some were stored in Pentagon vaults until the late 1960s. Secretary of State Christian A. Herter was quite explicit in a 1960 memorandum to the Atomic Energy Commission: "The Department of State has serious reservations about the release of these photographs because we have been concerned over the political impact in Japan, and because of our reluctance to present the Communists with a propaganda weapon they would use against us in all parts of the world."[122]

The void created by censorship was filled with misinformation and lies. On September 7, 1945, after visiting Hiroshima to survey the damage, the Deputy Chief of the Manhattan Project, General Thomas Farrell, told the press, "There is no possibility of delayed complications from exposure to radiation from an atomic bomb . . . . Everyone in Hiroshima and Nagasaki who was fated to die from the atomic bomb has already died. There are no longer any people suffering from radiation exposure." A decade later General Groves informed Congress that death from radiation was "very pleasant." *U.S. News & World Report* reported that only 100 Hiroshima survivors had developed leukemia, "no genetic damage was apparent in children born after the bomb," and it emphasized that "The Atomic Age is here, let's not be afraid of it."[123]

Sixty years after the atomic bombings of Hiroshima and Nagasaki people in Japan continue to ask how many died to save the imperial system, and they are beginning to demand that the US be held accountable for its crimes against humanity.[124] In the US, we have yet to ask why so many innocent Japanese were killed and made to suffer in order to achieve limited strategic advantages and to terrorize the Soviet Union. And, at the National Atomic Museum in New Mexico, tourists and students learn that the "lives of one million allied soldiers" were saved by the atomic bombings, and they can purchase A-bomb earrings for $20 a pair.[125]

3
Postwar Asia—Targeting Korea and China

There'll be fire, dust and metal, flying all around
And the radioactivity will burn them to the ground
If there's any Commies left they'll all be on the run
If General MacArthur drops the atomic bomb

Korean War-era song
Jackie Doll and His Pickled Peppers[1]

"[E]verything beginning with Taiwan and ending with Turkey [is the] American world. [The U.S. will] hold on to everything not wishing to let anything escape their grasp, not even our Chinese island of Quemoy."

Mao Zedung

It was in Asia, not Europe, that the Cold War repeatedly turned hot. There, as in Europe and the Middle East, terrorizing US nuclear dominance determined the framework and limits of diplomatic and military struggle. Beginning in the nineteenth century, while US elite and public opinion focused on relations with Europe and to a lesser extent Latin America, the US jockeyed with European colonial powers and later Japan for a share of Asia's markets and wealth, becoming the region's dominant power in the course of World War II.

Until the mid-1960s, Indochina was seen as a backwater, with North Korea and China being the primary objects of US attention and targets for threats and preparations to initiate nuclear war. North Korea (the Democratic Peoples' Republic of Korea) and China posed independent, but often intertwined, challenges to US regional dominance. Offshore, throughout the Cold War, Japan was Washington's "unsinkable aircraft carrier," providing bases and launching pads for "conventional" military interventions and for threatened US nuclear attacks against Asian nations and the Soviet Union. That Japan served the US in this way was no accident. Its postwar government was created and shaped to meet US needs.

To provide a framework for understanding US Cold War nuclear threats against North Korea and China, this chapter begins with a summary of the US ascent to become an "Asian power," and it describes the qualitative and quantitative dimensions of Washington's "commanding" nuclear superiority during the first decades of the Cold War. North Korea was the early object of US nuclear attention. We thus begin with President Truman's repeated Korean War nuclear threats against both North Korea and China, Pentagon preparations for these attacks, and General MacArthur's appeals for authorization to use as many as 20–30 atomic bombs to create a radioactive *cordon sanitaire* between Korea and China. This section concludes with President Eisenhower's nuclear threat, which won an armistice agreement acceptable to the US and which inspired his and later presidents' subsequent nuclear threats. It also taught Pyongyang's leaders that to ensure their security they needed to obtain nuclear weapons.[2]

After describing US preparations for—and, in at least two instances, threats of—US nuclear attacks against North Korea in the 1960s and 1970s, the chapter turns to China. Twice during the 1950s mainland China's efforts to reconquer the offshore islands of the rebellious province, and perhaps Taiwan itself, were repulsed by President Eisenhower's and Secretary of State Dulles' ostentatious nuclear threats of "massive retaliation." The chapter also describes how China attempted to cope with repeated US nuclear threats, including those related to the escalating war in Vietnam. The chapter closes by exploring how the Johnson administration struggled to come to terms with China's nuclear weapons program. Two little-known incidents are reported here. First is the Johnson administration's unsuccessful proposal to the Soviet Union that the two superpowers collaborate in a nuclear attack to prevent Beijing from becoming a nuclear power. The second draws on Daniel Ellsberg's recollection of the intense bureaucratic battle within the Pentagon and the highest reaches of the Cabinet over Secretary of State Dean Rusk's advocacy of an Indian proposal that it be given a US nuclear bomb which could be detonated in India to create the illusion of nuclear parity on the Asian continent.

BECOMING AN ASIAN POWER

For two centuries the US has been an Asian and Pacific "power." Much of the country's wealth in the nineteenth century, including the fortunes of the nation's first financial families, was built on the early Asia trade. Usually thought of in terms of trade in silk and spices, this commerce extended to other goods, from rhubarb and ceramics to opiates. Although ostensibly neutral, US warships and merchant vessels supported the British Navy during the Opium Wars of 1839–42, which were initiated by Britain to rectify its trade imbalance with the Middle Kingdom. Her Majesty's economy could be stabilized by "opening" China to the opium trade, which was dominated by British entrepreneurs.

Even before US naval forces arrived in Korea and Admiral Perry's Black warships "opened" Japan in 1856, William Seward, Secretary of State to both Lincoln and Andrew Johnson, advocated that if the US were to succeed Britain as the world's dominant power, it must first dominate Asia. In those days of coal-fueled vessels, war and merchant ships required bases or access to secure ports that could serve as coaling stations to reach Asian markets and resources. Seward's preferred route to Asia passed across mid- and South Pacific island nations including Hawaii, Guam, and the Philippines. These, however, were already occupied by Britain or Spain. To compensate, following the American Civil War, Seward negotiated the purchase of Alaska and the Aleutian Islands, "Seward's Folly," which guaranteed the US a northern bridge to Asia.

The late nineteenth and early twentieth centuries were marked by intense competition among the colonizing nations, particularly for control of Manchuria (the geopolitical key to control of northeast Asia) and China. Britain, Japan, Russia, France, and Germany vied for "concessions," colonies in all but name, along the Chinese coast. These served as sources of goods and as markets for the glut of manufactured goods being produced by the industrialized nations. US leaders, constrained by the country's anti-colonial political mythology and by coming late to the imperial game, countered with demands for an "Open Door"—equal access for all economic powers to China's markets and goods. Washington (in the form of Harriman railroad interests), Moscow, London, and Tokyo also struggled to control northeast Asia's rail systems, and thus for influence over the region's trade and strategic advantages.

Periodically, this competition exploded into warfare. In 1895, Japan defeated the Chinese Empress's forces in Korea, and seized the Liaoning Peninsula, Taiwan, and the neighboring Pescadores islands. However, under pressure from Russia, France, and Germany, Tokyo was forced to relinquish much of its ill-gotten gains, and settled for a Japanese protectorate over Korea and recognition of Taiwan as a Japanese colony. In 1898, the US, European powers, and Japan collaborated in sending troops to repress China's Boxer Rebellion, a populist and nationalist uprising aimed at ousting foreign occupiers. In 1905, the Meiji Emperor of Japan shocked the West by sinking the Russian Fleet and defeating Russian forces in Manchuria and Korea. President Roosevelt was less than neutral in mediating peace negotiations. The final deal included Japanese recognition of US sovereignty in the Philippines in exchange for US recognition of Japan's colonial control of Korea.

Until a series of mini-coups replaced what passed for Japanese "democracy" with uncompromising militarism in the early 1930s, Asia-Pacific "peace" was preserved by the "Washington system," a series of arms control agreements limiting the compositions of the competing imperial navies. It was the Japanese militarists' misreading of the global correlation of power and their belief that Anglo-Saxon dominance in the Asia-Pacific could be replaced by a Japanese "East Asia Co-Prosperity Sphere" that sparked "world war" in Asia.

As devastating as they were, the atomic bombings of Hiroshima and Nagasaki failed in their strategic objective of limiting Soviet influence in northeast Asia. To prevent Chinese Communists from gaining strategic advantage in the civil war, John McCloy organized one of the most ambitious military maneuvers in world history, by moving Chiang Kai-shek's morally bankrupt Nationalist armies north to accept Japan's surrender. The US, however, had no choice about sharing influence with the Soviet Union in Korea. And, with the Chinese Communist victory in 1949, the nation that for much of recorded history had been the center of human civilization, began to "stand up."

In 1952, to win an end to the US military occupation, the Japanese elite was forced to accept a constitution written and imposed on them by US forces and to secretly sign the US–Japan Mutual Security Treaty (MST), which provided for the continued presence of US military bases in Japan. The state created by the US rested on three contending forces: the pacifist constitution; the military alliance through which the US assumed preponderant responsibility for the military and diplomatic functions of the Japanese state; and "the somewhat surreptitiously but stubbornly preserved . . . prewar imperial state" in the form of Emperor Hirohito remaining on the throne and old-line militarists—including a Class-A war criminal serving as a US-sponsored prime minister. In this way, Japan was reconfigured to serve as "the keystone" of US power in Asia and the Pacific.

IMBALANCE OF TERROR

Having risen to power with, albeit limited, Soviet assistance, China's Communist leaders allied themselves closely with the Soviet Union for more than a decade. During this period, exaggerated US fears of Soviet nuclear capabilities and of communism were projected onto China and used to reinforce US Cold War political, economic, and military mobilization. Not infrequently, this led to disastrous US decisions.

The Truman administration was taken by surprise in 1949 when Stalin's first A-bomb shattered the US nuclear monopoly that most in the US elite had assumed would continue for at least a decade—an eternity in US political calculations.[3] Popular fears ignited by the Soviet bomb were heightened by the victory of Mao Zedong's forces that same year and by North Korea's invasion of the South in 1950. The US political climate quickly became ripe for the hysteria fueled by Senator Joe McCarthy and other anti-communist demagogues. Many believed that their lives and the continued existence of the US were threatened by nuclear-armed, godless, deceitful, and subversive Marxists led by Moscow and its junior partner in Beijing. A popular slogan in the 1950s and early 1960s was "Better dead than red."

In fact, the US was far more powerful—militarily and economically—than the Soviet Union and impoverished China, and remained so throughout the Cold War. In 1948, before the Soviets detonated their A-bomb and Mao's armies prevailed over Chiang's Nationalists, Secretary of State Dean Acheson won Truman's commitment to launch a massive US military build-up as outlined in National Security Council Memorandum 68. To complement the containment doctrine, US policy called for the creation of a "situation to which the Kremlin would find it expedient to accommodate itself, first by relaxing tensions and pressures and then by gradual withdrawal."[4] After the Communist victory in China, Washington pursued a dual policy toward Beijing: containment and—with high hopes for Chiang Kai-shek—regime change.

When North Korea invaded the South, some policymakers worried that Kim Il Sung's troops might be reinforced by Soviet nuclear threats. This was not a concern for Truman and Eisenhower, who understood that the US had "a commanding superiority over the USSR in strategic forces." Consider for a moment the meaning of "commanding superiority." It is the ability "to give an order or orders to" or to "direct with authority,"[5] in this case with fears of annihilation if orders were not respected. This nuclear supremacy soon came to permeate every dimension of US Cold War policy and practice. By 1953, the US had 329 nuclear-capable bombers that, from bases in Japan and Europe, could kill millions of people and eliminate the economic and military foundations of both Communist powers. Two years later the US Air Force began acquiring B-52 bombers which could annihilate key Soviet and Chinese targets from much greater distances.

The Eisenhower administration (1953–60) and the US Strategic Command were confident that US first-strike counter-force capabilities targeted against the Soviet nuclear arsenal could prevent Soviet retaliation not only against the US, but also against Japan and Washington's NATO allies. Soviet bombers were deployed at a limited number of bases whose locations were known to US military planners. With their warheads stored elsewhere and with no early warning systems, Soviet strategic forces were highly vulnerable to US first-strike attacks. Soviet bombers based in Moscow's Arctic region were theoretically capable of reaching continental US, but they were slow, taking up to 13 hours to arrive at their targets. They could thus be shot down by fighters with reasonable confidence. General Curtis LeMay, chief of the US Strategic Command, boasted that the US could eliminate Moscow's war-making capabilities "without losing a man to their defenses."[6]

After the deprivations of the Great Depression and World War II, President Eisenhower came to office committed to reducing the size of the military in order to encourage economic growth. His confidence in US nuclear superiority made it easier to engineer this shift in national priorities. To ensure that this took place without jeopardizing US allies and client states, Eisenhower and Secretary of State Dulles adopted the "massive retaliation" doctrine as the foundation of US military policy. By relying on the threat of "nation killing," and by "linking local conflicts to the specter of a global war of annihilation," they sought to ensure that neither Moscow nor Beijing would even consider challenging US dominance anywhere within its global "spheres of influence."[7] In his memoir, Eisenhower used the Korean example to describe how the doctrine worked:

> We let the Communist authorities understand that, in the absence of satisfactory progress, we intended to move decisively without inhibition in our use of weapons, and would no longer be responsible for confining hostilities to the Korean Peninsula. We would not be limited by any world-wide gentleman's agreement. In India and in the Formosa Straits area, and at the truce negotiations at Panmunjom, we dropped the word, discreetly, of our intention. We felt quite sure it would reach Soviet and Chinese Communist ears.[8]

Vice-President Nixon learned the "game" of nuclear terrorism as he observed Eisenhower and Dulles preparing and threatening first-strike massive "retaliation" during the Korean War (1953), the CIA-backed coup in Guatemala (1954), the Middle East War and Crisis (1956 and 1958), and against China (1955 and 1958).

How did Moscow and Beijing respond? *Very* cautiously. Both pretended that the Soviet arsenal was more powerful than it was, and in the case of the Soviet Union, a disproportionate amount of its limited economic resources were concentrated on developing weapons systems that would eventually redress the imbalance of terror.

After Stalin's death in 1953, both Nikita Khrushchev and his primary rival for power, Georgy Malenkov, distanced themselves from the Leninist belief in the inevitability of war between communist and capitalist forces. Instead, they called for "peaceful coexistence" and boasted that in time the Soviet Union would "bury" the West economically. They understood that with Soviet economic and technological capabilities lagging decades behind those of the US and with the Soviet people eager for improvements in their standards of living, restoration of Soviet military power was a long-term project. Economic development had to come first. To provide himself with political cover for this reverse course, Khrushchev stressed the need to prevent the "end of civilization," which necessitated "an accommodation with the United States."[9]

As Gareth Porter has documented, "Mao did not underestimate the economic or military might of the United States . . . and . . . . fully acknowledged the necessity for Chinese restraint in the face of U.S. power." Until 1960, because of China's dependence on Soviet strategic deterrence, "Mao had every reason . . . to want Khrushchev to publicly exaggerate Soviet strategic power."[10]

This "accommodation" involved more than rhetoric and respectful diplomacy. Khrushchev used Soviet leadership of the world's communist forces to contain possible challenges to the status quo which he feared could lead to a US–Soviet nuclear confrontation. During the 1954 Geneva Conference following the Vietnamese victory over the French at Dien Bien Phu, Soviet and Chinese leaders forced Vietnam's leaders to accede to US and French demands about where Vietnam would be divided and when national elections would be held. Khrushchev and Mao were sobered by Dulles' warning that the US had "a great capacity to retaliate instantly, by means and at places of our choosing."[11] In 1957, during the conference of the world's Communist parties held in Moscow soon after the exhilarating (and to many in the US frightening) launch of the world's first satellite, *Sputnik*, Khrushchev resisted Mao's call to proclaim that the Soviets had achieved a strategic advantage over the US. Mao's hope was that a declaration that the world's "correlation of forces" had been fundamentally changed would chasten Washington, buying time for Beijing. Instead, Soviet leaders argued that economic, not military, power was determinative, and that "the Soviet Union had no lasting edge in missile technology."[12]

KOREA

North Korea, like Vietnam and Japan, is among the nations that have been savaged by US "conventional" warfare and, in the case of Vietnam, repeatedly threatened with nuclear attack. During the Korean War (1950–53), nearly all of North Korea was burned to the ground or otherwise destroyed. Further, as Leon Sigal has documented, "No country has been the target of more American nuclear threats than North Korea—at least seven times since 1945."[13] Both South Korea (Republic of Korea) and North Korea (Democratic Peoples' Republic of Korea) have also seen the pursuit of nuclear weapons programs as a path to greater power, independence of action, and in the case of the North, as a possible deterrent against US attack. In the 1970s, South Korea's US-sponsored military government took serious steps toward developing a nuclear arsenal, and since the late 1980s North Korea's nuclear weapons program has been seen as one of the "greatest threats" to US security.

The origins of the Korean War were more complicated than are commonly understood.[14] Two days after the atomic bombing of Nagasaki, Colonels Dean Rusk and Charles Bonesteel were given 30 minutes to identify where a line could best be drawn to divide Korea into US- and Soviet-dominated zones. They selected the 38th parallel, although it was further north than US forces could reach if the Soviets were not cooperative. This had the benefit of including Seoul, Korea's capital, within the US zone. Like the Soviets, the US occupiers were less than fully committed to restoring true Korean independence and sovereignty. US forces initially designated Koreans as enemies "subject to the provisions and terms of [Japan's] surrender." Illustrative of the new order was the "meeting" at which the advance unit of US forces and Japanese military and colonial officials together arranged logistics for coming waves of US occupation forces. It reflected shared military and colonialist mentalities. Neither ceremonial nor business-like, it became a "glorious drunken brawl" that lasted for days and signaled something less than liberation was at hand for Koreans: "Any Korean who approached the U.S. personnel was 'summarily shown the door with a minimum of courtesy.' "[15]

Washington and Moscow soon established competing client states based in Seoul and Pyongyang. The Southern government's new ruling class was drawn from the impoverished nation's small landlord class and was led by Syngman Rhee, who had collaborated with both Japanese and US intelligence. Challenges to this unrepresentative government, in some cases armed uprisings, were brutally repressed, including massacres of thousands of civilians. In the North, Moscow rooted its client police state in cadres of returning guerrilla forces led by Kim Il Sung, who had fought the Japanese in Manchuria. Neither government respected the other's legitimacy, and each sought to reunify the nation under its exclusive leadership.

As long as US and Soviet forces remained in Korea, Syngman Rhee's and Kim Il Sung's ambitions and machinations were contained. But, when the occupying powers began their withdrawals in 1949, each side initiated guerrilla attacks and border clashes involving thousands of troops. In June 1950, Pyongyang struck first and most powerfully, launching a massive and initially successful invasion of the South.[16]

With South Korean and US troops reeling under the onslaught of the North's offensive, the Pentagon moved almost immediately to the planning of a nuclear counterattack. General Bolte, the US Chief of Operations, proposed that between 10 and 20 A-bombs be made available for use in Korea, and he was instructed to explore their possible use in "indirect support of ground combat" with General MacArthur. MacArthur liked the idea, and his response reflected his hope to use the war to reunify Korea under his leadership. To achieve both victory and reunification, he urged using nuclear weapons to sever North Korea from China and the Soviet Union, saying, "I visualize a cul-de-sac. The only passages leading from Manchuria and Vladivostok have many tunnels and bridges. I see here a unique use for the atomic bomb."[17]

Planning for nuclear attacks was temporarily suspended when the Joint Chiefs concluded that the proposed targets were too small, and they correctly concluded that MacArthur would soon prevail with "conventional" weapons. Throughout the summer, US air attacks rained hundreds of tons of explosives on North Korean forces, including 900,000 gallons of napalm, burning communities, including their civilian populations, to the ground.[18]

MacArthur's early victories and his ambitions led to disastrous miscalculations, to China's entry into the war, and to Truman's first nuclear threat against Korea. Not satisfied with having quickly driven North Korean forces back across the 38th parallel, and having been advised by the CIA that China would likely "be confined to continued covert assistance to North Korea," Truman authorized MacArthur to "roll back" the North Korean forces. To avoid inciting China, MacArthur was to deploy only Korean forces on the Chinese border. MacArthur's forces did successfully "roll back" the North Koreans, advancing 25 miles north of the 38th parallel in two days, seizing Pyongyang, and advancing to the Chinese border. However, the CIA, Truman, and MacArthur had erred seriously in taking the new Chinese government's measure. Fearing the loss of a buffer against US subversion and attacks, the revolutionary government in Beijing sent waves of Chinese "volunteers" across the Yalu River, leading to heavy US losses and forcing a desperate US retreat across much of the Peninsula.

MacArthur's response was to transform North Korea into a "wasteland." US air attacks were ordered to demolish everything lying between US positions and the Chinese border. They were "to destroy every means of communication and every installation, and factories and cities and villages. This destruction is to start at the Manchurian border and to progress south."[19]

The Chinese counter-offensive also panicked Truman and much of official Washington. Truman confided in his diary that "it looks like World War III is here," and at his November 30 press conference he implicitly threatened nuclear attack, saying that any weapon in the US arsenal might be used. To back up this threat, the Strategic Air Command was placed on alert, with orders "to be prepared to dispatch without delay medium bomb groups to the Far East . . . this augmentation should include atomic capabilities." MacArthur asked for authorization to use nuclear weapons at his discretion, and his journal indicates that he believed that he could win the war within ten days by dropping "between 30 and 50 atomic bombs . . . strung across the neck of Manchuria" to create "a belt of radioactive cobalt." This would ensure that "[f]or at least 60 years there could have been no land invasion of Korea from the North." On Christmas Eve, he requested 30 A-bombs to eliminate "a list of retardation targets" and "critical concentrations of enemy air power."[20]

Those weapons were not immediately forthcoming, but several months later, in March 1951, MacArthur and Truman moved precipitously toward nuclear war. With Moscow beginning to signal a threat to US air superiority by moving much of its Air Force to Manchuria and eastern Siberia, and with China massing still more "volunteers" north of the Yalu River, MacArthur requested "D Day atomic capability." The Pentagon and Truman responded positively, ordering that nuclear weapons be assembled within range of Korea at Kadena air base in Okinawa. Contrary to popular understanding, MacArthur was not cashiered by Truman because he recklessly wanted to use nuclear weapons, but to give Truman confidence that they would be used "reliably." He was replaced on April 6 by General Ridgeway. Truman now authorized their use.[21] Possible nuclear targets included Chinese and Soviet troop concentrations, Shanghai, Chinese industrial cities, and four North Korean cities. Despite their build-ups, Stalin and Mao wisely opted not to further escalate the war, and Ridgeway held his nuclear fire. The assembled nuclear bombs were retained in Okinawa for possible future use, and the Joint Chiefs again considered using tactical nuclear weapons just two months later.[22]

In January 1953, soon after his inauguration, President Eisenhower followed through on his election campaign promise to bring the war to an end on US terms by preparing, threatening, and if necessary proceeding with a nuclear attack. To put his strategy in place, he informed the National Security Council that the industrial city of Kaesong, just north of the demilitarized zone (DMZ), "provided a good target" for tactical nuclear weapons. On May 19, the Joint Chiefs followed up by recommending air and naval attacks—including the use of nuclear weapons—against Chinese targets. And in August, Eisenhower ordered General LeMay to implement "Operation Big Stick," augmentation of US nuclear war capabilities in East Asia, with the dispatch of 20 nuclear-armed B-36 bombers to Kadena air base. To ensure that the Chinese, Russians, and North Koreans got the message, LeMay invited the press to witness, record, and report the arrivals of the nuclear holocaust arsenal in Okinawa. Eisenhower thus won an armistice agreement which halted the fighting but did not formally end the war.[23]

This was not the end of nuclear threats in Korea. In violation of Armistice Agreement provisions that forbade deployment of new and advanced weapons on the Korean peninsula, in 1957, the Eisenhower administration reinforced US power by deploying nuclear-armed Matador missiles near the DMZ which straddles the 38th parallel. Over the next 43 years, the US nuclear arsenal in Korea grew to include Honest John, Davy Crockett, Lacrosse, Lance, and Sergeant missiles, howitzers with nuclear-armed shells, and nuclear bombs to be carried by Air Force fighters and bombers. F-4 fighter planes, armed with nuclear weapons, were kept on constant alert. These weapons were concentrated along the DMZ and at Kunsan and Osan air bases near Seoul.

Officers stationed along the DMZ had standing orders to respond to a North Korean invasion with their nuclear artillery, and they understood that they would be among the war's first casualties. Nuclear weapons based at Kunsan air base were integrated into the Pentagon's SIOP, and could be used against China and the Soviet Union, as well as against North Korea. In the 1970s, against the possibility that Seoul might be lost in the initial wave of a North Korean offensive, US war plans called for the possible use of neutron bombs, whose enhanced radiation would kill not only enemy forces but also much of Seoul's population, while leaving the city's buildings and infrastructure intact. To demonstrate US capabilities and thus intimidate Pyongyang, "Team Spirit" military exercises which brought together tens of thousands of US and South Korean troops included rehearsals for nuclear strikes against North Korea.[24]

Before Clinton and his senior advisors stumbled to the brink of nuclear catastrophe in 1994, nuclear forces were placed on alert during at least two additional crises. In 1968, when the US destroyer *Pueblo* and its crew were captured and held for nearly a year, the Johnson administration's initial response was to prepare a nuclear attack against Pyongyang. Eight years later, in 1976, a surreal nuclear crisis resulted from the dispatch of what was reported to be a small unit of US and South Korean troops with orders to "trim a poplar tree" in a forbidden area of the DMZ. North Korean troops challenged the "tree trimmers," killing two US soldiers when a North Korean seized their ax and used it against them. In response, US and South Korean forces were placed on "high alert." A nuclear-armed aircraft carrier task force was redeployed to Korean waters, and nuclear-capable B-52s, launched from Guam, flew across South Korea toward the DMZ, then "veer[ed] off at the last moment" as they approached North Korea. So serious was the crisis that the commander of US forces in South Korea thought it necessary to request President Ford's permission to use nuclear weapons if communication between South Korea and Washington were severed.[25]

Adding to the threats targeted against Pyongyang, and compounding Korean and northeast Asian tensions, was South Korea's nuclear weapons program launched by President Park Chung Hee in the 1970s. The project ended following intense pressure from Washington that resulted in a military coup implemented with US support. This may have included Park Chung Hee's assassination.[26]

Armed "peace"—in the case of the US, nuclear-armed peace—prevailed across Korea in the two decades that followed. Until the collapse of the Soviet Union, tensions were contained as North Korea and South Korea concentrated on economic development. Politically, little changed in the North, while in the South waves of political resistance led to the replacement of the military dictatorship with electoral democracy.

TAIWAN 1955 AND 1958

Taiwan has long been East Asia's second nuclear tinderbox. In 1949, in the face of defeat and with Washington's help, Chiang Kai-shek led tens of thousands (ultimately millions) of his forces and loyalists, along with much of his treasury, to Taiwan, an island roughly the size of Maryland or Switzerland, 100 miles across the East China Sea. For nearly three centuries, beginning in the mid-1600s, the island's indigenous Formosans were outnumbered and dominated by Han Chinese migrants, initially fishermen, outlaws, and merchants, followed by Chinese warlords, their armies, and land-hungry peasants. Having been liberated from 50 years of Japanese colonialism just four years earlier, Chiang's Nationalist invasion and the repressive dictatorship that followed were resented and in some cases resisted by the Taiwanese. Compounding the situation was the US. Not anticipating the Communist victory, throughout World War II Roosevelt and Truman recognized Taiwan as integral to Chinese territory. But Taiwan's potential role as a military, political, and economic outpost from which Communist China could be challenged, combined with Chinese Nationalist influence in Congress, the media, and in other elite US circles, led Washington to recognize the "Republic of China" in Taiwan as the government of all China.

Chiang's "Republic of China" was not limited to the island of Taiwan. It included tiny island clusters that had served as Chiang's stepping stones to Taiwan. These were soon used as bases from which to harass coastal China and its shipping. Most important were Jimmen (Quemoy), east of central Taiwan and just 2 miles from the mainland Chinese port of Xiamen (Amoy), and the Matzu (Matsu) islands, which lie 10 miles off the Chinese port city of Fuzhou, due east from northern Taiwan. The Dachen islands, 200 miles north of Matsu, were less defensible. Closer to Taiwan are the Pescadores just 30 miles west of Taiwan, which were also colonized by Japan.

In June 1950, with US public opinion and Washington's Asia-Pacific military forces being mobilized to roll back North Korea's invasion, both Washington and Beijing were confronted by Taiwan's potential vulnerability. Truman's response was to send an intimidating message in the form of the Seventh Fleet, which sailed through the Taiwan Strait. Mao understood that this "major event" was meant to communicate to China that it should not even dream of reconquering its former province.[27]

By 1954, with Chiang's government having been subsidized by Washington to the tune of $1.6 billion, the Nationalists had transformed their tiny offshore islands into "formidable positions." Preparing his reconquest of China, Chiang concentrated 58,000 troops on Quemoy and 15,000 on Matsu. Beijing was understandably concerned by these developments, by the US campaign to isolate it diplomatically and economically, and by Washington's policy which recognized the "renegade province" rather than China itself.

On September 3, the government in Beijing moved to change the prevailing "correlation of forces" that placed it on the defensive. Chiang's forces and the inhabitants of Quemoy were subjected to a withering, five-hour barrage, during which 6,000 artillery shells crashed onto the island. The assault was initially read by the Pentagon as the prelude to a Chinese invasion, and Eisenhower responded by deploying an armada of nuclear-capable aircraft carriers, destroyers, and their support ships to the Taiwan Strait. He also called for "all-out defense of the islands and the use of atomic weapons if the Communists launched a major assault."[28]

These initial displays of power were insufficient to silence the Chinese guns. The shellings were extended to Matsu. Across from the besieged islands, the People's Liberation Army (PLA) also turned to building airfields, roads, and artillery bunkers needed to support amphibious attacks. In Washington, where there was no consensus about the strategic importance of Taiwan's offshore islands, the Eisenhower administration, Congress, and the Pentagon debated what steps to take next. Eisenhower, a former general, doubted that the islands were essential to Taiwan's military defense, but he and Dulles feared that losing them would be a "mortal blow" to Chiang's perceived legitimacy and could lead to the collapse of his government. To reinforce Chiang, Eisenhower and Dulles thus negotiated a military treaty with the Nationalist government in December in which the US pledged to defend Taiwan, the Pescadores, and "other Nationalist-held territories on the mutual agreement of the two signatories." Chiang's sole concession to the US was a secret commitment to forgo offensive actions against mainland China unless they were authorized to do so by Washington. US prestige and the president's political future were now tied to the defense of Quemoy and Matsu.[29]

Beijing was still not intimidated. In January, it launched air attacks against the more distant Dachen islands, overwhelming Nationalist forces there and a small contingent of US advisors on nearby Yijang Island.

Dillon Anderson, Eisenhower's National Security Advisor, has since described the atmosphere and commitments that prevailed in the White House at the time: "our policy was to use them [nuclear weapons] wherever appropriate." Faced with the choice of using atomic weapons or landing "American forces on the Chinese mainland with 700 million Chinamen, it would not have been the latter. Good God, they can breed them faster in the zone of the interior than you can kill them in the combat zone."[30]

Consistent with this racist world-view, seven months into the deepening crisis, Eisenhower and Dulles went public with the nuclear threats they had already implicitly communicated to Beijing. After agreeing that if the Nationalists lost Quemoy and Matsu the consequences would be disastrous "for the rest of Asia," as well as for the stability of the Nationalist government, Eisenhower and his senior advisors committed to defending the offshore islands by all means necessary, including "atomic missiles" (i.e. nuclear weapons). To signal this to the Chinese and to prepare the US public for a one-sided nuclear apocalypse (Washington had no fear that the Soviets would intervene owing to its lack of long-range missiles and the inferiority of its long-range war planes), Dulles was instructed to use a speech scheduled for March 8 to communicate that in defending Quemoy and Matsu, the US would consider its nuclear arsenal "interchangeable with conventional weapons."[31]

As part of its preparations to follow through on its threatened nuclear attacks, the Strategic Air Command ordered, "on an urgent basis," selection of targets for an "enlarged atomic offensive" against China. Aware that a nuclear war would result in millions of Chinese civilian deaths and casualties, Eisenhower nonetheless reiterated Dulles' threat at a press conference held on March 16 saying that he didn't understand why nuclear weapons "shouldn't be used just exactly as you would use a bullet or anything else." Vice-President Nixon reinforced his president, saying that "tactical atomic weapons are now conventional and will be used against targets of any aggressive force." Two weeks later as China's shelling continued, the Navy's Chief of Staff, Admiral Robert Carney, turned up the heat when, without authorization, he informed the world that the US had "plans for an all-out attack on China," and that US military planning envisioned extensive nuclear attacks on China.[32]

These threats and pressures were too great for Beijing, and it moved to extract what diplomatic advantage it could as it defused the crisis. Premier Zhou Enlai used the Bandung Conference (which launched the movement of Nonaligned Nations) to announce that China did not want war with the US, and that it was willing to negotiate "reduction of tensions in the Taiwan area." In late April, Dulles responded that the US was willing to discuss a ceasefire with the Chinese. China's artillery soon fell silent. While Eisenhower and his advisors believed they had prevailed with their nuclear threats, China emerged with substantial diplomatic gains. In addition to winning friends at Bandung, the resolution of the crisis—short-term though it may have been—won the Beijing government a forum and platform for direct negotiations with the US.[33]

This was, however, less than a diplomatic victory. As Gareth Porter reports, "the PRC first began to display overt fear of a U.S. nuclear attack after U.S. public threats to use nuclear weapons against China over the offshore islands in mid-January 1955." Mao responded to what he experienced as US "nuclear blackmail" by beginning to prepare the Chinese people for a US-initiated war—including nuclear war—and in the years that followed Chinese military exercises were organized to respond to "sudden atomic attack."[34]

Even as the Chinese leadership absorbed the sobering lessons of the 1955 nuclear threats, with the PLA recommending redeployment of the nation's industrial infrastructure and population centers away from vulnerable coastal cities, Mao's compass continued to point toward *realpolitik* bravado. He pressed his comrades not to "show fear" lest "the enemy will consider us weak and easy to bully."[35] Three years after the Taiwan crisis appeared to have been resolved, Beijing fired it up again.

The Chinese were frustrated when the US unilaterally suspended the talks initiated in 1955. They were angry, too, that Moscow's revolutionary spirit seemed to be dimming, and that the Kremlin appeared to be moving toward détente with Washington after discovering common interests in negotiating a nuclear test ban treaty. Mao and his comrades were also deeply concerned by Chiang Kai-shek's continuing military build-up on Quemoy and Matsu. Nearly a third of the Nationalist Army—100,000 troops—had been moved to the offshore islands, from which they attacked Chinese shipping and launched guerrilla attacks against the mainland. With the US preoccupied with the Lebanese crisis, Mao and the PLA struck hard to overturn these realities. On August 23, 1958 Quemoy and Matsu were deluged by what was described as a deadly typhoon of steel—50,000 artillery shells. The murderous barrage and the US nuclear threats that followed continued for six weeks, during which "the world feared imminent war."[36]

Within a week of the beginning of the siege, the US mobilized for war, including first-strike nuclear attacks. Although the CIA doubted that China had the military capacity to seize the islands, Dulles and other senior administration figures feared that Chiang's forces could be starved into submission, a loss they believed might lead to Chiang's downfall and the loss of Taiwan. Eisenhower thus announced that defending Quemoy and Matsu was more essential for Taiwan's survival than in 1955. He placed US forces on alert and sent the nuclear-armed Pacific Fleet to the Taiwan Strait and adjacent waters. By August 29 two aircraft carrier groups, cruisers, 40 destroyers, a fleet of submarines, and additional support ships were in place and on alert. More than 200 nuclear-capable warplanes, at sea and nearby military bases, were also placed on alert.[37]

"Massive retaliation" was widely known to be the US war-fighting doctrine. Drawing lessons from the Korean War and the 1955 crisis, and with a potentially genocidal armada in place, Eisenhower ordered the Pentagon to "leak a 'few revealing words,'" which "would not escape the notice of the Communists." Consistent with their commander's approach, the Joint Chiefs urged the president that "the best hope of quickly and decisively stopping Communists attacks against the off-shore islands" and Taiwan itself was "an immediate counter-attack with atomic weapons." Dulles agreed, saying that "there was no use of having a lot of stuff and never be[ing] able to use it." Eisenhower, however, was concerned about international opinion and, as a result, was more cautious. Rather than delegating responsibility for initiating nuclear war to his field commanders as he had in 1955, the president reserved that power to himself and waited for events to unfold.[38]

Mao later conceded that the Chinese leadership was surprised by the intensity of Washington's response to this round of attacks against Quemoy and Matsu, and they took Eisenhower's nuclear threats very seriously. On September 6, to no avail, Zhou Enlai publicly urged resumption of US–Chinese talks in Warsaw. A week later Soviet Foreign Minister Andrei Gromyko journeyed to Beijing where he found that Mao fully expected Washington to go on the offensive. Mao's response was a plan which he proposed to Gromyko: PLA forces would retreat to the Chinese heartland as it had done throughout much of revolutionary "people's war," drawing US forces in behind them. The Soviets, Mao proposed, would then hit the invaders "with all its means," i.e. with Soviet nuclear weapons. The Soviets, however, were not prepared for nuclear war, and Gromyko wisely rejected Mao's proposal. Eisenhower held his fire, and on October 6 the Chinese siege was lifted.

Mao was sobered by this confrontation with the great capitalist power and shared a lesson that he took from the crisis with the Soviet Ambassador to China the following year: across Asia, "everything beginning with Taiwan and ending with Turkey [is the] American world." The US would work "to hold on to everything not wishing to let anything escape their grasp, not even our Chinese island of Quemoy." As he would soon advise his Vietnamese allies, China could not touch the Americans "even in places where they are weak."[39]

CHINA'S BOMB

In the immediate aftermath of the second Taiwan crisis, Chinese leaders obeyed Mao's dictum not to challenge the US directly. At the same time, they worked to rectify the imbalance of power by focusing on economic development and by building a Chinese nuclear weapon that could serve as a deterrent against the US, and, conceivably, against the Soviet Union. When John F. Kennedy assumed the presidency in 1961, he was advised that the "overall power balance in East Asia [was] even less favorable to the communist world than [it had been] in the previous five years." Chinese economic and military power had suffered massive setbacks as a result of the cut-off of Soviet subsidies and assistance and by the disastrous failure of Mao's "Great Leap Forward." China's industrial infrastructure was in ruins as nearly everything that could be used to produce poor quality steel had been cast into backyard furnaces in order to fulfill unrealistic quotas. Famine was widespread, with estimates of those who succumbed to starvation reaching 20 million or more. In this strategic environment, Kennedy was told to have no fear of falling dominoes. The worst that could happen if the puppet regime in Saigon fell would be that "Thailand and Malaysia would be tempted to adopt a neutralist posture."[40]

Kennedy was, however, given something new from China to worry about. He was told that Beijing could have a nuclear weapon by 1962 and a small nuclear arsenal by 1965. The president and his advisors responded by investigating whether the growing Sino-Soviet split could be exploited to subvert or destroy Beijing's nuclear weapons program. Toward this end, Kennedy used his Vienna summit with Khrushchev to probe Soviet interest in containing China's nuclear ambitions, but found that they were not yet ready to join in attacking their nominal ally. Two years later, as the US and the Soviet Union approached final negotiations for an atmospheric test ban treaty, Kennedy tried again. He signaled his agenda when he publicly raised the possibility of the treaty's text calling for the signatories to "use all the influence that they had in their possession to persuade others not to grasp the nuclear nettle." When Ambassador Harriman prepared for his July negotiations, he found that his briefing papers included a section titled "Military and Other Sanctions against Communist China." More, Harriman was instructed to approach the Soviets to explore possible "action to deny the Chicoms a nuclear capability," including "a joint U.S.–Soviet preemptive nuclear attack" against the Chinese nuclear weapons installation at Lop Nor. To ensure that Harriman took this part of his mission seriously, he was sent a cable as the negotiations opened to remind him to address the Chinese nuclear issue. He should, the cable read, "try to elicit Khrushchev's view of his willingness either to take Soviet action or to accept U.S. action aimed in this direction." By the time the successful treaty negotiations were concluded, Harriman was "crystal clear" that Moscow was anxious to isolate China, but when he raised the possibility of a joint attack on Lop Nor with Khrushchev, the latter "did not respond. [He] was clearly not ready to take the step with Washington."[41]

In August 1964, as China's nuclear scientists moved toward final preparations for their first nuclear test and the Johnson administration escalated the war against Vietnam, Mao warned party officials that "war is coming," and he understood that even with nuclear weapons China would long be on the defensive. At a meeting of the Chinese Communist Party's Central Secretariat, Mao warned that the US was preparing "a new war of aggression against China," and that to prepare for it, China needed to adopt a "three front strategy." Consistent with earlier PLA recommendations, the first two fronts were China's coastal and central provinces. Isolated provinces in China's southwest and northwest constituted the third. Mao "called for . . . the dramatic acceleration of the construction of industrial facilities in the interior provinces." The Air Force was pressed to build new air bases across southern China and the Vietnamese were advised "to avoid direct military confrontation with the invading military forces." Instead, they were to entice the US to "penetrate deep into their territory," where they would be vulnerable to a people's war.[42]

In mid-September, Johnson, his National Security Advisor McGeorge Bundy, CIA Director John McCone, and Secretaries Robert McNamara and Dean Rusk again turned to the disturbing question of China's preparations for an imminent nuclear weapons test. Senior figures in the Pentagon were urging preemptive overt or covert strikes to eliminate the Chinese nuclear program. Bundy recorded the outcome of their discussions as follows:

> "We are not in favor of unprovoked unilateral U.S. military action against Chinese nuclear installations at this time . . . We believe that there are many possibilities for joint action with the Soviet Government if that Government is interested . . . even a possible agreement to cooperate in preventive military action. We therefore agreed that it would be most desirable for the Secretary of State to explore this matter very privately with Ambassador Dobrynin as soon as possible."[43]

The Soviets, however, were not in a position to respond positively to the US proposal. On October 16, at about the same time that Khrushchev was being ousted for a host of failures, including the Cuban Missile Crisis and his "poor handling of the dispute with China," Beijing's first atomic bomb was detonated at Lop Nor. Leading US conservatives urged Johnson to "bomb Red China's bomb," but another scenario quickly became the focus of debate within the Johnson administration: an "Indian" bomb.

The Indian government, which had fought an intense border war with China two years earlier and which was shaken by the Chinese nuclear test, came forward with an unconventional proposal. As Daniel Ellsberg, then Special Assistant to Assistant Secretary of Defense McNaughton, has since reported, New Delhi believed the best way to offset the terrifying new Asian imbalance of power would be for the US to secretly give India an A-bomb that could be detonated as its own. India would chasten the Chinese by posing as a nuclear power.[44]

To the distress of senior Pentagon officials, the Indian proposal was initially well received. A year earlier, during a meeting in which Kennedy had resolved to defend India if it were attacked by China, McNamara had stressed that if "substantial commitment to defend India . . . [were to be given] we should recognize that . . . we would have to use nuclear weapons."[45] Senior figures in the Pentagon were nonetheless stunned when Secretary Rusk supported the Indian request. The plan was defeated only after intense debates in the highest circles of US power. Few, if any, involved in the debate anticipated that in less than a decade Maoist China would become Washington's tacit and most strategic ally.

Seven years later, to the amazement of the US people and much of the world, the fiercely anti-communist president, Richard Nixon, moved toward recognition of China and forged a tacit alliance with Beijing against the Soviet Union. In doing so, Nixon extended Washington's "nuclear umbrella" beyond South Korea and the western shores of the Japanese archipelago to Beijing and to the Usuri River which divided the two communist powers.

Nixon's 1972 visit to Beijing was more than an election year spectacle designed to diminish his Democrat challengers by the audacity of his diplomatic opening and the grandeur of ceremonies in the Chinese capital. It was also a classic expression of imperial *realpolitik*. Since the early 1950s, having learned from the Soviet–Yugoslav schism that nationalism could trump ideological commitments to communism, successive US administrations sought to exploit Soviet–Chinese tensions which remained largely hidden behind the world communist movement's façade of unity. Strains in their relations grew from differences over strategy and tactics about how best to defend and advance communism to border disputes dating from Tsarist intrusions and Soviet fears of Chinese ambitions in Mongolia. Between 1960 and the "savage outbreak" of fighting on the Usuri River in March 1969, there were as many as 5,500 often bloody border incidents between the two communist powers, at least one of which was backed by Soviet nuclear threats.[46]

The commitments and compromises that served as the foundation for the tacit US–Chinese alliance, possibly facilitated by US threats to permit Japan to develop a nuclear arsenal, were hammered out in a series of secret negotiations between Kissinger and China's leaders which preceded Nixon's triumphant journey to China. Washington's goals were clear: to gain greater freedom of action with Vietnam, to have more leverage over Moscow to win advantageous arms control agreements, and to contain both China and the Soviet Union. To gain these advantages, Nixon consciously treated Mao as an "emperor." He reversed the "One China" policy, committing the US to recognize Beijing and not Taipei, and he also promised to "restrain Japan."

Mao and Zhou Enlai came away from the summit with Nixon with a powerful buffer against Soviet demands and threats, an arrangement that endured until the end of the Cold War. US–Chinese relations would become more complicated with the decline of the Soviet Union. With the loss of the alliance's *raison d'être* and popular revulsion in the US in the face of Beijing's brutal repression of democratic protesters in Tiananmen Square and across China in 1989, the political foundations of this "most extraordinary relationship" were shattered beyond repair.

4
The Cuban Missile Crisis—Prestige, Credibility, and Power

Do not put a loaded rifle on stage if no one is thinking of firing it.

Anton Chekhov[1]

So long as we had the thumbscrew on Khrushchev, we should have given it another turn every day.

Dean Acheson [2]

My guess is, well, everybody sort of figures that, *in extremis*, everybody would use nuclear weapons.

John F. Kennedy[3]

On the evening of Monday, October 22, 1962, two weeks before the mid-term Congressional elections, President Kennedy addressed the people of the US and the world with solemn gravity from the White House. Surveillance flights over Cuba, the president said, had "established . . . that a series of offensive missiles sites" were being built by the Soviets on the "imprisoned island" of Cuba. Each of these missiles would be capable of "striking Washington, DC, the Panama Canal, Cape Canaveral, Mexico City, or any other city in the southeastern part of the United States . . . Central America, or . . . the Caribbean . . . . Neither the United States of America nor the world community of nations can tolerate deliberate deception and offensive threats on the part of any nation, large or small." The Soviet missile deployments were "a definite threat to peace" because they broke the tradition of "great care" which the US and the Soviet Union had long exercised in "never upsetting the precarious status quo . . . . this secret, swift, and extraordinary build-up of Communist missiles—in an area well known to have a special and historical relationship to the United States . . . cannot be accepted if our courage and our commitments are ever to be trusted again . . ." In some of the most frightening words ever uttered, Kennedy warned, "We will not prematurely or unnecessarily risk the costs of worldwide nuclear war in which even the fruits of victory would be ashes in our mouth—but neither will we shrink from that risk at any time it must be faced."

Kennedy informed his audiences that he had ordered the Navy to establish a limited "quarantine" around Cuba. US military forces would be reinforced and were prepared "for any eventualities." If the Soviets launched their missiles based in Cuba, the US would retaliate.[4]

The president was clear that the nation was on the brink of war, possibly nuclear annihilation, to maintain the predominance of US nuclear power and hegemony—that "special historical relationship"—in the Americas. Although it was not true, the popular understanding was that 180 million US Americans could be incinerated in the course of the crisis.[5]

The superpower confrontation, whose origins lay in the preceding months, years, and decades, climaxed before most people could meaningfully respond. On the morning of October 28, six days after Kennedy threatened "whatever action is needed" to force the removal of Soviet missiles from Cuba,[6] Soviet Premier Nikita Khrushchev announced that Moscow would comply with Kennedy's demands. His sole apparent condition was that the US should provide assurances that Cuba would not be invaded. Khrushchev's announcement also contained obscure diplomatic phrasing that was inaccessible to most people, including members of Kennedy's Cabinet and Congress, signaling a second secret condition: that the US withdraw its nuclear-armed Jupiter missiles from Turkey.

The US and the Soviet Union had gone "eyeball to eyeball" in their unequal "game" of nuclear chicken before Khrushchev's humiliating reversal in the face of Washington's overwhelming military power. So close had the superpowers come to nuclear war that, at the height of the confrontation, Kennedy believed the chances that the US would initiate nuclear war were "somewhere between one out of three to even."[7] Dean Rusk, Kennedy's Secretary of State, later remarked that the missile crisis was the "moment in history when we came closest to nuclear war," apparently overlooking the atomic bombings of Hiroshima and Nagasaki.[8] These apprehensions were mirrored in the stated and silent fears of ordinary people across the US, in the Soviet Union, Cuba, Japan, and many other nations. The Cuban novelist Edmundo Desnoes put it succinctly: we feared "It's all over."[9]

The Kennedy administration's handling of the Cuban Missile Crisis was immediately hailed in the US as a great diplomatic and political victory for the president and the nation. It became essential to the myth of the Camelot presidency. The crisis had not spread to Berlin, Turkey, or Asia. It was widely believed that Kennedy and his advisors had forced the Soviets to back down without the US making any concessions, and with Kennedy's senior advisors believing that they had mastered the practice of nuclear-enforced "coercive diplomacy." The Cuban Missile Crisis thus helped to pave the way for Kennedy and Johnson's disastrous escalation of the war in Vietnam.[10]

A decade later, when the Soviet Union finally achieved the rough nuclear parity that McNamara had long predicted was inevitable, few reflected publicly about the madness of US policymakers in 1962. The political viability of the Kennedy presidency had been preserved, as had national pride and prestige, by risking a thermonuclear exchange which McNamara estimated could have killed 200 million people in its first hour,[11] and at the cost of accelerating the already catastrophic nuclear arms race. From the perspective of history, the reckless nuclear terrorism practiced by the "best and brightest" US leaders, and to a lesser extent by Soviet and Cuban leaders, illuminates the ideological insanity and "rational" madness inherent in "security" based on preparations for, and threats of, nuclear war.

Because the Cuban Missile Crisis grew out of the history of US colonialism and neocolonialism, as well as the US–Soviet Cold War confrontation, this chapter begins with a review of the "special relationship" between the US and Cuba. It describes Eisenhower's and Kennedy's fears that the Cuban revolutionary government threatened US dominance of Latin America first envisioned in the Monroe Doctrine and how both John and Robert Kennedy were obsessed with overthrowing Fidel Castro. As is explained in the following pages, Khrushchev's campaign to secretly deploy ballistic missiles in Cuba that could target the entire US was designed to both defend the besieged Cuban revolution and to overcome what the Soviets experienced as the humiliating imbalance of nuclear terror.

The chapter then documents this near-cataclysmic example of how Kennedy, his advisors, and lieutenants risked unleashing a holocaust that could have claimed the lives of more than 500 million people in a classic example of the use of the US nuclear arsenal to intimidate those whom Washington was "determined to attack."[12] Contrary to popular understandings that the Cuban Missile Crisis was a great US victory, Kennedy and his advisors were risking cataclysmic nuclear war to preserve US prestige, to extend their nuclear dominance for little more than a decade, to avoid the possible impeachment of the president, and to enforce the principle that the US, but not the Soviet Union, could base nuclear weapons—even obsolete ones—on its enemy's periphery.

The Cuban Missile Crisis also illuminates other disturbing truths which are described here. President Kennedy and his Secretary of State were unable to fully control their military. At the height of the crisis, Kennedy succumbed to demands by the Joint Chiefs to invade Cuba if the Kremlin failed to back down within 48 hours. A senior general dangerously increased the level of the nuclear alert on his own authority. And, in violation of directives from the Secretary of Defense, the Navy came within seconds of launching a nuclear war. Similarly, years after the Cuban Missile Crisis, surviving leaders of the Kennedy administration and scholars were shocked to learn that Khrushchev had delegated authority to launch tactical nuclear weapons to his field commander in Cuba. Debate continues to rage over whether that delegation of authority remained functionally in place on the eve of the planned US invasion. Finally, there is the profoundly disturbing news that in the final hours of the Missile Crisis Castro urged Khrushchev to use his nuclear arsenal to destroy the Yankee imperialists, even if that meant annihilating the Cuban people.

A SPECIAL HISTORICAL RELATIONSHIP

In the fall of 1960, former US Ambassador to Cuba Earl E. T. Smith described the twentieth-century history of US–Cuban relations in less than diplomatic terms: "Until the advent of Castro, the United States was so overwhelmingly influential in Cuba . . . the American Ambassador was the second most important man in Cuba, sometimes even more important than the [Cuban] President."[13] The journalist Tad Szulc was more direct: since being granted its "independence" in 1902, Cuba was more of "an appendage of the United States" than a sovereign country.[14]

Long before the Spanish-American War, "Manifest Destiny" and geostrategic considerations turned US ambitions to the fertile island 90 miles south of Florida. Cuba's harbors could serve or threaten US dominance in the Caribbean. In 1823, Secretary of State John Quincy Adams observed that Cuba had "become an object of transcendent importance to the political and commercial interests of our union." He ventured that "it is scarcely possible to resist the conviction that the annexation of Cuba to our federal Republic will be indispensable to the continuance and integrity of the Union itself."[15]

Cuba was at the time a Spanish colony. Although Spanish imperialism was a spent force, an intense political conflict stood between Adams' ambitions, the president he served (James Monroe), and the annexation of Cuba. The island had more slaves per capita of the free population than any other nation in the world, and the defining and immobilizing debate within the US was whether newly annexed territories would enter the Union as "slave" or "free" states. For that reason, Congressmen from the North opposed Cuba's immediate annexation. Partially as a result of his political need to buy time for the eventual annexation of Cuba, Monroe enunciated the Doctrine that still bears his name. All of the Western Hemisphere lay within the US sphere of influence. European nations, and Britain and

France particularly, were placed on notice not to challenge US dominance (or ambitions) in this region.[16]

Official sanction has not always been required for political penetration or symbiotic union. By 1895, when the long-suppressed Cuban revolution for independence from Spain reignited, US businesses and banks owned Cuban sugar plantations, mines, and other resources estimated to be worth $30 million in late nineteenth-century dollars.[17] When the revolution came, the Spanish Crown moved with determination, brutally repressing the people and interning Cubans by the hundreds of thousands in concentration camps. They died there in staggering numbers from torture, neglect, starvation, and disease. On the mainland the "yellow press" competed with reports of the most agonizing accounts of Spanish atrocities, urging support for Cuban nationalists. Instead, President Cleveland chose neutrality, an option that required Spain to continue to protect US property in Cuba.[18]

In much the same way that Presidents Bush and Clinton used the rhetoric of "humanitarian interventions" to build popular support for their wars in Iraq, Yugoslavia, and Afghanistan, the misnamed "Spanish-American" war was ostensibly fought to relieve human suffering. Those who look carefully today in New England can glimpse the ideological foundations and rhetoric used to mobilize popular support for the war. In addition to revenge for the sinking of the *Maine*, the rationale for the war is seen in nearly identical monuments in town commons and parks across the region. Atop a cement plinth stands a lone yeoman soldier holding a rifle across his torso. Below, is a plaque that pictures a desperate woman kneeling on a beach with her arms outstretched, imploring help from abroad. Behind her US soldiers and sailors come ashore, bringing relief from distant ships in the bay. The words "Cuba," "Puerto Rico," and "Philippines" frame an engraving, naming the countries "saved" by US forces.

In the 1890s, desperation was not limited to the *campesinos* and dissidents of the Spanish empire. The US was in the grip of a severe economic depression. On farms, in mining districts and cities people were without work, losing their homes, hungry, and threatening revolt. And since the 1870s depression, access and exports to Latin American and Chinese markets were seen as one of the few means to revitalize the economy.[19] In addition to their agricultural resources and markets, control of Cuban and Puerto Rican ports would guarantee US military supremacy in the Caribbean. Subic Bay in the Philippines, 5,000 miles away, was seen as the essential stepping stone to China's markets.

In January 1898, apparently in response to renewed fighting across Cuba, the naval cruiser *Maine* was sent to Havana as "a visible expression of United States' concern." Within days it was sabotaged by attackers whose allegiance remains a mystery. Despite the failure to identify the saboteurs, the sinking of the *Maine*, with the resulting heavy loss of US lives, fueled war fever. President McKinley's response was a declaration of war against Spain. His goal, he said, was "to put an end to the barbarities, bloodshed, starvation, and horrible miseries" in Cuba, and to right "the very serious injury to the commerce, trade and business of our people . . . [the] wanton destruction of property and devastation of the island," and the "enormous expense" caused by the turmoil. Significantly, he made no reference to Cuban nationalists and their independence struggle. When the guns of the Spanish–American war finally fell silent, hundreds of thousands were dead, and the US had conquered, occupied, and colonized Cuba, Puerto Rico, the Philippines, and Guam, the last another stepping stone to China.

Washington was not satisfied with simply expelling Cuba's Spanish oppressors. US occupation forces remained until 1902, when the US sponsored government in Havana accepted the Platt Amendment, a law that functionally precluded Cuban sovereignty and transformed the island into a US economic colony and political protectorate.[20] The amendment gave the US the right to "intervene for the preservation of Cuban independence, the maintenance of a government adequate for the protection of life, property and individual liberty," and it required that Cuba "sell or lease to the United States the land necessary for coaling and naval stations."[21] During the next six decades successive US administrations demonstrated that the "preservation of Cuban independence," the "protection of life," and "individual liberty" were not US policy priorities.

In this way the US naval base at Guantánamo Bay, now best known for US torture of "enemy combatants," was secured. US agents gained routine access to the economic, political, and personal secrets stored in Cuban tax, banking, and public works records. US ambassadors were appointed because they were "essential to the protection of American investments in Cuba."[22] While the Platt Amendment provided the legal rationale for repeated military interventions, the ideological foundation was laid with Theodore Roosevelt's 1905 corollary to the Monroe Doctrine: "wrong-doing, or an impotence which results in a general loosening of the ties of civilized society, may in America . . . ultimately require intervention by some civilized nation." The "civilized" nation that would right wrongs would of necessity be the US.[23]

As Maurice Zeitlin has documented, during "the next twenty-five years, at least five attempted revolutions were suppressed or influenced by the presence of U.S. Marines." Countless other "warnings" from Washington or the US ambassador had a similar impact.[24] The last gasp of this tradition of gunboat diplomacy came early in Franklin Roosevelt's administration. Washington was unwilling to tolerate the economic reforms proposed by the government of Ramón Grau San Martin, which would have restructured Cuba's debts and limited the freedom of US corporations to exploit Cuban labor and resources. Grau's government was overthrown through a combination of diplomatic and military maneuvers.

By the 1930s, after a century of conquest, intervention, and imperial administration, "Lake Monroe" (the Caribbean Sea) and its environs were secured. The US had consolidated control over the hemisphere, and Roosevelt astutely moved to soothe simmering anti-US sentiments with his "good neighbor" policy, which explicitly renounced the right of any nation to intervene in the affairs of others. With US economic influence, military bases, and loyal elites assiduously assembled throughout Latin America, there was less to this policy than met the eye.

The Platt Amendment was finally abrogated in 1934, but the Navy's lease of Guantánamo Bay in perpetuity was not. With its military base, its dominant role within the Cuban economy, its loyal dictators, and its powerful ambassadors, the US continued to exert tremendous influence over nearly all aspects of Cuban life.[25]

The last of Washington's and Wall Street's brutal Havana minions was the dictator Fulgencio Batista, an army sergeant who consolidated his power within the military while ruling Cuba through elected proxies. In 1936, he overthrew his former ally, President Miguel Gomez, and with US support terrorized Cuban politics for most of the next 22 years. Batista was not the stereotypical banana republic dictator. In the Americas, he was ahead of his time. He understood "the refinements of twentieth-century totalitarianism," keeping a tight rein on labor unions, the universities, and the press. His regime thus had more in common with Spanish and Italian fascism and Latin American military dictatorships of the 1970s and 1980s than with the postcolonial *caudillo* strongman tradition. Cubans were killed, tortured, or maimed by the thousands to maintain Batista's hold on power. By 1958, when he was finally overthrown by the Cuban revolution, it was estimated that his regime had murdered 20,000 of Cuba's 7 million people.[26]

Fidel Castro was never "our man in Havana." He and the Cuban revolutionaries were widely viewed in the US as the democratic alternative to Batista's repression, but President Eisenhower provided weapons to Batista and his army until the spring of 1958, six months before the guerrilla forces victoriously entered Havana. It was thus understandable that when Castro came to power, he was convinced that Eisenhower would attempt to turn back the clock. Castro warned, "If you send Marines, thousands of them will die on the beaches."[27]

Castro's economic policies soon alienated Washington. An estimated $1 billion worth of US-owned Cuban assets were nationalized, including sugar plantations, oil refineries, and tobacco, tourist, and real estate resources. Castro launched literacy campaigns, armed the populace, drafted doctors to serve the people, "destroyed the oligarchy and curbed the bourgeoisie."[28] Many Batista loyalists were summarily tried and publicly executed. And, on December 19, 1960, Castro formally aligned Cuba with the increasingly fractured Sino-Soviet bloc.

Eisenhower's response was to sever diplomatic relations with Havana and impose limited economic sanctions. Quickly upping the ante, the newly inaugurated Kennedy administration escalated the one-sided confrontation by eliminating Cuba's sugar quota in order to deprive Cuba of access to its most important market, and he succumbed to pressures from the CIA and the outgoing Eisenhower administration to approve the self-defeating invasion of Cuba at the Bay of Pigs.[29] When it came time to apportion blame, the president pointed to the CIA; the CIA pointed to the Joint Chiefs . . . and the Joint Chiefs pointed to the president.

AN ENDURING IMBALANCE OF TERROR

During the Cuban Missile Crisis and in the decades that followed, most Americans believed that two, nearly equal nuclear powers had confronted one another. At the same time, they feared that they and all humanity were in danger of being killed in an omnicidal thermonuclear exchange. Hundreds of millions of lives were in jeopardy, but most were Russian, European, and Cuban lives. The primary motive driving Khrushchev's  attempt to deploy nuclear-armed missiles in Cuba was the desperation that he and many Soviet military leaders felt at their vulnerability to a first-strike US attack. During the crisis, the disparity of US and Soviet nuclear forces led former President Eisenhower to comment that Soviet leaders "must be scared as hell" and to again recommend that the US invade Cuba.[30]

Despite Soviet attempts to intimidate the US and world opinion with increasingly powerful atomic and hydrogen bomb tests, before 1955 neither Stalin nor his successors could pretend to have the ability to successfully attack the US. Moscow's nuclear Potemkin village did little more than pacify domestic critics in the USSR and to spur the Pentagon to accelerate the expansion of its nuclear arsenal. By 1960, when the US first began deploying nuclear-armed missiles on Polaris submarines, Washington had 1,735 strategic bombers capable of eliminating the Soviet Union. In strictly numerical terms, US nuclear superiority was 17:1.[31] This understates the imbalance of power and obscures the intoxication of many US leaders who argued that the US was capable of launching a totally disarming first-strike nuclear attack against the Soviet Union. The historian Paul Kennedy has documented that US and Soviet military disparity, "total fire power, manpower . . . mobility of conventional forces . . . diversity, lethality, and precision of strategic weapons systems" was 40:1 in the mid-1950s and nearly 10:1 a decade later after military build-ups on both sides. "This disparity," Kennedy explained, "was far greater than any other . . . between the strongest power and its strongest rival, or group of rivals," since the modern state system came into existence in the seventeenth century.[32]

Despite Washington's rhetoric of a "missile gap" and "falling dominoes," the US establishment appreciated its spectacular military superiority. A 1955 National Intelligence Estimate reported that Moscow's conciliatory approach resulted from its "realization of . . . the fact that at present U.S. nuclear capabilities greatly exceed those of the USSR" and that "as long as this gap exists the Soviet leaders will almost certainly wish to minimize the risk of general war." In 1958, after U-2 spy flights demonstrated that the Kremlin still had no ICBM launch sites, Eisenhower explained it more graphically to Lyndon Johnson, then Majority Leader in the Senate: "If we were to release our nuclear stockpile on the Soviet Union, the main danger would arise not from retaliation but from fallout in the earth's atmosphere."[33]

By the time of the Cuban Missile Crisis in 1962, the Kremlin may have had as many as 20 primitive intercontinental ballistic missiles (ICBMs) theoretically capable of reaching the US, but to prevent corrosion, their fuel tanks were left empty, thus requiring several hours of fueling before they could be launched. Like sentries along the Great Wall of China, the missiles' guidance systems necessitated signal installations at 300-mile intervals along their flight paths, and the Soviet military had limited information about the location of US targets. This compared with Washington's 284 ICBMs and 2,000 nuclear-capable bombers, which made "the entire land-based Soviet strategic force . . . highly vulnerable to a U.S. first-strike attack" and left the entire Soviet Union vulnerable to "counter-value" annihilation (i.e. destruction of Soviet cities and their populations). As one Soviet missile designer complained, "nothing would be left of us" before Moscow could launch a retaliatory strike.[34]

It was difficult for Soviet generals and committed Communist revolutionaries to stand aside, seeming to kowtow to the capitalists, during the Korean War, the Taiwan crises, and the initial US escalation in Vietnam. Yet, throughout the 1950s, Khrushchev held firm, warning that a "small imperialist war can develop into a world nuclear war," and urging Communist forces not to resort to warfare. In 1958, when Gamal Abdel Nasser, the Egyptian leader, urged Moscow to threaten the US in response to Marines landing in Beirut, Khrushchev refused, saying, "We are not ready for World War III." A year later, when Iraq's military leader, Abdul Karim Kassem, killed hundreds of Communists following their failed attempt to gain a share of power, Moscow again stood on the side-lines.

Admonishing communists from Vietnam to Cuba, Khrushchev warned that the Iraqi calamity was a result of "premature slogans of socialist transformation . . . where conditions for them have not yet matured."[35] In 1962, when Khrushchev appointed Anatoly Dobrynin Ambassador to the US, his instructions were that "war with the United States was inadmissible—this was above all."[36]

KENNEDY CONTEXTS

Poetic vision can reflect the collective unconscious and illuminate reality. Thus when the celebrated poet Robert Frost read his inaugural poem at "the beginning hour" of the Kennedy presidency, he celebrated both the young president's persona and much of the nation's expectation:

> The glory of a next Augustan age
> Of a power leading from its strength and pride
> Of young ambition eager to be tried.[37]

With these words the old poet anticipated the imperial arrogance, militarism, hubris, and inexperience that paved the way to the Cuban Missile Crisis and to the catastrophic escalation of the Indochina War.

John F. Kennedy and his cohort of East Coast can-do academics marked a generational transition from the Eisenhower era, but their arrival was less than the total break with the past trumpeted to the public. Kennedy had long straddled both wings of the Democratic Party: liberals loyal to their twice-defeated presidential candidate Adlai Stevenson and hard-liners still clustered around Dean Acheson, the architect and executioner of Truman's confrontational Cold War foreign policies. David Halberstam's description of Kennedy as he assumed office was apt: "there was . . . an element of the hard-liner in him, as there was to almost everyone in politics at that point . . . He was the epitome of the contemporary man in a cool, pragmatic age, more admiring of the old, shrewd, almost cynical Establishment breed . . . than of the ponderous do-good types . . ." Kennedy admired the "guts and toughness" of the aging "Wise Men" of the establishment, men like Acheson, McCloy, and Harriman, all of whom served Kennedy through his administration's travails.[38]

Like the mythic Icarus who flew too close to the sun, dangerous and tragic currents flowed beneath Kennedy's public image of heroism, youth, and ambition. Like Franklin Roosevelt before him, he labored to conceal his ill health, chronic pain, and now notorious womanizing.[39] And, like others before him, Kennedy was not above demagoguery, raising popular fears, and distorting reality to advance his political career. Michael Beschloss, the presidential historian, was right when he wrote, "No candidate risked more by shilling for votes than John F. Kennedy who . . . sowed the seeds of the gravest crises of his Presidency." Kennedy urged that the US support "fighters for freedom" who sought to oust Castro, and he "hamstrung himself" by wrongly accusing Eisenhower of permitting the Soviets to threaten US security by allowing a nonexistent missile gap that favored Moscow to emerge.[40]

In fact, Pentagon and CIA briefings during and after the election were clear that there was a serious missile gap, but one that favored the US. Ten months after Kennedy's inauguration, Deputy Secretary of Defense Roswell Gilpatric described the real missile gap, saying that Washington "has a nuclear retaliatory force of such lethal power that an enemy move which brought it into play would be an act of self-destruction."[41] Official US estimates were that Moscow had "fewer than fifty" ICBMs, while the US had 185 and more than 3,400 deliverable nuclear bombs. According to a 1961 National Intelligence Estimate, "fewer than fifty" was a diplomatic way of saying "four."[42]

Nonetheless, having aroused the public's existential fears during the campaign, Kennedy found it politically necessary to accelerate the one-sided nuclear arms race. Within months of assuming office he won a 15 percent increase in military spending, accelerated production of nuclear-capable missiles, and made training for anti-guerrilla war a priority for the Army and Marines.[43] This deepened Soviet fears of a US first-strike nuclear attack and contributed to Khrushchev's decision to deploy nuclear-armed missiles in Cuba.

Kennedy's inner circle was dominated by younger men, most of whom were self-described "pragmatic rationalists." McGeorge Bundy came from Harvard where he was dean of a government department dedicated to "ultra-realism." Like many in the administration, he had served senior policymakers during World War II. Unlike his colleagues, he was an admirer of, apologist for, and had been a collaborator with Henry L. Stimson, Secretary of War, who had played a central role in the decision to bomb Hiroshima and Nagasaki. Robert McNamara, who had served on General Curtis LeMay's staff during the fire bombings of Japanese cities, brought the profit-oriented logic of systems analysis from Ford's offices in Michigan to Pentagon and Cabinet counsels. Dean Rusk, who had drawn the line dividing Korea and who as Assistant Secretary of State had negotiated the fine points of the US–Japan Mutual Security Treaty, returned to the State Department at Foggy Bottom as Secretary of State. Retired General Maxwell Taylor had written the bestselling book *The Distant Trumpet*, advocating a new strategic doctrine that relied more heavily on counter-insurgency ground forces, reinforced by threats of limited or general nuclear war. Taylor initially joined the inner circle as Kennedy's "military advisor" in the wake of the Bay of Pigs disaster, but was soon promoted to become Chairman of the Joint Chiefs. Robert Kennedy, the president's younger brother who served formally as Attorney General and informally as prime minister, cut his political teeth as a member of Senator Joe McCarthy's staff.[44]

US–Soviet relations in the first years of the Kennedy presidency were characterized by intense rivalry, fear, and miscalculation. Even as Kennedy's advisors were fascinated by the emerging Sino-Soviet split and believed it could provide valuable opportunities to advance US power,[45] they were challenged by Khrushchev's constant taunts and testing as he sought to gain advantage in Berlin, Southeast Asia, elsewhere in the Third World, in outer space, and in nuclear technologies, which Khrushchev boasted were "equal, if not superior" to Washington's. In the public mind and in the minds of many of Kennedy's advisors, Moscow seemed to be on the offensive as it sought to ally itself with the rising Third World wretched of the earth, and dared to challenge traditional US primacy in Cuba and elsewhere in Latin America.[46]

Though powerful, Kennedy and his circle were insecure and inflexible. Roy Medvedev, the dissident Soviet historian, was particularly perceptive, writing that:

> the abortive coup in Cuba coincided with the defeat of pro-American, right-wing forces in Laos .... The pro-American Government of Ngo Din Diem was also finding it difficult to retain power in South Vietnam. Among Washington's ruling circles these indignities abraded a certain sensitivity, particularly in view of recent reversals in Middle East and Africa. American politicians were unaccustomed to such setbacks and were prepared neither to retreat nor to reconcile themselves to the prospect of a reduction of their influence over international politics."[47]

At the June 1961 summit in Vienna, Khrushchev judged Kennedy to be "an inexperienced young leader," who could be bullied, intimidated, and blackmailed.[48] He also assumed that Washington "had learned some lessons from [its] defeat" at the Bay of Pigs but "wouldn't refuse a chance to repeat their aggression."[49] There was some truth in Khrushchev's reading of Kennedy, but there were also dangerous miscalculations not shared by some of his closest colleagues on the Soviet Presidium.[50]

Influenced by Kissinger's thinking, by Maxwell Taylor, and by the then little-known Pentagon advisor Daniel Ellsberg, the Kennedy administration broke with the Eisenhower–Dulles military doctrine of "massive retaliation." Late in the Eisenhower presidency, the doctrine had begun to lose its credibility. Moscow had been building its nuclear arsenal for a decade, and it was popularly believed to be capable of launching a retaliatory attack after suffering a US first strike. Politicians, the public, and strategic analysts also questioned the proportionality, risks, and credibility of relying on first-strike nuclear attacks in response to every "conventional" challenge to US power and influence. Were Guatemala, Quemoy and Matsu, or Laos worth nuclear cataclysms or the pariah status that would follow if the US initiated nuclear war during any but the most dire circumstances? Nonetheless, as Ellsberg later wrote, Kennedy and his successors believed "that past and current threats [to use nuclear weapons] had succeeded, this was why . . . they and their successors kept making such threats and buying more and more first-use and first-strike nuclear weapons systems to maintain and increase the credibility and effectiveness of threats they expected to make in the future."[51]

Kennedy's response to the critique of "massive retaliation" was Maxwell Taylor's "flexible response." This was a synthesis of Kissinger's advocacy of threatening, and if necessary fighting, limited nuclear wars, combined with calls for greater reliance on counter-insurgency and ground forces. Kennedy's cutting-edge weapons system was the "Green Beret" infantryman, reinforced by "escalation dominance" and a diversified nuclear arsenal that could theoretically "trump" the Soviets (or any other enemy) at every step on the ladder of military escalation.

Kennedy had reason to be confident about US first-strike capabilities and escalation dominance. In July 1961, the same month that he was informed of a proposed first-strike attack on the Soviet Union, which "appear[ed] to be more than a contingency plan,"[52] the CIA transmitted a report to the president from Oleg Penkovsky, a CIA mole in Moscow. It confirmed that the Soviet Union had built virtually no missiles and that Khrushchev was bluffing when he implied that Moscow was ready for war. Kennedy's strategic arms advisor, Carl Kaysen, also informed him that a "disarming first strike" against Soviet strategic forces could be carried out with a high level of confidence that it would catch them all on the ground. This report demonstrated that "[t]he whole Soviet ICBM system was suddenly obsolescent."[53]

Kennedy's "flexible response" doctrine was premised on the belief that Soviet leaders and other potential adversaries were rational. Instead of opting for suicide, they would back down in confrontations with the US, leaving the field open to the Pentagon's "conventional" ground forces. But, should the system be tested, as Kennedy's *alter ego* Theodore Sorensen explained, "John Kennedy . . . was still willing to face the ultimate risk of nuclear war . . . He neither shrank from that risk nor rushed out to embrace it."[54] That said, despite overwhelming US nuclear superiority, when he faced pressures to escalate the Cuban Missile Crisis and the Vietnam War, he was far more cautious about threatening or initiating nuclear war than were many in his Cabinet and certainly the Pentagon's Joint Chiefs. Kennedy properly feared irrationality in both Washington and Moscow.[55]

A year after assuming office, Secretary of Defense McNamara revised the SIOP (Single Integrated Operational Plan) for nuclear war. In addition to targeting Soviet, Chinese, and Albanian cities,[56] the US war plan also called for eliminating "Soviet missiles, bomber bases, submarine tenders, air defenses . . . and control systems." Consistent with flexible response, McNamara believed that nuclear weapons could be used in a limited nuclear war, and that the US "must be in a position to bring the war to a conclusion on terms favorable to Washington." Confident that this could be done, McNamara informed Congress that the entire Soviet strategic arsenal was "vulnerable to attack." As the Pentagon later concluded, "At the time of the Cuban Missile Crisis," Moscow's ability to respond to a US first-strike attack was doubtful. "[T]he Soviet strategic situation in 1962 might have been judged as a little short of desperate."[57]

With the strength, energy, and limited experience of younger men, Kennedy and many of his advisors were insensitive to the fears that their rhetoric and activism engendered in Moscow. Despite his diplomatic successes and boastful rhetoric, Khrushchev was profoundly aware of the weakness and limits of Soviet military power. He ruled, as Max Frankel observed, "with a deep sense of inferiority, aware of the frailty of the Soviet 'union' of nationalities. He feared a resurgent Germany. And he never outgrew his view of capitalists as predatory." Khrushchev's aggressive confrontational diplomacy at the 1961 Vienna summit and elsewhere were largely designed to obscure Soviet deficits and to put the US on the defensive.[58]

Khrushchev was anxious as the new administration accelerated its nuclear warhead and missile production. He resented Washington's encirclement of the Soviet Union with nuclear-armed Jupiter missiles in Turkey and Italy and nuclear-armed Polaris submarines at sea. After the Bay of Pigs fiasco, Khrushchev remained sure that "the Americans would never reconcile themselves to the existence of Castro's Cuba."[59] Nor could Khrushchev ignore Kennedy's warning that if Moscow resorted to military means to resolve the continuing confrontation over Berlin, "we might have to take the initiative." Kennedy had threatened nuclear attack. This, as much as anything, drove Khrushchev to his desperate attempt to equalize the imbalance of terror with missile deployments in Cuba. Kennedy's first-strike threat, Khrushchev warned, was a "very bad mistake—for which he would have to pay."[60]

"OPERATION MONGOOSE"

John and Robert Kennedy were obsessed with Cuba. While Castro haunted the Kennedys as "a reminder of deep humiliation and a target for revenge,"[61] it was his commitment to free Latin America from US hegemony that most concerned policymakers in Washington. Having removed Cuba from the US imperial domain, Castro and his comrades wanted to liberate other Latin American nations as well. Speaking in Havana on February 4, 1962, he "virtually declared war" in what later became known as the Second Declaration of Havana. He condemned the impacts of US imperialism, saying that an "unending torrent of money" was flowing "from Latin America to the United States: some $4,000 per minute, $5 million per day . . . A thousand dollars per corpse . . ." Castro declared that "It is the duty of every revolutionary to make the revolution."[62] Two weeks later, at the president's request, Brigadier General Lansdale presented his six-phase proposal for the US destabilization and overthrow of the Cuban government.

Earlier, during his election campaign, when he first called for an "Alliance for Progress" with Latin America, Kennedy envisioned a campaign patterned after Roosevelt's good neighbor policy. It would be designed to provide political, economic, social, and military alternatives to Castro's call to overcome hunger and US dominance through revolutionary communism and radical redistribution of power and wealth. Plans and the proclamation for the "Alliance" developed slowly as a result of the fall-out from the Bay of Pigs fiasco and the inherent difficulties of creating a credible proposal. The challenge, as Sorensen explained, was to conceive a program to address "a life expectancy less than two-thirds of our own, a lack of schools and sanitation and trained personnel, runaway inflation in some areas, shocking slums in the cities, squalor in the countryside, and a highly suspicious attitude toward American investments . . . ." When it was finally launched at a special meeting of the Inter-American Economic and Social Council in Punta del Este, Uruguay, in August 1961, the US promised $20 billion over the next decades if Latin American governments took the "necessary internal measures."[63]

"Reality," as Sorensen later conceded, "did not match the rhetoric which flowed about the Alliance on both sides of the Rio Grande." Kennedy's commitment to the program and to democratic governments in the hemisphere was limited. Like their predecessors, he and "his advisors were less consistent . . . in their attitude toward military takeovers." Sorensen wrote that Kennedy believed that in many countries "the military often represented more competence in administration and more sympathy with the U.S. than any other group." Kennedy's contradictions were understood throughout much of Latin America. As one prescient official at the Punta del Estes conference said, "the United States is trying to stop Castro, nothing more. That it may do; money and guns can stop a man. But it will never stop Castroism."[64]

The Kennedys were, in fact, "hysterical about Castro." They were obsessed by their failure at the Bay of Pigs and constantly pressed the Pentagon and CIA to develop new plans to topple the Cuban leader. They were also haunted by Castro's growing influence in Latin America.[65] During the presidential transition, Eisenhower encouraged the president-elect to support efforts to oust Castro "to the utmost"—including the not-so-secret training of CIA-sponsored right-wing Cuban guerrillas in Guatemala.[66] In the spring of 1962, at the behest of the White House, Brigadier General Edward Lansdale conceived and began implementation of "Operation Mongoose," a plan to invade Cuba and to overthrow Castro. Earlier, as the formerly secret 1,500 pages of "Possible Actions to Provoke, Harass or Disrupt Cuba" testify, Kennedy and his advisors developed a series of actions designed to delegitimate and remove Castro. Among them was "Operation Dirty Trick," a plan to cover the possible failure of the "Mercury" space mission. If the astronaut John Glenn and the Mercury space capsule failed to return safely to Earth, the Kennedy administration intended to use manufactured evidence to "prove" Cuban responsibility. "Operation Good Times" "involved showering Cuba with faked photos of 'an obese Castro' with two voluptuous women in a lavishly furnished room 'and a table brimming over with the most delectable Cuban food.' " The flyer was to be captioned "My ration is different." Finally, "Operation Bingo" involved a faked attack on the Guantánamo naval base to justify a US invasion.[67] Aware that the US was not simply seeking to isolate his government, but to overthrow it, Castro turned increasingly to Moscow to reinforce and protect his revolutionary government. Thus, while the State Department and the Agency for International Development offered carrots to Latin America, the Pentagon prepared sticks for Cuba. In the summer and early autumn of 1961 the Joint Chiefs of Staff initiated planning for a blockade and a full-scale invasion to "destroy Castro with speed, force and determination."[68] In November, Robert Kennedy informed the planning group that "higher authority wanted higher priority for Cuba." In February 1962 Lansdale presented his plan for "Operation Mongoose."

US agents were to "start moving in" to Cuba the following March. Between April and July "operations inside Cuba for revolution" were to begin, while "political, economic, and military-type support" were to come from the US. On August 1, the planning group was to receive authorization for the operations, and this was to be immediately followed by guerrilla attacks within Cuba. A revolt, supported by substantial US military force, was to begin two months later, in October, and climax in the creation of a new client Cuban state.[69]

Believing that if the Soviets "picked up rumblings of these plans . . . So much the better," the Pentagon's approach was anything but subtle. No efforts were made to disguise an "Operation Mongoose"-related military exercise in April, which mobilized 40,000 Marines and sailors from North Carolina to the Caribbean. The ostensible goal of this mock invasion was to unseat the mythical dictator "Ortsac" (Castro spelled backwards) and culminated with an amphibious assault on the Puerto Rican island of Vieques.

McNamara and Bundy have since conceded that if they "had been in Moscow or Havana at that time, [they] would have believed the Americans were preparing for an invasion." They have argued, however, that despite Kennedy's decision in March 1962 to "respond promptly with military force to aid" the planned Cuban revolt, the purpose of "Operation Mongoose" was "not . . . stronger action but a substitute for it." Others close to the planning disagree. Pierre Salinger, Kennedy's press spokesman, for example, has been clear that the aim "was to destabilize Cuba and bring down the Castro regime before October 20, 1962."[70]

Some essential elements, however, were lacking. Most critical was the inability of Lansdale's agents in Cuba to find popular support for a revolt that could be reinforced by the promised US invasion. The operation fell hopelessly behind schedule. When October came, Robert Kennedy was still pressing senior planners, including Lansdale and CIA Director McCone, to develop "new and more dynamic approaches," urging that "sabotage should be brought forward immediately" and that plans for "mining harbors should be developed."[71]

Seen from abroad, the operation's weaknesses were less visible than its military mobilizations. When Khrushchev traveled to Bulgaria in the spring of 1962, he was thinking about more than Eastern Europe, for he was deeply concerned about the obvious US preparations to invade Cuba and anxious about Chinese challenges to Soviet leadership of the Communist movement. He later wrote that "[O]ne thought kept hammering away at my brain: what will happen if we lose Cuba? . . . We had to establish a tangible and effective deterrent to American interference in the Caribbean . . . . The logical answer was missiles." As General Anatoly I. Gribkov, who coordinated the secret deployment of Soviet missiles and war materials to Cuba, later recalled, "Although Khrushchev worried a great deal that the ratio of strategic weapons—300 on the Soviet side to 5,000 in the United States' arsenal—was heavily against the Soviet Union . . . his main purpose . . . [was] to help the young Cuban Republic defend the freedom it had won, to deter the U.S. aggression actively being planned against it." It was Castro's fear of the anticipated US invasion, reinforced by a desire to contribute to the advance of socialism, that led him to accept Khrushchev's proposal for the secret deployment of the Russian missiles. An agreement for the missile deployments in Cuba was reached in June.[72]

THE POPULAR HISTORY

The popular lore of the Cuban Missile Crisis was developed in the US through Kennedy's televised statements and uncritical press coverage at the time. Robert Kennedy's best-selling memoir, *Thirteen Days*, memoirs of trusted Kennedy associates, particularly Sorensen and Arthur M. Schlesinger, Jr., and Khrushchev's memoirs rounded out the picture. Since the mid-1990s, with the release of transcripts of Kennedy's secret White House recordings, declassification of official documents, and conferences involving the era's decision-makers have shed new light on the US, Soviet, and Cuban leaders' calculations and near-catastrophic miscalculations.

As Robert Kennedy portrayed it, "Neither side wanted war over Cuba . . . but it was possible that either side could take a step that, for reasons of 'security' or 'pride' or 'face' would require a response by the other side . . . and eventually an escalation into armed conflict."[73] The scholars Richard E. Neustadt and Graham T. Allison described and reinforced the popular perception in their afterword to Kennedy's book: "Robert Kennedy . . . like McNamara . . . was haunted by the prospect of nuclear doom. Was Khrushchev going to *force* the President into an *insane* act?" In the popular imagination, US leaders have been, by definition, beneficent. If the US precipitated a nuclear war, it could be only the Kremlin's fault. As the Pulitzer prize-winning journalist Max Frankel wrote, "It all began with a Russian ploy worthy of the horse at Troy in the summer of 1962."[74]

With the exception of Khrushchev's memoirs, popular history paints a picture of a confrontation between two great powers with destructive nuclear arsenals. For the most part, the Russians are depicted as being dangerously reckless, willing to "force" the US president to take "insane" action. The Kennedy administration and its advisors are consistently described as careful, deliberate, and courageous. The Soviets are presented as seeking to offset a slight nuclear inferiority, or perhaps even attempting to achieve superiority, through the outrageous missile deployments. This version of events ignores the massive US nuclear superiority that prevailed. "Operation Mongoose," and the fears it created in Cuba and Moscow, are similarly neglected. Castro is portrayed as accepting the

Russian missiles simply because of his commitment to international communism.

The popular lore of the crisis has been concisely summarized by Neustadt and Allison:

* September 6, 1962—Four months after Khrushchev's decision, Moscow lands nuclear-capable missiles in Cuba.
* October 14—A U-2 reconnaissance aircraft flying over Cuba photographs the missiles, initiating what U.S. policymakers experience as a 13-day crisis.
* October 22—President Kennedy initiates the public confrontation with his televised speech, during which he announces the presence of the Soviet missiles, demands their withdrawal, declares the military "quarantine" of Cuba, and places U.S. military forces on alert. Khrushchev responds by placing Soviet forces on alert and threatening to "sink U.S. ships if they interfere with Soviet ships en route to Cuba."
* October 24—At the climax of one of the two most harrowing periods of the confrontation, Soviet ships bound for Cuba stop short of the quarantine line. Some return to the Soviet Union.
* October 26—Nikita Khrushchev sends President Kennedy a rambling, "existential" threatening letter proposing withdrawal of Soviet missiles from Cuba in exchange for a U.S. pledge not to invade Cuba.
* October 27—Khrushchev's letter of October 26 is superseded by a tougher letter demanding U.S. missiles in Turkey also be withdrawn. President Kennedy indicates his willingness to accept Khrushchev's initial offer to trade the Cuban missiles for a no invasion pledge. He warns that if withdrawal of the Soviet missiles does not begin the following day, a U.S. air strike or invasion would follow on Monday or Tuesday, the 29th or 30th.
* October 28—The confrontation climaxes when the Kremlin announces its missiles will be withdrawn.[75]

Despite its limitations, there is much that is revealing and terrifying, if little remarked, in the official history. To begin with, the freewheeling debate within Excom (the Executive Committee of the National Security Council) has been honored for providing options and fluidity during the crisis.[76] In fact, several senior figures, including McNamara, careened from one extreme to the other in their recommendations. Throughout the confrontation, Excom was consistently divided into two camps. One, led by Chip Bohlen and Llewellyn Thompson, former Ambassadors to the Soviet Union, and by Robert Kennedy, believed Soviet leaders were rational and would back down in the face of US will and theoretical ability to overwhelm them at each step up the ladder of escalation. However, they also understood that the logic of "prestige and power" could create situations in which "neither side [w]ould withdraw without resort to nuclear weapons."[77]

One of the more likely escalation scenarios that most frightened Robert Kennedy was that "If we carried out an air strike against Cuba and the Soviet Union answered by attacking . . . Turkey, all NATO was going to be involved. Then . . . the president would have to decide whether he would use nuclear weapons against the Soviet Union, and all mankind would be threatened."[78] Similar scenarios began with fighting at sea after the sinking of a Soviet freighter or naval vessel that attempted to break the US blockade.

Kennedy's frightening scenario assumed that Khrushchev might have been unwilling, or unable, to withdraw Soviet missiles from Cuba following the president's October 27 warnings. With little political room of his own in which to maneuver, Kennedy would then have approved air strikes against Soviet missiles, nuclear weapons bunkers, and Ilyushin bombers in Cuba. In response to the public humiliation of devastating US air strikes against its forces in Cuba, Khrushchev would have ordered the destruction of US missile bases in Turkey. Moving to the next rung of escalation, this would, at a minimum, have triggered US and NATO attacks on Soviet missile bases. Finally, fearing further US attacks and driven by the "logic" of "use them or lose them," Moscow would likely have launched its remaining nuclear arsenal against US and European cities, and Washington would have retaliated with its intercontinental and sea-based ballistic missiles.[79]

The second powerful, but ultimately less influential, camp within Excom was dogmatic in its belief that the Soviets would respond "rationally" to the decisive imbalance of forces and accede to US demands. This group, led by Dean Acheson, Treasury Secretary Dillon, and Assistant Secretary of Defense Paul Nitze, believed that the US strategic and tactical military advantage was so overwhelming that if there was a risk, "it lasted only until our destroyers, troops and aircraft were deployed in the Atlantic and Florida." As Acheson put it, "So long as we had the thumbscrew on Khrushchev, we should have given it another turn every day." This group's values and commitments were similar to the Joint Chiefs', one of whose members, General Curtis LeMay, told the president that "there would be no reaction from Moscow to a U.S. invasion."[80] Throughout the crisis, unaware of both the number of Soviet troops in Cuba and that Moscow's commanding general in Cuba was authorized to use his tactical nuclear weapons to defend the missile deployments, the

Joint Chiefs consistently pressed the president to approve a military attack against Soviet and Cuban forces in Cuba.[81]

The Kennedy administration's response reflected its commitment to maintain its nuclear superiority. Throughout the crisis, the White House relied on its "flexible response" and escalation dominance doctrines, and repeatedly demonstrated its willingness to risk apocalyptic nuclear war. At the height of the crisis, Kennedy instructed Adlai Stevenson, the US Ambassador to the United Nations, that "the United States would not be shaken in its determination to get the missiles out of Cuba. There was to be no wobbling. The time had come to turn the screw."[82] Days later, the president's October 27 letter to Khrushchev concluded with an ultimatum from which it would have been impossible to back down.

What led Khrushchev to risk a nuclear confrontation? His memoirs confirm that his primary motivation was fear that the US would further exploit the absence of a Soviet nuclear deterrent, including the possibility that Kennedy might order a first-strike attack.[83] By deploying nuclear weapons in Cuba, Khrushchev sought to rectify the imbalance of terror, achieving mutual assured destruction (MAD) a decade earlier than proved the case. From Khrushchev's perspective, "the Americans would think twice before trying to liquidate our [Cuban] installations by military means . . . . If a quarter or even a tenth of our missiles survived—even if only one or two big ones were left—we could still hit New York . . . . an awful lot of people would be wiped out." He wanted to give Washington "a little bit of their own medicine." This sobered Kennedy, if not all of his advisors.[84]

DECEPTION, PERCEPTION, AND ESCALATION DOMINANCE

Paralyzed by cognitive dissonance throughout the summer of 1962, Kennedy and his senior officials discounted intelligence reports and rumors circulating among the Cuban immigrant community about the arrival of Soviet troops and missiles in Cuba. The Soviets had always respected US hegemony in the Western hemisphere, and they understood the dangers of trying to challenge it. The president concluded that these claims were exaggerated and designed to entice the US to attempt to reconquer its former colony.

Throughout August and September Kennedy refused to take seriously alarms being raised by John McCone and his assistant Ray Cline at the CIA. Almost a month before the first missiles arrived in the port of Mariel on September 15, McCone sent Kennedy a memorandum explaining that the "arrival of four to five thousand Soviet Bloc technicians and possibly military personnel" and the "arrival of many shiploads of equipment and material" in July and August meant that "the Kremlin planned to use Cuba as a base of medium-range ballistic missiles."

McCone recommended three courses of action: 1) awaken "all of Latin America and all of the free world as to the extreme dangers inherent in the present Cuban situation"; and 2) make an "instantaneous commitment of sufficient armed forces to occupy the country, destroy the regime, free the people." His third recommendation remains classified.[85] Two days later he warned that "If Cuba succeeds, we can expect most of Latin America to fall." In early September, Cline reported that "U-2 photography confirms extensive Soviet military deliveries to Cuba in recent weeks."[86] On September 10, five days before the Soviet missiles arrived, McCone sent a desperate telegram from his honeymoon:

> MEASURES NOW BEING TAKEN ARE FOR PURPOSE OF INSURING SECRECY OF SOME OFFENSIVE CAPABILITY SUCH AS MRBM'S TO BE INSTALLED BY SOVIETS AFTER PRESENT PHASE COMPLETED AND COUNTRY SECURED FROM OVERFLIGHTS.[87]

Under mounting election year pressure from Senator Kenncth Keating, who charged that the Kennedy administration had turned a blind eye to Soviet missile deployments in Cuba, and McCone's hammering the same theme, the administration devoted September 4 to containing the growing political crisis. The day began with Kennedy's Cabinet rehearsing debates that would become existential six weeks later: McNamara complained that even the outmoded MiG fighter-bombers that Moscow was shipping to Cuba undermined Latin American confidence in the US. Bundy argued that if the Soviet Union deployed nuclear-armed missiles in Cuba, it would create a "turning point," transforming the Soviet presence there from defensive to offensive. But, he cautioned, this would still leave the US with a 15:1 nuclear advantage. Rusk argued that missile deployments would be unacceptable, necessitating a "systematic blockade to weaken Cuba" which could also provide a way to avoid an invasion that would end in a "bloodbath."[88]

Meeting later in the day with Congressional leaders, Kennedy assured them that he was monitoring the situation in Cuba and was concerned that if he ultimately found it necessary to declare a blockade, they had to be prepared for renewed Soviet pressure on West Berlin. Pressed by Democratic leaders as well as by Republicans, Kennedy promised that if the Soviets deployed surface-to-surface missiles in Cuba, "the situation would then be quite changed and we would have to act." Finally, to reassure the public made anxious by Senator Keating's charges, Press Secretary Sallinger issued a statement that there was no evidence of Soviet bloc combat forces in Cuba, nor any indication that the Soviets were establishing military bases or "offensive ground-to-ground missiles" there. "Were it to be otherwise," he pledged, "the gravest issues would arise."

On learning of Sallinger's announcement, Khrushchev began to fear that his nuclear gambit had been detected. He responded by ordering reinforcement of Soviet troops already en route to the island, including nuclear-armed artillery shells to "resist or deter an invasion."[89]

Khrushchev's fears were premature. An unauthorized U-2 intrusion of Sakhalin island east of Siberia had led the president to suspend all U-2 flights until operational procedures could be reviewed. Spy flights over Cuba were thus halted for more than a month and did not resume until October 14. The shock came the following day when it was reported that U-2 reconnaissance film demonstrated that the Kremlin was indeed deploying medium-range missiles to Cuba. Construction of two, or possibly three, missile sites had begun. To regain the element of surprise, Kennedy insisted that the news and the deliberations of what became the Excom remain entirely secret.

The range of the administration's immediate and reflexive responses was breathtaking. Possibly playing the role of devil's advocate, Kennedy wondered aloud if the deployments made any difference, saying incorrectly, "They've got enough to blow us up now anyway," but complaining that "It makes them look co-equal with us."[90] McNamara reported that the Pentagon opposed any negotiations with the Kremlin. The Joint Chiefs were convinced that diplomacy would delay and possibly prevent the US from prevailing. They "wanted to hit all Soviet and Cuban planes, airfields, guns and nuclear storage sites, then erect a naval blockade to prevent new weapon deliveries and [to] finish the job with a full scale invasion."[91] Rusk was nearly as belligerent, arguing that the US had not intervened during the aborted 1956 Hungarian uprising because Budapest was within the Soviet sphere, while "[t]his action in this hemisphere violates . . . the historic well known foreign policies of the United States in this hemisphere."[92]

Edwin Martin, Assistant Secretary for American Republics Affairs, crystallized the administration's understanding of the crisis by arguing that "it's a psychological factor that we have sat back and let them do it to us. That is more important than the direct threat."[93] This view was reinforced by revised National Intelligence Estimates that warned:

> A major Soviet objective in their military buildup in Cuba is to demonstrate that the world balance of forces has shifted so far in their favor that the US can no longer prevent the advance of Soviet offensive power

> even into its own hemisphere. At the same time, they expect their missile forces in Cuba to make an important contribution to their total strategic capability vis-à-vis the U.S.[94]

The psychological underpinnings of US imperial domination of the Americas and beyond were now in jeopardy. Seeing Cuba as "a pistol aimed at the Western hemisphere," Excom's initial consensus was that "an air strike against the missile sites could be the only course." Two days into the crisis, Robert Kennedy suggested that the *casus belli* could be "sinking the *Maine* again, or something." Suggestions for what "something" could be included "a fake attack on . . . Guantánamo."[95]

Three days into the crisis Sorensen summarized Excom's thinking:

> It is generally agreed that these missiles, even when fully operational, do not significantly alter the balance of power . . . .
>
> Nevertheless it is generally agreed that the United States cannot tolerate the known presence of offensive nuclear weapons in a country 90 miles from our shores, if our courage and commitments are ever to be believed by either allies or adversaries . . . . the following possible tracks or course of action have each been considered . . .
>
> Track A—Political action, pressure and warning, followed by a military strike if satisfaction is not received.
>
> Track B—A military strike without prior warning . . . accompanied by messages making clear the limited nature of this action.
>
> Track C—Political actions and warning followed by a total naval blockade . . .
>
> Track D—Full-scale invasion, to "take Cuba away from Castro."
>
> Obviously any one of these could lead to one of the others . . . .[96]

Before becoming a leading advocate for a naval "quarantine" of military equipment bound for Cuba, Secretary of Defense McNamara had won the "general agreement" of Excom that the Soviet missiles in Cuba would not significantly alter the global imbalance of power. The deployments reduced the warning time of a Soviet attack, but this would not seriously diminish US ability to retaliate with a nation-killing second-strike nuclear attack. From McNamara's perspective, "the missiles . . . represented an inevitable occurrence: narrowing the missile gap between the United States and the U.S.S.R. It simply happened sooner rather than later." McNamara initially believed that it mattered little whether the US had 17 times more or fewer nuclear weapons than the Soviet Union. In either case, the number of "*American casualties*" would be unacceptable.[97]

McNamara's early rationality wilted under arguments that the Soviet missile deployments undermined US credibility and commitments, and he conceded that the "political effect in Latin America and elsewhere would be large." The president concurred, saying he "was less concerned about the missiles' military implications than with their effect on the global balance . . . it represented a provocative change in the . . . status quo. Missiles on Soviet territory or submarines were very different from missiles in the Western Hemisphere, particularly in their political and psychological effect on Latin America."[98]

Domestic political considerations also preoccupied the president throughout the crisis. Ironically, as Adlai Stevenson argued, the potential *political* impact of the missile deployments, not their military or existential implications, was a decisive factor. "No politician," he argued, "could have missed the significance of Russian missiles in Cuba. We just had to get them out of there. This was the first time that the Latin Americans were also directly involved or threatened."[99]

This was not a new argument for the Kennedys, who understood the crisis as a threat to the presidency. On first receiving news of the missile deployments, John Kennedy's response had been "He can't do that to me!" *New York Times* journalist Max Frankel later wrote that the missile deployments "made Kennedy appear not just weak but also dangerously gullible." Like Khrushchev, both domestic political and imperial imperatives required that he prove that he and his nation were not weak.[100]

The Kennedys were thus desperate to contain the psychological political damage of having been publicly humiliated by Khrushchev's deceptions and the possibility that if he prevailed, much of the world would be in awe of Moscow's ability to challenge the US on its "home ground"—the Western hemisphere. Kennedy underscored the role domestic politics played in his calculations and nuclear threats when, on October 24, as US naval forces prepared to confront Soviet ships approaching the "quarantine" zone, he confided to his brother Robert that they had no choice. The alternative to escalating the nuclear confrontation, he believed, was impeachment: "That's what I think," the president said, "I would have been impeached."[101]

Within days, Excom narrowed the options to two: blockade Cuba or bomb the missile sites before their construction was complete (with the possibility of following the attack with an invasion to overthrow Castro). McNamara, joined by Robert Kennedy and George Ball, argued that a blockade was a form of "limited pressure, which could be increased as the circumstances warranted." Kennedy could move up the ladder of escalation to air strikes, invasion, or, in a worst-case scenario, war with the Soviet Union.[102]

Former Ambassador Thompson played a key role in tipping the balance toward a blockade, arguing that it was "highly doubtful that the Russians would resist a blockade" with military action. In crises over Berlin, the Soviets had backed away from their military threats. In Cuba, 5,000 miles further away, Thompson explained, Moscow faced even greater military disadvantages. By showing restraint with a blockade rather than moving immediately to military attacks, Kennedy would also win support in Western Europe, whose peoples and governments had lived within range of the Soviet nuclear arsenal for most of the previous decade. Most importantly, a quarantine provided Khrushchev with the least humiliating and politically threatening way to back down and remove his missiles.[103]

Throughout the crisis the Joint Chiefs and their allies in Excom pressed for aggressive military action. From the beginning, Acheson, Taylor, and Nitze argued for air strikes. They thought a blockade could not guarantee that the missiles would be withdrawn. Air strikes, they argued, would focus the confrontation on Castro and Cuba, while a blockade courted the danger of Moscow moving to horizontal escalation by blockading West Berlin.[104] Challenging Robert Kennedy's doubts that air strikes would be entirely successful and were reminiscent of Tojo's surprise attack against Pearl Harbor, Acheson hammered away that the Monroe Doctrine "made clear to all the world the United States would not tolerate the intrusion of any European power into the Americas." The president, Acheson argued, had warned Moscow that the US would be forced to act if it moved offensive weapons to Cuba, and Congress had publicly authorized the president to prevent such deployments "by whatever means may be necessary, including the use of arms."[105]

Kennedy consulted former President Eisenhower, who backed the more aggressive approach. He feared that a blockade would be indecisive and pointed to the difficulties of enforcing it. Eisenhower preferred "military action which would cut off Havana and therefore take over the heart of the government." He proposed that it "be done by airborne divisions" rather than storming beachheads in a conventionally slow invasion.[106]

Advocates of military attacks or an invasion believed that the US had an overwhelming military advantage. As Maxwell Taylor advised on October 26 as the crisis neared its climax, "We have the strategic advantage . . . This is no time to run scared."[107]

Initially, advocates of a blockade, renamed a "quarantine" to avoid the appearance of a formal act of war, prevailed. They succeeded only because a blockade did not rule out the possibility of later escalation. Within days US nuclear forces were placed on alert. Planning for 2,000 bombing sorties against Cuba was completed; 250,000 troops were mobilized for an invasion of Cuba; and the leaders of "Operation Mongoose" were ordered "to create a political office to plan for a post-Castro Cuban government." On the night of October 27, when Robert Kennedy met with Soviet Ambassador Dobrynin at the height of the crisis, he warned that "We had to have a commitment by tomorrow that those bases would be removed . . . if they did not remove those bases, we would remove them."[108]

THE DISCRIMINATORY PRINCIPLE OF NUCLEAR INEQUALITY

Few in the US were aware of how great the US nuclear advantage was or of Pentagon estimates of the number of people who would be killed in a first-strike attack. While Kennedy could order 284 ICBMs to be launched against Soviet and Chinese bases and cities, Khrushchev had four that were theoretically operational.[109] Nuclear war would be fought—if that is the right word—primarily with hydrogen bombs. In an all-out nuclear war 275–325 million people would die within the first six months of a US nuclear attack. Over time, 100 million more would die in Eastern Europe. Depending on the time of the year and the direction of the wind, as many as another 100 million people could die in Western Europe. Afghanistan and Japan, which were in the path of the fallout, would be "wiped out."[110]

There was also the political reality of appearances. Khrushchev was preoccupied by the affront that the "United States had already surrounded the Soviet Union with its own bomber bases and missiles . . . . American missiles were aimed against us in Turkey and Italy, to say nothing of West Germany."[111]

Unknown to the public, during the crisis considerable debate within Excom focused on the fate of these obsolete missiles and the insistence that the US protect the discriminatory principle that it could base nuclear missiles along the Soviet Union's borders, but that the Soviet Union could not reciprocate. At the height of the confrontation, Excom was nearly unanimous in preferring the risk of apocalyptic nuclear war over compromising this principle.[112]

The possibility of exchanging the withdrawal of missiles in Turkey for those in Cuba was first raised three days into the crisis by George Ball, who proposed making "a deal with the bases for Turkey. We substitute Polaris for the missiles we've got there . . . It doesn't have to be all-out war."[113] Two days later, Adlai Stevenson joined Ball in advocating this strategic compromise which would in no way diminish US nuclear dominance.

Unknown to most Excom members, before the crisis Kennedy had twice issued instructions for the 15 Jupiter missiles in Turkey to be removed.

Secretary of Defense McNamara had earlier described the Jupiters as "a pile of junk";[114] they were "unreliable, inaccurate, obsolete, and too easily sabotaged." The Turkish government had opposed their removal, and Kennedy's instructions were lost in the diplomatic morass. Shortly before the Missile Crisis, the Joint Congressional Committee on Atomic Energy returned to the issue by recommending Jupiter and Thor missiles in Turkey and Italy be withdrawn.[115]

Despite this history, Kennedy bluntly rejected Ball's and Stevenson's recommendations. Withdrawing the missiles in response to a Soviet threat, he believed, would communicate that "we were in a state of panic,"[116] undermining US alliances and credibility. Kennedy was supported in his initial rejection of the Ball–Stevenson proposal by Ambassador Hare in Istanbul who wrote that "removal [of] Jupiters from Turkey in [the] context of [the] Cuban situation would present major problem not only in terms of bilateral Turkish–American relationship but also NATO association . . . Turks deeply resent any coupling of Turkey and Cuba on [the] ground that [the] situations [are] completely different . . . ."[117]

On October 25, ten days into the crisis, as the US and the USSR approached the brink of nuclear war, debate over the Jupiter missiles broke unexpectedly into the public domain. Walter Lippman, the dean of liberal journalists, possibly encouraged by Ball, opened the day with a politically explosive proposal in the *Washington Post* which was read by President Kennedy, Soviet Ambassador Dobrynin, and many others.[118] Lippman proposed that the president seek a "face-saving agreement." He was clear that he was not advocating a " 'Cuba–Berlin' horse trade," explaining that the two were not analogous. "The only place that is truly comparable with Cuba," he wrote, "is Turkey. This is the only place where there are strategic weapons right on the frontier of the Soviet Union." Lippman went on to describe a second similarity between the military bases in Cuba and Turkey: both were "of little military value."

Lippman's proposal was given little consideration in Excom or in the media that day. Instead, attention focused on the first, and uneventful, interception of a Soviet ship in the quarantine zone.[119]

Two days later, as the Soviets were completing construction of their Cuban missile bases, and as pressure in the White House and Congress mounted for an immediate invasion of Cuba, the fate of the missiles in Turkey moved to center stage. The Kremlin's tough and formal October 27 letter to President Kennedy, broadcast internationally, declared that the Jupiter missiles would have to be withdrawn from Turkey if the crisis was to be resolved peacefully. The Soviet leaders wrote:

> You are worried over Cuba. You say that it worries you because it lies at a distance of 90 miles across the sea from the shores of the

> United States. However, Turkey lies next to us. Our sentinels are pacing up and down and watching each other. Do you believe that you have the right to demand security for your country, and the removal of such weapons that you qualify as offensive, while not recognizing this right for us?[120]

Robert Kennedy later recalled that "the proposal the Russians made was not unreasonable and did not amount to a loss to the U.S. or to our NATO allies," it was simply unacceptable, and left the president feeling "vulnerable," troubled, and angry. Until he secretly joined Khrushchev in blinking on October 28, he continued to resist withdrawing the missiles from Turkey under Soviet threat, but he was loath "to involve the U.S. and mankind in a catastrophic war over missile sites in Turkey that were antiquated."

Within Excom, former Ambassador Thompson warned that the Soviet proposal "had a glittering symmetry," but that accepting it would be seen as "proof" of Washington's weakness. Rusk and Bundy agreed. "If we appear to be trading the defense of Turkey for the threat in Cuba," the NATO alliance, and thus US global dominance, would be severely undermined. McNamara and Dillon concurred that the missiles should not be withdrawn to reach a settlement.[121]

The president and Excom, most of whose members now pressed for an invasion of Cuba, agreed to make one last effort to avoid war by accepting a formula that was never in fact proposed by the Soviets. In a letter to Khrushchev, Kennedy signaled that if the Soviet Union withdrew its missiles under UN supervision and pledged not to repeat the deployment of missiles to Cuba, the US would "give assurances against an invasion of Cuba." Kennedy's secret offer also made an oblique reference to the Jupiter missiles. Withdrawal of Soviet missiles from Cuba, he wrote, "would enable us to work toward a more general arrangement regarding 'other armaments' as proposed in your second letter, which you made public." Soviet failure to accept this proposal, Kennedy continued, "would surely lead to an intensification of the Cuban crisis and a grave risk to the peace of the world."[122]

The October 27 Excom meeting adjourned with the belief that the next day Kennedy would order air strikes and the invasion of Cuba to begin on October 29 or 30.[123] Even as he worried that he might not see another Saturday, Secretary McNamara reminded Robert Kennedy that they would need to organize a government for Cuba. Someone even joked that Robert Kennedy should be appointed mayor of Havana.[124]

That evening Robert Kennedy was dispatched to meet with Ambassador Dobrynin to ensure that the Russians fully understood the proposal and that time was running out. Unknown to all but the president, during the meeting Robert Kennedy confirmed that the president was willing to make an additional concession to secure the withdrawal of the Soviet missiles.

The "other armaments" were, he stressed, the Jupiters in Turkey. They would be removed within three months, but only if Khrushchev preserved the secret. With no assurances that Moscow would respond favorably, when Robert Kennedy returned to the White House, the president ordered 24 Air Force Reserve troop-carrier squadrons to active duty. They would be needed for an invasion.

Khrushchev proved less willing to gamble with the lives of hundreds of millions of people than were Kennedy and his advisors. The following morning he and the Kremlin blinked a second time. They "rationally" agreed to the humiliation of publicly withdrawing their missiles from Cuba in exchange for guarantees that Cuba would not be attacked and for the highly secret anticipated "thoughtful appraisal of the international situation."[125]

OTHER TRUTHS

With the end of the Cold War, US and Soviet archives began to disclose their secrets. In the 1990s, long-secret documents were finally made public, and the surviving *dramatis personae* of the Missile Crisis had opportunities to meet in conferences, sharing their memories and exploring each side's calculations and miscalculations.

While confirming many details of the official history, the secret memoranda and encounters revealed that the dangers of escalation to nuclear war were far greater than most people—including many policymakers—understood at the time. The confrontation was, indeed, the most dangerous crisis in human history. More than once, individual or collective actions had brought the world precariously close to nuclear cataclysm. Similarly, little-known decisions by those who precipitated the crisis and by a Soviet submarine commander saved hundreds of millions of lives.

It is widely assumed that, as the US Constitution provides, the president is the Commander-in-Chief of US military forces and that they are fully under his command. In fact, as illustrated by divisions between civilian and uniformed military leaders over the A-bombings of Hiroshima and Nagasaki or over the wisdom and strategies of invading Iraq in 2003, White House and Pentagon agendas do not always coincide. Worse, unauthorized actions by senior military officers during the Cuban Missile Crisis provided a stark reminder that the military is a human institution whose members can act and have acted independently of the president and his most senior advisors.

As General William Smith recounted during the 1992 Havana conference which brought together surviving US, Russian, and Cuban Missile Crisis decision-makers, the Joint Chiefs and the White House pursued similar *and* different goals during the crisis. President Kennedy had one primary goal, the withdrawal of the Soviet missiles from Cuba. The Joint Chiefs shared that goal, but they also sought to use the crisis to oust Castro, to regain the respect of the White House, and to meet the parochial needs of the individual services.[126]

Tensions between Kennedy and his generals over whether to invade Cuba were so great that General LeMay "all but call[ed] the President a coward to his face." The president's secret tape recordings also reveal that after Kennedy deferred the Joint Chiefs' proposal for an invasion, Marine Commander David Shoup cursed him, and General Wheeler was so upset by Kennedy's refusal to authorize an invasion that he told Maxwell Taylor, "I never thought I'd live to see the day when I would want to go to war."[127]

Even before Kennedy's secret tape recordings were made public, Raymond Garthoff, a special assistant in the State Department during the Kennedy years, reported something that "even Excom didn't know at the time." It was long known that immediately prior to his October 22 speech Kennedy ratcheted up the alert status of US nuclear forces to a Defcon 3 alert. In addition to heightening the alert for US missiles, 66 nuclear bombers were constantly airborne, and eight aircraft carriers were deployed with 180 other warships to the Caribbean.[128] Garthoff's revelation was that two nights later, on October 24, the commander of the Strategic Air Command, General Thomas Power, on his own authority, "sent out the 'Defcon 2' alert instructions to all SAC [Strategic Air Command] units . . . *in the clear* . . . just so the Soviets could pick it up . . . . General Power had simply taken it upon himself to rub the Soviets' noses in their nuclear inferiority."[129]

Earlier that day, under orders from Moscow, Soviet ships stopped dead in the water moments before sailing into the "quarantine" zone. With a military confrontation at sea at least temporarily postponed, Kennedy had stressed to Secretary of Defense McNamara the imperative of giving Kremlin leaders time and political space to think; the last thing he wanted was an unauthorized shot or unanticipated incident to intensify the crisis. McNamara's attention had been, understandably, concentrated on the Navy, not the Strategic Command. As McNamara later recalled, "No matter how hard you tried, no matter how much rationality you tried to inject into the process, it just never turned out the way you anticipated."[130]

In addition to General Powers' reckless escalation of the nuclear threat, at least two incidents served as catalysts for "McNamara's law": "It is impossible to predict with a high degree of certainty the consequences of the use of military force because of the risk of accident, miscalculation, inadvertence and loss of control."[131]

The first is now legendary and has been recounted by both McNamara and his then deputy, Roswell Gilpatric. On the night of October 24, still focused on the need to enforce US naval tranquility in the Caribbean, McNamara became concerned that he was "not being well informed." He and Gilpatric went unannounced to the "Flag Plot," the Navy's command center in the Pentagon, a "naval sanctuary" that was traditionally off-limits to civilians, including the Secretary of Defense. The two civilian officials crossed the threshold and questioned the duty officer before Admiral Anderson, the Navy's chief of staff, appeared and worked to divert the Secretary of Defense's attention.[132]

McNamara had noticed a marker that indicated that a US ship was "in the ocean by itself, far from the quarantine line." He asked Anderson its significance and was told that the marker represented a ship monitoring a Soviet submarine. McNamara's questions became an interrogation. What was the US ship doing there? Was there a chance of a confrontation between the two ships? What were the ship commander's orders in the event of an engagement? Anderson's reply was near insubordination: "[the] Navy knew all there was to know about running a blockade since the days of John Paul Jones." McNamara's third degree then became a lecture: "the object was not to shoot anybody but to communicate a political message to Khrushchev. The operation must be run to avoid humiliating the Russians, if at all possible, otherwise Khrushchev might start a war . . ." Gilpatric marked the exchange as a turning point within the Pentagon. "From that point on they were submitting, asking approvals."[133]

After the Missile Crisis, but before he was banished from the Pentagon to serve as US Ambassador to Portugal, Admiral Anderson more accurately described the meaning of the marker. The "presence of many Russian submarines in the Caribbean and Atlantic waters provided perhaps the finest opportunity since World War II for U.S. Naval anti-submarine warfare to exercise their trade, to perfect their skills and to manifest their capability to detect and follow submarines of another nation." During the crisis, six Soviet submarines were harried "mercilessly" and forced to surface.[134] On one occasion, unknown to Anderson and his civilian commanders, this "finest opportunity" brought Washington and Moscow within minutes of a nuclear exchange.

The potential dangers of not being fully in control of its military were revisited three days later, at the height of the confrontation on October 27. Already shaken by the news of a U-2 being brought down over Cuba when Soviet forces believed the US invasion had already begun, and struggling to determine how to respond to the Kremlin's demand for the withdrawal of US missiles from Turkey, President Kennedy and Excom received news of a second U-2 incident. A plane based in Alaska had inadvertently flown over Soviet air space while on an "air sampling mission." Soviet planes had unsuccessfully given chase. After concluding that the Kremlin was "unlikely to interpret the incursion as the prelude to an attack," the president remarked, "There is always some son of a bitch who doesn't get the word." Khrushchev was also made aware of the incident, writing the next day that "Is it not a fact that an intruding American plane could easily be taken for a nuclear bomber, which might push us to a fateful step?"[135]

As Kennedy read about intruding US warplanes, neither he nor Khrushchev was aware that a single Soviet submarine captain had courageously prevented nuclear war. It was later revealed that the "most dangerous moment of the Cold War," possibly, as Kennedy historian Arthur Schlesinger has written, "the most dangerous moment in human history," came on the evening of October 27. While policymakers and diplomats worked to avert nuclear war on terms that served their imperial and political interests, a naval confrontation in the Caribbean resulted in an incident which McNamara has conceded "could easily have escalated into a full-scale nuclear exchange."[136]

Off the Cuban coast, a submerged Soviet submarine armed with nuclear torpedoes was "trapped and . . . bombarded by a US warship patrolling off Cuba." The US destroyer's crew were perfecting their skills by pounding the submarine with depth charges but were unaware that they were tormenting a nuclear-armed warship. The depth charge explosions created pandemonium aboard the Soviet submarine, and resulted in panic as its oxygen supply was exhausted and crew members began to faint.

Two of the submarine's three commanders ordered preparations for retaliation with nuclear torpedoes, with one saying, "We're going to blast them now! We will die, but we will sink them all. We will not disgrace our Navy." As Thomas Blanton of the National Security Archive wrote, "A guy named Arkhipov saved the world." Agreement of all three of the submarines' captains was required to authorize the firing of nuclear torpedoes, and Arkhipov insisted on waiting for orders from Moscow.[137]

There was more. At the 1992 conference in Havana, General Anatoly I. Gribkov, the man responsible for coordinating the deployments of Soviet missiles, troops, and other war materials to Cuba, sparked a debate that still churns over how close the US and the Soviet Union came to nuclear war in the closing hours of the Missile Crisis. As Gribkov testified, the Soviet arsenal in Cuba included tactical (battlefield) nuclear weapons to be used to repel a US invasion of Cuba. The debate is whether General Pilyev, the commander of Soviet forces, was authorized to use them without additional clearance from Moscow throughout the entire crisis.[138]

According to Gribkov, in the last days of the confrontation just half of the R-12 medium range ballistic missiles (MRBMs) deployed to Cuba were ready to be fueled (an 18-hour process) and none had targeting technologies installed. Nor had any longer-range M-14 MRBMs reached this stage of readiness. However, 12 Luna rockets and 80 FKR cruise missiles were "in place and targeted on likely beachheads and ocean approaches" of a possible US invasion.[139]

Gribkov revealed that in July 1962, as Pilyev prepared to leave for Cuba, in the presence of the Soviet Defense Minister Khrushchev "had personally given General Issa Pilyev . . . authority to use his battlefield weapons and their atomic charges if, in the heat of combat, he could not contact Moscow." This authority did not extend to the intermediate-range missiles which could reach the US mainland. Gribkov carried a reconfirmation of these orders to Pilyev when he joined the Soviet forces in Cuba in early October.

In mid-October, as Khrushchev began to fear that his secret gambit had been discovered and that the first shipments of Soviet missiles "could be destroyed from the air at one blow," he revised Pilyev's orders. The general was to "take immediate steps to raise combat readiness and to repulse the enemy together with the Cuban Army and with all the power of the Soviet forces, except for STATSENKO's means and all of BELOBORODOV's cargoes." "STATSENKO's means" were the MRBMs that could reach the United States; "BELOBORODOV's cargoes" were the Luna rockets, cruise missiles, four atomic mines, and atomic bombs for the Ilyushin 28s. Faced with the imminent danger of war, Khrushchev was sufficiently "rational" to reduce the nuclear risk.[140]

But the revision of Pliyev's orders did not remove the possibility that Soviet troops in Cuba would fire their tactical nuclear weapons if the US invaded Cuba (which Kennedy signaled was a distinct possibility in his October 27 letter to Khrushchev). Gribkov has since maintained that US air strikes would have destroyed all the MRBM sites in Cuba and all the Ilyushin bombers. US attackers, he wrote, would "have cut the Soviet and Cuban defense forces to pieces, disrupting communications on the island and severing contact with Moscow." He has been less certain that tactical nuclear weapons' warheads would have been found and destroyed. Because they were inspired by the spirit of the Cuban revolution and had orders to "fight independently . . . until the enemy was completely destroyed," Gribkov has argued that "a desperate group of Soviet defenders, with or without orders from above [might] have been able to arm and fire" a Luna warhead or a more powerful cruise missile. "If such a rocket had hit U.S. troops or ships," Gribkov asked, "would it have been the last shot of the Cuban crisis or the first of a global nuclear war?"[141]

Had either the Lunas or cruise missiles been fired, US forces would have moved quickly up the ladder of escalation. The US invasion plan required that tactical nuclear weapons be "readily available" and *used* "in retaliation for the employment of nuclear weapons against U.S. forces."[142]

Castro's contribution to the intensity of the crisis and to Khrushchev's decision to withdraw the missiles was also elaborated at the 1992 conference. On October 27, as the crisis became acute, Cuban anti-aircraft batteries were ordered to fire on US reconnaissance planes. When the Cuban batteries began to fire, Soviet officers thought "combat had begun and that the previous restraints on Soviet forces had been superseded." Soviet gunners thus launched the surface-to-air missile that destroyed a U-2 spy plane and killed its pilot. Excom's initial response was that the US had no option but to launch air attacks against Cuba. Kennedy wisely declined to be swept up into the war fever.

More disturbing was the confirmation that Castro, facing an imminent invasion, pressed Khrushchev to launch a preemptive nuclear attack in the event of the US attack. Castro recalled:

> We started from the assumption that if there was an invasion of Cuba, nuclear war would erupt. We were certain of that . . . Everybody here was simply resigned to the fate that we would be forced to pay the price, that we would disappear . . . . Before having the country occupied—totally occupied—we were ready to die in the defense of our country. *I would have agreed, in the event of invasion . . . with the use of tactical nuclear weapons . . . . I wish we had had the tactical nuclear weapons. It would have been wonderful.*[143]

In his memoirs, Khrushchev recorded that Castro in fact had pressed him to launch a preemptive strike in the closing days of the Missile Crisis. Castro's October 26 letter to Khrushchev advised:

> aggression is almost imminent within the next 24 or 72 hours . . . . If . . . the imperialists invade Cuba with the goal of occupying it, the danger that aggressive policy poses for humanity is so great that following that event, the Soviet Union must never allow the circumstances in which the imperialists could launch the first strike against it . . . . the imperialists' aggressiveness is extremely dangerous and if they actually carry out the brutal act of invading Cuba in violation of international law and morality, that *would be the moment to eliminate such danger forever through an act of clear and legitimate defense, however harsh and terrible the solution would be, for there is no other.*[144]

This helps to explain Oleg Troyanovsky's account of Khrushchev's decision to end the confrontation. Troyanovsky, who played a key role in drafting Khrushchev's letters to Kennedy during the crisis, reported that when Khrushchev was told that Kennedy would address the US public on October 28, "Everyone agreed that Kennedy intended to declare war, to launch an attack . . . . Khrushchev hurriedly drafted a message to Kennedy agreeing to withdraw Soviet missiles from Cuba. He did so without informing or consulting Fidel, and thus solved his own predicament without regard for Castro's."[145]

FALLOUT

Having precipitated humanity's gravest crisis to preserve imperial prestige and power, as well as their personal political careers, Kennedy and Khrushchev were at times more cautious and inventive than many of their advisors. Parrying pressure for an immediate invasion of Cuba, Kennedy opted for the blockade. In his first secret crisis communication to Khrushchev, he indicated his willingness to resolve the crisis through negotiations. Although at times inebriated by their staggering nuclear advantage, both Kennedy and McNamara rightly worried that even if just one or two Soviet missiles reached US cities, the US would win a pyrrhic victory. Having initially ruled it out of hand, thus prolonging and deepening the crisis, Kennedy later secretly negotiated the withdrawal of US missiles from Turkey.[146] Once his strategic missiles were detected in Cuba, Khrushchev took steps to regain full command and control over his still secret and already operational tactical nuclear weapons in Cuba. He also rejected advice to retaliate against the blockade by imposing a similar stranglehold on West Berlin. And, in the last hours of the crisis, when communication delays threatened to sabotage the secret diplomatic process, Kennedy and Khrushchev went public, broadcasting their terms, conditions, and acceptances on state-controlled radio networks.

In the US, the initial popular responses to the end of the Cuban Missile Crisis were relief that nuclear war had been averted and admiration for the president's victorious confrontation with the Soviets. Fears aroused by the crisis were somewhat calmed with the announcement of the creation of a telephone "hotline" between the White House and the Kremlin to facilitate communication during future crises and by negotiating the limited test ban treaty which outlawed nuclear testing in the atmosphere and ocean. Although these steps went a long way toward demonstrating that the superpowers were backing away from brinkmanship, the crisis demonstrated the unavoidable reality that Hiroshima, Nagasaki, and worse could indeed become the world's fate.

Although Khrushchev was ousted in 1964, in part because of his Missile Crisis miscalculations, his nuclear gamble achieved one of its two goals: Kennedy's assurance that Cuba would not be invaded was honored, thus protecting the Cuban revolution. In time, the Jupiter missiles were also withdrawn from Turkey, but this had minimal impact: they were, as Kennedy and Congress knew, obsolete.[147]

The crisis had at least three enduring and particularly dangerous legacies. First, as was entirely predictable, the Soviets refused to accept US nuclear domination and their second-class status. Instead, Soviet leaders opted to invest whatever was required to overcome their nuclear inferiority. By the early 1970s they had achieved rough nuclear parity, ensuring mutual assured destruction would be the outcome, if not the purpose, of a US–Soviet nuclear war. This in turn spurred US campaigns to regain first-strike capability.

Second, the inability to fully control their militaries and Castro's actions during the crisis demonstrated that neither the nuclear powers nor their opponents could always be expected to respond according to the "rational" rules of game theory. Such irrationality was not confined to Castro's ambitions or to the political and strategic calculations of Kennedy, Khrushchev, and their immediate circles. To reinforce their hegemonic powers and their prestige, senior US and Soviet leaders were willing to risk catastrophic nuclear war and the loss of hundreds of millions of lives. Like Vice-President Johnson, Senator J. William Fulbright, later known as a Vietnam-era dove, advised Kennedy that "a blockade is the worst of the alternatives" and urged an "all-out" invasion of Cuba "as quickly as possible." Senator Richard Russell echoed Fulbright, pressing the president to risk nuclear war by saying, "We've got to take a chance somewhere, sometime, if we're going to retain our position as a great world power." And General Wheeler spoke the minds of the Joint Chiefs when he complained that "I never thought I'd live to see the day when I would want to go to war." In Moscow, too, irrational responses were urged on Khrushchev. Following Kennedy's announcement of the blockade, Ambassador Dobrynin urged retaliation by reimposing the blockade of Berlin.[148]

Finally, the popular perception in the US, and the lesson learned by many politicians and strategic analysts, was that US nuclear threats and the practice of escalation dominance had forced the Kremlin to back down. The US commitment to, and practice of, preparing and threatening to use its first-strike nuclear arsenal were thus reinforced.

5
Vietnam: Failures of Nuclear Diplomacy

> McNamara's interest in signaling to Hanoi about possible use of nuclear weapons was galvanized by a meeting with Eisenhower on February 17 at which the former President recounted how he and Dulles had used an indirect nuclear threat to end the Korean war.
>
> Gareth Porter[1]

> I call it the Madman Theory . . . I want the North Vietnamese to believe I've reached the point where I might do anything to stop the war.
>
> Richard Nixon[2]

> I refuse to believe that a little fourth-rate power like North Vietnam does not have a breaking point.
>
> Henry Kissinger[3]

In August 1970 Mrs. Misao Nagoya addressed the World Conference against Atomic and Hydrogen Bombs. Her words reflected broad Japanese opposition to the war in Indochina. They also carried her memories of Hiroshima 25 years earlier: "We A-bomb victims can feel the agony of the people of Okinawa, Vietnam and Cambodia . . . . No atomic bomb should ever be dropped again anywhere on this earth. No one should encroach on other people's territory and destroy the wealth and peace of the people in other lands . . . ."[4]

Unknown to all but a very few people outside the most elite political circles in Washington, Moscow, and Hanoi, President Nixon and his national security advisor, Henry Kissinger, repeatedly threatened and prepared to end the Vietnam War with nuclear weapons. In October, during the most intense period of the confrontation, the Strategic Air Command and other US military forces were placed on a high, but undeclared, nuclear alert to signal Nixon's threat to both Hanoi and Moscow. B-52 bombers and other nuclear-armed aircraft "were placed in take-off duty on runways across the United States, fully armed, fueled, ready to fly attack missions" and were placed on alert at municipal airports in places like Atlantic City.[5]

These preparations for and threats of nuclear war were known at the time as the "November ultimatum," but they were not the first time the US threatened nuclear war against Vietnam.

As this chapter describes, in spite of France's refusal in 1954 to accept the Eisenhower administration's offer of two nuclear weapons to break the decisive Viet Minh siege at Dien Bien Phu, the United States' "commanding nuclear superiority" framed its efforts to add Indochina to its empire from the negotiation of the Geneva Accords through the Johnson administration's massive escalation of the war in 1965. It recounts the steady escalation of the US war in Vietnam as France was pushed aside and the US assumed responsibility for creating a client regime, the Kennedy administration's unsuccessful efforts to fight what they described as a limited counter-insurgency war, and the Johnson administration's massive escalation of that war. As explained here, the last came with a commitment to respond with nuclear attacks if China intervened as it had in North Korea, and with the belief that a US nuclear threat could limit North Vietnam's support for the South Vietnamese National Liberation Front.

After framing the conflict for more than a decade, both Johnson and Nixon prepared and threatened nuclear attacks to decisively affect the outcome of the war. First, in 1967, facing the potential loss of 6,000 Marines at Khe Sanh in a possible repeat of the French disaster at Dien Bien Phu, the Pentagon prepared plans and leaked warnings that, if necessary, nuclear weapons would be used to break the siege at Khe Sanh fortress. Whether or not this threat played a decisive role in the redeployment of North Vietnamese and NLF forces remains a subject of debate. Second, in 1969, President Nixon implemented his secret plan to end the war by replicating Eisenhower's nuclear dictation of the Korean armistice agreement. Nixon failed. Despite a massive and secret worldwide nuclear mobilization designed to intimidate North Vietnamese and Soviet leaders, it was Nixon who blinked in the potentially catastrophic game of chicken. Like the Vietnam War itself, the chapter closes with his 1972 pledge to preserve the client regime in Saigon with nuclear weapons if necessary, despite the terms of the Paris Peace Accords. In the event, Nixon proved unable to fight two simultaneous wars successfully: Vietnam and Watergate.

THE UNITED STATES IN VIETNAM

Three decades after the US defeat in Vietnam competing interpretations of the most divisive US conflict since the Civil War still echo through Congress, the media, schools and universities, and movie theaters. Flag poles draped with POW/MIA banners are reminders of the unresolved debate. The Vietnam War Memorial in Washington perhaps best reflects the mainstream view: no glory, no honor, and the starkly etched names of the 58,132 US American war dead. The millions of Vietnamese, Laotian, and Cambodian civilians and soldiers killed in the war are present only in their absence, as are the dead of US wartime allies from countries such as South Korea and Canada. That successive administrations considered, prepared, and threatened to use nuclear weapons to affect the war's outcome remains essentially unknown.

Presidents from Harry Truman through Richard Nixon engaged, deepened, and escalated the US war in Vietnam. Their reasons were many and changed over time. *The Pentagon Papers*[6] stressed US economic interests in Southeast Asia, the need to hold Indochina as a market for Japan after forbidding Japanese trade with the Chinese mainland, the anti-communism of the era, and the need to "preserve U.S. prestige."[7] For many policymakers, Vietnam was a "test case of U.S. capacity to help a nation meet a Communist 'war of liberation,' " and it soon became a war "to avoid humiliation."[8] Senior Kennedy and Johnson advisors, as well as Nixon, worried that if Washington abandoned the Saigon government, irreparable damage "would be done to other nations' confidence in our reliability."[9] In essence it became a "war to teach people elsewhere the lesson that the United States had many weapons in its arsenal to destroy revolutionary movements and that revolutions don't pay."[10]

There were also political calculations. As Daniel Ellsberg wrote, each of these presidents "aimed mainly to avoid a definitive failure, 'losing Indochina to Communism,' during his tenure."[11]

Even as Vietnam has largely put the war behind it in order to concentrate on the nation's future needs, the war's legacies remain carved deeply into the lives and memories of the war's survivors. Of Vietnam's wartime population of 40 million, an estimated 2 million were killed between 1954 and 1975; 2 million more were wounded; and 14 million people were made refugees.[12] After the 1973 Paris Peace Accords and the 1975 rout of the Saigon government, the war continued as peace. Successive US governments labored to isolate Vietnam and to squeeze it economically "like a ripe plum," much as the US has done to Cuba since 1960. The goal was to achieve in "peace" what had eluded them in war.[13]

Two-thirds of Vietnamese people alive today have been born since the end of the war and have learned about the war from their families, in their schools and museums. The principal lesson they are taught about the war is that it was but a moment in the 1,000-year history of struggle for independence from China and, later, France. The defeat of the US was the culmination of a 100-year struggle begun in resistance to French colonialism.

In the course of Washington's two-decade war against Vietnam's communist nationalists, the US used its nuclear superiority to limit Soviet and Chinese support for the North Vietnamese government (DPRV) and the National Liberation Front (NLF) in the South. US strategic dominance encouraged the Eisenhower administration to propose nuclear attacks to break the decisive Viet Minh siege of French forces at Dien Bien Phu. It encouraged Kennedy's senior advisors and the Joint Chiefs to press for and win the president's initial military commitments to the Saigon government and Johnson's massive escalation of the war. Drawing inspiration from the nuclear threats used by Eisenhower to force an end to the Korean War, Presidents Johnson and Nixon prepared and threatened nuclear attacks against Vietnam.

EISENHOWER, NUKES, AND DIEN BIEN PHU

The US prepared for nuclear attacks against Vietnam during the final days of the futile French colonial war to reconquer Vietnam in the aftermath of World War II. By the time Dwight D. Eisenhower became president in 1953, the US was already sending 30,000 tons of war matériel a month to French forces in Vietnam. Over the next year, the US share of the war's costs grew to 80 percent. Eisenhower inherited the war from Truman, whose ambivalence about French colonialism ended with the triumph of the Chinese Communist revolution in 1949. From then on, US policy was to provide "political, economic and military assistance and advice 'to areas threatened by communist aggression.' " Special attention was devoted to Indochina.[14]

US funding of the French war effort was not sufficient to defeat the Viet Minh (League for the Independence of Vietnam) led by Ho Chi Minh. By 1954, French-controlled zones in Vietnam were limited to the capital, Hanoi, its immediate environs, and the interior of southern Vietnam bordering Laos and Cambodia. Believing that the outcome of the Geneva Conference, convened to negotiate an end to the war, would ultimately reflect the imbalance of power on the battlefield, and with advice from the Chinese, Vietnam's General Giap moved from guerrilla to conventional warfare after luring French forces into a massive setpiece battle at what French General Navarre thought was an impregnable fortress at Dien Bien Phu. In a calculated gamble, Navarre believed that superior French technology would decimate the Viet Minh.

Navarre would have done better to limit his gambling to the casino. By March, the French airfield at Dien Bien Phu had been destroyed. Unable to reinforce the 3,000 isolated and besieged troops, who faced starvation and deadly attrition, General Paul Ely was dispatched to Washington to request direct US intervention to break the siege.[15]

By the time Ely arrived in the US, the Eisenhower administration and the Joint Chiefs were debating how best to support the French. The US political climate was still molded by popular mobilization for the Cold War, by Senator Joe McCarthy's rabid anti-communism, and by the imperatives of *realpolitik*. These led to deep concerns about how "the unified world communist movement" might build on a Vietnamese victory. Eisenhower and Secretary of State Dulles both opposed committing ground troops to save or to replace the French. Eisenhower understood that the French colonial war was a lost cause. In response to pressures to intervene militarily, he countered that it would lead the Vietnamese to "transfer their hatred of the French to us." He let his National Security Council know that he was "bitterly opposed . . . to such a course of action." Anticipating the possibility of French defeat, Dulles believed the US could influence the outcome of the Geneva Conference with its nuclear superiority in ways that would provide openings for greater US influence in Indochina.[16]

This was the era of "massive retaliation." Eisenhower's threatened use of nuclear weapons in Korea seemed to have worked, and Dulles saw the doctrine as "an easy way to conduct diplomacy."[17] US "air power, and carrier-based air power with nuclear weapons or perhaps simply the threat of nuclear weapons would determine the global balance . . . an inexpensive *Pax Americana* . . ."[18] Drawing on the lessons they had taken from Korea and the US ability to "bomb Chinese military targets and population centers with impunity," the Pentagon and the White House responded to General Ely's request.[19]

In response to the French appeal, the Pentagon developed "Technical and Military Feasibility of Successfully Employing Atomic Weapons in Indochina," later named "Operation Vulture." The plan called for massive bombing of Viet Minh positions by 60 B-29s, to be followed by attacks with three atomic bombs.[20] Air Force Chief Nathan Twining argued that "[y]ou could take all day to drop a bomb, make sure you put it in the right place . . . and clean those Commies out of there and the band could play the Marseillaise and the French could come marching out in great shape."[21] The Joint Chiefs, with the exception of Army Chief of Staff General Matthew Ridgeway, endorsed the proposal.

Dulles, Vice-President Nixon, and Atomic Energy Commission Chairman Lewis Strauss enthusiastically supported "Operation Vulture." With the support of the Joint Chiefs, they won Eisenhower's conditional support. Eisenhower's caveat was that France and Britain should first endorse the nuclear attacks. To prepare the political and diplomatic ground, Senate Majority Leader Johnson was consulted and his support for the offer secured. All of this was done in the name of what Eisenhower and Dulles would later call the "domino theory." If Vietnam fell, the rest of Asia, including possibly Taiwan and Japan, would soon fall to Communism in a "chain reaction."[22]

Dulles and Admiral Radford of the Joint Chiefs were dispatched to London and Paris, where they presented two options. One or two US A-bombs could be detonated in China to disrupt Viet Minh supply lines, or two atomic bombs could be dropped on the Viet Minh at Dien Bien Phu. Eisenhower's ambassadors "were stunned and disappointed" by the responses they received. Churchill did not believe British public opinion would support the use of atomic bombs in Vietnam, and he challenged the applicability of the domino theory. The French were no more receptive to Dulles' arguments that nuclear "weapons must now be treated . . . as having become conventional." French Foreign Minister Georges Bidault declined the US offer, thinking it impossible to predict China's response and fearing that "if those bombs are dropped near Dien Bien Phu our side will suffer as much as the enemy."[23]

Pentagon leaks that it was "definitely considering the use of small atomic bombs in that area" failed to entrap Churchill and Bidault or to intimidate the Viet Minh.[24] On May 7, after 56 days of desperate fighting, French forces at Dien Bien Phu were overrun. The French government sued for peace the next day in Geneva, and after weeks of intense diplomacy, reinforced by the threats implicit in US nuclear dominance, an agreement was reached.[25] The Geneva Accords provided for French military withdrawal, the establishment of "regroupment zones" in North and South Vietnam, a ban on the introduction of foreign military bases and alliances with foreign powers, and a general election to reunify the country in 1956. The Declaration of the Geneva Conference was endorsed by all but one of its participants: the US refused to sign. It had played a double game, influencing the negotiations, but refusing to be bound by them.

IMPACTING THE GENEVA ACCORDS

In the run-up to the Geneva Conference, the Soviets heeded Dulles' warning that the US would not accept "the imposition on Southeast Asia of the political system of Communist Russia and its Chinese Communist ally." Dulles' speech, which warned of Washington's "great capacity to retaliate instantly, by means and at places of our choosing," was understood in both Moscow and Beijing as a warning that the US would "use its strategic superiority for coercive purposes."[26]

As the Geneva Conference opened, Soviet Foreign Minister Molotov warned his Chinese counterparts not to "expect too much . . . because the imperialist countries had 'unshakeable interests' in the outcome." Bowing to US pressure, Soviet and Chinese leaders forced the Viet Minh to accept Washington's terms for the Geneva Accords which were designed to buy time and space for the creation of an anti-communist South Vietnamese government. At US insistence, the size of the southern "regroupment" zone was expanded at the North's expense by moving the "temporary" line between the two zones from the Soviet's initial proposal of the 16th parallel north to the 17th. Similarly, in response to US demands, the general election for national reunification was delayed for two years until July 1956, later than even French Prime Minister Pierre Mendès-France had dared to hope.[27] With this additional territory and time, Washington hoped to create and consolidate a client state in South Vietnam.

Knowing that they would win the promised election, the Viet Minh initially abided by the Accords. But their nonviolent victory was not to be because, as President Eisenhower later wrote, "had elections been held . . . possibly 80% of the people would have voted for the communist Ho Chi Minh."[28] As 1956 approached, under pressure from both Moscow and Beijing, Ho Chi Minh was willing to accept the most extreme electoral demands prepared by Dulles' advisors, which, Ho understood, would not have immediately reunified the divided nation. But, believing that he had the power to dictate to the Soviet Union, China, and North Vietnam, Dulles refused to even put forward a long-term road map for elections. Cowed by US nuclear superiority, Moscow and Beijing failed to respond.

By 1956, the US Military Assistance Advisory Group replaced the French forces in Vietnam. Instead of continuing to subsidize French influence, Eisenhower and Dulles halted funding for the French legions. To reinforce its client state, led by Ngo Dinh Diem who returned from exile, and a 50,000-strong South Vietnamese army,[29] by the late 1950s the US had created an infrastructure of repression manned not by US troops, but by the military and police forces it "assisted."

This apparatus was designed to destroy the Viet Minh, which, in 1959, was still holding out for the promised elections. These hopes were reinforced by Hanoi, which remained dependent on the still cautious Soviet Union and China. North Vietnam remained committed to negotiating peaceful coexistence with the Diem government in Saigon. As Vietnam's Foreign Minister Nguyen Co Thach later reported, at the time both the Chinese and Soviets believed that the US was invincible, and "that led to the desire for peace at any price."[30]

Under pressure from Moscow and Beijing, Hanoi dictated policy for its allies in the South. "Armed struggle" was essentially to be limited to defending former members of the Viet Minh being hunted by the South Vietnamese Army (ARVN) and South Vietnamese police forces. This was not to include guerrilla warfare, nor were fighters in the South "to liberate zones and to establish a government as at the time of the resistance." In May 1959, with growing numbers of Viet Minh members and their sympathizers being imprisoned and murdered, the Viet Minh finally launched a widespread campaign of armed self-defense. Uprisings occurred in 800 Mekong Delta villages. Although the Saigon government was able to maintain a continuing presence in all but 100 of these communities,[31] the "whole Saigon government apparatus fell apart . . . because it was . . . based on nothing but a monopoly of violence."[32] By 1962, the repressive and corrupt Diem regime's hold on power was precarious, and the Viet Minh had transformed itself into the National Liberation Front (NLF), which promised freedom, national independence, and economic justice.

KENNEDY'S WAR: NUCLEAR SUPERIORITY AND COUNTER-INSURGENCY

John F. Kennedy assumed the presidency committed to Eisenhower's approach to Vietnam. During his first year in office his public statements routinely "emphasized the importance of taking a stand in Vietnam"[33] as he held to a policy line consistent with his campaign promises and the expectations of his senior advisors.

Despite his rhetoric, Kennedy arrived at the White House reluctant to increase US military commitments to salvage Diem's failing regime. Having visited Indochina as a congressman during the Franco-Vietnamese war, he had a deep appreciation for the power of Vietnamese nationalism and respected Ho Chi Minh's popular support. During the siege of Dien Bien Phu, Kennedy had warned that "no amount of American military assistance in Indochina can conquer an enemy which is everywhere and at the same time nowhere and . . . which has the sympathy and covert support of the people."[34]

Yet, as president, Kennedy's political calculations led to disastrous compromises. He won the 1960 election in part on the basis of anti-communist demagoguery, by stressing the nonexistent missile gap and putting forward his strategy for challenging national liberation movements with highly mobile Green Beret counter-insurgency forces. Despite McNamara's personal commitment to "minimum deterrence," the belief that a very few atomic or hydrogen warheads could inflict unacceptable damage, under pressure from their generals, Kennedy and McNamara supported Pentagon demands for vast increases to the US arsenal of ICBMs. Throughout Kennedy's brief presidency, Washington enjoyed the overwhelming nuclear superiority that dictated Khrushchev's "peaceful coexistence" doctrine and precipitated his calamitous effort to rectify the imbalance of power by basing nuclear weapons in Cuba. With the Pentagon's missile build-up, the nuclear disparity between Washington and Moscow continued to grow, reaching its apex between 1964 and 1966, which were not coincidentally the years of Johnson's escalation of the Vietnam War.[35] The Pentagon's calculation was that "[t]he more stockpiling, the greater the sense that the U.S. 'will go first' during a confrontation with the Soviet Union [and that] will make the Soviet Union more likely to avoid non-nuclear confrontations in situations that do not directly involve its interests."[36]

China's military power lay in its ability to threaten to overwhelm by throwing masses of Chinese troops against US forces as it had done in Korea. But, with the US ability to destroy China's cities at will and the massive economic and political dislocations caused by Mao's disastrous "Great Leap Forward," Chinese military power was not a major factor in Kennedy administration strategic planning. Beijing, it was believed, would not become a nuclear power until 1964, and even then it was not expected to pose a threat to the US for decades to come.[37]

Consistent with his campaign promises, in the first days of his administration Kennedy warned of the threat of "international Communism" in Vietnam and Laos. Nonetheless, he resisted pressure from McNamara, Bundy, Rusk, and Taylor to intervene in the Laotian civil war and thus halt the trickle of supplies coming from North to South Vietnam along the "Ho Chi Minh Trail." But, in May 1961, with Diem's hold on power increasingly precarious, Kennedy secretly dispatched 400 Green Berets and another 100 "advisors" to experiment with his much vaunted strategy for defeating communist insurgencies. Kennedy also secretly approved his advisors' proposals to begin a low-intensity covert war against North Vietnam. South Vietnamese forces were trained, assisted, and infiltrated into North Vietnam and Laos. And, in November 1961, under pressure from both McNamara and Rusk, Kennedy transformed the nature of the incipient war by approving deployments of helicopters and warplanes to South Vietnam and the creation of a new US force, the Military Assistance Command Vietnam. The former greatly increased the deadly force targeted against the NLF, and the latter increased the US military's "influence over how the war would be fought."[38]

The Kennedy administration thus deepened the US military commitment to prevent "Communist domination of South Vietnam." In fact, the only North Vietnamese presence south of the 17th parallel was a trickle of material aid that came down what came to be called the "Ho Chi Minh Trail." While Kennedy continually pressed Diem to reform and to broaden the base of his regime, US efforts concentrated on defeating the NLF (referred to by US leaders as the Vietcong).[39]

The Kennedy administration's idealistic belief was that they could keep the US military commitment limited. US forces, they believed, would help the

Vietnamese to help themselves. Instead, the president's rhetoric and repeated public rationales for US military intervention raised the profile of the war in US political consciousness and led the Pentagon to demand greater influence in policymaking for the war.[40]

Throughout this period, the lessons of the Korean War and the implicit threat represented by US first-strike capabilities set parameters for the administration's Indochina war planning. With still fresh memories of waves of Chinese "volunteers" pouring across the Yalu River Valley, Kennedy and his civilian advisors were loath to commit to another major ground war in Asia. The apparent successes of Eisenhower's nuclear threats also reverberated in Washington's war councils. As Kennedy's senior advisors pressed for ever-deepening military commitments to defend the Saigon government, they believed that they could intimidate North Vietnam by refusing to rule out the use of nuclear weapons. At the same time, the implicit threat of Washington's nuclear superiority continued to lead the Soviets and the Chinese to press North Vietnam and the NLF to proceed cautiously. Not wanting to spark a catastrophic military confrontation with Washington, throughout the war Moscow and Beijing provided only limited military assistance to their Vietnamese allies. Weapons that would have permitted Hanoi to carry the war directly to the US were never provided. Thus, the US Seventh Fleet, which was positioned offshore, was never attacked with ground-to-sea missiles or by Soviet-supplied MiG-fighters. The strategic imbalance of power thus framed the rules of the 15-year war.[41]

As the Pentagon had anticipated, 500 Green Berets and advisors were hardly sufficient to turn the tide of the escalating conflict. By 1962, the NLF's growing support across South Vietnam and its diplomatic initiatives to create a neutral government in Saigon panicked Washington. The Joint Chiefs, backed by McNamara, Bundy, and Rusk, successfully pressed for more troops, the freedom to use napalm (ostensibly for defoliation), and creation of "free-fire zones," in which anyone was considered an enemy and thus a legitimate target. Accepting Mao Zedong's dictum that in guerrilla war the insurgents are fish nurtured by the surrounding sea of peasants, the Pentagon sought to drain the sea, leaving the guerrilla fighters isolated, exposed, and vulnerable. Essential to this strategy was the creation of "strategic hamlets," internment camps based on the British colonial model in Malaysia and the CIA-led campaign against the Huks in the Philippines. Peasants were removed from their land and held in what were essentially prison camps.

By September 1962, the Diem government claimed that more than one-third of its rural population had been "resettled." French journalist and historian Bernard Fall described the strategic hamlets as "the most mammoth example of 'social engineering' in the non-communist world."

Resettlement was imposed by coercion and terror and had profound and unanticipated consequences:

> Vietnamese peasants worshipped their ancestors and expressed their reverence by tending ancestral graves. The land where they lay was sacred and formed part of the peasants' social identity. When they were driven from that land, the links with their ancestors were snapped . . . Their feeling of disorientation often produced results diametrically opposed to those intended.[42]

By the end of 1962 NLF forces had grown in number from 16,500 to 23,000 cadres, supported by an additional 100,000 militia forces. Early in 1963, Washington concluded that, despite the strategic hamlets, half the South Vietnamese supported the NLF.[43]

Kennedy's efforts to reverse course by exploring the possibilities of negotiating the neutralization of South Vietnam with Hanoi were stymied by the Diem regime's endemic repression and by the assassinations of two presidents. In May 1963, under orders from the Catholic Diem, South Vietnamese government forces attacked South Vietnamese Buddhists protesting government restrictions that severely limited the celebration of the Buddha's birth, killing nine people. The ensuing confrontation between Diem's forces and the Buddhists became a searing international crisis when Thich Quag Duc, a Buddhist monk, immolated himself to protest Diem's repressive regime.

Thich Quag Duc's silent, motionless body engulfed in flames was filmed and broadcast internationally. Diem's response horrified international opinion. He would, he said, be "glad to supply the gasoline" for others, and his wife termed the monk's sacrifice "a barbecue." Rather than heeding Kennedy's advice to settle with the Buddhists, Diem ordered coordinated raids against Buddhist pagodas in Saigon, Hue, and other cities. Thousands of monks were arrested; some were killed; and many were brutally beaten.

This, combined with Washington's anger over Diem's effort to create an independent channel for negotiating short-term accommodations with Hanoi,[44] proved to be Diem's final outrage. His foreign minister resigned after shaving his head in solidarity with the Buddhist leadership, and Ambassador Lodge did not refuse ARVN generals who approached him to learn if the US would support a *coup d'état*. By mid-September, Lodge and the Pentagon were signaling their support,[45] and on November 1, Diem and his family were killed. Three weeks later another bullet claimed the life of President Kennedy.

Kennedy advisors Theodore Sorensen and Arthur Schlesinger, Jr., and the historian Gareth Porter have demonstrated that before Diem's assassination,

Kennedy understood "that withdrawal was the viable option." In 1962, he began to frame "elements of a three-part exit strategy, one that his assassination would prevent him from pursuing." Even before the Cuban Missile Crisis, on March 1, 1962, Kennedy won McNamara's and the very reluctant Joint Chiefs' agreement to develop a "contingency plan for South Vietnam in the event our present efforts fail." Kennedy's astute political strategy was to have the first contingency plans for US withdrawal from Vietnam come over the signatures of his most senior leaders, not his own.[46] By March 1963, the Joint Chiefs developed the plan. Several thousand troops would be withdrawn by 1964 (in time for the presidential election), while 12,200 troops would remain through most of 1965. Half of these would be withdrawn in 1966, with the last US forces returning home in 1967.

Having the ability to deflect blame to the Joint Chiefs, Kennedy began speaking about the possibility of withdrawal, telling Senate Majority Leader Mike Mansfield that he would "begin pulling troops out on the first of the next year," and informing journalist Charles Bartlet that "[w]e don't have a prayer of staying in Vietnam." By September, Joint Chiefs Chairman Taylor and McNamara were warning Diem that "unless you do certain things we have described, we are going to pull out in a relatively short time." This, Taylor later explained, was to get Diem "to do certain things, which, if done, we believed would make possible the termination of the [U.S. troop presence] . . . in about two years."[47]

Believing that Diem regime failures could provide "a favorable moment" to withdraw US forces, Kennedy initially opposed the plot to overthrow the South Vietnamese president, and on September 3 he ordered US officials to break off contact with General Minh and his fellow conspirators. Diem's assassination was a setback for Kennedy. Understanding that his plans for withdrawal had been jeopardized, he turned to developing new strategies. On the eve of his assassination, Kennedy confided in Michael Forrestal of the National Security Council that he wanted to begin a "complete and very profound review of how we got into this country . . . I even want to think about whether or not we should be there."[48]

JOHNSON'S WAR

Unlike Truman, Lyndon Johnson assumed the presidency with considerable foreign policy experience and having learned many lessons from recent wars. True, Kennedy and his entourage sidelined their vice-president, a man chosen to attract voters in Texas, a state whose Electoral College votes were essential to Kennedy's election. But, as majority leader in the Senate, Johnson had long been involved in shaping US foreign policy.

He had been consulted by presidents when they considered or launched wars and lesser military interventions. Johnson was tormented by the Vietnam War from his first days in office: it subverted his efforts to build on Roosevelt's "New Deal" with a "Great Society," and his escalation of the war cost him the presidency.

Johnson inherited Kennedy's senior advisors, many of whom believed that South Vietnam would fall to Communism unless the US increased its military commitments. Only two days before Kennedy's assassination, while meeting with his military commanders, McNamara pressed for "full-fledged" covert operations to be led by the Pentagon, not by the CIA.[49] Needing to buy time and to communicate continuity to the country's political elite, to his senior advisors, and to the public to ease the national trauma following Kennedy's assassination, Johnson immediately let it be known that he was "not going to lose Vietnam." Within four days of Kennedy's assassination, Johnson stated that he would support the new government in Saigon and ordered that plans be made for covert operations against North Vietnam.[50]

Johnson was, however, the same man who, on becoming vice-president, had said that "barring an unmistakable and massive invasion of South Vietnam from without we have no intention of employing combat U.S. forces in Viet Nam or even naval or air support."[51] His goal was to get the South Vietnamese "off their butts and [to] get out in those jungles and whip the hell out of some Communists." He confided to his press secretary, Bill Moyers, that he was "determined to avoid a U.S. takeover of the war." McNamara has since confirmed that Johnson was "grasping for a way to hurt North Vietnam without direct U.S. military action." Thus, the day before ordering plans for covert operations, Johnson signed NSAM 273, which "explicitly endorsed the aim of withdrawing the bulk of U.S. military personnel from Vietnam by the end of 1965."[52]

In spite of Johnson's reluctance to become more deeply involved in Vietnam's civil war, his senior advisors, the Joint Chiefs, and Ambassador Lodge in Saigon seized the opportunity provided by the presidential transition period. Within a month of Kennedy's death, McNamara was pressing General Harkins, his commander in Vietnam, and Ambassador Lodge for covert operations that would signal that "the United States will not accept a Communist victory in South Vietnam and that we will escalate the conflict to whatever level is required to ensure their defeat." Two months into Johnson's presidency, Maxwell Taylor was calling for US bombing of North Vietnam, to be disguised as South Vietnamese attacks.

Under pressure from McNamara, Bundy, and the Joint Chiefs, Johnson authorized Operation Plan 34A. It called for surveillance flights over North Vietnam, kidnapping North Vietnamese for intelligence purposes, infiltrating sabotage teams to blow up rail lines and bridges, and bombing coastal sites from patrol torpedo boats. Attacks would be planned by the US and South Vietnamese militaries and carried out by Vietnamese and Asian mercenaries with support from US forces. Bombing in Laos was also intensified to block North Vietnamese material assistance from reaching the NLF.[53]

A month later McNamara upped the ante, urging that Johnson approve bombing "key industrial complexes" and "key rail lines to Communist China" to block supplies from the Soviet Union and China.[54] McNamara's will had been reinforced in the course of consultations with the Joint Chiefs and the CIA. The Joint Chiefs wanted to launch a naval blockade of North Vietnam and bombing attacks to destroy its economic and military infrastructure. Both the JCS and the CIA agreed that Moscow would not intervene unless the survival of the North Vietnamese government was at stake, because of its fear of taking retaliatory action that "would increase the likelihood of nuclear war."[55]

In South Vietnam, McNamara found the situation worse than he had anticipated. He reported that the situation had

> unquestionably been growing worse . . . about 40% of the territory is under Viet Cong control or predominate influence. Large groups of the population are now showing signs of apathy and indifference . . . the ARVN and paramilitary desertions rates . . . are high and increasing . . . while Viet Cong are recruiting energetically and effectively . . .

To turn the tide, McNamara urged increasing US military aid to the South Vietnamese government and sending another 50,000 US troops.[56]

Throughout the late winter of 1963 and spring of 1964, Johnson responded to mounting pressures to escalate the war by stalling for time. He reminded his senior advisors that he had an election to win, that "[i]t's their war and it's their men." Appreciating that he was unlikely to commit to a major war during the election campaign, in mid-May, without authorization from the president, Bundy, Secretaries Rusk and McNamara, CIA Director McCone, and Taylor reconstituted themselves as the Executive Committee of the National Security Council and used its meetings to devise a strategy to win Johnson's and the nation's commitment to a massive escalation of the war. Their two-part plan focused on intensifying the fighting in the South and bombing of the North. The bombing, they believed, could "get the North to use its influence to call off the insurgency in the South."[57] They called this "diplomacy through violence," now termed "coercive diplomacy," a derivative of escalation dominance. Their plan called for secretly warning Hanoi of imminent attacks if it did not capitulate to Washington's demands, winning Congressional authorization for the war's escalation, to be followed almost immediately with the bombing of North Vietnamese military and industrial targets.[58]

As Daniel Ellsberg and others have since reported, the "war planners . . . presumed that we would initiate nuclear war against China" if taking the war to North Vietnam resulted in massive Chinese military intervention. The Korean War's legacy was "Never again land war with China *without nuclear weapons*." The reliance on nuclear war against China was more than theoretical. In his May 30 meeting with South Vietnam's ruler General Nguyen Khanh, Rusk was clear that "[w]e would not allow ourselves to be bled white fighting them with conventional weapons." As Ellsberg reports, Khanh responded that he "certainly had no quarrel with American use of nuclear arms," and he appreciated the "decisive use of atomic bombs on Japan had in ending the war."[59]

Excom's planning reflected something of a bipartisan approach. While they were secretly making war plans for their Democratic administration, Republican presidential candidate Barry Goldwater was publicly urging the use of nuclear weapons. Goldwater wanted to empower field commanders to use their tactical nuclear weapons on their own authority.[60] Meanwhile, General Curtis LeMay urged "bombing Vietnam back into the Stone Age." Even as Johnson presented himself as the peace candidate against the "trigger-happy" Goldwater, in June word was sent to the North Vietnamese Prime Minister Phan Van Dong that "the United States' patience was not limitless," and that it understood North Vietnam's control over the "Vietcong." Hanoi was warned that should the US find it necessary to escalate the war, "the greatest devastation would of course result for the D.R.V. itself."[61]

The 2003 US invasion of Iraq was hardly the first time the US launched a war on a tide of lies and deceit. On August 2, 1964, it was reported that the US destroyer *Maddox* had been attacked by Vietnamese warships. No serious damage was done, and in response to recommendations that he retaliate, Johnson urged patience. He did not believe the attack reflected a conscious policy change in Hanoi and assumed it was a local response to the OPLAN 34 attacks. Two nights later, before Ellsberg, the night officer at the Pentagon, received reports of another clash in the Tonkin Gulf, McNamara alerted Johnson about an imminent North Vietnamese naval operation. Hours later Ellsberg began receiving what he soon understood were dubious reports of a second attack on the *Maddox* and its sister ship, the *Turner Joy*. The next morning, when McNamara briefed Johnson about the new crisis, Ellsberg's doubts were not communicated to the president.

Instead, with Johnson's approval, the Pentagon went into high gear, planning immediate retaliation for the nonexistent attack.

Unknown to the president, at the time McNamara was winning Johnson's agreement for the attack, the *Maddox*'s captain was informing the Commander-in-Chief in the Pacific (CINCPAC) that he was no longer certain an attack had occurred. Confusion, he reported, might have been caused by "freak weather effects." He urged a "complete evaluation" before the US retaliated. The captain's message was delivered to McNamara, but he opted not to inform Johnson. Instead, he ordered the military to proceed with the attack that evening. Moments before giving the final order for the US attack, McNamara went public with a press statement: "two [US] destroyers were attacked by patrol boats. The attacks were driven off . . . . We believe several of the patrol boats were sunk. Details won't be available till daylight." Daylight brought news of the US bombing of the Vietnamese naval base.[62]

In the days that followed, Johnson moved simultaneously in two directions. Even as he acted on his suspicions that no attack had taken place by tasking Bundy with a "major inquiry into the *alleged* attack on U.S. ships and the way in which decisions had been made,"[63] he also forced the Tonkin Gulf Resolution (drafted months earlier by the Excom) through Congress. The resolution, which would serve as Johnson's declaration of war, authorized the president to take "all necessary measures to repel any armed attack against the forces of the United States . . . including the use of armed force."[64] Thirty-five years later McNamara finally conceded that the Tonkin Gulf incident never occurred.[65]

In December 1964, little more than a month after his landslide election victory, Johnson began carrying out the threat communicated earlier to Phan Van Dong. US forces were ordered to conduct "reprisal" attacks against NLF forces in the South, and these were followed by a sustained air war against North Vietnam, initially dubbed "Operation Rolling Thunder."

In South Vietnam, General Westmoreland, now commander of US forces in Vietnam, continued the futile effort to separate the NLF from the indistinguishable peasantry. "Free fire zones" proliferated. US and South Vietnamese ground and air forces destroyed vast numbers of Vietnamese homes and villages using everything from cigarette lighters to napalm and B-52 bombers. Body counts became the measure of success. The "official unconcern with Vietnamese lives and property" led to atrocities from "turkey shoots," "skunk hunting," and "popping dinks," to the use of villages for target practice, massacres at the village of My Lai and other communities, and to the near-total destruction of the South's second largest city, Hue. In the final years of the Johnson administration, the secret "Phoenix" program coordinated the undercover murder of tens of thousands of reputed members of the NLF.[66]

The day-to-day rhythms of the war in the South were reflected in the 33:1 ratio of Vietnamese to US deaths was described well by Brigadier General William C. DePuy and Clare Culhane, the administrator of a Canadian hospital in Quang Hay. The "solution in Vietnam," said DePuy, "is bombs, more shells, more napalm . . . till the other side cracks and gives up."[67] Culhane described "Endless cases of women and children being run down by tanks, of GIs picking off children as they swam out to pick up food cartons from an overturned supply truck, of pilots inviting passengers for human 'turkey shoots.' "[68]

The air war against the North, "Operation Rolling Thunder," began on March 2, 1965 with B-52s and fighter jets bombing Xam Bong. By April, 1,500 sorties were being flown each month—an average of 50 massive aerial bombardments a day.[69] The air war was fought according to the doctrine of "diplomacy through violence." Although North Vietnamese troops in South Vietnam numbered only 400 at the beginning of the bombing campaign, the strategy was to "strike for the purpose of changing the North Vietnam decision on intervention in the south . . . [to] use selected and carefully graduated military force . . . on a very large scale, from the beginning so as to maximize their deterrent impact and their menace."[70] Maxwell Taylor urged that "bombing was . . . to be given away at the negotiation table for something concrete in return, not abandoned beforehand merely to get negotiations started."[71] Between 1965 and 1969, 4,500,000 tons of bombs were dropped on North and South Vietnam, about 500 pounds for every Vietnamese.[72]

US pilots understood that the purpose of their missions was to disrupt and prevent supplies being moved south to the Vietcong. This "gradually broadened to include supply depots—fuel dumps, ammo dumps, etc.—where re-supply material is collected." Other targets included oil refineries, communications centers, and transportation systems—in particular bridges, which served as "choke points."[73] These were often located in or near populated communities, including cities. By 1966, *The New York Times* reported extensive bombing of civilian targets in Hanoi, Phy Ly, Nam Dinh, and across North Vietnam.[74]

Thousands of "Operation Rolling Thunder" sorties were flown by B-52 bombers, which also rained destruction across broad swathes of the South. Ngo Vinh Long has explained that "B-52s typically flew in formations of 4, 8 or 16 airplanes per mission. Each B-52 carried enough bombs to destroy an area ½ mile in width and a mile and a half in length . . . . B-52s could destroy more than the nuclear bomb used over Hiroshima with much less political fall-out."[75]

Truong Nhu Tang, a senior figure in the NLF, described what it was like to be on the receiving end of a B-52 attack:

> [N]othing the guerillas had to endure compared with the stark terrorization of the B-52 bombardments.
>
> From a kilometer away, the sonic roar of the B-52 explosions tore eardrums, leaving many of the jungle dwellers permanently deaf. From a kilometer, the shock waves knocked their victims senseless. Any hit within half a kilometer would collapse the walls of an unreinforced bunker, burying alive the people cowering inside. Seen up close, the bomb craters were gigantic—thirty feet across and nearly as deep . . .
>
> The first few times I experienced a B-52 attack it seemed . . . . that I had been caught in the Apocalypse. The terror was complete. One lost control of bodily functions as the mind screamed incomprehensible orders to get out.[76]

John Gerassi, who traveled to North Vietnam for the Bertrand Russell Foundation, documented the consequences of 33 air raids on the city of Nam Dinh in 1965 and 1966:

> The Americans bombed and strafed many densely populated districts of the city like . . . the workers' living quarters and so on. They bombed the textile complex when the weavers were working and blew up the dyke protecting the city. The U.S. went to the length of destroying hospitals, schools, nurseries, kindergartens and even churches and pagodas.[77]

The terror imposed by "Operation Rolling Thunder" did not lead to the capitulation of North Vietnam as anticipated by McNamara and Taylor. Instead, it deepened the loyalty of the North Vietnamese to their government and stiffened their resolve. Rather than forcing the NLF to withdraw from the battlefield, Hanoi began augmenting its forces in the South. By the end of 1967, the Ho Chi Minh Trail had been widened to accommodate the heavy weapons and thousands of troops: 55,000 North Vietnamese soldiers now assisted the NLF's 240,000 armed cadre.[78] With the air war failing to change the course of the war, and under pressure from McNamara, Bundy, and the Joint Chiefs, in July 1965, Johnson secretly increased the number of US forces in Vietnam from 75,000 to 125,000. It became what Assistant Secretary of State George Ball termed "a white man's war."[79] Two years later 525,000 US troops would be at war in Vietnam.

The threat of, and preparations for, nuclear coercion were woven into the fabric of the US escalation. In February 1965, as McNamara and the hawks in Johnson's Cabinet pressed to increase the US troop commitment beyond the symbolic 100,000 figure, Johnson and his senior war planners consulted with former President Eisenhower. Eisenhower reminded them that he had warned North Korea and China that "failing a satisfactory armistice, we would remove the limits we were observing as to the area of combat and the weapons employed." Eisenhower mistakenly advised that if Johnson let it be known that he would not be limited to the traditions of "conventional warfare," the North Vietnamese would "not come in great strength." Two months later McNamara took Eisenhower's advice, using a background briefing to warn that the "inhibitions" on US use of nuclear weapons in Vietnam "might be eventually lifted." Within days, this "speculation" by an "unnamed senior government official" quickly found its way into the *New York Times* and thus to Vietnam.[80]

Pentagon thinking about how nuclear weapons might best be used in the war was refined the following year. Freeman Dyson, a scientist and Pentagon consultant, had heard rumors about the possible use of nuclear weapons in Vietnam. His interest was piqued in the spring of 1966 when he heard "a high-ranking Pentagon official with access to President Johnson" suggest that "[i]t might be a good idea to toss a nuke from time to time, just to keep the other side guessing." Dyson's response was to gain McNamara's approval for the JASONs, a group of 40 scientists, to prepare a secret report on the utility of nuclear weapons in the war. Their conclusions, which were passed to McNamara, were complex: because guerrilla forces were usually widely dispersed across South Vietnam, the JASONs believed they made poor targets for nuclear weapons. There were, however, exceptions to the main thrust of the report: Vietnamese airfields, "troop concentrations, tunnel systems, and Viet Cong bases in the South" would, they concluded, be appropriate targets. Although nuclear weapons might not deliver a "decisive blow," they would be "helpful," serving as "a major increase in the strength of B-52 bombardments." The JASONs also advised that "[t]he use of theater tactical nuclear weapons on [Vietnamese] troop targets would be effective in stopping the enemy from moving large masses of men in concentrated formation"—a circumstance that applied when tens of thousands of North Vietnamese and NLF forces besieged the US fortress at Khe Sanh.[81]

KHE SANH: NO "DAMN DINBINPHOO"

Lyndon Johnson was profoundly marked by his memories of Dien Bien Phu. In 1965, as he prepared to increase US troop levels in Vietnam to 200,000, he hesitated in response to questions about the causes of the French defeat raised by George Ball, his most dovish senior advisor. Johnson's doubts led Bundy to write an extended memorandum for the president "specifically rejecting the Dien Bien Phu analogy for the Vietnam commitment."[82] Three years later 6,000 US troops at the old French fortress Khe Sanh found themselves surrounded by at least 40,000 North Vietnamese and NLF fighters.[83] Seeking to entrap one another's forces, Generals Westmoreland and Vo Nguyen Giap, who had led the Vietnamese siege of Dien Bien Phu, prepared for a battle that each hoped would prove decisive. Equally important would be the role that the siege of Khe Sanh played in drawing US forces away from South Vietnam's most heavily populated cities, opening the way for the psychological and political victories of the North's Tet Offensive.

North Vietnamese planning for the battle for Khe Sanh and the Tet Offensive began in 1967 as a response to fears that the US was preparing to invade the North. In the tradition of the best defense being a powerful offense, a military campaign was designed to reverse "the achievements of the U.S. pacification program, expand their control in the countryside, end any U.S. plans to invade the North, destroy U.S. faith in its ability to achieve a military victory, and nudge the Americans in the direction of negotiations."[84] US forces would be lured to the isolated former French fortress at Khe Sanh for a decisive battle near Laos and the 17th parallel, while opening the way for a broad North Vietnamese and NLF offensive against all of South Vietnam's major coastal cities.

The military value of the Khe Sanh fortress remains a matter of debate. Built by the French in a mountainous area, it served as an observation post to monitor North Vietnamese movements along the Ho Chi Minh Trail in Laos and across the DMZ. Its runway allowed it to serve as a base for aerial reconnaissance, and it provided US ground forces with the ability to attack North Vietnamese supply lines in Laos. General Westmoreland has argued that an additional strategic reason for holding Khe Sanh was that it blocked North Vietnamese access to the coastal plains that lay to the east, beyond the mountains.[85] The first minor skirmishes around Khe Sanh, which were designed to attract Westmoreland's attention, began in April 1967 with North Vietnamese troops cutting the supply route to the base and hitting the fortress with rocket, artillery, and mortar attacks. Westmoreland responded by sending more Marines to help defend the base.

As US sensors detected the movement of thousands of North Vietnamese forces moving toward and around Khe Sanh, Westmoreland believed General Giap's forces intended to replicate the siege of Dien Bien Phu. Having more advanced technologies and deadlier weapons than had been available to General Navarre, Westmoreland planned to turn the tables. He would transform Khe Sanh into a decisive killing field. In order not to scare off gathering Vietnamese forces, he reinforced Khe Sanh gradually, sending his "best Army units" and deploying mobile forces from the coastal cities and plain.

So convinced was he of the potential importance of a battle for Khe Sanh, that he stripped "the rest of the country of adequate military reserves."[86] General Giap thus won invaluable tactical advantages for the Tet Offensive, which began in the opening days of the battle for Khe Sanh.

Like chess players, Giap and Westmoreland drew one another's forces toward what they hoped would be a climactic battle. Westmoreland used the Marines as bait, deploying them around the Khe Sanh region to draw North Vietnamese and NLF guerrillas from their sanctuaries to the "Indian country" of Khe Sanh. The plan was "to allow the enemy to surround us closely, to mass about us, to reveal his troop and logistic routes, to establish his dumps and assembly areas, and to prepare his siege works as energetically as he desires." This would reveal "an enormous quantity of targets . . . ideal for heavy bombers."[87] Giap did his part in building the greatest concentration of opposing forces on a Vietnamese battlefield since the siege of Dien Bien Phu, bringing on more than Westmoreland anticipated. The four divisions Giap deployed were reinforced with tanks and artillery regiments.

President Johnson, some of his advisors, and many in the press agreed the battle could be a turning point, but in whose favor they were not so sure. The president was certain of one thing: he didn't "want no damn Dinbinphoo" at Khe Sanh.[88] Despite his reservations, he accepted the Joint Chiefs' recommendation to join the battle on January 29, as Vietnamese infantry forces began storming US positions.

During the 77-day siege, with Khe Sanh fully encircled by Vietnamese trenches and tunnels, the isolated garrison endured barrages, mortar attacks, ambushes, and assaults. Giap's assault began with a devastating rocket and missile attack that hit US ammunition dumps, setting off thousands of artillery shells, plastic explosives, and tear gas. The dramatic scene instantly made the battle for the once isolated fortress the major story for the world's press in the weeks that followed. The siege was intense, with Vietnamese forces hitting the encircled Marines with up to 1,600 rockets and artillery shells a day. Several Marine outposts were overrun, while others went without food or water for days. As Westmoreland accelerated the resupply of the base, he also signaled his expectations and determination by sending two tons of body bags.[89]

Westmoreland attacked with B-52s and fighter bombers, raining nearly 100,000 tons of bombs, rockets, and napalm on the Vietnamese positions. "Indian country" was transformed into a terrifying "mass of fire," the non-radioactive equivalent of a 1.3 kiloton atomic bomb every day, roughly six Hiroshima-size bombs, killing as many as 15,000 Vietnamese.[90] The Vietnamese experience was described in the last diary entry of Hoai Phong:

> Fifteen days after the siege began, things turned out to be more atrocious than ever and even by far fiercer than . . . Dien Bien Phu . . . . From the

> beginning until the 60th day, B-52 bombers continually dropped their bombs in this area with ever growing intensity and at any moment of the day. If someone came to visit this place, he might say that this was a storm of bombs which eradicated all living creatures . . .[91]

Despite the "storm of bombs," the North Vietnamese maintained their pressure and at times threatened to overrun the garrison. As the initial victories of the Tet Offensive began to overwhelm US forces across Vietnam, Johnson began to wonder if US troops at Khe Sanh could be resupplied and if they might be defeated. He began to fear a second Dien Bien Phu. On February 1, after reassuring the president, General Wheeler dispatched an "eyes only" cable to his commanding general in Vietnam. Westmoreland was informed that there was "a considerable amount of discussion . . . comparing Khe Sanh to Dien Bien Phu" in Washington. On behalf of the Joint Chiefs, he inquired "whether there are targets in the area which lend themselves to nuclear strikes, whether some contingency nuclear planning would be in order, and what you consider to be some of the more significant pros and cons."[92]

Westmoreland's response was cautious: "the use of nuclear weapons should not be required in the present situation," but he did not rule out their use. "Should the situation in the DMZ area change dramatically, we should be prepared to introduce weapons of greater effectiveness against massed force. Under such circumstances I visualize that either tactical nuclear weapons or chemical agents should be active candidates for employment."[93]

Later, Westmoreland regretted in his memoirs that nuclear weapons had not been used to break the siege:

> Because the region around Khe Sanh was virtually uninhabited, civilian casualties would be minimal. If Washington officials were so intent on "sending a message" to Hanoi, surely small tactical nuclear weapons would be a way to tell Hanoi something, as two atomic bombs had spoken convincingly to Japanese officials during World War II and the threat of atomic bombs induced the North to accept meaningful negotiations during the Korean War. It could be that use of a few small tactical nuclear weapons in Vietnam—or even the threat of them—might have quickly brought the war to an end.[94]

Although nuclear weapons were not detonated on the battlefield, nuclear threats were made in the Eisenhower tradition. In response to Westmoreland's cable, General Wheeler created a secret Pentagon group to study the possibility of using nuclear weapons at Khe Sanh. That secret was poorly kept. On February 9, in response to a question from Senator Fulbright, Dean Rusk "denied the existence of any plans for nuclear use or of stockpiles of nuclear weapons in Vietnam." The White House followed with a press statement that "no *recommendations* had been received for the use of nuclear weapons in Vietnam." The message carried between the lines was that if recommendations were received, nuclear weapons could be used.[95]

The threats continued. On February 10, the *Washington Post* reported that General Wheeler had informed senators that the Joint Chiefs would recommend the use of tactical nuclear weapons if they came to believe they were essential to defend the 6,000 besieged Marines. Wheeler "did not *think* nuclear weapons would be *required*." But thinking and the requirements of the war could, it was understood, change. Battlefield use of nuclear weapons was also considered at a meeting between McNamara, Rusk, Wheeler, and the president.[96]

Finally, on February 16, in a statement ostensibly designed to end speculation, Johnson stated publicly that "[t]he president must make the decision to deploy nuclear weapons . . . No recommendation has been made to me. Beyond that, I think we ought to put an end to that discussion." This statement quieted the media, congressional, and international debate, but it did not silence it. The president, some noticed, had not ruled out the possibility of a nuclear attack, something he could have done easily.[97]

There is conflicting evidence about whether these nuclear threats influenced the outcome of the battle for Khe Sanh. The siege continued into early March. As Vietnamese bombardments abated and North Vietnamese troops disappeared, General Westmoreland concluded that the battle had been won.

Intelligence analysts differed about what had happened and why. Some believed that the battle was a ruse from the beginning, and that the North Vietnamese had moved most of their forces away from Khe Sanh in time to help launch the Tet Offensive. At least one North Vietnamese division at Khe Sanh was confirmed to have participated in the Tet Offensive's battle for Hue, Vietnam's historic and cultural capital.[98] General Phillip Davidson, Chief of US Intelligence in Vietnam, thought otherwise, believing that General Giap was aware of Washington's nuclear threats and understood the probability of nuclear attack was greater than at Dien Bien Phu. Davidson argued that it "may have been more than just coincidental that PAVN [People's Army of Vietnam] attacks against the Marine outposts . . . ceased at the same time as nuclear weapons were being considered for use in the area."[99]

The price Vietnamese paid with their lives at Khe Sanh was enormous, but as Nguyn Huu Vy, who fought with the Viet Minh against the French and later against the US, reflected, Tet's casualties were "not a very high price . . . We wanted to make a political statement . . . . Without the Tet Offensive, the killing would have been greater."[100] US military leaders disagreed, believing that they had inflicted "a crushing operational defeat for the Vietnamese, crippling" the North Vietnamese Army. The Pentagon estimated 10,000 of 70,000 North Vietnamese and NLF fighters were killed at Khe Sanh and across the country as they were driven back from every major city they attacked.[101]

This was not, however, a traditional war. The offensive delivered a transformative political shock through the US political landscape. The scope, intensity, and duration of the Tet Offensive stunned the US people, the political establishment, and even the Pentagon. The US political and economic elite, mindful of the growing power of the anti-war movement across the country, faced a stark choice: "Either we go to war like in the Second World War, or we pull out."[102]

Khe Sanh and Tet proved to be the turning point Hanoi's leaders hoped for. In their aftermath, General Westmoreland requested another 200,000 US troops be sent to Vietnam. Instead, Johnson's policy review concluded that additional troops would not win the war, and that increased deployments could provoke "a domestic crisis of unprecedented proportions" across the US.[103] This was not an overstatement. Polls indicated that more than half of the US people now opposed the war. On March 31, Johnson announced that he would not seek re-election. Three days later came the concession that negotiations with the Vietnamese would soon begin in Paris.[104]

NIXON THE "MADMAN"

Richard Nixon will be remembered as one of the most complex, vulgar, and brutal of US presidents. On coming to power in 1969, he faced two major international challenges: extricating the US from its disastrous war in Vietnam and reinforcing US global strategic dominance. His response on each front was to up the nuclear ante. By his own count, he seriously considered first-strike nuclear attacks on four occasions: in a "massive escalation" of the Vietnam War, during the 1973 Israeli–Arab "October War," during "an intensification of the Soviet–Chinese border dispute," and during the 1971 India–Pakistan war.[105]

The strategic terrain confronting Nixon was significantly different than that faced by his immediate predecessors. After the Cuban Missile Crisis and Khrushchev's related ouster, Moscow diverted massive economic resources away from economic development to overcome its military inferiority. The Soviet Union was beginning to approach rough nuclear parity with the US, making mutual assured destruction a near-certainty in the event of a nuclear exchange.

In response, Nixon and his National Security Advisor (later Secretary of State) Henry Kissinger opted for a carrot-and-stick containment policy.

In the name of détente, they worked to enmesh the Kremlin by offering economic and diplomatic opportunities with the US in exchange for more compliant behavior. Meanwhile, Nixon, Kissinger, and their allies raced to reestablish US strategic dominance by "MIRVing" US missiles (i.e. arming them with multiple independently targeted nuclear warheads) and by accelerating research and development for a new generation of first-strike missiles. With the mistaken belief in the continued existence of a unified global communist movement, Nixon and Kissinger believed that they could use détente to leverage Moscow to force North Vietnam to accept US terms for ending the war. In 1969, North Vietnam was receiving 85 percent of its weaponry from the Soviet Union, which was shipped via China and by sea.[106]

For both personal and strategic reasons, Nixon was committed to preserving General Thieu's government in Saigon. Thieu's refusal to participate in the Paris peace talks on the eve of the 1968 presidential election had been an important factor in Nixon's victory.[107] Nixon also shared McNamara's early fears that abandoning his Vietnamese client would undermine US credibility and power on a global level. He thus sought to do the impossible: keep Thieu in power while withdrawing nearly all US troops from Vietnam and negotiating the release of US prisoners of war.

Essential to Nixon's vision was the necessity of improving the balance of power on the battlefield in order to strengthen his negotiating power in Paris. This was easier said than done. In addition to the determination of NLF and North Vietnamese forces, Nixon had to overcome powerful constraints. US economic dominance was not what it had been immediately after World War II. Economic competition resulting from Japanese and Western European postwar regeneration required the "downsizing of US imperial commitments" and refining US strategy.[108] The popular opposition to the war, which had forced Johnson to resign, also limited Nixon's options. His answer was the Nixon Doctrine: on the peripheries of the US empire, Washington's allies and clients would fight to defend shared interests, with the US providing the weapons. In Vietnam this meant "Vietnamization": "changing the color of the corpses" by replacing US troops with a larger and more aggressive South Vietnamese army. It also meant "irresistible military pressure" on North Vietnam, much of it from B-52 and other air attacks. Elsewhere, the Nixon Doctrine meant relying on sub-imperial powers, such as Indonesia, Israel, and Iran.

During the 1968 election campaign, like Johnson in 1964, Nixon presented himself as a peace candidate with "a secret plan to end the war in Vietnam." His well-kept secret stratagem was built on lessons learned as vice-president when Eisenhower forced North Korea to accept US terms for ending the Korean War. As his chief of staff, H. R. Haldeman later recalled:

> Nixon not only wanted to end the Vietnam war, he was absolutely convinced he would end it in his first year . . . He saw a parallel in the action President Eisenhower had taken to end another war. When Eisenhower arrived in the White House, the Korean War was stalemated. He secretly got word to the Chinese that he would drop nuclear bombs . . . In a few weeks, the Chinese called for a truce and the Korean War ended.[109]

Nixon's path to this belief and strategy came naturally. The historian Fawn Brodie observed that Nixon was "a man shaped by the racism of his era, including the demonology of Asians and the 'Yellow Peril' concept . . . . Nixon—as Vice-President—had anticipated an 'eventual confrontation of white- vs. dark-skinned races.'"[110] Marginalized by Eisenhower since the 1952 election controversy over accepting illicit gifts, Nixon as vice-president forged an alliance with John Foster Dulles, learning from a man he described as "one of the great diplomats of our time."[111] In 1954, when Dulles first enunciated the policy of "massive retaliation," Nixon immediately supported it. "We have adopted a new principle," he said at the time. "Rather than let the communists nibble us to death all over the world in little wars, we will rely in the future on massive, mobile, retaliatory powers."[112] Nixon advocated using nuclear weapons at Dien Bien Phu without consulting the French and British. And, after briefing him about the apocalyptic capabilities of nuclear weapons, Oppenheimer reported that he had "just come from a meeting with the most dangerous man I have ever met."[113]

Following his 1968 election, Nixon chose Kissinger to serve as his national security advisor, believing that this would allow him to govern with the support of the more liberal Eastern establishment.[114] There was another reason for Kissinger's appointment: the Harvard professor had served on Johnson's negotiating team with the Vietnamese in Paris. Those negotiations continued through most of the 1968 election season, during which Kissinger also secretly served the Nixon campaign by planting obstacles to reaching an agreement and providing information about the ostensibly secret negotiations.[115] Similarly, the fact that Kissinger had written a seminal work advocating US use of tactical nuclear weapons, *Nuclear Weapons and Foreign Policy*, was not unrelated to Nixon's choice or to his agenda.[116]

It is now widely recognized that if Nixon had not been committed to keeping General Thieu in power, he could have ended the war during his first year in office by agreeing to a withdrawal on the basis of a publicly announced schedule. This would have meant admitting what Johnson had recognized: the war was a lost cause. Instead, like Johnson during his first days as president, Nixon resolved that he would "not be the first president of the United States to lose a war." He threatened North Vietnam with "savage" assaults and the possibility of nuclear attacks. When those threats and his escalation of the war failed to "break" the Vietnamese, he secretly widened the war to Cambodia "to demonstrate to Hanoi that the Nixon Administration [was] 'tougher' than the previous administration."[117]

Since the publication of Haldeman's diary, the broad outlines of Nixon's "secret plan" to end the war in Vietnam have been a part of the public record. Subsequent research has filled out the picture.[118] Because Nixon lacked the military experience to make his nuclear threat credible, he compensated with what he called his "Madman Theory." He boasted that he could coerce the Kremlin and Hanoi into accepting his will by leading them "to believe I've reached the point where I might do *anything* to stop the war. We'll just slip the word to them that, 'for God's sake, you know Nixon is obsessed about Communism. We can't restrain him when he's angry—and he has his hand on the nuclear button'—and Ho Chi Minh himself will be in Paris in two days begging for peace."[119]

Nixon had earlier signaled this approach in what he thought was an off-the-record briefing at the 1968 Republican National Convention. Asked by Southern delegates how he would end the war, he responded, "I'll tell you how Korea was ended . . . . Eisenhower let the word go out—let the word go out diplomatically—to the Chinese and the North Koreans that we would not tolerate this continual ground war of attrition. And within a matter of months they negotiated." He also told his speech writer, Richard J. Whalen, "I would use nuclear weapons."[120]

Not learning the lessons from the first years of the Kennedy administration, that Moscow's leverage over its Vietnamese ally was severely limited, like McNamara, Bundy, and Rusk, Nixon overestimated Moscow's willingness and ability to intervene. He also underestimated the will of the Vietnamese to prevail. Additionally, Nixon failed to appreciate Hanoi's superior ability to discern the correlation of political forces within the US.

During the pre-inaugural transition period, Kissinger arranged for the Rand Corporation to develop a set of options for the war. Daniel Ellsberg, who had recently completed research on the Pentagon's secret history of the war, was given the assignment, and he reported that US military victory in Vietnam was not an option. This was not acceptable to Kissinger, and under pressure from Kissinger's aides, Ellsberg agreed to add a threat option to his report. He cautioned, however, that he "did not see how threatening bombing is going to influence the enemy, because they have experienced four years of bombing." The only threat that Ellsberg thought the NLF and North Vietnamese might find credible was the threat to "stay there for a long time; not to win." Kissinger was not satisfied, responding: "How can you conduct negotiations without a credible threat of escalation?"[121]

A second report prepared by Ellsberg for Kissinger became NSSM 1. Preparing the study required posing questions to the Pentagon, the State Department, and the CIA about the progress of the war, ostensibly to identify differences in analyses and bureaucratic tensions that might affect the president's exercise of power. The study revealed deep pessimism within the government. Doubts were expressed about the efficacy of bombing and pacification, and about ARVN's ability to defeat the North Vietnamese and Vietcong forces without heavy American air support. The "most optimistic estimates envisioned a period of 8.3 years before the U.S. could pacify NLF-controlled areas. The more pessimistic projections were 13.4 years."[122]

Kissinger's power and status depended on pleasing his prince, a vocation that would not be advanced by honoring Ellsberg's conclusions. Kissinger thus ignored the studies he had commissioned and followed the administration's guiding principle: South Vietnam would "remain non-Communist forever." Hanoi would be shown that "the Nixon Administration would stop at nothing—not even the physical destruction of North Vietnam's cities and waterworks—to end the war on terms it [Washington] declared to be honorable." Moscow would be warned that détente was not Washington's first priority, "that its relationships with the United States in all areas, especially foreign trade, would be linked to its continuing support for Hanoi." The US anti-war movement would also be challenged to buy time to pursue military victory.[123]

Nixon and Kissinger wasted little time. During his first month as president, Nixon pressed his strategy, telling Soviet Ambassador Dobrynin that he hoped the Soviets would "do what they could to get [the] Paris Vietnam talks off dead-center." In early April, Nixon ordered "timetables for incremental American troop withdrawal" be developed, and in early June General Thieu was informed that 25,000 of the 550,000 US troops in Vietnam would be repatriated over the course of the summer. Having tested the public's patience by ruling out total and unilateral US withdrawal from Vietnam, Nixon's initial troop withdrawal won him some time, but it also illuminated a problem that would plague his conduct of the war. Secretary of Defense Melvin Laird and Secretary of State William Rogers wanted to accelerate the pace of withdrawal.[124]

To prevent Laird from placing obstacles in their path, Nixon and Kissinger began planning for "Operation Duck Hook" in extreme secrecy.

Even as they drew senior military officials into the planning, Laird was excluded. "Duck Hook" was conceived as a campaign that could include the mining of Haiphong harbor, the bombing of Hanoi, destruction of North Vietnam's dike system, an invasion of North Vietnam, and nuclear attacks to eliminate railroad lines linking Vietnam with China and the Soviet Union. By applying Kissinger's nuclear war-fighting concepts, Nixon planned to challenge the North Vietnamese with a "carefully orchestrated series of threats, culminating in dropping a tactical nuclear weapon . . . if they ignored a final ultimatum set for November 1, 1969." This was referred to as "the November ultimatum."[125]

Over the course of the summer, Nixon and Kissinger prepared the way. To pacify the home front, the president rolled out the Nixon Doctrine to reassure the public that the US would not again be "dragged into conflicts such as the one we have in Vietnam." In mid-August, Laird was authorized to announce that the US objective in Vietnam was not the defeat of North Vietnam but, consistent with the Nixon Doctrine, the strengthening of South Vietnam's "ability to repel a North Vietnamese attack." Rumors were also leaked to the press about a possible breakthrough in the Paris negotiations.[126] Finally, in September, with the peace movement's October Moratorium demonstrations approaching, Nixon announced that an additional 35,000 US troops would be brought home from Vietnam.

Behind-the-scenes planning and diplomacy for "Operation Duck Hook" proceeded apace. On July 7, Nixon reiterated his commitment to winning the war through negotiations or on the battlefield. "In either case," he told Kissinger, "we'll bomb the bastards." Four days later, Kissinger passed the word to Dobrynin that Nixon could turn to "other alternatives" if North Vietnam failed to cooperate in Paris. On July 15, he sent a bland letter to Ho Chi Minh "renewing his offer to negotiate an end to the war but proposing no new peace terms." Two weeks later Nixon advised Thieu that he planned to send "a warning" to Hanoi "in an unorthodox way." The French were warned by Kissinger that "it was important that the United States not be confounded by a fifth-rate agricultural power," and, Jean Sainteny, a French diplomat who had served in Hanoi and was close to Kissinger, was entrusted with the mission of telling Ho Chi Minh that "unless some serious breakthrough had been achieved by November l," the president would be "obliged to have recourse 'to measures of great consequences and force.' " In early August, Nixon used a meeting with the Rumanian dictator, President Nicolae Ceausescu, to reinforce his message to Hanoi. Ceausescu was urged to let Ho Chi Minh know that "[w]e cannot indefinitely continue to have two hundred deaths a week in Vietnam and no progress in Paris. On November 1 this year . . . if there is no progress, we must re-evaluate our policy." Two days later, Kissinger personally and secretly delivered the threat to the North Vietnamese in Paris: "If by November 1 no major progress has been made toward a solution, we will be compelled—with great reluctance—to take measures of the greatest consequence."[127]

Kissinger used August to assemble a working group to continue refinements of "Operation Duck Hook." In addition to military personnel assigned to the National Security Council, civilians, including Anthony Lake, Winston Lord, Roger Morris, and Helmut Sonnefeldt, were instructed to develop plans for "the bombing of military and economic targets in and around Hanoi, the mining of Haiphong and other ports, air strikes against North Vietnam's northeast line of communications, as well as passes and bridges at the Chinese border, and air and ground attacks on other targets." Kissinger instructed his team that it was to be "a savage blow . . . you are not to exclude the possibility of a nuclear device being used for purposes of a blockade in the pass to China if that seems to be the only way to close the pass . . . I refuse to believe that a little fourth-rate power like North Vietnam does not have a breaking point."[128]

Roger Morris, Kissinger's aide responsible for coordinating "Duck Hook's" targeting proposals, later testified that the operation provided for attacks by at least two low-yield nuclear weapons, one of them a mile and a half from the Chinese border.[129] Within the White House and the "Duck Hook" planning group, Morris recalled, "Savage was a word that was used again and again . . . a savage unremitting blow on North Vietnam to bring them around . . . That was the whole point."[130]

In early September, even as he announced additional troop withdrawals, Nixon warned of the possibility of blockading Haiphong harbor or invading North Vietnam. He was frustrated. Ho Chi Minh had rejected his terms, and Nixon believed "the doves and the public" were undermining his negotiating position in Paris. He thus resolved to implement "Duck Hook." Later in the month, with both the moratorium and the November ultimatum deadline approaching, Nixon stepped up the pressure and the theatrics. During a White House meeting between Kissinger and Dobrynin, by pre-arrangement, the president phoned Kissinger. When they finished their conversation, Kissinger turned to Dobrynin and told him, "[t]he president has told me in that call that as far as Vietnam is concerned, the train has just left the station and is now headed down the track."[131] At about the same time, to attract Hanoi's attention, Nixon met with a group of Republican senators and, as he recounted in his memoirs, deliberately leaked his plan for the mining of Haiphong and an invasion of North Vietnam. As he hoped, the threat was soon reported in the media.

Seymour Hersh has reported that on October 1, with still no response from the Vietnamese, Nixon ordered a Defcon 1 alert status, maximum force readiness. For 29 days, Nixon used the highest form of controlled violence or force short of nuclear war to intimidate Hanoi via Soviet messengers. As Hersh described it:

> Aircraft were pulled off their routine training and surveillance duties and placed in take-off position on runways across the United States, fully armed, fueled, ready to fly attack missions anywhere in the world. No public announcement was made of the special alert . . . [it] amounted to a secret between the White House and the Soviet Union . . . the United States had gone, without announcement and for no obvious reason, to the most advanced alert status possible.[132]

It was later learned that there was more to the story. The release of previously classified documents to the National Security Archives indicates that Nixon had second thoughts about following through with "Operation Duck Hook," and that he implemented a more complex—but no less threatening—nuclear threat to intimidate the Soviet leadership into forcing Ho Chi Minh's hand.

As William Burr and Jeffrey Kimball, National Security Archive analysts, have explained, in the face of Laird's and Rogers' continued opposition to escalating the war, and challenged by the still growing public opposition to the war, Nixon's commitment to "Duck Hook" "melted." As early as October 6 he may have decided against it. Nixon remained convinced, however, that "the Soviets would need a special reminder."[133]

Taking action that could serve as either the opening move of "Duck Hook" or as a threat directed solely at the Soviet Union, Nixon ordered Laird to begin "a series of increased alert measures designed to convey to the Soviets an increasing readiness by U.S. strategic forces." The operation was to be secret to all but the Soviet leadership, in part to "protect Soviet prestige," thus "making it less necessary for Moscow to counter with nuclear threats of its own." Not even National Security Council staff who specialized in the Soviet Union or Vietnam were informed. In the White House, only Nixon, Kissinger, Haldeman, and Haig knew of the alert, while at the Pentagon only Laird, General Pursley (who planned the alternative alert), and the Chairman of the Joint Chiefs, General Wheeler, fully understood the operation. To make sure that Moscow received the message, Nixon used a meeting with Dobrynin to signal that "unless there is real progress in Vietnam, U.S.–Soviet relations will continue to be adversely affected."[134]

On October 10, the Commanders in Chief (CINCs) of the US Strategic, European, Pacific, Atlantic, and Southern Commands, the Strike Command, the Alaska Command, and the North American Defense Command were each informed that "higher authority" (i.e. the president) had ordered "a series of actions to test our military readiness in selected areas world-wide to respond to possible confrontation by the Soviet Union . . . these actions should be discernible to the Soviets but not threatening in themselves." Three days later, tactical training flights were canceled so that as many nuclear-capable bombers and support aircraft as possible could be placed on alert.[135] ICBMs were already at launch on warning alert status. Soon 144 B-52 bombers, 32 B-58 bombers, and 189 KC-135 refueling tankers were readied for possible nuclear attacks, reinforced by the cancellation of more than 4,000 Strike and Tactical Air Command training sorties to raise combat readiness. Within days European and Pacific Command forces also canceled training flights and increased the number of aircraft prepared for SIOP alert. On October 17, General Wheeler ordered the CINCs to further increase readiness for possible nuclear attacks. Middle East naval forces were ordered to conduct exercises off the Gulf of Aden, and a nuclear-armed aircraft carrier and a hunter-killer anti-submarine warfare fleet were sent into the North Atlantic signaling a threat to Soviet nuclear forces concentrated on the Kola Peninsula. Days later the Pacific Command was ordered to closely monitor Soviet ships en route to Vietnam and "to increase the number of [nuclear-armed] Polaris missile submarines on patrol in the Pacific."[136]

The CINCs, who were implementing Nixon's and Wheeler's commands, wondered why the undeclared nuclear alert had been ordered. Some correctly concluded that it was related to the Paris negotiations. White House staff aware of increased activity and tension might have remembered what they had been told by Charles Colson, Nixon's notorious senior advisor: "We'll be out of Vietnam before the year is out . . . the Old Man is going to have to drop the bomb. He'll drop the bomb before the year is out and that will be the end of the war."[137]

In the Executive Office Building basement, members of Kissinger's staff—some of whom had been involved in the planning for "Duck Hook" and who were unaware of the alert that had been ordered—were less optimistic. Roger Morris, William Watts, and Anthony Lake reinforced one another's doubts and scruples. On October 13, two days before the peace movement's national moratorium, Watts, who had the authority of having worked at the Ford Foundation and having been a member of Nelson Rockefeller's staff, addressed a top-secret memorandum to Kissinger. He warned that, if implemented, the November ultimatum could provoke widespread domestic violence. African-Americans in ghettos and others in the US would believe that Nixon was committed to his foreign agenda, but not to solving domestic problems. "The resultant feeling of disappointment and rage could be hard to contain." Young people, including students, would join Black rioters. "Widespread mobilization of the National Guard could become inevitable, and use of U.S. army units . . . could also ensue. The Administration would probably be faced with handling domestic dissension as brutally as it administered the November plan."[138]

On October 21, as the still-secret nuclear alert intensified, Lake and Morris sent Kissinger another memorandum arguing that Vietnamization could not work. The administration, they advised, should cut its losses with the Thieu government and negotiate a caretaker government acceptable to both Washington and Hanoi. If necessary, Thieu might have to be assassinated like Diem had been before him.[139]

Documents released to the National Security Archive and Nixon's memoirs provide conflicting, but not necessarily incompatible, accounts of the climax of Nixon's Madman threat.

Consistent with Hersh's earlier reports of nuclear-armed B-52s being placed wing to wing on SAC runways so that they could be seen and photographed by Soviet spy satellites, while other nuclear-armed warplanes were placed on alert in civilian airports, the documents reveal that Wheeler ordered SAC aircraft to the "highest state of maintenance readiness" no later than October 25 and to remain on alert "through the first week of November and possibly longer." Nixon took his nuclear brinkmanship further on October 27 when he ordered implementation of "Operation Giant Lance," nuclear-armed bombers flying continuously over Alaska and the Bering Sea along the Soviet frontier for four days to ensure that Moscow received his coercive message.[140]

There are various, though not necessarily contradictory, explanations of how and why the nuclear alert was terminated. Burr and Kimball report that on "October 30 . . . after 17 days of ground alert, stand-downs, surveillance, heightened naval activity, and airborne alert, the test ended on schedule" without having aroused an observable Soviet response. They report that Dobrynin's response was that "[t]he reaction in the Kremlin to tactics of this kind would always be the opposite of what Washington desired."

Nixon blamed the peace movement. As he later recorded in his memoirs: "I had to decide what to do about the ultimatum . . . . after all the protests and the Moratorium, American public opinion would be seriously divided by any military escalation of the war . . . On October 14, I knew for sure that my ultimatum failed . . . . A quarter of a million people came to Washington."[141]

In their secret Paris meetings, Nguyen Co Thach, North Vietnam's foreign minister, reportedly informed Kissinger that he had read his books: "It is Kissinger's idea," Thach said, "that it is a good thing to make a false threat the enemy believes is a true threat. It is a bad thing if we are threatening an enemy with a true threat and the enemy believes it is a false threat. I told Kissinger that 'False or true, we Vietnamese don't mind. There must be a third category—for those who don't care whether the threat is true or false.' " Kissinger, Thach later maintained, was unable to threaten North Vietnam because, if he did so, "we would turn our backs . . . we knew that they could not stay in Vietnam forever, but Vietnam must stay in Vietnam forever."[142]

Scapegoating the peace movement, Nixon argued that it had "destroyed whatever small possibility there may have existed for ending the war in 1969."[143] He had found himself, he conceded, in a difficult position. If he did not follow through on his threats, "the Communists would become contemptuous of us and even more difficult to deal with." To compensate for the failure of his November ultimatum, Nixon discarded the draft of his previously scheduled November 3 speech announcing the escalation that he had secretly threatened. In what became known as his "silent majority" speech, Nixon warned that he would "not hesitate to take strong and effective action" to prevent a US defeat that would "result in a collapse of confidence in American leadership." He appealed to "the great silent majority of . . . Americans" to support him in preventing the "massacres" and repression that he claimed would inevitably follow a US withdrawal from Vietnam. With aides manipulating the press through orchestrated telegrams of support, polls indicated that Nixon won the support of 77 percent of his audience and time to prolong and widen his war in pursuit of "peace with honor."[144]

END GAME

Nixon, Kissinger, and their allies resisted their inevitable defeat. For three years they pursued "peace with honor," a public relations slogan used as political cover for their murderous effort to preserve the credibility of US coercive force. They intensified and expanded the war across Indochina. The secret bombings of Cambodia planted the seeds of Nixon's ultimate and humiliating downfall,[145] and were followed by the US invasion and a CIA-sponsored military coup. Nixon's efforts to deny NLF and North Vietnamese forces sanctuary in Prince Sihanouk's kingdom opened the way for the genocidal Pol Pot regime to come to power in that abused and once idyllic nation.[146] In neighboring Laos, the Plain of Jars was bombed until it became a cratered moonscape, and millions of tons of deadly ordnance were dropped on the Ho Chi Minh Trail.

Consistent with "Vietnamization," the numbers of US ground forces and their daily death toll in Vietnam were steadily reduced. To offset this loss of firepower, the client, ARVN, was vastly expanded. It become a highly dependent million-man army, reinforced by more than a billion dollars of the era's most modern weaponry. To augment the power of his diminishing ground forces, Nixon ratcheted up the intensity of the air war, making much of South Vietnam a free-fire zone. To expose NLF positions and movements, defoliants, including the carcinogenic "Agent Orange," were used across wide expanses. In addition to clearing swathes of jungle, the defoliants poisoned people—US troops as well as Vietnamese, their future offspring, and the land for generations to come. Nixon and Kissinger's faith in "coercive diplomacy" led them to mine Haiphong harbor, North Vietnam's principal port, and to decimate the North's economic, military, and cultural infrastructures with B-52 attacks.

During the Nixon years, more than 2 million Indochinese were killed or wounded to "win" the Paris Peace Accords, which were not signed until January 1973. In essence, the agreement consisted of terms and conditions the NLF and North Vietnamese had offered in 1969, and the signatories understood that they were "designed to be a fraud by both sides."[147]

By 1972, Nixon's and Kissinger's strategic priorities had changed. There was a presidential election to be won, and they saw important political and strategic openings in the chasm and tensions that had grown from the Sino-Soviet split. They believed that a tacit alliance with Beijing could be used to force Moscow to make concessions in arms control agreements and to force accommodations by North Vietnam. A triumphant journey to Beijing, "Opening China," would politically trump almost any imaginable initiative by the Democratic Party's candidate. Nixon's meeting with Mao Zedong, they thought, would also signal to North Vietnam that it had little choice but to negotiate a face-saving agreement in Paris.

As had been the case during the 1954 Geneva Conference, realities on the ground in Vietnam largely determined the outcome of the Paris negotiations. With the July 1971 announcement of Kissinger's secret Chinese diplomacy and of Nixon's forthcoming trip to Beijing, General Thieu began to fear that his government might be sacrificed in Washington's pursuit of greater strategic advantages. Across the DMZ, recalling how its battlefield victories in 1954 had been compromised in Geneva by both Moscow and Beijing, Hanoi's leadership moved to strengthen their negotiating hand.

Nixon and Kissinger sought a Vietnam "peace" agreement that could be signed before the election, and that would provide for the withdrawal of US forces, the return of prisoners of war, and the ability (even if not in the terms of an accord) to keep the Thieu government in power in Saigon by resuming the air war. Faced with waning Congressional and public support for the war, Kissinger and Nixon believed that they could better preserve the anticommunist regime in Saigon if North Vietnam signed a peace agreement and then violated it. Once the 1972 election was won, Nixon could use

Provisional Revolutionary Government (formerly the NLF) and North Vietnamese treaty violations as rationales for a renewed air war fought from US air bases in Thailand and Japan and from US aircraft carriers.

In Paris, negotiations focused on a PRG proposal that provided for withdrawal of US forces, the return of prisoners of war, and the creation of a tripartite coalition government. Called the Council of Reconciliation and Concord, it was to be composed of members of the South Vietnamese government (excluding General Thieu), the PRG, and neutralist forces. The Council was to operate on the basis of consensus, and was charged with organizing an election of a new government in South Vietnam responsible for negotiating reunification of Vietnam. This was essentially what Ho Chi Minh had been prepared to accept in 1956! The PRG's proposal also called for Vietnamese troops to remain in place following the ceasefire and allowed North Vietnamese forces and supplies to move freely across the DMZ.

Predictably, the negotiations stalled, then broke down, and all parties to the war turned to "politics by other means." More than 100,000 North Vietnamese troops soon poured across the DMZ for a spring offensive which nearly routed the far better equipped "Vietnamized" ARVN. With US ground forces greatly reduced, Nixon and Kissinger's response was to escalate the air war. At an April 25 meeting, in response to Kissinger's proposals for intensifying the air war with B-52 attacks against North Vietnam's power plants and harbors, Nixon urged more: "I'd rather use the nuclear bomb. The nuclear bomb." When Kissinger demurred that nuclear weapons "would just be too much," Nixon pressed, "Does that bother you? . . . I just want you to think big . . . . I don't give a damn about civilians being killed."[148]

Without resort to nuclear weapons, the intensified air war halted the North Vietnamese offensive, and the sobered negotiators returned to Paris. In the months that followed, Nixon and Kissinger found Thieu to be the greatest obstacle to negotiating the treaty, which they wanted in place before the US presidential election. Thieu, who understood that terms initially accepted by Kissinger spelled the demise of his government, demanded changes in the draft treaty. Nixon's response was to name him as the primary obstacle to peace, to threaten to sign the treaty without him, and to warn him of assassination by reminding him—in writing—of the late Ngo Dinh Diem's fate.[149]

Ultimately, with Nixon's "assurances of continued assistance" to defend Thieu's government "in the post-settlement period and that we will respond with *full force* should the settlement be violated by North Vietnam,"[150] underscored by the savage 1972 Christmas bombings of North Vietnam, and with renewed leaks of US nuclear threats, the Paris Peace Accords were signed. The Accords recognized that Vietnam was one country and provided for the withdrawal of all US troops and the release of all US prisoners of war. North Vietnamese and PRG military forces were permitted to remain in place across South Vietnam. Thieu's political prisoners were to be released, and the US pledged to assist in the reconstruction in North Vietnam and other Indochinese nations.

Nixon and Kissinger may not have been in full agreement about what they had achieved. Kissinger believed that the Accords had bought South Vietnam's government "a decent interval" of two years to demonstrate its viability or to fall in ways that would obscure US responsibility.[151] Nixon, as Ellsberg and others have argued, appears to have been sincere in his commitment to use "full force"—which Thieu understood to mean B-52 attacks and Ellsberg the re-mining of Haiphong harbor and possible nuclear attack—to keep Thieu in power throughout his second term in office.

Nixon, however, proved unable to fight two wars—one military and one political—simultaneously. US and North Vietnamese violations of the Peace Accords began almost immediately. Washington provided weapons to Thieu's army illegally, and North Vietnam sent fresh troops across the DMZ. In mid-April 1973, Thieu was welcomed at Nixon's California White House in San Clemente to demonstrate the continued alliance, but, as Kissinger understood, their "strategy for Vietnam was in tatters." The Watergate scandal had begun to monopolize the nation's and the White House's attention and energies. Nixon's "diminishing prestige" and his lack of credibility left him unable to mobilize the popular or Congressional support needed for renewed bombing.[152]

During the two-year indecent interval that followed, the National Council of Reconciliation and Concord predictably failed to function. The promised elections were not held. Thieu's corrupt government, economy, and army, each dependent on US support, atrophied as Congress cut funding for the war and the PRG pressed home its political and military victories. Despite commitments made by Nixon and his successor, Gerald Ford, to defend Thieu's regime, the end came in the spring of 1975. In March, General Giap launched a general offensive that sent Thieu's demoralized army into an undisciplined retreat. Two weeks later, as Thieu futilely attempted to cut his losses and consolidate his forces in and around Saigon, Secretary of Defense James Schlesinger understood that he was witnessing the collapse of South Vietnam. He advised Ford that there was only one way to halt the North Vietnamese offensive: tactical nuclear weapons. Ford wisely decided not to pursue that option.[153]

6
The Middle East: Monopolizing "The Prize"

> "Axiom One of International Affairs [is] that the United States will take any possible steps to ensure that its allies do not gain independent access to these [Middle East oil] resources to any significant degree, and surely that the Soviet Union does not. All other issues will be subordinated to this concern."[1]

Throughout the twentieth century the Middle East was, in Eqbal Ahmad's words, "the geopolitical center of the struggle for world power." The US military saw it in much the same way. For them, it was the "jugular vein" of Western capitalism, not to mention an essential source of fuel for the US and allied war machines. In the decade following World War II, through often corrupting and militarized diplomacy, combined with the decline of the British and French Empires, the US replaced the former colonial powers as the regional hegemon, albeit one that struggled to suppress rising nationalist forces. Throughout the Cold War, beginning with the 1946 clash over Azerbaijan in northern Iran, the US reinforced its support for loyal monarchs and other client regimes by repeatedly preparing and threatening to initiate nuclear wars against the Soviet Union, and on one occasion against Lebanon and Iraq.[2]

This chapter explores the repeated US use of nuclear terrorism to guarantee its continued control over and privileged access to "the prize" of Middle East oil. The chapter begins with an introduction to the centrality of Middle East oil to twentieth-century economies and militaries, and how, in the immediate aftermath of World War II, Washington dealt with having won "one of the greatest material prizes in world history."[3] It then reviews the tragic, often criminal, history of the Middle East wars the final outcomes of which the US dictated with its nuclear threats. It traces how President Eisenhower cemented US regional dominance by responding to the joint Israeli, British, and French invasion of Egypt with ultimatums and an attack on the British currency and how he answered a rhetorical Soviet nuclear threat with a more meaningful one of his own. Two years later, as described here, the US dispatched tactical nuclear weapons along with the Marines to Lebanon to reinforce a puppet president there. Those nuclear weapons were initially intended to contain the Arab nationalist revolution in Iraq, but Eisenhower's special envoy found that using them to threaten the destruction of Beirut proved helpful in ensuring the continued loyalty of the Lebanese army. US nuclear threats during the 1967 Israeli–Arab Six Day War set a pattern that was repeated six years later in the October War of 1973 and invoked to ensure that Syrian forces did not intervene in the Black September civil war in Jordan: dispatching the nuclear-armed Sixth Fleet to the eastern Mediterranean to send a message to Moscow that "no translator would need to interpret to the Kremlin leadership." The chapter concludes with President Carter's response to the Iranian revolution and to the Soviet invasion of Afghanistan, a doctrine that committed the US to use "any means necessary"—nuclear weapons included—to ensure its continued dominance in the Middle East.

ANTECEDENTS

Throughout the twentieth century, the peoples of the Middle East were dominated by foreign powers. Contrary to the rhetoric that World War I was a "war to end all wars," it was fought primarily to determine whether Germany or the more entrenched European colonial powers, Britain and France, would carve out colonies from the oil-rich corpse of the Ottoman Empire. As oil replaced coal as the most efficient source of energy, control of Middle East oil became, in Winston Churchill's words, "the prize" of global mastery and thus of World War I. Centuries of Ottoman rule were followed by British, and to a lesser extent French, hegemony, sealed in the secretly negotiated terms of the 1916 Sykes–Picot Agreement, which divided much of the Arab world into spheres for the two colonial powers.[4]

European concepts of nation and nationalism were exported to support "divide and conquer" rule. New structures of power were created to facilitate European rule through old elites. Then as now, "the key to the international politics of the Middle East [lay] in the relations between outside powers and local forces, whether governments, rulers, tribal chiefs or warlords."[5] National boundaries, like those of Iraq and Kuwait, were drawn in the sand and across mountains, while, on the margins, France ruled Syria, Lebanon, and much of North Africa, and the US established a foothold on the Arabian Peninsula.

Britain remained master of "the prize" until it was succeeded on numerous fronts by the US at the end of World War II. As the war drew to a close, US planners understood they were about to win what the State Department described as "a stupendous source of strategic power, and one of the greatest material prizes in world history." It advised that this treasure would "undoubtedly be lost to the United States unless [Washington acceded] to the reasonable requests of King Ibn Sa'ud."[6] As the US gradually replaced Britain as the preeminent Middle East power, its influence was not unrivaled. In the first decade of the Cold War, the US shared power and divided responsibilities with Britain and France while also working to reduce their influence. Resistance to British and French authority, and opportunities for greater US influence and power, intensified in the course of their invasion of Egypt, the 1958 Lebanese civil war and Ba'athist coup in Iraq, and Algeria's war for independence, which began in 1954. Of greater strategic importance was Washington's preoccupation with Soviet ambitions in the region.

Until the end of the Cold War, US Middle East policy was defined by three goals, which were usually mutually supportive but at times in tension: 1) controlling the production and distribution of the region's oil; 2) marginalizing Soviet influence; and 3) ensuring Israeli survival and security. Within this framework, US policymakers had their differences. Cold Warriors saw Russians—or their agents—behind every sand dune and tended to view Israel as "a bulwark against Soviet penetration and a bastion of regional order." "Regionalists" sought stability by addressing the sources of conflicts, such as the Israeli–Palestinian–Arab conflict and the rise of al-Qaeda, on their own terms.[7] There were also those, including some Christians, whose identity and commitments lay primarily with Israel.

AXIOM NUMBER ONE

Noam Chomsky has written that "Axiom One of International Affairs" is "that the United States will take any possible steps to ensure that its *allies* do not gain independent access to these resources to any significant degree, and surely that the Soviet Union does not. All other issues will be subordinated to this concern . . . ."[8] He recalled that as early as 1949 George Kennan reinforced his call for reindustrializing Japan by noting that when necessary the US would be able to exercise "veto power" over future Japanese policies. US control of Middle East oil gave it "a stranglehold on Europe and Japan."[9] The primacy of maintaining this stranglehold largely explains the last six decades of US Middle East policy. Today, it applies to containing Chinese influence in the Middle East and Africa as much as it did to the Soviet Union.

When the Allied victory in Europe appeared increasingly inevitable, US strategists turned their attention to the use of the Middle East "prize" for the longer term. In 1943, Secretary of State Cordell Hull recommended that Britain be allowed to expand its Middle East oil facilities "only if such increase is clearly necessary from the military view-point and the need could not be met by providing for increased supplies of American Middle

East oil." The following year the broad outlines of US postwar strategy were outlined in a State Department memorandum recommending that, where possible, the import of Middle Eastern oil should be substituted for US-produced oil in Europe, Asia, and South Asia. An agreement should be negotiated with Britain on the development and distribution of Middle Eastern oil, so that "the unilateral political intervention that has characterized Middle Eastern petroleum affairs heretofore" (i.e. British influence) be eliminated. It also urged that the US "forestall those factors" that might lead to the loss or "failure to exploit" US oil concessions in the Middle East, and that it should "guard against political complications that might develop."[10] In 1945, the concern about British "unilateral political intervention" was explained more fully:

> We want a cessation of British political interventionism in the process of obtaining petroleum concession in areas directly or indirectly dependent upon British sovereignty. This political interventionism . . . has taken the form of interposing innumerable and ingenious obstructions . . . in the path of efforts by United States nationals to obtain concessions in areas within the British sphere of political influence.[11]

These strategies were based on the centrality of the tacit US alliance with Saudi Arabia, which controls the world's largest known petroleum reserves. Shortly before his death, Franklin Roosevelt sealed the alliance with commitments to the Saudi monarchy memorialized in a photograph of the president and King Ibn Saud aboard a US battleship in the Red Sea. Two years later, Acting Secretary of State Robert Lovett cabled the US ambassador in Riyadh that "one of the basic policies of [the] United States in [the] Near East is unqualifiedly to support [the] territorial integrity and political independence of Saudi Arabia." Lovett advised the ambassador that "If Saudi Arabia should . . . be attacked by another power or be under threat of attack, the U.S. through medium of [the] U.N. would take energetic measures to ward off such aggression."[12] Irene Gendzier has written that with the founding of ARAMCO (an alliance between Standard Oil of New Jersey, Socony-Vacuum [later Mobil], Texaco, and Standard Oil of California with the Saudi monarchy) in 1947 "the geopolitics of oil and U.S. Middle East policy were joined."[13]

The long-term foundations of US Middle East hegemony were thus in place by 1952: the US had a "special relationship" with the Saudi monarchy, whose survival it guaranteed. A "Tripartite Agreement" had been negotiated with France and Britain, which committed them to resist "any attempt to alter Middle East borders by force." And, with Greece and Turkey integrated into NATO, a barrier against Soviet influence and intervention was erected.

In 1955, this infrastructure was reinforced by the Baghdad Pact, a series of US- and British-inspired bilateral "agreements between Turkey and Iraq, Britain and Iraq, and Pakistan and Iran."[14] Until the 1967 Israeli–Arab War, US Middle East policy was largely implemented by the "Seven Sisters" oil companies[15] with the assistance of State Department staff and CIA agents. They were reinforced by presidential initiatives and doctrines, a network of US military bases, covert operations and overt military interventions, and on numerous occasions by the threat of US nuclear attack.

The proximity of the Middle East to the Soviet Union inevitably meant that regional developments would impact Soviet (now Russian) security. Yet, ever since Truman had nightmares in 1945 of a "giant pincer movement against the oil-rich areas of the Near East and the warm-water ports of the Mediterranean," US presidents have shared his fear and built on his commitments to block any expansion of Soviet (or Russian) influence in the Middle East.

Because the Soviets understood the centrality of Middle East oil to US imperial power, as well as their strategic inferiority, with rare exceptions the Kremlin was cautious, avoiding actions that could be interpreted as challenging US power in the region. Despite its support for Middle East monarchs, dictators, and tyrants, Washington's ostensible commitment to "democracy and freedom" has coincided neatly with its imperial ambitions. Before al-Qaeda, it was the Russian threat that was repeatedly invoked "to scare the Hell out of the country,"[16] and to provide presidents with political cover to justify whatever action they thought necessary to implement "Axiom Number One." In the name of freedom and anti-communism, the Truman, Eisenhower, and Carter Doctrines were proclaimed. Under the Truman Doctrine, the US would intervene "to support free people who are resisting attempted subjugation by armed minorities or by outside pressures." The Eisenhower Doctrine called for "employment of the armed forces of the United States to secure and protect the territorial integrity and political independence of nations requesting such aid against . . . aggression from any nation controlled by international communism."[17] The Carter Doctrine asserted that "Any attempt by any outside force to gain control of the Persian Gulf will be regarded as an assault on the vital interests of the United States of America, and such an assault will be repelled by *any means necessary* . . ."[18] And, when neither weapons of mass destruction nor links between Saddam Hussein and al-Qaeda could be found to justify the twenty-first-century US war or occupation of Iraq, the articulated rationale was simply changed to exporting "democracy and freedom."

Thus, when the Soviet Union was slow to withdraw from northern Iran after World War II, Truman informed the Soviet ambassador that "Soviet troops should evacuate Iran within 48 hours—or the United States would use the new superbomb that it alone possessed."[19] In 1948, when the CIA informed Truman that "a victory for the Greek guerrillas would endanger U.S. control over Middle East oil, 40% of the known world reserves," the president initiated a counter-insurgency effort on behalf of Greek royalists who had collaborated with the Nazis. In the civil war that followed, 160,000 people lost their lives.[20]

During the Eisenhower administration, fear of communism was used to justify the CIA-directed coup in Iran which restored the Shah, the unsuccessful attempt to topple Gamal Abdel Nasser of Egypt, and the dispatch of nuclear-armed Marines to Lebanon. Marginalizing the Soviets also dominated the Nixon–Kissinger approach to the region. It also served as the rationale for President Carter's creation of the Rapid Deployment Force (later to become the Central Command).[21]

Just as the Balfour Declaration's commitment of British support for "the establishment in Palestine of a national home for the Jewish people" was an act of British "national interest," so US support for Israel has been less than fully altruistic. US economic, political, and military aid, and the maintenance of a regional military balance of power in Israel's favor, have been rooted in a multitude of foreign policy and domestic political considerations.

Cold Warriors saw Israel as a "bulwark against Soviet penetration."[22] Before the 1969 Nixon Doctrine formally transformed Israel and Iran into the hammer and anvil of US regional power, the Johnson administration understood that Israeli military power could be used to contain and weaken Arab nationalism which threatened oil-rich conservative monarchies allied with the US.[23] And, under the Carter Doctrine and Reagan's "Strategic Cooperation" framework, Israel served the US as an "unsinkable aircraft carrier" for the Rapid Deployment Force.

Israel's shared Western values and origins as a colonial settler state, the role Israel plays in Christian theology and imagination, and the need to atone for anti-Semitic guilt, have all served as ideological underpinnings for the strategic US–Israeli relationship. They also reinforced the power of the American Israel Public Affairs Committee (AIPAC) and other powerful Zionist political action committees, widely known as the "Israel lobby."[24] Its power has rivaled, and at times surpassed, that of oil interests in framing and influencing US foreign policy.[25]

Until the 1991 Gulf War, the goals of assuring US control over Middle East oil, marginalizing other powers' influence in the region, and supporting Israel regardless of its conquests and occupations usually reinforced one another. That most Arab nations have seen Israeli repression of the Palestinians, and not the Soviet Union or al-Qaeda, as the greatest threat to their security has long been the central contradiction of US Middle East policy.

SUEZ

The causes of the 1956 Suez War, and the war itself, were as simple as colonialism—and necessarily complex. The Eisenhower administration, which had decided to weaken and possibly overthrow the Egyptian government, unintentionally precipitated the chain of events that culminated in Nasser's decision to nationalize the Suez Canal. It later reversed course and supported Nasser following the British, French, and Israeli invasion in their effort to retake the Suez Canal and drive the Arab nationalist government from power. When the Soviet Union responded with threats of "missile attacks" against London, Paris, and Israel, the US immobilized Moscow by threatening nuclear war.

The crisis took place during the rule of an exceptionally aggressive US administration. Despite Eisenhower's later condemnation of the "military industrial complex," his repeated threats to initiate nuclear war, his administration's "anti-communist" *coups d'état* in Iran and Guatemala, and its counter-insurgency warfare across Southeast Asia resulted in the Eisenhower years being among the most militarized in US history.[26] The Suez War also took place at a time when the Soviet Union and Eastern Europe were enjoying the first freedoms resulting from Khrushchev's de-Stalinization program. Even as Washington understood that the USSR would pursue "a less tense relationship with the Western powers" while it focused on economic development, there were deep fears that the Kremlin would "increase efforts . . . to extend the area of Communist influence or control."[27]

In the Middle East this translated into a US policy fixated on removing what little influence the Soviets had and preventing any possibility of its expansion. As in Southeast Asia, neutrality was interpreted as undermining US interests and was to be opposed. Soon after being appointed Secretary of State in January 1953, Dulles traveled to the Middle East, where he was impressed by the "disadvantages of collaborating with an ally [Britain] so clearly marked with the emblem of empire." Deaf to the reality that there were few communists in the Arab world and that Israel was seen as a greater security threat to Arab nations than was the Soviet Union, he returned home frustrated by regional governments' refusal to accept his understanding of the dangers of communism or the importance of creating a "northern tier" barrier against Soviet influence in the region.[28]

Eisenhower and Dulles did not initially oppose the Egyptian Free Officers Movement, which brought Nasser to power in 1952. The ousting of Britain's client, King Farouk, presented the US with the opportunity to expand its influence at Britain's expense. Nasser's government was given economic assistance, and the CIA unsuccessfully attempted to purchase the new leader's loyalty.[29] Nasser was initially more moderate than many anticipated. In 1955 and early 1956 he engaged in secret peace negotiations with Israel sponsored by the US. These peace efforts were sabotaged by a series of what Ambassador Hare described as Israeli "military, quasi-military and political actions aimed at keeping frontiers in turmoil."[30]

The US nuclear war-fighting doctrine of the time was outlined in the "Basic National Security Policy." It proposed that the US would "integrate nuclear weapons with other weapons . . . . Nuclear weapons will be used in general war and in military operations short of general war as authorized by the President . . . . The United States will not preclude itself from using nuclear weapons even in a local situation."[31] The policy and contingency plans called for "massive retaliation."

Britain and France were dying empires and were only beginning to acknowledge the traumatic changes that would inevitably follow the decline of their global power. Resistance and desperate efforts to retain as much of the old order as possible characterized their responses to the emerging postcolonial world. Britain had nuclear weapons; France was working to develop them and, beginning in 1951, collaborated intermittently with Israel to this end.[32]

Despite the Egyptian revolution and Britain's subsequent, if reluctant, agreement to withdraw its troops from the Suez Zone, the waterway continued to serve as the lifeline for what remained of the British Empire, and it was essential to the economies of Europe. Two-thirds of Britain's oil and half of France's passed through the Suez Canal, and the 10,000 ships that used it each year transported oil to Europe. Furthermore, 60,000 British troops moved annually between England and British military bases "east of Aden" through the Canal. The closure would, as British Foreign Minister Harold Macmillan reported, "finish Britain as a world power."[33]

Nearly all Arab nations were nominally independent, but France was again resisting a nationalist revolution, this time in Algeria. The Algerian revolutionaries, the Front Nationale de Libération (FNL), were supported by Nasser's Egypt and other Arab nationalists. In addition to its investment in, and economic dependence on, the Suez Canal, the French government was increasingly preoccupied with Nasser's Pan-Arabism and his support for the FNL.

The situation became more complex in September 1955, when Israeli border attacks against the Egyptian Army sabotaged peace negotiations, humiliated Nasser, and led his government to turn to Britain, France, and the US in search of weapons to achieve parity with Israel.[34] Nasser's requests were denied, ostensibly in keeping with the 1950 Tripartite Agreement which limited arms sales to the region. In desperation, Nasser solicited weapons from the Soviet Bloc and, to the West's amazement, Nasser reached an agreement with Moscow for "more tanks, guns and jets than . . . all the Middle East's armies combined."[35] Nasser had circumvented Dulles' "northern tier" barrier, but he repeatedly stated that his goals were self-defense, independence, and non-alignment. Yet Dulles and Eisenhower saw Nasser's action as betrayal. From their perspective, he had "opened the Middle East to penetration by the Soviet Union," and they now moved to weaken, if not overthrow, his government.[36]

In July 1956, Eisenhower instructed Dulles to inform the Egyptians that the US was withdrawing its offer to finance the construction of the Aswan Dam, the project on which Nasser's dreams of economic development depended. The plan for what became the Baghdad Pact was developed to surround and isolate Egypt with an informal network of pro-Western nations: Iraq, Jordan, Libya, Saudi Arabia, and Syria. Dulles also replaced Hank Byrode, the US Ambassador to Egypt, who later recalled that when he informed Nasser that he was being recalled, Nasser's "face went black. He stared at me for a full two minutes . . . He just stared. I am sure he feared we were going to assassinate him and I was being removed because we had been so close."[37]

When the US publicly announced its decision to withdraw from the Aswan Dam project, Nasser described the action as "an attack on the regime and an invitation to the people of Egypt to bring it down."[38] He had reason to be concerned. Three years earlier the CIA had overthrown another independent-minded nationalist, Mohammad Mossadeq, in Iran.

Nasser's response was to finance construction of the Aswan Dam by nationalizing the Suez Canal. The Canal's revenues would subsidize the economic, social, and political transformation of Egypt. His plan was carefully designed to avoid any legal justification for the violent retaliation he anticipated. It respected international law and provided that the company's share- and bond-holders be compensated for their losses. Free rights of passage through the Canal would continue to be respected. On the first day after nationalization, 49 ships passed through the canal, four more than the average, including ships chartered by Israel.[39]

The British Prime Minister, Anthony Eden, responded with panic and outrage that Nasser had "his hand on our windpipe." Despite reports that Nasser's actions were legal, Eden ordered the British military to devise a campaign to retake the Canal. When the British Cabinet met, the major question it faced was whether the US would support British-led economic sanctions and military action.

The French response was tougher than Eden's. Foreign Minister Christian Pineau accused Nasser of "plunder" and publicly stated that Paris would not accept Nasser's unilateral action. Prime Minister Guy Mollet announced that there would be a "severe counterstroke."[40] French and British leaders agreed to a joint invasion to take the Canal.

Weeks before Nasser's nationalization, the Israeli Prime Minister, David Ben-Gurion, and his protégé, Moshe Dayan, had agreed on the necessity of preemptive war against Egypt before the acquisition of Soviet bloc weapons changed the regional balance of power. By destroying Egypt's army, they expected to end Nasser's support for Palestinian *fedayeen*. They also anticipated that a humiliating defeat of Egypt would lead to Nasser's fall and weaken Pan-Arabism, which they believed was the greatest threat to Israeli security.[41] What they needed was a *casus belli* acceptable to the Western powers.[42] Nationalization of the Suez Canal provided Shimon Peres, another of Ben-Gurion's protégés, the opening he had been instructed to find. By August an agreement was negotiated whereby Israel would attack Egypt across the Sinai Peninsula in alliance with France and Britain. Following the Israeli invasion, France and Britain would demand that both Egypt and Israel withdraw 10 miles from the Suez Canal. When Nasser refused to withdraw from what was, in fact, Egyptian territory, France and Britain would invade, reconquer the Canal and drive Nasser from power.

In September, Eisenhower informed his European allies that "our views on the situation diverge . . . American public opinion flatly rejects the thought of using force." He let the Israelis know that he would not pander to their ambitions despite the approaching presidential election. He calculated that the US had little to lose. The British were "invit[ing] on themselves all the Arab hostility to Israel," and he wondered if Eden, Mollet, and Ben-Gurion were really "going to *dare* us—dare *us*—" to defend the Tripartite Agreement, which provided that action be taken in support of Middle East victims of aggression. As the invasion and elections approached, Eisenhower again warned his allies that "The United States has pledged itself to assist the victim of any aggression in the Middle East. We shall honor our pledge."[43] All possible outcomes of the crisis seemed to bolster US power in the oil-rich region.

The Israeli invasion began on October 29 and, unable to defend his forces in the eastern Sinai, Nasser ordered their withdrawal to the Canal Zone. Two days later, with Egyptian forces in retreat, Eisenhower honored his pledge. All US military, development, technical and agricultural assistance to Israel were suspended. When Britain and France followed with their attack, the US introduced a resolution in the UN General Assembly condemning the invasion and demanding their withdrawal. Combined with a US attack on sterling and threats to cut their oil supplies, Eisenhower quickly forced the British–French–Israeli alliance to accept a ceasefire and military withdrawal,[44] but not without a US–Soviet exchange of nuclear threats.

In response to the Anglo-French invasion, Soviet Premier Bulganin warned Eisenhower that "if this war is not stopped, it . . . can grow to a third world war." Because the US and USSR had "all modern types of arms, including atomic and hydrogen weapons," the alternative he proposed was that Washington and Moscow should together "crush the aggressors."[45] In separate letters to Eden and Mollet, Bulganin threatened to attack London and Paris with missiles if they did not immediately withdraw from Egypt. Soviet aircraft were reportedly dispatched to Syria, and "the danger of a great-power confrontation suddenly was looming larger and was more significant and frightening than the crisis in the Middle East." The White House concluded that the Kremlin was bluffing, but there were fears that Soviet bombers could attack Israel, if not Britain and France, with nuclear weapons.[46] At the very least, the Russian threats distracted attention from Moscow's invasion of Hungary, where it repressed popular demands for an end to the Soviet occupation.

Eisenhower publicly denounced Bulganin's proposal for joint action, calling it "unthinkable," and he warned that the US would oppose the Soviet Union if it moved its forces into the region. Less publicly, to enforce "Axiom Number One," Admiral Radford, the Chairman of the Joint Chiefs of Staff, provided the president with recommendations to increase US military readiness. These were to be "implemented by degrees." Fighter planes were placed on advanced alert, and two aircraft carriers and their accompanying fleets of cruisers and destroyers were dispatched to reinforce the nuclear-armed Sixth Fleet. Eisenhower told his senior advisors that "If those fellows start something, we may have to hit 'em—and, if necessary, with *everything* in the bucket."[47] He made certain that the Kremlin's leaders understood his intent. As Nixon later recalled:

> In 1956 we considered using the Bomb in Suez, and we did use it diplomatically . . . Eisenhower's response was very interesting. He got Al Gruenther, the NATO commander, to hold a press conference, and Gruenther said that if Khrushchev carried out his threat to use rockets against the British Isles, Moscow would be destroyed "as surely as day follows night." From that time on, the U.S. has played the dominant role in the Mideast.[48]

To ensure that the US, and not the USSR, filled the vacuum created by the French and British defeat, the Eisenhower Doctrine was subsequently proclaimed, promising US assistance to "any nation or group of such nations requesting assistance against armed aggression from any country controlled by international communism."

Nasser snatched political victory from his military defeat. His prestige and the power of Pan-Arabism soared, although his independence led to continuing US efforts to isolate and contain his ambitions. Nasser did, however, understand that the Egyptian military had been defeated by a superior Israeli force and that renewed military confrontations would have to wait until Arab armies became more powerful. Though forced to surrender the Sinai Peninsula, Israel also emerged from the war as a "victor." Nasser had committed to keep the Gulf of Aqaba open to Israeli shipping, and UN forces (UNEF) were deployed to the Peninsula to serve as a buffer between the two countries. Dulles also promised that the US would consider any future Egyptian blockade of the Tiran Straits as an act of war to which Israel could respond militarily in self-defense. France and Israel also derived a dubious lesson from the war: they would be vulnerable in the future without nuclear weapons. This deepened their commitment and cooperation to developing nuclear arsenals.

LEBANON AND IRAQ 1958

The origins of the initial spasms of the Lebanese civil war and the 1958 Iraqi revolution were more convoluted than those of the Suez Crisis. Like the 1956 war, the crises grew from European colonialism. They were complicated by US–British rivalries, and to a greater degree by US–Soviet competition. And, in response to both crises, Eisenhower prepared and threatened nuclear attacks to protect the United States' growing Middle East empire.

Mid-century Lebanon was in many ways a French creation. Beirut served as "the Paris of the Middle East." It was an opening to the West, a banking center, and a resort for the Arab elite. Western districts of Syria had been fused with the predominantly Maronite Christian-dominated Mount Lebanon region. French influence in Lebanon was buttressed by disproportionate privilege accorded to the Maronite minority. The National Covenant of 1943 codified this confessional balance of power: the Muslim majority would not press to unify Lebanon with other (i.e. Muslim) Arab states, and Lebanese Christians would recognize the Arab (i.e. Muslim) "dimension of Lebanon and not ally themselves to any Western power."[49] The posts of president and prime minister and parliamentary seats were allocated proportionately to reinforce this agreement.

In 1948, a joint State Department and War Department country report on Lebanon emphasized "the strategic importance of the country, with its port, air bases, railway and oil pipeline. The commercial and military importance of Near East oil reserves, the deterioration of Britain's strength, the emergent interest of the Soviet Union in the Near East" all pointed to "the importance to the U.S. of a politically stable and economically prosperous Lebanon."[50] Eight years later the Joint Chiefs elaborated Lebanon's military role in continued US domination of the region's oil reserves. Lebanon provided "atomic support forces" and an expanded "logistic base complex to support the strategy." Lebanon served these priorities as a communications hub for the military. Lebanon was also valued because, as the US Embassy reported, the Lebanese were "less fanatical than other Arabs and more disposed to rational conduct . . . due . . . to their better education, their commercial mentality, and their agreement on the necessity for maintaining religious equilibrium." Others, including Ben-Gurion, saw Lebanon as "the weakest link in the Arab League" and believed an allied Christian state could be carved out of the fractured nation.[51]

In 1952, choosing among candidates who were "without exception friendly to America," the Lebanese parliament selected Camille Sham'un as president. Sham'un was served by the equally pro-US Christian Foreign Minister, Charles Malik. Within a month of coming to power, Sham'un acceded to US oil company demands and pledged to exclude Kamal Jumblat, the leader of the Druze minority, who was influenced by Mosadeq's nationalization of Iranian oil, from his Cabinet. Sham'un also signaled that in the event of the US going to war with the Soviet Union, Lebanon would be "100 percent on the side of the West." The problem for Sham'un and Washington was that leading members of the Lebanese ruling class, including Christians, were not in full agreement with him. Many feared that his pro-US commitments violated the National Compact, and that Lebanon's resulting isolation from much of the Arab world would be costly.[52]

Sham'un found himself in trouble soon after coming to power. His "reformist" Cabinet gave women the vote, challenged landed interests, reduced the size of the parliament, and failed to distribute the nation's wealth in ways that benefited the majority of Lebanese. His pro-US foreign policy, including efforts to mediate the Suez crisis, endorsement of the Eisenhower Doctrine and Baghdad Pact, and his deepening ties with Saudi Arabia all further alienated essential constituencies. Even as the US Embassy considered Sham'un the "best possible President for Lebanon" whose rule was "clearly in U.S. interest," by the mid-1950s the Embassy was sending disturbing reports to the State Department: "[L]ocal Communists were more active than ever and . . . had effectively infiltrated the press." Palestinian refugees, Armenian and Greek Orthodox Christians, Shiite *ulema* in the south, and urban intellectuals were all susceptible to communism. There was an "awakening social and political consciousness" among increasingly militant Muslims who understood that "the Christians . . . are fighting a losing battle as far as numerical strength is concerned." The Embassy reported that the Maronite leader Pierre Jemayyel was stoking the fire by telling his Muslim peers that Lebanese

Christians "contribute 80 percent of the Lebanese budget . . . Moslems of Lebanon should be willing, if necessary, to give up all government positions in favor of Christians."[53] A year into his presidency, Sham'un thought it necessary to request US aid for the Beirut police and for a gendarmerie accountable to him alone.

Lebanon's crisis crystallized in 1957, as the nation turned to parliamentary elections which would determine the selection of the country's president the following year. Sham'un's opponents united to form the United National Front (UNF) coalition. Its leaders, who backed demands for an interim government to ensure a fair election with strikes and mass protests, could not be tarred as Nasserites or radical leftists. They were members of "the Lebanese bourgeoisie" who had long been the foundation of Western influence, and who now favored greater solidarity with the Palestinians and opposed Sham'un's embrace of the Baghdad Pact. Even Lebanon's leading general, Chehab Shihab, distanced himself from Sham'un, warning him that his repressive tactics were forcing "an otherwise loyal Muslim constituency . . . in[to] the ranks of the opposition." In Washington, Dulles had nightmares of the emergence of a neutralist-oriented government that would be vulnerable to Egyptian and Syrian pressures.[54]

Washington's answer was money and military planning. Three months before the June elections, Sham'un was told that the US would provide $13 million in development and military aid, and "an undisclosed contribution for the forthcoming election."[55] Throughout the election campaign, Wilbur Crane Eveland, the second-ranking CIA official in the region, commuted regularly between the US Embassy in Damascus and the presidential palace in Beirut to deliver hundreds of thousands of dollars to Sham'un.

Money made the difference. Sham'un and his allies won a landslide victory. The US Embassy reported that the "next parliament will be composed of 'nonentities' [Sham'un's lackeys, etc.] and is designed to re-elect President [Sham'un] in 1958." The United Front appropriately charged that the victory of Sham'un "lackeys" was the result of widespread bribery.

In the first months of 1958 Lebanon was preoccupied by two events. First was the selection of the country's president which, despite Parliament being packed with "lackeys," did not guarantee Sham'un's appointment. Second was the creation of the United Arab Republic, the ostensible union of the Egyptian and Syrian governments (and their militaries) under Nasser's leadership. The optimism inspired by this dynamic Pan-Arab nationalism ignited hopes across the Arab world, including Lebanon, where Sham'un thought it necessary to ban pro-Nasser rallies and propaganda, but to no avail.

The political struggle for power in Lebanon thus became increasingly intense, complex, and violent. Despite Sham'un's charge that the UNF was led by Nasserites, the US Ambassador, Robert McClintock, understood that Lebanon was tangential to Nasser's project. McClintock saw no alternative to continued support for Sham'un, reporting that he had assumed a central position in the region's anti-Nasser forces, and that "western failure to support him will have repercussions among all most moderate and responsible friends and allies of west in ME area . . . "[56]

With spring came a general strike calling for Sham'un to resign and the splintering of the nation into semi-autonomous communal regions: Druze, Maronite, Sunni, and Shi'a. Sham'un lost control as hundreds were killed and wounded, and the country descended into civil war. The crisis came to a head in mid-May when the UNF appealed to the military and to Sham'un's gendarmerie, as well as to ordinary citizens, to "withdraw completely from Sham'un and the clique of plotting rulers."

In Washington, the Joint Chiefs agreed on a rationale for US military intervention that circumvented the Eisenhower Doctrine requirement of demonstrating foreign aggression before US forces could intervene and dispatched the Sixth Fleet with two Marine battalions to the Lebanese coast. Having been advised by Dulles that "gunboat diplomacy . . . no longer represented acceptable practice, unless the forces went at the invitation of the government," Eisenhower and Dulles prepared the ground by arranging for British forces to collaborate in restoring peace to Lebanon and by instructing Sham'un precisely how to issue the invitation. He should ask the US to "protect American life and property." Sham'un was to appeal to the UN, "alleging interference from without in its internal affairs and the consequent threat to its integrity and independence." Sham'un was also instructed to line up "at least some Arab states . . . prepared publicly to support Lebanon . . . in its appeal to the Security Council." Eisenhower's directive came with a caveat: if Sham'un's continued candidacy continued to divide the nation, Washington would not be bound to support him.[57]

In mid-July, as US forces prepared to land near Beirut airport, the situation was greatly complicated by the overthrow of the British-sponsored monarchy in Iraq in a military coup modeled on Nasser's Free Officers revolution. Pro-Western regimes across the Middle East found themselves immediately on the defensive as one of General Qasim's first acts was to withdraw from the Baghdad Pact, leaving Dulles' northern tier barrier in ruins. Washington and London refused to believe that the revolution reflected a popular rejection of monarchy and neocolonialism. Instead, they blamed Nasser and used the Iraqi coup as the political cover Sham'un needed to "invite" the US–British intervention into Lebanon's growing civil conflict. Eisenhower authorized implementation of "Operation Blue Bat," and the Marines landed on July 18.

For US troops, the occupation of Lebanon was a bloodless, if nuclear, affair. What were probably apocryphal reports announced that the 5,000 Marines who first landed on Beirut's beaches were greeted by people selling popsicles. Although none of Lebanon's warring forces turned their guns against the regional hegemon, the Marines were not initially widely welcomed. Wilbur Eveland later explained how Robert Murphy, Eisenhower's special emissary, guaranteed the loyalty of General Shihab's increasingly rebellious army. Meeting with the general, he "quietly explained that just one of its aircraft, armed with nuclear weapons, could obliterate Beirut and its environs from the face of the earth .... Murphy quickly added that he'd been sent to be sure that it wouldn't be necessary .... That ... ended the conversation. It now seemed that the general had 'regained control' of his troops."[58]

By the end of the month, Washington had ushered Sham'un out of the presidential palace, replacing him with General Shihab. Without having resolved the inequities and tensions that had spawned this initial outbreak of what later became a catastrophic 16-year civil war, "peace" was restored. In Washington, as Dulles lied to Congress that the US intervention had been preceded by "125 direct acts of aggression by Syria and the United Arab Republic," the myth that the Marines had prevented an illegitimate Nasserite regime from coming to power was widely encouraged. In the Middle East, with the British having been ousted from Iraq, the US was "the uncontested power in the region."[59]

What role did nuclear weapons and Eisenhower's nuclear alert play?

As in the past, Washington's nuclear dominance ensured that Khrushchev did little more than complicate war-related diplomacy. As US forces intervened, the Chairman of the Joint Chiefs, General Nathan Twining, was confident that the "Soviets would do no more than wring their hands and deliver verbal protests. We knew this because U.S. military forces could have destroyed the USSR—and Russia knew it."[60] Eisenhower had also taken steps to ensure that the Kremlin got the message; he placed the Strategic Air Command on alert and let it be known that it would be "desirable" that the Soviets be aware of the nuclear alert. At least "1,100 aircraft were positioned for takeoff, and for several days the alert kept the show-of-force going." Twining was also ordered to "be prepared to employ, subject to my personal approval, whatever means might become necessary to prevent any unfriendly forces from moving into Kuwait."[61]

Nasser feared that the landing of the Marines in Beirut was part of a larger operation designed to oust General al-Karim Qasim's revolutionary government, and he insisted that Moscow make a deterrent threat. Khrushchev's response was that "he thought the Americans had gone off their heads." "Frankly," Khrushchev continued, "we are not ready for a confrontation. We are not ready for World War III." Khrushchev urged Nasser "to lean with the storm, there was no other way because Dulles could blow the whole world into pieces."[62]

Once again, the US invaded a nation confident that others would not move militarily to protect those it was determined to attack.

When the time came for the Marines to take their nuclear weapons onto Beirut's beaches, Under-Secretary of State Christian Herter had second thoughts, worried that displaying them publicly might further inflame Arab public opinion. He ordered that "what goes with them [Marines] in its most violent form aboard ship" not be offloaded. Instead, they were redeployed to Turkey.[63] Nonetheless, the forward deployment and threatened use of tactical nuclear weapons had a powerful impact. In June, news that Secretary of Defense Neil McElroy had raised the possibility of using nuclear weapons during the Lebanon crisis helped General Shihab understand the gravity of Robert Murphy's nuclear threat the following month. Knowledge that three US nuclear-capable aircraft carriers were within range of Iraq may also have influenced General Qasim's decision to honor Iraq's contracts with US oil conglomerates and other Western corporations.

THE SIX-DAY WAR

In 1967 and 1970, Presidents Johnson and Nixon respectively threatened first-strike nuclear attacks to ensure continued US predominance in the Middle East. William Arkin estimates that, as in Lebanon in 1958, in each case the US brought "more than one thousand nuclear weapons" to bear on the crisis: approximately 100 atomic bombs aboard each aircraft carrier, an estimated 50 nuclear weapons carried aboard accompanying ships, and 400 warheads on Polaris submarines. The Sixth Fleet also drew on the arsenal of atomic bombs, nuclear depth bombs, Honest John rockets, and nuclear artillery shells based at US military facilities in Spain, Italy, Greece, and Turkey.[64]

Both Johnson and McNamara remained discreet about their 1967 nuclear threat, and the notion that the US leaders would have thought it necessary to threaten nuclear war during Israel's six-day devastation of the Arab world's combined armies seems counterintuitive. Nixon was more forthright, stating that the possibility of Syrian, Israeli, and Soviet intervention in the 1970 Jordanian civil war "was like a ghastly game of dominoes, with a nuclear war waiting at the end."[65]

The tensions, complex alliance structures (formal and informal), intrigues, and miscalculations that triggered the Six-Day War were not unlike those that triggered World War I. While debate continues over who actually started the war, it is clear that, encouraged by the Soviet Union and his leading general, Nasser provoked an intense confrontation that provided the Israeli military with the occasion to implement long-standing plans to destroy the Egyptian and other neighboring militaries. It is also increasingly recognized that a major contributing factor in Israel's decision to destroy the Egyptian military was the fear that Israel's nuclear weapons facilities at Dimona could be a primary target of a preemptive attack. Having launched its nuclear weapons program in earnest following the Suez War, by 1967 Israel "had a rudimentary, but operational, nuclear weapons capability."[66] As would be the case again in 1973, it was at the very end of the war, when the Kremlin threatened to intervene to impose a ceasefire, that US nuclear threats were made to prevent the expansion of Soviet influence in the oil-rich region.

At the core of the complex structure of tensions that triggered the Six-Day War lay the "Palestinian Question": continued conflict between Israel and the Arab states; conflicts among Arab states; and the struggle for control of water which was essential for development.

By the early 1960s, growing numbers of Palestinians who had been forced into exile began armed resistance as *fedayeen*, attacking Israeli frontier settlements. Israeli retaliatory attacks in the Jordanian-occupied West Bank, the Egyptian-occupied Gaza Strip, and in Syria often had a second purpose: pressing the territorial ambitions of the new Israeli state that had yet to define its borders. Israel and the Arab states remained in a formal state of war, having ended the 1948–49 war with an armistice, not a peace agreement. There were also volatile tensions, including military conflicts, among Arab states. As part of their continuing war against Israel, and as a dimension of their postcolonial competition for status and power, Egypt, Syria, and Iraq encouraged and often manipulated competing Palestinian *fedayeen* and political forces, exploiting them for their own ends. The Palestine Liberation Organization (PLO), for example, was created by Nasser in 1965, during an Arab summit meeting. Nasser installed his loyal "stooge," Ahmad al-Shuqari, to lead the PLO in ways that would avoid drawing Cairo into a war with Israel for which Cairo was ill-prepared. It was to create an independent Palestinian resistance and to draw the Arab states into a liberation war against Israel that Yasir Arafat and his colleagues established *al Fatah*. At various times *al Fatah* was supported by the Saudis, who were at war with Nasser in Yemen, and by Syrian Ba'athists.

The struggle for control of the Levant's limited water compounded Israeli–Arab and inter-Arab tensions. Israel's decision to channel water from Galilee for irrigation threatened Jordanian and Syrian water supplies and heightened Arab anxieties that the diverted water would reinforce

Israel's power by sustaining millions of new Jewish immigrants. Competing with Egyptian nationalism, Syrian leaders called for a "people's war" to destroy Israel, winning diplomatic if not military support from the Jordanian monarchy, more than half of whose subjects were Palestinian.[67]

The last structural layer of Middle East tension and conflict which permeated and, in many ways, set the parameters for all of the others was US–Soviet competition.

Seeking to outflank Washington, the Soviets poured billions of rubles into military and economic aid for the region, most of it directed to Ba'athist Syria, which included communists in the ruling coalition, and to Nasser, who was seen by the Kremlin as a "noncapitalist revolutionary democrat." In the years leading up to the 1967 war, Moscow pursued a "bifurcated" policy toward its Syrian and Egyptian allies. Given US strategic dominance and the proximity of the nuclear-armed US Sixth Fleet, Premier Alexei Kosygin and Foreign Minister Andrei Gromyko worked to prevent conflicts that could escalate into confrontations with the US. However, Communist Party Secretary General Leonid Brezhnev's allies in the military believed that with the US bogged down in Vietnam, Middle East opportunities should be exploited to their limits. The greater the tension in the region, the more Moscow's Arab allies would be reminded of their dependence on Soviet assistance.[68]

President Kennedy remained committed to Eisenhower's Middle East balancing act, albeit with modifications. In addition to supporting Israel diplomatically, he worked to lure Nasser into transferring his dependence from Moscow to Washington. Kennedy offered massive shipments of wheat and other essentials for Egypt's impoverished people, and by 1962 40 percent of Egyptians were being fed by the US.[69] Kennedy and his senior advisors opposed many of Israel's military retaliations, its water diversion plans, and its refusal to repatriate Palestinian refugees. While providing limited economic assistance to Israel, Kennedy also pressed Ben-Gurion to allow US and neutral inspections of Israel's Dimona nuclear reactor so that the world, and especially the Arabs, could be reassured.[70]

Kennedy's assassination resulted in a greater US tilt toward Israel. Although he served the interests of major oil companies throughout his political career, Johnson was not tied to the Saudis or other Arab elites, and he was the first US president to officially receive an Israeli prime minister at the White House. Soon after assuming the presidency, Johnson told an Israeli diplomat, "You have lost a very great friend. But you have found a better one." During his meeting with Prime Minister Levi Eshkol, Johnson pledged that, "The United States is foursquare behind Israel on all matters that affect their vital security interests."[71] Like Eisenhower and Dulles, containing Arab nationalism was a priority for Johnson and his advisors. His White House had little patience for Nasser's opposition to the US war in Vietnam, Cairo's cold war with Israel and proxy war with Saudi Arabia in Yemen, or his demands that the US withdraw from its strategically important air base in Libya. Johnson halted wheat shipments to Egypt and pressed "regime change" by undermining the Egyptian economy.

Throughout his final years in office, Johnson was preoccupied with Vietnam. To offset the massive military, economic, and political commitments to Southeast Asia, his administration anticipated the Nixon Doctrine in the Middle East, forging an "unprecedented, covert military-security relationship" with Israel to contain Arab nationalism. This policy was informed in part by a State Department report that "[T]rue Arab unity will not be achieved for many years, if then." Federations of Arab political and military power, the report advised, "would not detract from Israel's military superiority over the Arabs." As part of this arrangement, Washington gradually became Israel's primary weapons supplier.[72]

The tensions and attacks that triggered the Six-Day War intensified in late 1966. In November, Israel launched its largest military operation since the Suez War, with punitive attacks by hundreds of troops and 40 tanks against West Bank villages surrounding Hebron. In the course of punishing Palestinian villages from which *al Fatah* had launched its attacks, the unexpected happened. A Jordanian reconnaissance unit stumbled on the Israelis and was routed in the "pitched battle" that followed. Nasser now had an opening to charge that CIA-sponsored King Hussein had prepared the way for Israeli aggression by refusing Syria's and Saudi Arabia's less than altruistic offers to help defend the West Bank. Damascus' rhetorical attacks were worse: Jordan's defeat resulted from "the sinister cabal between 'the reactionary Jordanian regime and imperialist Zionism.' "[73]

King Hussein defended himself and his regime by going on the offensive against Nasser. Weeks later, when Egyptian MiGs straying over Israel were shot down, he denounced Nasser's hypocrisy to Arab leaders assembled for a summit and in radio broadcasts across the Arab world.[74] Nasser was vulnerable to Hussein's verbal assaults. His claims to Arab leadership were being challenged by Syrian Ba'athists; his military establishment and economy were sapped by a war with Saudi Arabia in Yemen; and, at home, he faced challenges from the Muslim Brotherhood, many of whose leaders he imprisoned, and from his struggling economy. Some said that there was little left of the old Nasser but his pride.[75]

Moscow's encouragement of Syrian shelling of Israeli settlements below the Golan Heights contributed to deepening regional tensions, as did widely accepted but false Soviet warnings that Israel was massing troops to invade Syria. Reinforcing Damascus' fears, in April 1967 Prime Minister Eshkol ordered Israeli forces (the IAF) to retaliate against Syrian-sponsored guerrilla attacks by bombing villages and military installations on the Golan Heights. The results were devastating. Worse for Syria's leaders was that MiG fighters sent to challenge the Israeli Mirages were shot down within sight of Damascus. The people there watched the Israelis destroy the warplanes and establish Israeli aerial supremacy within 30 seconds. Adding political insult to psychological injury, the Israeli jets flew a victory loop around the Syrian capital.[76]

In Cairo, with the Soviets pressing reports of a planned Israeli invasion of Syria in mid-May, and even King Hussein challenging his leadership, Nasser found himself in an increasingly difficult situation. If Israel invaded Syria and Egypt failed to respond, his government would lose what legitimacy remained. If the Syrian government was toppled, Nasser feared that progressive governments across the Arab world—including his own—would fall like dominoes; and he knew that behind Israel stood the United States. In response, Nasser and his advisors developed a plan to silence critics and to avert a disastrous regional war: UNEF would be ordered back from its forward positions in the Sinai; and the Egyptian army would move into defensive positions on the Peninsula, forcing Israel to redeploy troops that Nasser incorrectly believed were preparing to invade Syria.

Nasser's stratagem failed to take into account his field marshal's deceits and the rot in the Egyptian military. Nasser's friend, leading general, and rival Abd al-Hakim 'Amer repeatedly assured him that the Egyptian military was not only strong enough to repulse an Israeli offensive, but that it could fight its way across the Negev to Jordan, splitting sparsely populated southern Israel from its metropolitan center. In fact, the war in Yemen, the economic crisis, and political corruption had taken a terrible toll on the Egyptian military.

The crisis began to spin out of control when, contrary to Nasser's orders, General 'Amer ordered the complete withdrawal of UN forces from Sinai, rather than simply pulling them back from the border. As ordered, thousands of Egyptian troops—many unarmed—soon paraded through Cairo, past the US Embassy, and across the Nile on the march to reoccupy Sinai. The Egyptian legions moved with less than military precision and still less planning. "[C]ontinuous and contradictory orders" sent them racing back and forth across the Sinai, exhausting Nasser's ill-fed and poorly armed troops and their already compromised war machines.[77]

After ousting UNEF from the Sinai, Nasser agonized over how the crisis would end, and thus how best to respond to the competing pressures that assailed him. He believed that Egypt's reassertion of sovereignty by ordering UNEF's withdrawal, the deployment of Egyptian forces onto the Sinai, and the closing of the Straits would result in a bloodless diplomatic coup that would buttress his power in Egypt and his standing in the Arab world. But he also feared that General 'Amer could be wrong, that Egypt's military would not be a match for Israel's. The die, however, had been cast. He could not recall his troops without losing face and jeopardizing his rule.[78]

Tragically, Nasser had miscalculated that the Israelis would suffer the closing of the Straits. The 7-mile wide waterway between Saudi Arabia and the Sinai served vital economic and psychological roles for Israel. Tankers passing through the Straits supplied Israel with Iranian oil, and the port city of Elat served as the Israeli hub for trade with Asia and Africa.

Confident that they could defeat Egypt in two days, the Israeli military refused to tolerate the Straits' closing. With Egyptian radio propaganda blaring "It is our duty to prepare for the final battle in Palestine," and worried that an Egyptian first strike would destroy Israel's nuclear weapons facility, Yitzhak Rabin, Chief of Staff of the IDF, mobilized the country's military reserves. The IDF alert was further increased on November 17, following Egyptian reconnaissance flights over Dimona. Fearing that Egypt would use diplomacy to extend the crisis and thus sap the Israeli economy, or that they would provoke Israel into a retaliatory attack to establish a rationale for bombing Dimona, Aahron Yariv, head of Israeli military intelligence, began urging that Israel take the offensive and destroy the Egyptian military. It was "Israel's fear *for* the reactor" that was "the greater catalyst for war."[79]

On May 21, having been reassured by General 'Amer that the Egyptian Army was prepared for war against Israel, Nasser formally ordered the closing of the Tiran Straits. This sparked popular demonstrations across the Arab world and two weeks of intense international diplomacy.

In Washington, Johnson and his advisors feared that if Israel retaliated against Egypt for closing the Straits, the crisis could build to a US–Soviet confrontation. Johnson was informed by the CIA that regardless of which side began the fighting, the Israelis would defeat Egypt within a week. Secretary of State Rusk informed the president that he had a choice: either "unleash" the Israelis or mediate the crisis. Johnson chose the latter.[80] As he would reiterate during the coming weeks, Johnson wrote Eshkol that he understood that Israeli "patience" was being "tried to the limits," but he warned him that there were limits to US support: "I want to emphasize strongly that you have to abstain from every step that would increase tension and violence in the area . . . the United States cannot accept any responsibility for situations that are liable to occur as a result of actions in which we are not consulted."[81]

Having been criticized for moving too quickly when he accepted Egypt's demands to withdraw UNEF observers, UN Secretary General

U Thant now bought time to negotiate a diplomatic solution to the crisis by calling for a three-week moratorium during which Egypt's blockade would not be enforced and Israel would take no military action. Nasser accepted the moratorium, repeating that Egypt had "no intention of attacking unless we are attacked . . . . We will not attack first."[82]

The Israelis initially honored the moratorium, but it was opposed by the Israeli military. General Mattityahu Peled, then a member of the Israeli Chiefs of Staff, later described the eagerness of the Israeli military—confident of its capabilities—for war. They knew that they could quickly defeat the combined Arab armies and pressed Eshkol to resist Johnson's entreaties to allow time for the US to mediate the crisis, permitting Israeli forces to go on the offensive.[83] Rabin, who was eager to destroy the Egyptian military, told his General Staff that with the closing of the Straits, Nasser had permitted "a *casus belli* [to fall] into place . . . the ball [is] now in our court." During their meetings with Eshkol, Generals Yariv, Sharon, and Weizman were unremitting in their demands for authorization to launch their offensive.

Johnson, however, used pressure on Eshkol and inducements to "manifest steady nerves." He informed Eshkol that the Soviets were willing to help the US resolve the crisis, and he demanded that Israel give the US time to explore organizing an international convoy to escort Israeli ships through the Straits. Johnson also offered Israel tens of millions of dollars of military and economic assistance if it allowed time for a diplomatic solution to be brokered.[84]

Nasser was also under pressure. Soon after his order to close the Straits, Johnson termed the blockade "illegal" and accused him of committing an "aggression" which impacted US interests negatively. If Egypt struck Israel militarily, Johnson warned, it would face the "gravest international consequences." Johnson's offer to send Vice-President Hubert Humphrey to Egypt to mediate the crisis provided Nasser little encouragement. Humphrey had described Israel as "a beacon to all people in the Middle East and elsewhere." The Kremlin also voiced serious concerns. Although the official Soviet press celebrated Egypt's remilitarization of the Sinai, Moscow was not happy with the closing of the Tiran Straits. They had not been consulted, and Nasser again was informed that the Soviets were not ready for a war with the US. Nasser was warned not to up the military ante, and to rely on diplomacy.[85]

In Washington, Israeli Foreign Minister Abba Eban reminded US officials of Dulles' 1957 pledge that the US would view a blockade of the Tiran Straits as an act of war to which Israel could respond militarily. His arguments had little impact, and he was consistently warned "not to put a match to this fuse." Eban learned that Johnson was preoccupied by the

Vietnam War and opposition to it, and that the last thing he and his advisors wanted was a second war. In his May 26 meeting with Johnson, Eban was informed that "there is no Egyptian intention to . . . attack, and if there were, Israel would win . . . it is a necessity that Israel should never make itself seem responsible in the eyes of America and the world for making war." Five times Johnson told the Israeli envoy, "*Israel will not be alone unless it decides to go it alone*."[86]

With the Straits still mine-free and Nasser signaling that his purpose was to demonstrate leadership, not to start a war, on May 27 his emissaries began meetings with the Kremlin's leaders. Premier Kosygin continued to urge caution. With US forces bogged down in Vietnam, he feared that the US might respond to the growing crisis with nuclear weapons. While reiterating his support for the Egyptians, he urged them to pursue a diplomatic compromise: "[Y]ou have made your point and won a political victory . . . . It is better to sit at the negotiating table than to wage a battle by the sword." While the Egyptians were still in Moscow, Kosygin received an urgent message from the White House which was crafted to underline the seriousness of the crisis and to put the Soviets and Egyptians on notice that Egypt should not launch a preemptive attack against Israel.

The Israeli and Egyptian delegations returned home to accelerating preparations for war. On May 27, as the Israeli War Cabinet met to consider Eban's report, Eshkol was again forcefully challenged with arguments that if Israel waited for Egypt to strike first, Dimona would be destroyed and "Nasser could portray himself as the hero who saved the Middle East from nuclear weapons," that Israel was in danger of becoming a US protectorate, and that if Israel waited, King Hussein might fall to Nasser. But the Cabinet's divisions were reinforced by two messages from President Johnson. One reiterated his intention to use "any and all measures in his power" to end the blockade; the second warned that "It is essential that Israel not take any preemptive military action and thereby make itself responsible for the initiation of hostilities . . . . Preemptive action by Israel would make it impossible for the friends of Israel to stand at your side." Later that day, in response to an appeal from U Thant for all parties to the crisis to "exercise special restraint," the Israelis announced that they would demobilize 40,000 reservists, but no action was taken to implement this. Nasser was thus lulled into the belief that he had won time to consider his options.[87]

With the Israeli public increasingly frightened that the Arab states would soon launch a war to destroy Israel, and with widespread concern that Eshkol could not fulfill his dual roles of prime minister and defense minister, his military commanders pressed for change within the Israeli government. They were unremitting, insisting that "the honor of the army of Israel had been sullied" and challenged Eshkol and his Cabinet with reports that Israeli intelligence was "predicting a surprise attack on Dimona and Israeli airfields, an onslaught of missiles, poison gas, and even primitive radioactive devices." Johnson, they said, had failed to break the blockade and would not intervene. No one came to the prime minister's defense, and he conceded by appointing the war hero and former commander-in-chief, Moshe Dayan, as the new defense minister.[88]

Despite Johnson's continued efforts to find a diplomatic solution, it was no longer possible. Dayan was set on war and was reinforced by reports from the Israeli Ambassador in Washington that Johnson had denied that he had committed to use "all and every measure" to end the blockade.

On June 4, Dayan received Eshkol's authorization to attack. The goal would be to seize as much Egyptian territory as possible for use as a bargaining chip in future negotiations, before international pressures forced a ceasefire. After Egypt was defeated, the IDF would turn its offensive against Jordan and Syria.[89]

The Egyptian military was not prepared for the Israeli onslaught. It was already exhausted and depleted, and its leaders and air defenses ill prepared. On the eve of the Israeli offensive, Field Marshal 'Amer had partied through the night, and had ordered Egyptian air defenses to stand down to ensure that they didn't accidentally shoot down his plane when he visited forces on the Sinai the following day. The Air Force commander spent the night at his daughter's wedding. And, "[t]he commander of the Sinai front wasn't in place and the army's commander wasn't in place, and neither were their subordinates." No one knew where to find President Nasser.[90]

On the morning of June 5, Israeli bombers began their devastating attacks. In simultaneous waves, they trapped the Egyptian warplanes and fighters on the ground, first destroying runways, then returning to eliminate the immobilized aircraft. In the first half hour, 204 Egyptian planes, half the country's air force, were destroyed. An hour later Rabin was informed that "The Egyptian Air Force has ceased to exist." This was followed immediately by an armored Israeli offensive launched along the eastern frontier of the Sinai which thoroughly routed the Egyptians, fighting its way across the Peninsula to the Suez Canal in three days.[91]

With his generals afraid to inform him of their staggering losses, Nasser initially believed 'Amer's claims that Egyptian forces had inflicted "crippling Israeli casualties" and were going on the offensive. This message was broadcast across Egypt and the Arab world, leading King Hussein to enter the war. Jordanian forces began shelling West Jerusalem and moved to isolate Israeli sites above East Jerusalem. Dayan responded by improvising on his war plan, ordering the destruction of the Jordanian Air Force and opening the battle for the Old City of Jerusalem.[92]

Syria did little better than its allies. Damascus' war plans called for air attacks against Israeli forces, bombarding settlements below the Golan Heights, and a massive armored and infantry *blitzkrieg* to conquer Haifa and the Galilee. The Syrian military proved little better prepared than Nasser's. Political purges had depleted its officer corps; its modern Soviet tanks and artillery pieces were in disrepair; and the air assault never got off the ground. Damascus' air bases and most of its planes were quickly destroyed and Syrian forces could not find their way to the jumping-off point for the *blitzkrieg*. The shelling of Israeli settlements, however, took a heavy toll on Israeli lives and infrastructure, which in turn generated popular and military pressure within Israel to conquer the Golan Heights.[93]

As Dayan had anticipated, both Johnson and the Soviets moved to halt the fighting as quickly as possible. Within hours of the first Israeli attacks, Kosygin was on the hotline, urging Johnson to join him in working to impose a ceasefire. Rusk responded that the US would "exercise all our influence to bring hostilities to an end" and pointed to the UN Security Council as the forum for negotiating the terms of a ceasefire.

That night's Security Council session did not go well. The Israeli Ambassador's instructions were to prevent adoption of a ceasefire resolution for as long as possible to allow time for the IDF to expand its conquests. He was inadvertently assisted by the Egyptian Ambassador, who had been seduced by 'Amer's propaganda accounts of Cairo's powerful counter-offensive. And, despite instructions from Moscow, the doctrinaire Soviet Ambassador was in no hurry to impose a ceasefire on his Egyptian allies.[94]

As the war's first day came to a close, Walt Rostow, President Johnson's Special Assistant for National Security Affairs, forwarded reports of the day's fighting to the president with the message: "Herewith the account, with a map, of the first day's turkey shoot."[95]

Day two of the war, June 6, spelled further disaster for the Egyptians, Palestinians, and Jordanians. Fearing that their situation was worse than it actually was, the Egyptian legions in the Sinai were ordered to begin what became "a wholesale and wildly disorganized retreat." Chaos and disaster soon prevailed as the desert's few roads were clogged to the point of being impassable, and thousands of trucks and tanks and tens of thousands of soldiers competed in the race to escape Israel's advancing columns and warplanes. On the eastern front, all of East Jerusalem, except the encircled Old City, was captured, while the Jordanian army and thousands of Palestinians were driven from the West Bank.[96]

Nasser refused to concede defeat. Instead, he cabled Kosygin that the Sixth Fleet, "together with U.S. bases in the region," were supporting the Israelis, and he urged the Soviets to replenish his air force and to provide additional assistance to avoid an Arab defeat.[97] Nasser's hope of being saved by the Soviets or by the "Arab masses" made matters worse by providing the Israelis time to expand and consolidate their conquests. When the Security Council met that night, the Soviet Ambassador was under orders to support a simple ceasefire, and the Council adopted a US call for an end to the blockade, for talks on separation of forces, and for "certain 'territorial changes.'" Israel, claiming to be fighting a defensive war, had little choice but to agree in principle. The Egyptian Ambassador, however, rejected it, giving Dayan still more time to occupy the Old City of Jerusalem and the Golan Heights, setting the stage for a US–Soviet confrontation.[98]

In addition to its territorial ambitions and Egyptian and Syrian intransigence, a third factor encouraged the Israelis to continue pressing home their advantage: US public opinion. Most people in the US believed the Soviets had engineered the war to alleviate pressure on Communist forces in Vietnam.[99] On June 7, day three of the war, Israeli forces captured Sharm El Sheikh, overlooking the Tiran Straits, and by the end of the day were within striking distance of the Suez Canal. On the eastern front, Israeli forces consolidated their conquest of the West Bank and ecstatically captured the historic Old City of Jerusalem from the tiny remnant of Jordanian forces left to defend it. These Israeli gains came with immediate, as well as long-term, risks. As the scale of the defeat of their Arab allies became apparent, and with Nasser publicly charging Soviet complicity in Israeli victories, the Kremlin became more aggressive in confronting Tel Aviv and Washington in order to salvage what it could of its reputation. Eshkol and Johnson were informed that if Israel did not immediately comply with the ceasefire resolution, the Kremlin would "review" its relations with Israel and take "other necessary steps."

Neither Tel Aviv nor Washington was initially impressed by such threats. Israeli troops reached the Suez as the disintegrating Egyptian army continued its desperate and chaotic flight. In the Gaza Strip, Jerusalem, and the West Bank, Palestinians were reeling under the assaults and shocks of the first days of the Israeli occupation. And, with Israeli settlements below the Golan Heights being systematically destroyed by Syrian artillery, popular Israeli demands to drive the Syrians from the Heights received a powerful boost from what was seen as a green light from Washington. Bundy was quoted as saying that he thought it strange that the Syrians, having sparked the war and caused so much suffering, had gone unpunished.[100]

Day five spelled more disaster for the Egyptians and Syrians. Cairo was traumatized by the scenes of its decimated army staggering—and in some cases literally swimming—across the Nile. Up to 15,000 Egyptian soldiers were dead; thousands more were wounded, and 5,000 had been taken prisoner, with an equal number missing. In the face of the undeniable scale of the disaster, Nasser resigned, condemning the "forces of imperialism" and urging the Egyptian people never to submit. His resignation proved short-lived and was withdrawn when hundreds of thousands of Cairenes poured into the streets, distraught that they would be losing their powerful, if flawed, leader.

On the northern front, the Israelis launched their battle for the Golan. Syrian resistance was stiff, but with no major obstacles lying between the advancing Israeli forces and Damascus only 30 miles away, Syria's leaders feared the Israelis would soon occupy their capital. In panic, they turned to Moscow, appealing for the UN to impose an unconditional ceasefire. Again Moscow's UN Ambassador misplayed his hand by demanding that the second ceasefire resolution condemn Israel and order its forces back to the 1948 Armistice lines. The US balked, and Israel had another 24 hours to complete its conquest of the Golan.

The sixth and final day of the war held greatest potential for catastrophe. Even before the Syrian military began the day by retreating *en masse* from the Golan Heights, Kosygin sent a dire message to Washington via the hot-line: "A very crucial moment has now arrived which forces us, if military actions arc not stopped in the next few hours, to adopt an independent position . . . these actions may bring us into a clash which will lead to a grave catastrophe." Kosygin demanded that the US force the Israelis to accept an unconditional ceasefire. If not, Moscow would take "necessary actions, including military." Kosygin's threat was reinforced by another from the KGB: the Soviets were prepared "to violate Turkish, Iranian, and Greek air space in order to fly troops into the region." These warnings were received in Washington with "great concern and utmost gravity."[101]

Johnson responded that the US was encouraging Israel to comply with the ceasefire, and that it expected Israel would do so. At McNamara's urging, Johnson sent Moscow a second message with the Sixth Fleet: Moscow would not be permitted to intervene. As Johnson, McNamara, and Ambassador Thompson considered what could be done other than reaffirm support for a ceasefire, McNamara suggested that "[W]e make it clear . . . that we don't intend to take this lying down." The Sixth Fleet and its two nuclear-armed aircraft carriers, he urged, should be dispatched to the eastern Mediterranean. With Thompson confirming that this would get the message "to Moscow in a hurry," Johnson ordered the deployment. As he would later write, Johnson understood "that message, which no translator would need to interpret to the Kremlin leadership, was that the United States was prepared to resist Soviet intrusion in the Middle East."[102]

Johnson's concern was not limited to Moscow. His message to Prime Minister Eshkol was blunt: Israel had to "prove its acceptance of the ceasefire on the ground before the Security Council meets this afternoon, otherwise it will jeopardize its gains on all other fronts." This was reinforced by a message from the State Department: "[T]he United States government does not want the war to end as the result of a Soviet ultimatum. This would be disastrous for the future not only of Israel, but of us all. It is your responsibility to act now . . ." Eshkol and Dayan got the message. By that evening the conquest of the Golan had been completed and Israeli guns fell silent.[103] As news of the Israeli implementation of the ceasefire spread, the US–Soviet confrontation dissipated. Only a few among the US and Soviet elites knew that the war had ended with a nuclear threat.

"BLACK SEPTEMBER"

Three years later, Richard Nixon's "Black September" nuclear threat resulted from his inability to distinguish indigenous threats to the Middle East status quo from his obsession with the Soviet Union. As Seymour Hersh put it, his administration believed that there were Russians "behind every sand dune."[104]

The Hashemite Kingdom of Jordan was carved by the British from the Mandate of Palestine in 1922 and was never a model of political stability. This was particularly true in 1970. Palestinian refugees, seeking safe haven during and after Israel's conquest of the West Bank, had fled there, swelling the Palestinian "state within a state." King Hussein had been unable to prevent competing *fedayeen* forces from using Jordan as a base for guerrilla raids against Israel. The King was a loyal ally of the US and, as Nasser had charged, received regular gratuities from the CIA, beginning in 1956.[105] Although support from the US was significant, his power was ultimately based on the intense loyalty of his army, comprised principally of Bedouin troops.

On coming to power in 1969, Nixon and Kissinger framed their Middle East policies in Cold War terms. The next Middle East war would, they feared, lead to another nuclear confrontation in which the unthinkable would be the likely outcome. "If the Arabs were to lose again, the Soviets might feel obliged to intervene; if the Israelis were under severe military pressure, the Americans could not stand aside. The intervention by one superpower would almost automatically trigger a reaction from the other." To promote US interests in the region, to avoid the dangers of a regional war, and as an expression of the Nixon Doctrine, they concluded that the "military balance . . . must be maintained in Israel's favor."[106] They were not, however, entirely committed to the status quo.

The Jordanian civil war in 1970 was precipitated by the Popular Front for the Liberation of Palestine (PFLP), which was frustrated by the agreement ending the Israeli–Egyptian "war of attrition," the ongoing artillery duel across the Suez that followed Israel's 1967 conquest of the Sinai Peninsula. The PFLP was anxious to revive the Arab world's—and particularly Jordan's—confrontation with Israel by engineering a crisis. Toward that end, in early September, PFLP guerrillas hijacked four airliners taking nearly 500 passengers and crew (most of them American) hostage. Three planes and most of the captives were taken to a remote airfield in Jordan.

On September 12, having released most of the hostages in response to rumors that US troops had been ordered to move against them, the PFLP destroyed the airliners on the ground. A brief lull followed, during which King Hussein consulted Nasser and then moved to end the confrontation with an unexpected climax. As part of his preparations, the King informed Nixon that he planned to appoint a military government which would launch a civil war designed to destroy the power of the PLO, then controlled by Arafat's *al Fatah*.[107]

Nixon and Kissinger reaffirmed their support for the King, but they feared that behind the Palestinians lay the Syrians, and behind the Syrians lay Moscow, and that all were committed to overthrowing Hussein. It was this fear that led Nixon to envision a "ghastly game of dominoes with a nuclear war waiting at the end." If Hussein were overthrown, Nixon feared that Israel would attack "a Syrian-dominated radical government in Jordan, resulting in a renewed regional war followed by Soviet intervention and a U.S.-Soviet confrontation."[108]

King Hussein initiated the war in Amman on September 17, and fighting soon spread to northern Jordan. Syria's divided government responded by moving tanks to the border. It was at this point that Nixon, preoccupied with election campaigning, and Kissinger, whose energies were focused on Vietnam and planning for a coup in Chile, warned Damascus, Moscow, and Tel Aviv to keep their distance. Communicating through the press, Nixon warned that if Syrian tanks invaded Jordan, only Israel and the US could stop them, and he preferred that the US do it alone. Briefly setting aside the Nixon Doctrine and replacing it with his "Madman" approach, Nixon confided to journalists that it might be helpful if the Soviets remembered that he was "capable of irrational or unpredictable action."[109]

In Washington, unencoded orders were transmitted to ensure that the Soviets were aware of the US mobilizations that were to follow. Paratroopers in Europe were placed on alert, as was the 82nd Airborne Division. The Sixth Fleet, with its nuclear arsenal and 1,200 Marines, was deployed to the eastern Mediterranean.[110]

Unlike in 1967, when they had shadowed the Sixth Fleet, Soviet warships gave the Sixth Fleet a wide berth as it assembled off the Lebanese coast.[111]

The crisis continued for nearly a week. Syrian tanks, hastily painted with Palestinian colors, briefly crossed the border into northern Jordan. Israeli forces, at Kissinger's instigation, were then massed along the Jordanian border and the Golan Heights. On September 23, under Soviet pressure, Syrian tanks rolled back toward Damascus.[112] The PLO was forced to accept its defeat and expulsion from Jordan. Nixon and Kissinger exulted in their victory, still believing that the Soviets, not the Israeli–Palestinian–Arab conflict, were the primary source of Middle East turmoil.

OCTOBER 1973—KISSINGER'S NUCLEAR BRINKMANSHIP

On October 6, 1973, heavy concentrations of Egyptian and Syrian aircraft simultaneously attacked Israeli positions in the Sinai Peninsula and the Golan Heights. Soon Egyptian troops were crossing the Suez, a feat Israelis thought was impossible because of their fortifications, which included rigging the Canal with oil pipes that could transform it into "a murderous mass of fire."[113] Egypt, thought by the Israelis to be a "dead body," had risen with a vengeance. In Israel and in much of the US, it was widely believed that "the Arabs" were again attempting to destroy Israel and to "drive the Jews into the sea." In reality, as President Sadat announced early in the war, Egyptian and Syrian war aims were limited to breaking the diplomatic deadlock that had persisted since their 1967 defeat.

Nasser had died shortly after helping to mediate the "Black September" crisis and was succeeded by General Anwar Sadat, who moved quickly and radically to alter Egypt's approach to the Israeli–Arab–Palestinian conflict. In early 1971, he responded positively to UN mediator Gunnar Jarring's inquiries about how to proceed diplomatically, while Israel refused to return to the pre-1967 war boundaries as mandated by UN Resolution 242.[114] Sadat had also launched a diplomatic initiative of his own, offering an interim agreement providing for partial Israeli withdrawal from the Sinai Peninsula in exchange for Egypt reopening the Suez Canal.

The diplomatic ground for Sadat's initiatives was less than fertile. After the Six-Day War, Israeli leaders believed they could ignore the Egyptian corpse for the next 50 years. In Washington, Johnson had adopted a policy that placed greater demands on Arab states than did UN Resolution 242: before the US would press Israel to negotiate, Egypt and other Arab countries had to recognize Israel's "right of national life." There would be justice for Palestinian refugees—not self-determination, free maritime passage, limits on the arms race, and "independence and territorial integrity" for all states in the region.[115]

Nixon and Kissinger built on Johnson's policy and, consistent with "Political Axiom Number One," worked to purge Soviet influence from the Middle East. Given Israel's Nixon Doctrine role, the US administration was in no hurry to press for a comprehensive settlement of the Israeli–Palestinian–Arab conflict or to challenge Israel's increasingly harsh military colonization of East Jerusalem, the West Bank, the Gaza Strip, and Golan Heights. During his first term, Nixon joined Israel in rejecting Sadat's diplomatic initiatives. The joint US–Israeli policy was "to let Sadat sweat it out . . . until he had little choice but to sue for peace on Israel's terms."[116]

The "no peace, no war," deadlock was untenable for the Egyptians economically, politically, and in terms of national self-respect. Rather than capitulate, Sadat opted to restructure the prevailing imbalance of power as a means to break the diplomatic deadlock. He believed that Washington held "ninety-nine percent of the cards," and he structured his approach accordingly. In August 1972, with Moscow refusing to sell Egypt the weapons Sadat believed he needed, he took the radical action of expelling Soviet advisors. Kissinger and Nixon were not impressed and rewarded Sadat with little more than a back channel of dubious value for communication with the Secretary of State.[117]

In September 1973, Sadat unexpectedly convened the Egyptian National Defense Council. There, at his request, General Ahmad Isma'il briefed government leadership about the planned Egyptian–Syrian offensive, which would "pressure Israel into accepting the conditions for a peaceful solution." Because "reinforcements and supplies from the Soviet Union were limited," the Egyptian plan was to reconquer the whole of Sinai. "[I]t would be a long war" and Sadat anticipated heavy losses, but Israel "would suffer even greater losses." He planned to shock the superpowers into taking responsibility for negotiating a comprehensive settlement between Israel and its Arab neighbors.[118]

Once the war began, Nixon was marginal to US decision-making and diplomacy. When Egyptian forces began pouring across the Suez, he was in Florida, agonizing over how to respond to legal demands that he surrender Watergate-related tape-recordings. During the three-week war, Vice-President Spiro Agnew was forced to resign, Gerald Ford was appointed as his successor, and Nixon escalated the constitutional crisis by firing the Attorney General and Special Prosecutor in the "Saturday Night Massacre." Although Kissinger had to deal with rivals in the Pentagon who, unlike him, had closer ties to the oil industry than to Israel, he had a relatively free hand in framing US policy. This was kept secret to protect Nixon's waning reputation, but as the war moved to the end-game and a nuclear confrontation, Kremlin proposals and ultimatums were addressed to the Secretary of State, not to the inebriated president.[119]

Kissinger approached the war preoccupied, as always, with the Soviet Union. Consistent with his pursuit of détente and reliance on "linkages," on October 6 he promised Soviet Ambassador Dobrynin that the White House would continue to press for congressional support of most-favored-nation trade status for Moscow if it "showed restraint" during the war. Brezhnev responded quickly that Moscow would "act in cooperation with you," a formula designed to maintain or augment Soviet regional influence. In the war's first days, Kissinger assumed that Israel would quickly regain the offensive, and he worked to delay calls for a ceasefire until the Israeli army retook its pre-war positions. If Israel "came out a little ahead but got bloodied in the process, and if the US stayed clean" in terms of Arab perceptions of Washington, Kissinger believed that US influence in the Middle East would be greatly augmented, with the Soviets further marginalized.[120]

Kissinger's Defcon 3 alert on the night of October 24–25 was not the first or only nuclear threat of the war. On October 9, Prime Minister Golda Meir placed Israeli military forces on a nuclear alert which continued secretly until October 16.[121]

The previous night, with Israeli forces still on the defensive, Meir convened her "Kitchen Cabinet" for an all-night meeting. Fearful that Israel might succumb to the Egyptian and Syrian offensives, they made three critical decisions: Israeli forces would be rallied for a major counterattack; the Israeli nuclear arsenal (the "Temple weapons") would be armed and targeted against the possibility of continuing military defeats; and Israel would notify Washington of its nuclear preparations and reiterate demands for the urgent resupply of weapons and munitions. Israel's nuclear-capable Jericho missiles were armed, as were eight US-supplied F-4 aircraft, with Egyptian and Syrian military headquarters as their targets.

The Israeli leaders assumed that Soviet agents in Israel would inform Moscow of the nuclear alert, and that the Soviets in turn would press Egypt and Syria not to advance beyond the 1967 pre-war boundaries. Meir's advisors also assumed that this "drastic step would force the United States to begin [the] immediate and massive resupply of the Israeli military" that had been requested, promised, and repeatedly delayed.[122]

Although the Israeli nuclear threat had little apparent effect on Egyptian and Syrian decision-making, this was not the case in Washington. Israeli Ambassador Simcha Dinitz met with Kissinger in the early hours of October 9, exhorting him to provide new weapons and resupply Israel's diminishing reserve of munitions. Given the disparity of Israeli and Arab manpower, Kissinger was told that Israel would have to "do something decisive." He was also informed that Meir was willing to come to Washington secretly for a one-hour meeting with the president, an offer that Kissinger interpreted as "either hysteria or blackmail." Kissinger ended the meeting with assurances that the US would replace all Israeli war matériel consumed during the war, assuming that this would provide Israel the confidence to move to the offensive.[123]

The war matériel did not flow as quickly as Kissinger anticipated. He did not want it carried by US aircraft, lest it further alienate the Arab states. The Pentagon created obstacles by preventing Israeli transports from landing at US supply bases, and charter airlines prevaricated in the face of the risks of flying weapons into a war zone. Meir again rattled her nuclear sabers. "Israel," she wrote Kissinger, "had suffered very heavy casualties and its resources were running very low . . . . If the United States did not begin immediately to resupply it on a massive scale, it *might soon be forced to use every means at its disposal* to ensure its national survival."[124] Meir's appeal and threat lit a fire under Kissinger and the Pentagon. In response to Kissinger's frantic demands, the obstacles to resupplying Israel were quickly dismantled. And, in spite of Kissinger's concerns about alienating the Arab world, Secretary of Defense Schlesinger ordered US warplanes to airlift 80 tons of weaponry and munitions directly to Israel.

William Quandt, Director of Middle East Affairs in Jimmy Carter's National Security Council, later wrote that Kissinger responded out of fear that Israel might use its nuclear weapons: "[W]e knew that a desperate Israel might activate its nuclear option. This situation by itself, created a kind of blackmail potential . . . . But no one had to say it." Herman Eilts, US Ambassador to Egypt, also confirmed that, for Kissinger, "there was concern that the Israelis might go nuclear. There had been intimations that if they didn't get military equipment and quickly, they might go nuclear." During his postwar shuttle diplomacy, Kissinger told Sadat that the US airlift to Israel had been initiated to prevent escalation to nuclear war. Sadat quoted Kissinger as telling him that the Israelis had three nuclear warheads which they were prepared to use, and that "It was serious, more serious than you can imagine."[125]

The war's second nuclear threat came on the night of October 24–25, well *after* the tide of battle had turned, and resulted in large measure from Kissinger's manipulative dishonesty.

Within a week of the US airlift, Israeli forces crossed to the western shore of the Suez, threatening to surround and isolate 25,000 Egyptian Third Army troops in the desert. It was at this point that Kissinger traveled to Moscow, at Soviet urging, to begin ceasefire negotiations.[126]

Without consulting the Israelis, Kissinger and the Soviets quickly reached an agreement. A ceasefire would be imposed by the UN Security Council. Reference would be made to Resolution 242, although no specific demands would be made for Israel to withdraw from Arab territory. At the behest of the superpowers, negotiations "between the parties concerned" would be urged.

En route to Israel to apprise its leaders of the agreement, Kissinger anticipated that he would be met by Meir's rage. Israeli army commanders had been pressing her to postpone a ceasefire until the Third Army was fully encircled. Their arguments were received sympathetically, given Israeli eagerness to gain strategic advantages for postwar negotiations. As Kissinger labored to persuade the Israelis to accept the US–Soviet agreement, he reminded Meir that "in Vietnam the cease-fire didn't go into effect at the exact time it was agreed on." Some "slippage" in implementing the ceasefire was possible.[127]

Not surprisingly, there was "slippage" on the Sinai Peninsula. As UN Security Council Resolution 338 was scheduled to go into effect, Israel renewed its offensive, completing the encirclement of the Third Army. Predictably, Egyptian and Soviet leaders protested bitterly, believing that Kissinger had deceived them to buy time for Israel. Kissinger in turn tried to appease Brezhnev and Sadat by joining in a renewed UN call for a ceasefire requiring the warring parties to return to their positions of October 21. When Meir threatened continued non-cooperation, Kissinger pacified her by asking, "How can anyone ever know where a line is or was in the desert?"[128]

On October 24, when the ceasefire was supposed to be in force, the Egyptians reported renewed Israeli attacks. Soviet leaders responded by warning Israel that it faced "the gravest consequences" if it failed to halt its siege of the Third Army. Simultaneously, US intelligence detected Soviet airborne divisions being placed on alert—an indication that the Soviets might intervene. Sadat, with his military forces facing the possibility of annihilation by thirst and starvation, was desperate. Privately, he urged Kissinger to dispatch troops to protect his forces. When there was no response, he called publicly for US *and Soviet* forces to enforce the ceasefire.

Kissinger and Brezhnev had created a situation in which they had little room for maneuver. As Kissinger perceived it, "If the United States held still while the Egyptian army was being destroyed after an American-sponsored ceasefire and a Secretary of State's visit to Israel, not even the most moderate Arab could cooperate with us any longer." He also faced political constraints as Meir charged US "collusion" with Cairo and Moscow, while Senators Jackson and Javits claimed that Kissinger had sacrificed Israel's needs for the imperatives of détente. Sadat's appeal also placed Soviet leaders in a difficult situation: "Their credibility was on the line: with the Egyptians . . . with the Syrians, who had not yet accepted the cease-fire; and indeed, with all the Arabs. The Soviets were not pursuing a forward diplomatic strategy, they were simply trying to hold on."[129]

The crisis climaxed on the night of October 24–25. That evening, Dobrynin informed Kissinger that his government would endorse a UN resolution calling for the dispatch of US and Soviet troops to enforce the ceasefire. Kissinger responded that the US would veto such a resolution, to which Dobrynin replied that minds in Moscow "had probably been made up." He was correct. At 9:30 p.m. he phoned with a message from Brezhnev: "If you find it impossible to act jointly with us in this matter, we would be faced with the necessity urgently to consider the question of taking appropriate steps unilaterally."[130]

Kissinger interpreted Brezhnev's response as "an ultimatum" challenging US hegemony in the geopolitical center of the struggle for world power. He later wrote,

> We had not worked for years to reduce the Soviet military presence in Egypt only to cooperate in reintroducing it as the result of a UN resolution. Nor would we participate in a joint force with the Soviets which would legitimize their role in the area . . . . we were determined to resist by force if necessary the introduction of Soviet troops into the Middle East . . . .

He concluded that the only way to ensure that Soviet forces did not return to Egypt was to "shock the Soviets into abandoning the unilateral move they were threatening . . . "[131]

With Nixon's Chief of Staff Alexander Haig advising Kissinger that the president was "too distraught" to be consulted, Kissinger convened a rump session of the National Security Council. He was joined by Secretary of Defense James Schlesinger, CIA director William Colby, and Joint Chiefs Chairman, Thomas Moorer. They made three important decisions: 1) Urge Sadat to withdraw his request for US and Soviet forces and encourage him to call, instead, for UN peacekeeping forces. By definition this would exclude the superpowers. 2) Dispatch a message to Brezhnev informing him that the US "could in no event accept unilateral action . . . . such action *would produce incalculable consequences* which would be in the interest of neither of our countries and which would end all we have striven so hard to achieve." 3) Demonstrate the meaning of "incalculable consequences" by placing US nuclear forces and troops across the globe on nuclear alert.[132]

The alert included the Strategic Air Command, the North American Air Defense Command and field commands. The aircraft carrier *Franklin Delano Roosevelt* and its support squadron were redeployed from the Straits of Gibraltar to the eastern Mediterranean where they joined the *Independence* and other nuclear-armed warships. The aircraft carrier *John F. Kennedy* and its escorts were also ordered to the Mediterranean. Sixty B-52s were moved from Guam to the US to join the SAC alert, and the 82nd Airborne Division was placed on alert, as were other US-based units.[133]

Kissinger's diplomatic *démarches* and his nuclear threats achieved their aims. On the morning of October 25, Kissinger was informed that Egypt would withdraw its earlier request and instead call for the UN to send an international force. Brezhnev responded by supporting the revised Egyptian call and communicated his hopes for continued US–Soviet cooperation. UN Security Council Resolution 340 was adopted. This no longer urged, but now demanded, that Israelis and Egyptians return to their positions of October 22.[134] Although the confrontation in the Sinai continued for several more days, the US nuclear alert ended the following day.

Kissinger continued to press the Israelis to break the siege, but to little avail. Finally, it was Sadat who ended the impasse by agreeing to initiate direct Egyptian–Israeli military talks, provided that a supply convoy was first allowed through the Israeli siege to save the Third Army. The Israelis agreed, and General Abdel Gamasy and Major General Ahron Yhariv quickly met to negotiate disengagement terms.[135]

The October War, caused largely by US diplomatic intransigence designed to preserve an unjust status quo in the Middle East, brought the world to the brink of nuclear cataclysm twice within a two-week period. By risking escalation to "general war," which would have dwarfed the unimaginable destruction of Hiroshima and Nagasaki, Kissinger achieved his imperial objectives: the Soviet Union was further marginalized in the Middle East; Egypt was moved into the US sphere and soon integrated into the Nixon Doctrine; and, diplomatic and strategic frameworks for managing the Israeli–Palestinian–Arab conflict in ways that were consistent with US and Israeli objectives had thus been created.

The war and its role in deepening US regional hegemony came as no surprise to Kissinger and other senior figures in the Nixon administration. As both an NSA official and an anonymous Rand analyst have since explained, "We knew [the October 6 Egyptian–Syrian attack] was coming. We knew when. We knew where. We were told to shut up and let it happen." The Rand researcher had advised that the surprise attack on a Jewish holiday would not give the Egyptians and Syrians the advantage they anticipated, because Israel's military reservists would be at home and more easily mobilized.[136]

THE CARTER DOCTRINE

Now widely thought of as a relatively inoffensive era of US foreign and military policies, the realities of the Carter years (1976–80) were not in fact benign. Rising to power with the assistance of the Trilateral Commission[137] in the wake of the Vietnam War and the Watergate crisis, the Christian peanut farmer, Georgia governor, and former nuclear submarine commander helped the US people feel that they had returned to a more compassionate and democratic era. He took important steps toward institutionalizing US human rights commitments. He tilted tax laws to encourage energy conservation and conversion to renewable sources of energy. He turned back Pentagon and corporate efforts to build costly B-1 bombers. And, in what seemed to be the continuation of détente, his administration negotiated SALT II (the second Strategic Arms Limitation Treaty) with the Soviet Union.

At the same time, the demands of empire and pressures from Republicans and from the right wing of his own party dictated that other, less benevolent, political traditions be reinforced. Thus, despite his election campaign remarks about the hypocrisy inherent in the nation's nuclear nonproliferation policies that committed the US to nuclear dominance while denying other countries access to nuclear weapons, the Carter years witnessed US research for the development of a neutron bomb that could kill millions while not destroying property. It was during the Carter era that the US moved to deploy nuclear-armed cruise missiles and doubled the number of nuclear warheads targeted against the Soviet Union. It was Carter, too, who encouraged the brutal Contras in Nicaragua and the Salvadoran military with military and economic assistance.

Structurally, the greatest challenge to US global power during the Carter years came with the Islamic revolution in Iran, which shattered the Nixon Doctrine as the Shah was replaced by a clerical regime. The response was the Carter Doctrine, which explicitly reaffirmed the US commitment to use "*any means necessary*" to maintain its Middle East dominance. This policy was reinforced by Presidential Directive 59, which moved US nuclear war-fighting doctrine from mutual assured destruction to "flexible" and more "limited" nuclear war fighting.[138]

The US military presence, including bases in and surrounding the Persian Gulf, was deeply entrenched. By 1950, the US was not only committed to defending the Saudi monarchy and "one of the greatest material prizes in world history," but was well on the way to building a regional network of military bases to enforce its commitments. When, in 1967, Britain announced its military withdrawal from east of Suez, the US moved to fill the anticipated military vacuum by constructing air and naval bases on the Indian Ocean island of Diego Garcia, and as part of the Nixon Doctrine, the Shah was promoted to become Washington's regional enforcer, along with Israel.[139] To assist him in that role, the Shah was extended the privilege of being allowed to purchase more than $10 billion ($40 billion in 2005 dollars) worth of the world's most sophisticated and deadly weapons.

Successive presidents relied on the Shah to defend US interests as oil continued to increase in economic and strategic importance. Throughout the 1970s, the Gulf region was the source of 60 percent of the world's known reserves. Oil revenues permitted the Middle East to become a vital export market for US manufacturers, and billions of "petrodollars" were reinvested in US banks and businesses, reinforcing the US economy and Washington's global dominance. Many strategic analysts came to believe that the Middle East was as important to US global power as were Europe and East Asia, with some arguing that the region was more important. Without the US hand on the Middle East oil taps, they argued, Western Europe and East Asia would become increasingly independent.[140]

The overthrow of the Shah in December 1978 and the subsequent "hostage crisis," in which 52 US citizens and officials were held captive by Iranian revolutionaries for more than a year, removed Iran as the eastern pillar of the Nixon Doctrine. Fear that the Soviet Union would intervene to fill the resulting military vacuum propelled the Carter administration to respond militarily. Twenty-five warships were dispatched to the Persian Gulf, including three nuclear-armed aircraft carriers and 1,800 Marines. Despite Iranian hostility to the US, plans were developed to defend Iran against a potential Soviet invasion, a scenario that would reestablish US dominance over the country.

Anxiety in Washington escalated to hysteria when Soviet forces invaded Afghanistan in late 1979, although Afghanistan's mountainous terrain precluded it from serving as an invasion route between Moscow and Teheran. Carter's National Security Advisor Zbigniew Brzezinksi understood that Moscow had fallen into a US trap, and that a "third front" of the US–Soviet confrontation had been joined. Even as Brzezinski hoped that Afghanistan would prove to be Moscow's Vietnam, the president moved to proclaim the Carter Doctrine in his 1980 State of the Union address: "Any attempt by an outside force to gain control of the Persian Gulf region will be regarded as an assault on the interests of the United States and will be repelled by the use of *any means necessary* . . ."[141] The imperial "prize" was not to be threatened.

In addition to its futile effort to functionally annex the Persian Gulf as the sixth US Great Lake, there were other major faults with the Carter Doctrine. Even with the decision to deploy Pershing II and cruise missiles in Western Europe, Washington's ability to recreate first-strike nuclear forces that would allow it to break out of MAD and to threaten the Soviet Union with "any means necessary" was doubtful. Also, as illustrated by the overthrow of the Shah, the takeover of the Grand Mosque in Mecca by religious extremists in November 1979, and the continuing turmoil of the Israeli–Arab–Palestinian conflict, the principal threats to US Middle East hegemony were indigenous and had little to do with the Soviet Union.

The Carter Doctrine was, of course, dual-capable, providing the rationale for a military build-up that could be used against the nations and peoples of the Middle East as well as against the USSR. As his doctrine replaced Nixon's, Carter pressed for the creation of a Rapid Deployment Force (RDF) to speed projection of US military power into the Gulf region in times of crisis. To reinforce the RDF, new basing agreements were negotiated with Oman, Somalia, and Kenya. And, to avoid the appearance of recolonization, the Carter and Reagan administrations secured political agreements from friendly regimes guaranteeing the US access to bases in their countries. The model for these agreements was Saudi Arabia, where "Saudi" bases had been built to US specifications under the supervision of the US Army Corps of Engineers, and stocked with pre-positioned US weapons and munitions.[142]

The Reagan administration built on the Carter Doctrine. The Pentagon's mid-1980s formulation of US military priorities placed maintaining influence in the Middle East second only to Western Europe: "Our principal objectives are to assure continued access to Persian Gulf oil and to prevent the Soviets from acquiring political-military control of the oil directly or through proxies . . . . we should be prepared to introduce American forces directly into the region should it appear that the security of access to Persian Gulf oil is threatened."[143]

To this end, nuclear-armed cruise missiles were deployed in Comiso, Italy, whence they could strike targets across the Middle East and North Africa. One billion dollars were allocated to modernize military bases in a dozen Middle East countries, in southwest Asia, and in North Africa. The RDF was renamed the "Central Command" and was assigned responsibility for US military operations from North Africa to Central Asia, giving the Middle East equal status in the Pentagon with Europe and East Asia.[144]

One aspect of the Central Command was given little publicity: it was armed and routinely trained to fight with tactical nuclear weapons. As one embarrassed commander explained in the mid-1980s, "We taught our troops two things: to dig their trenches *real* deep, and to keep their units spread far apart, so that if the wind blows the wrong way we don't lose everyone."[145]

7
Nukes and the New World Order—What We Say Goes

> What we say goes.
>
> George H. W. Bush[1]

> I purposely left the impression that the use of chemical or biological agents by Iraq could invite tactical nuclear retaliation.
>
> James Baker[2]

> We will continue to maintain nuclear forces of sufficient size and capability to hold at risk a broad range of assets valued by . . . political and military leaders.
>
> Bill Clinton[3]

On the night of January 17, 1991, a barrage of 400 sea-launched cruise missiles struck the technological, military, and economic infrastructures of Baghdad on the orders of President George Bush. Complemented by aerial bombardments, the US and its French and British allies struck Iraq's power plants, its communications grid, and critical centers of the Iraqi military hierarchy. To demonstrate that in the New World Order, "what we say goes,"[4] Bush had ordered the attacks to sever Iraq's political and military leadership from its army in Kuwait and southern Iraq. This opening assault was followed by an estimated 100,000 sorties by war planes, which hit Iraq with more bombs in two months than were used against Europe in World War II. Iraqi troop concentrations in the south were annihilated by fuel-air explosives, whose concussive power approached that of nuclear weapons. The combination of high-technology and saturation bombings created a situation in which, as Jürgen Habermas observed, "the victims remain shadow figures; we can only speculate whether there were a hundred thousand, two hundred thousand, or more."[5]

The reduction of human beings to "shadow figures" was not the only, or even the primary, link between the devastation of Iraq and the atomic bombings of Hiroshima and Nagasaki. The quick, awesome, and overwhelming defeat of Iraq, like the first atomic bombings, was designed to reconsolidate strategically important resources into the structures of the

US global empire for the anticipated competitions of the post-Cold War era. Just as Hiroshima and Nagasaki heralded the Cold War era, the high-tech bombing of Iraq back into the "pre-industrial age" warned the world of US capabilities and its will for a new postwar period.

Despite the war's high-tech weaponry and the innovative use of the United Nations to manipulate the US Congress and public, the war itself demonstrated how little had really changed. Through the assembly of Bush's "Desert Shield" and the unleashing of his "Desert Storm," the president demonstrated, as had his predecessors of the previous 45 years, that the US would use "any means necessary," including nuclear weapons, to maintain its dominance of Middle East oil, "the jugular vein of Western capitalism."[6] As in the past, the US repeatedly used its nuclear arsenal during the conflicts to ensure escalation dominance. During the first Gulf War, Iraq was encircled with an estimated 1,000 nuclear warheads, and Bush, Vice-President Dan Quayle, Defense Secretary Dick Cheney, and British Prime Minister John Major all "diplomatically" threatened to use them. As McGeorge Bundy reflected in the pages of *Foreign Affairs* after the "Desert Storm" victory, that US nuclear weapons targeted against Iraq had "not exploded does not of itself exhaust the more subtle question of whether they are used."[7]

This chapter describes how the Bush I and Clinton administrations made the transition from Cold War empire to "New World Order." It begins by reviewing the series of arms control agreements that ended the Cold War and reinforced US nuclear superiority even before the collapse of the Soviet Empire. It then explores how the first President Bush, Quayle, Cheney, and Major prepared and threatened nuclear attacks against Iraq in the war that not only reinforced US control over and privileged access to Middle East oil for the post-Cold War (dis)order, but provided rationales for revitalizing US alliances, disciplining recalcitrant allies, and maintaining Cold War levels of military mobilization and weapons production. Its description of how the little-known General Glossom sought authorization to attack Iraqi biological warfare production facilities with tactical nuclear weapons illuminates the degree to which nuclear weapons have been integrated into what have become the routines of US "conventional" war-fighting. Glossom's proposal also anticipated what would become the neoconservatives' drive to produce and use more "usable" nuclear weapons. This section concludes with an introduction to the use and growing dangers of depleted uranium weapons, which were used liberally by US forces in southern Iraq.

The Clinton administration was more than a "bridge to the twenty-first century." It provided many of the foundations for the Bush–Cheney administration's reckless military and nuclear war-fighting doctrines.

This section begins by summarizing the debates within the US "national security" establishment over what the implications of "Desert Storm" were for US nuclear war policies, and it explains how the Clinton Nuclear Policy Review resolved the debate: embracing the nuclear arsenal and doctrines it had inherited from the Bush administration. One major innovation, however, was "counter-proliferation," diplomatic and military commitments to prevent unwanted nations from joining the nuclear club.

The chapter also describes how, in 1995, the Clinton administration, assisted by other nuclear powers, forced the world's nations to accept the unconditional extension of the Nuclear Nonproliferation Treaty as it worked to limit proliferation and resist demands that it fulfill its Article VI obligations to negotiate the elimination of the world's nuclear arsenals. Also included here is how, five years later, in order to avoid the collapse of the 2000 NPT Review Conference, the US and other nuclear powers were forced to reaffirm their irrevocable commitments to eliminate their nuclear arsenals and to implement steps toward abolition. Not surprisingly, even as the Clinton administration made these affirmations, its ambassador to the NPT Review Conference announced they would never be fulfilled.

After the excesses of the second Bush administration and its denunciations of the Clinton years, memories of Clinton's nuclear recklessness have largely been forgotten. This chapter's history of how he almost blundered into a catastrophic nuclear war against North Korea and his nuclear threats against China, Libya, and Iraq will hopefully serve as a corrective.

THE END OF THE COLD WAR

The end of the Cold War did not remove the dangers of catastrophic nuclear war. It changed them. The possibility of a nuclear winter-inducing US–Russian thermonuclear exchange was greatly diminished. However, US nuclear threats to expand and consolidate its postmodern empire, the emergence of new nuclear powers, and possibilities of non-state nuclear terrorism combined to increase the likelihood of nuclear war.

After defining so much of the human experience for two generations, a perfect storm of economic, political, and social forces brought the Cold War to an end with a whimper, not a bang. For several years before East Germans breached the hated Berlin Wall, Soviet President Mikhail Gorbachev aggressively pursued disarmament with the West and revitalization of the moribund Soviet economy and stagnating political life. His tools were inspired diplomacy, encouragement of popular disarmament movements in the West, as well as *glasnost* (openness) and *perestroika* (restructuring) in the Soviet Union and its satellites. In Eastern Europe, détente had provided openings for human rights advocates and nationalists to resist repression more confidently and thus the underpinnings of the Warsaw Pact alliance. In the West, fears that Reagan administration brinksmanship, war-fighting rhetoric, and new first-strike weapons would climax in a thermonuclear exchange and "nuclear winter" spilled over into the streets in demonstrations to halt the nuclear arms race. By 1987, this political pressure cooker of hopes, fears, popular mobilizations, and political changes produced the Intermediate Nuclear Forces (INF) Treaty, which symbolized and spurred the end of the Cold War.

The INF Treaty eased the hair-trigger confrontation in Europe. The US agreed to forgo deploying first-strike Pershing II missiles, designed to "decapitate" the Soviet leadership by vaporizing the Kremlin and severing surviving Soviet leaders from their command-and-control systems needed to order a retaliatory second strike. The US also committed to withdraw its nuclear-armed ground-launched cruise missiles from Europe. Moscow, in turn, agreed to decommission its SS-20 missiles targeted against Western Europe and Washington's East Asian allies. INF was followed by START I (Strategic Arms Reduction Treaty) in 1991, reducing the superpowers' *deployed* strategic weapons by a third.[8]

To further diminish the dangers of miscalculation and to reap what additional gains it could as the Soviet Empire approached collapse, President Bush challenged Gorbachev to make still deeper cuts. In October 1991, Bush announced that the US would unilaterally remove its tactical nuclear weapons (excluding airborne nuclear bombs) from their forward deployments, and would abandon several missile systems then on the drawing board. More dramatically, Bush canceled the decades-old alert of US strategic bombers.[9]

Gorbachev responded in kind, promising to go beyond START I's limits by reducing his arsenal to 5,000 nuclear warheads. Moscow's tactical nuclear weapons would also be retired. Development of new missile systems was halted, and Soviet nuclear-armed missiles and aircraft were also taken off alert.[10] Gorbachev upped the arms control ante by announcing a moratorium on nuclear weapons testing and the demobilization of 700,000 Soviet troops. The Cold War was over; "peace" had broken out.

Two months later the Soviet Union was consigned to Karl Marx's dustbin of history. The combined assaults of Gorbachev's top-down democratic opening and the uncompromising ambitions and opportunistic political attacks by Boris Yeltsin and his allies in other Soviet "republics" unleashed centrifugal forces that shattered the "Union," fragmenting the USSR into 15 nations, which were led, for the most part, by nimble survivors of the *ancien régime*.[11]

Peace brought both opportunities and dangers. Of immediate concern was the fate of Soviet nuclear weapons and related materials left in the newly independent republics. With a shared interest in preventing nuclear weapons proliferation, Washington and Moscow worked in tandem, using a stick-and-carrot strategy to win Ukrainian, Kazakh, and Belarusian agreements to destroy or return to Russia the nuclear weapons they had inherited and to sign the Nuclear Nonproliferation Treaty.

When he was sober, Yeltsin had to address serious challenges at home. The Russian economy was in free fall, plummeting to the size of Holland's, limiting Moscow's ability to prevent its military and social infrastructures from imploding. Yeltsin thus moved to cover political necessity with diplomatic grace. Claiming that he sought "full nuclear disarmament," early in 1992 he concluded negotiations with the US for the START II Treaty committing the superpowers to a goal that neither would fulfill: reducing their strategic arsenals to no more than 3,500 each by 2003. START II did, however, provide Yeltsin with a rationale for cutting the Soviet arsenal to levels it might be able to manage while further ingratiating the Russian president with Washington and the international financial institutions it controlled. As Yeltsin's nationalist opponents and the *New York Times* reported, START II served the US well. The *Times* editorialized that it "wipe[d] out the centerpiece of the Russian arsenal, its land-based missile force, while preserving much of the sea-based force that the United States military strategists consider this nation's greatest strength."[12]

While much of the mainstream media celebrated the new era of peace, Daniel Ellsberg described the new order in more pessimistic terms: the US and Russia each continued to retain 5,000–8,000 nuclear warheads, including those in readily accessible stockpiles. There was "no Comprehensive Test Ban, a first-use threat policy, and no [IAEA International Atomic Energy Agency] inspections of U.S. nuclear facilities." And, to reinforce the hierarchy of nuclear terror, US leaders sought "indefinite extension of the Nonproliferation Treaty."[13]

NUCLEAR THREATS AND THE NEW WORLD ORDER

To ensure the continuation of what many in the US "national security" elite saw as the "unipolar moment," the foundations and systems of US global dominance needed to be restructured, reinforced, and consolidated. Imperial omelettes could not be made "without breaking eggs," and Saddam Hussein's August invasion of Kuwait provided the needed opportunity.

Like the atomic bombings of Hiroshima and Nagasaki, the 1990–91 Gulf War served to impose the parameters for a new era. The Bush administration orchestrated its responses to the invasion of Kuwait in ways that reaffirmed and restructured US control of Middle East oil, revitalizing an essential lever of power over its competitors and allies, particularly Japan, Western

Europe, and newly emerging China. The war was also used to reinforce Washington's alliances and its access to bases and military facilities from Shannon Airport in Ireland to Marine bases in Okinawa. In a world of three economic superpowers (the US, the European Union, and Japan) and a single military superpower, the Bush administration sought to demonstrate that use and threatened use of brute military force would be the determining factors in the post-Cold War era.[14]

In the wake of the "Desert Storm" victory, fought with repeated US nuclear threats, the new wisdom in Tokyo was that "Japan is Number Two." Across the Atlantic, the lesson taken by Jacques Delors, former president of the European Commission, was that unless Europe developed an integrated and independent military by 1995, it would be unable to compete with the US. Those in the US who had feared that the end of the Cold War meant the loss of their military-industrial complex jobs, profits, and privileges were reassured. Everything had changed, but everything seemed to remain essentially the same.

So powerful was the return to history that the US drive to war reminded some of European colonialism. Even King Hussein, the former CIA asset, warned that "the real purpose behind this destructive war . . . is to destroy Iraq and rearrange the area in a manner far more dangerous to our nations' present and future than the Sykes–Picot Agreement."[15]

Borders drawn in 1918 by British Oriental Secretary Gertrude Bell with "consideration of Britain's need for oil"[16] provided the rationale for the Iraqi invasion, but there was more to Saddam Hussein's military gamble than rectifying a colonial injustice. The Iraqi offensive was a response to the preceding eight-year Iraq–Iran war, launched by Saddam Hussein with a green light from Washington. Iraq's goal in invading Iran in 1980 was to reestablish control over the Shatt al-Arab waterway which flows into the Persian Gulf and is a vital route for Iraqi oil exports. Hussein also sought to assert Iraq's primacy in the region and to halt Iranian efforts to replace his secular dictatorship with a Shi'ite-dominated Islamic state modeled after and influenced by Iran's.

The Reagan administration backed Saddam in hopes that this would lead to the overthrow of Teheran's insurgent clerical regime and prevent it from challenging US regional domination. At the least, by supporting each warring nation in different ways and at different times, the US played both ends against the middle, bleeding each of its potential regional rivals. Yet, by the time the war ended in 1988, the US was fighting Iran in a tacit alliance with Iraq, providing it with intelligence on the location of Iranian troop concentrations and even shooting down an Iranian passenger plane. Saddam's Iraq was no longer perceived by Washington as a Soviet-oriented state; instead, it was a valued "junior partner in preserving the status quo in the

Gulf." In what would become a family tradition, Bush Sr. and his principal advisors embraced the Reagan administration's misreading of Iraqi political realities and dynamics. In their first year in office, despite CIA reports that Iraq was covertly seeking to purchase nuclear weapons technology, Bush ordered "closer ties to Baghdad."[17]

In addition to its staggering human costs, the Iraq–Iran war left Baghdad deeply indebted to Kuwait and other Gulf states. To ease this debilitating financial burden, Saddam's government pressed the Kuwaiti sheikdom to waive its debt. It opposed increased Kuwaiti oil production which was contributing to a global glut thus reducing Iraqi oil revenues. Saddam also protested that Kuwait was stealing Iraqi oil from the Rumalia oil fields (5 percent of which extended into Kuwaiti territory), and he pressed for resolution of long-standing border disputes. More dangerously, he began to view Kuwaiti wealth as a shortcut for Iraq's economic reconstruction and to finance his dictatorship.[18]

It has yet to be definitively determined if the Bush administration was inexplicably blind to the warning signs of Iraqi aggression or if it consciously lured Saddam into invading Kuwait. The "usually compliant" al-Sabah family that ruled Kuwait was uncharacteristically inflexible in resisting Iraqi demands, leading some to conclude that there "might have been a Kuwaiti–US conspiracy," with the US "secretly promising to support Kuwait."[19]

The Bush administration knew that Saddam was using Iraq's oil revenues to reconstruct its military, and that this included research for nuclear weapons and production of chemical and biological weapons. In January 1990 the world press reported Saddam's warning that the decline of the Soviet Union meant that the US would become the unrivaled superpower in the Middle East. "If Arabs were not vigilant," he proclaimed, "everything, including oil prices, would be ruled by the United States." Four months later, he went on to threaten Israel with chemical weapons in the event of war. Yet, within ten days, a US delegation, led by Senator Robert Dole (later the Republican Party's presidential nominee), assured Saddam that the Bush administration hoped to improve US–Iraqi relations. In late April, Saddam could only have been reassured when US Assistant Secretary of State John Kelly publicly opposed Congressional efforts to impose economic sanctions on Iraq, arguing that they would penalize US exporters.

The determinative signal may have been sent in the July 15 meeting between US Ambassador to Iraq April Glaspie and Saddam Hussein, during which the Iraqi dictator was informed that the US had "no opinion on the Arab–Arab conflicts like your border disagreement with Kuwait." This message was underlined a week later when, with Iraqi forces massing on the Kuwaiti border, Kelly informed Congress that the US had no treaty obligations to defend Kuwait.[20]

The Bush administration's position regarding the "Arab–Arab conflict" and the lack of sanctity of Kuwait's borders changed dramatically after the Iraqi invasion. The administration's early commitment to rely on military force rather than diplomacy was, however, obscured. Public attention focused initially on dramatic scenes of Kuwaiti refugees desperately fleeing their country and on less dramatic debates in the UN about how to respond to the invasion. The Bush administration, however, had already resolved that "[n]o outcome would be tolerated other than [Iraqi] capitulation to force."[21]

Central Command Forces were initially deployed to Saudi Arabia, ostensibly to protect Saudi oilfields. The Saudis, in fact, had little fear of an Iraqi invasion. Like Saddam Hussein, they had scant regard for the Kuwaiti government and had recently concluded a non-aggression pact with Baghdad. They had no evidence and little concern that Iraq's ambitions extended beyond Kuwait. Only *after* Washington exhorted the Saudi monarchy to permit the deployment of US forces to Arabia did the first wave of 500,000 US "Desert Shield" troops arrive in the Saudi desert.

In late August, the *New York Times*' Thomas Friedman summarized the Bush administration's approach: diplomacy would be avoided to ensure against rewarding Iraq with token gains. Jordan was isolated and punished for urging diplomacy, as were the PLO and Yemen. Saddam Hussein's August 12 proposal to simultaneously resolve "all cases of occupation, and those cases that have been portrayed as occupation in the region"—code for linking Israeli withdrawal from the West Bank, Gaza Strip, Golan Heights, and southern Lebanon to an Iraqi retreat from Kuwait—was immediately ruled out. Saddam's call did, however, highlight US double standards. Another Iraqi proposal, described as "serious" and "negotiable" by a State Department Middle East specialist, which called for withdrawal from Kuwait in exchange for minor border adjustments, was similarly dismissed. And, as General Norman Schwarzkopf finalized US preparations to rout Iraqi forces, the Bush administration rejected renewed Iraqi proposals for linkage and for French and Soviet mediation. Even James Webb, Ronald Reagan's aggressive navy secretary, declared that the Bush administration had "relentlessly maneuvered our nation into a war."[22]

The commitment to launch the 1991 Gulf War was consistent with the 50-year history of US military interventions and wars for oil in the Middle East and the more recent Reagan–Bush "discriminate deterrence" doctrine. Bush may have been genuinely outraged by Iraq's invasion of Kuwait, but greater strategic concerns were present from the start. Four years earlier, in 1987, as it became clear in elite circles that the Soviet

Empire would end in a "grand failure,"[23] there were related concerns about what the end of the Cold War would mean for the US. *The Rise and Fall of the Great Powers* had stirred debates across the country, and the Congressional Joint Economic Committee had warned that the US could not long remain both a great power and a debtor nation.[24] It was in this environment that the Reagan administration assembled its Commission on Integrated Long-Term Strategy, whose members included Henry Kissinger, Zbigniew Brzezinski, Samuel Huntington, former members of the Joint Chiefs of Staff, and other "national security" luminaries. Their charge was to recommend modifications in US military strategy to ensure that the country remained the world's dominant power in the first decades of the anticipated post-Cold War era.

The Commission's report stressed that the US should not spread its military resources too widely. Continued US control of the Persian Gulf, the Mediterranean, and the Pacific were essential to US dominance for "the long haul." The Commission also reported deep concern that US military power was decreasing relative to increasingly well-armed Third World nations, and that in the "next century, forty or more countries in Europe, Asia, the Middle East will have the means to build nuclear arsenals." Military spending priorities, the Commission urged, should be for air- and sea-lift capabilities and for high-tech weaponry for "precisely controlled strikes against distant military targets" in Third World nations. The rationales and strategy of the 1991 Gulf War were thus laid out when George H. W. Bush was still vice-president.

Iraq's incipient nuclear program was not initially a part of the president's mobilizing agenda, but before long he turned it to his political advantage. Memories of the 1981 Israeli bombing of Iraq's Osirak reactor and of Saddam Hussein's repeated statements about achieving military parity with Israel provided opportunities for pollsters and then for the president. A November 1990 *New York Times*/CBS poll indicated that "Americans saw the destruction of Saddam Hussein's nuclear, chemical and biological weapons capabilities as a compelling reason to go to war with Iraq,"[25] a lesson the president's son would reprise a decade later.

Bush carried awareness of this poll with him to Saudi Arabia where he used Thanksgiving with US troops to mobilize the US people for war. In four carefully staged and widely reported rallies, Bush concluded each speech with the argument that "[e]very day that passes brings Saddam Hussein one day closer to his goal of a nuclear weapons arsenal. And that is another reason . . . why more and more of our mission is marked by a real sense of urgency."[26]

By raising the specter of Iraqi nuclear weapons, Bush not only built popular support for his war, he also prepared the way for what would become the Clinton administration's aggressive "counter-proliferation" policy. In the nearer term, his public relations campaign laid the political and diplomatic ground for UN Security Council Resolution 687, which defined the terms Iraq would be required to accept to halt what became the "turkey shoot" destruction of Iraq's military. Significantly, when Bush gave the final order for the US attack, eradication of Iraq's nuclear weapons infrastructure was given equal, or possibly greater, priority than Kuwait's "liberation." Freeing Kuwait was the *last* war aim listed in Operations Order 91-001.[27]

There were more immediate nuclear dimensions to "Desert Shield" and "Desert Storm." Washington and London each relied on nuclear threats as they prepared for war. In a classic example of "escalation dominance" that has since been integrated into declared US policies, nuclear attacks were threatened to ensure that chemical and biological weapons were not used in desperation against US forces.[28] Nuclear threats also provided a shield for vulnerable US and allied advance units as they assembled in Saudi Arabia during the first chaotic weeks while the invasion force was deployed.

To back up the nuclear threats, a naval flotilla armed with more than 700 tactical and strategic nuclear weapons was dispatched to the Gulf. Another 300 land-based nuclear weapons in Turkey reinforced the nuclear fleet. There were also credible reports that land-based tactical nuclear weapons were shipped to US forces in Saudi Arabia. Britain contributed five nuclear-capable ships, each carrying between 8 and 16 nuclear weapons.[29]

The first veiled US nuclear threat was delivered just six days after the Iraqi invasion of Kuwait when the Bush administration was ostensibly still relying on diplomacy. Bush warned that Iraqi use of chemical weapons "would be intolerable and would be dealt with very, very severely." Two days later, "Whitehall sources [in London] made it clear that the multinational forces would be ready to hit back with every means at their disposal . . . [including] using tactical nuclear weapons."[30]

As the "Desert Shield"—including nuclear forces—was assembled, the muffled drumbeat of nuclear threats rumbled on. Under-Secretary of State Paul Wolfowitz warned that "[i]f we have to fight a war, we're going to fight it with all we have." Secretary of Defense Cheney told the international press that the US would use the "full spectrum" of its weaponry: "Were Saddam Hussein foolish enough to use weapons of mass destruction, the U.S. response would be absolutely overwhelming and devastating." When asked if he would rule out the possibility of a nuclear strike in response to Iraqi use of weapons of mass destruction, Cheney refused to reiterate US declared policy that nuclear weapons would not be used against non-nuclear nations.[31]

According to Bundy, the president's "most clear-cut" nuclear warning was delivered by Secretary of State James Baker when he handed Iraqi Foreign Minister Tariq Aziz a letter from the president during their highly publicized meeting in Geneva on January 7, ten days before "Desert Storm" was launched. The missive warned that if Hussein used chemical weapons, "[t]he American people would demand the strongest possible response," and "you and your country will pay a terrible price."[32]

More was to come. In February, during the transition from air war to ground war, Cheney publicly threatened Iraq when, during a televised interview, he referred to Hiroshima and repeated the lie about US lives being saved by the first atomic bombing. "I basically think," Cheney said, "that President Truman made the right decision when he used the bomb on Hiroshima . . . . Speculation goes that [US] casualties may have exceeded a million people." Soon thereafter Cheney commented that he "would not *at this point* advocate use of nuclear weapons." Vice-President Quayle also chimed in, warning that the US would not rule out the use of nuclear weapons: "Our policy is very clear and that is we simply don't rule options in and out."[33]

Nuclear war planning was not limited to official suites in Washington and London. In Saudi Arabia, as General Schwarzkopf oversaw planning for the US offensive, he urged that Washington "send a *démarche* to Baghdad . . . [that] if you use chemicals, we're going to use nuclear weapons on you." Possibly more significant for future US policy was the recommendation made by Air Force Brigadier General Glossom, who was responsible for identifying US bombing targets and the weapons to be used against them. He recommended that nuclear weapons be used to destroy Iraq's biological weapons infrastructure. Only the blast's intense heat, he advised, could ensure complete destruction of their pathogens. Radioactive fallout was apparently a lesser concern. Schwarzkopf did not object and forwarded Glossom's recommendation to the Pentagon without comment. Fortunately Colin Powell, then Chairman of the Joint Chiefs, had the wisdom to veto the request, but it presaged one of the driving forces of US post-Cold War nuclear weapons development and planning, especially during the Bush II presidency.[34]

The Gulf War also marked the first wartime use of a deadly radioactive derivative of the US nuclear program: depleted uranium (DU). During the 100-hour war, US warplanes and tanks fired 860,000 rounds of DU munitions to destroy Iraqi tanks and kill their crews. British forces fired 100 rounds.

DU is an extremely dense and hard metal which is produced as a by-product of the enrichment of nuclear fuel rods for nuclear power generation and nuclear weapons production. Its density makes it an ideal material for the armor of ships and tanks and for armor-piercing shells that explode on impact creating "clouds of uranium oxide dust." This dust is carried in the air, exposing those who come in contact with it to alpha and beta radiation. For years the Pentagon denied that DU weapons could have contaminated US troops and Iraqi civilians. Not until a decade after the war did the Armed Forces Radiobiology Research Institute concede that, "even though alpha radiation from depleted uranium is relatively low . . . [it] can induce DNA damage and carcinogenic lesions in the cells that make up the bones in the human body."[35]

Many US troops were exposed to more than the low-level radiation of their DU armor and unexploded ordnance. Victorious warriors were poisoned as they peered into Iraqi tanks they had destroyed or inhaled battlefield air.[36]

DU has taken a far greater toll among Iraqi civilians. Even before US warplanes and tanks returned to Iraq in 2003 with more DU destruction and fallout, Iraqi doctors and scientists sought to understand, contain, and alleviate the suffering caused by DU munitions. Dr. Jawad Al-Ali, Director of the Oncology Center in Basra, reported that "more than 300 tons" of DU weapons were used "extensively" in western districts of Basra. Studies by the University of Baghdad's College of Engineering determined that "levels of radiation in the area reached hundreds of thousands of times the normal background levels in the Iraqi soil." The consequences, Al-Ali reported, were fatal cancers and congenital malformations. Twelve years after "Desert Storm," cancer deaths in the Basra area "increased 19 times the rate of death in 1988. The congenital malformations in newly born babies had increased 7 times the rate in 1990." Doctors also confronted the "new and strange phenomenon of cancers appear[ing] like clusters of cancer in families," including "double and triple cancers in one person." While Al-Ali conceded that malnutrition and lack of medicines and medical equipment compounded suffering and the death rate, he stressed that "[t]he only cancer-producing factor that has been added to our environment after 1991 is the radiation factor."[37]

THE CLINTONIAN "BRIDGE"

The popular acclaim that followed the "Desert Storm" victory was not sufficient to carry Bush through the 1992 presidential election. His inability to identify with the needs of ordinary people struggling with an economic recession left him vulnerable to the younger and effervescent former governor of Arkansas, Bill Clinton. Clinton would later define his presidency as "a bridge to the twenty-first century," but his administration's foreign, military, and nuclear war policies were for the most part extensions of the path laid by his immediate predecessor. He threatened nuclear attacks against China, Libya, and Iraq before surrendering the

Oval Office in 2001 to perhaps the worst and most destructive president in US history, George W. Bush.

Clinton rose from his middle-class roots to the presidency by bending himself and his commitments to power, accommodating the needs of those whose power, influence, and resources could advance his ambitions.[38] Having been, like Cheney, a Vietnam era draft evader, on moving into the White House he understood that to secure his political power he needed to reassure the Pentagon and the military-industrial complex. Despite popular hopes for a post-Cold War peace dividend, he immediately promised that there would be no cuts in military spending. When highly publicized crises with China, Libya, and Iraq needed to be addressed, Clinton understood that his political survival depended on maintaining the façade that, as one senior advisor put it, he awoke each morning to "run the world."[39] If endorsing continued preparations for nuclear war and making nuclear threats were the price of power, that price would be paid. During at least four crises, Clinton ostentatiously and dangerously reminded those challenging US power that Washington's nuclear arsenal was capable of enforcing "full spectrum dominance."

In October 1993, after nine months in office, Clinton's first Secretary of Defense, Les Aspin, launched the administration's Nuclear Posture Review, which stated that the "post-Cold War world is decidedly not post-nuclear." He was correct. At any given moment, the US had a minimum of 2,300 strategic nuclear weapons, with the explosive power of 44,000 Hiroshimas on alert, and "a greater capacity to destroy Russian nuclear forces" than a decade earlier. The unprecedented Gulf War decimation of Iraq's military, economic, and public health infrastructures by "conventional" weapons (the UN reported Iraq had been bombed "back into the pre-industrial age") reinforced *Discriminate Deterrence*'s priority of research, development, and deployment of high-tech weaponry. Yet, as in the Eisenhower era, the belief that US nuclear weapons remained essential "to sustain our commitments overseas" was shared by Democrats and Republicans alike.[40] The US nuclear arsenal continued to ensure US "escalation dominance," to provide the means for first-strike attacks, and to reinforce US nuclear blackmail. Washington did, however, have reason to believe that the world was changing and that its nuclear preeminence might not be never-ending.

In addition to continuing concerns about Russia, there was China which, with 20 long-range nuclear-armed missiles capable of reaching continental United States, was still playing catch-up economically and militarily, and initially refused to join a moratorium on nuclear weapons testing. Worse, the science and technologies of nuclear weapons were half a century old and widely understood by the world's physicists. This led CIA Director James

Woolsey to warn that "more than 25 countries, many of them hostile to the U.S. and our allies, may have or may be developing nuclear, biological and chemical weapons—so called weapons of mass destruction—and the means to deliver them." The discrepancy between what Iraq had previously revealed about its nuclear weapons program and what IAEA inspectors found after the "Desert Storm" war further disturbed the CIA, US policymakers, and others as they contemplated the possibilities of nuclear weapons proliferation. Of primary concern were Pakistan's and India's undeclared nuclear arsenals; nuclear weapons programs in North Korea, Iran, Algeria, and Libya; and possible "leakage" of nuclear materials, technology, and expertise from the former Soviet Union.[41]

In the post-Cold War era, Hiroshima, as Ellsberg reminded his audiences, had resumed its initial meaning. After representing the possibility of an "all-out nuclear war" threatening destruction of the Northern hemisphere and possibly nuclear winter, Hiroshima again symbolized the possibility of "limited," regional nuclear cataclysms. The likelihood of another Hiroshima, Ellsberg explained, had *increased*. Alexi Arbatov, the Kremlin veteran who had served as a senior advisor to Gorbachev, concurred: "In both Russia and the United States . . . nuclear strategists are discussing the idea of hitting rogue Third World nations that might try to develop their own nuclear weapons. The . . . lists . . . are almost identical: North Korea is followed by such countries as Iran, Iraq, India and Pakistan."[42]

NUCLEAR DOCTRINES

In the Pentagon and higher echelons of the US nuclear priesthood, debate raged over the conflicting "lessons" of the 1991 Gulf War. Some, like Army Chief of Staff Carl Vuono, believed that "it was America's conventional forces, not its nuclear arsenal . . . [that] ultimately decided [the war's] outcome." Others, including General Lee Butler of the Strategic Command, argued that the US nuclear threat had prevented Saddam Hussein from using weapons of mass destruction (WMD). "It's not a mistake," he told the *New York Times*, "that Saddam Hussein never used chemical or biological weapons in the Persian Gulf." Accordingly, Butler, who would later advocate nuclear weapons abolition, revised the Strategic Command's computer programs "to aim nuclear weapons at third world nations that threaten the interests of the United States or its allies." Other US war planners focused on a lesson learned in several Third World capitals: conventional weapons could not deter nuclear-armed nations, so nations should "never fight the US without nuclear weapons."[43]

A 1991 review headed by Butler, which included Bush Sr. loyalists and men who would later serve in the Clinton administration, warned that it was "premature" to assume that the former Soviet Union would not again threaten the US, or that Russian imperialism was a spent force. In addition to retaining a nuclear "hedge" to contain Russia, they proposed creating a "nuclear expeditionary force" for possible use against "China or Third World targets." Los Alamos analysts also remained on the offensive, anticipating Bush II priorities with a call for development of mini- and micro-nukes, "true battlefield weapons," that could be used in the Third World to "prevent Dunkirk-like traged[ies]."[44]

Dangers of nuclear weapons proliferation were a common theme in these studies and became a preoccupation of the elite that rose to power with Clinton. In his confirmation hearings, Secretary of State Warren Christopher testified, "We must work assiduously with other nations to discourage proliferation through improved intelligence, export controls, incentives, sanctions, and even *force when necessary*." Clinton's National Security Advisor Anthony Lake similarly urged isolation of "backlash states . . . likely to sponsor terrorism and traffic in weapons of mass destruction and ballistic missile technology." When US *interests*—not necessarily the US itself—were threatened, Lake warned, "*we clearly must be prepared to strike decisively and unilaterally*."[45]

The Clinton administration quickly manifested an aggressive approach to non-proliferation. In May 1993, Martin Indyk, of the National Security Council, articulated the new administration's approach to the Middle East. It included "an abiding interest in the free-flow of Middle Eastern oil at reasonable prices . . . stemming the flow of weapons of mass destruction to this volatile region," confronting Iranian and Iraqi efforts "to rebuild their arsenals, particularly in the nuclear and ballistic missile fields," and containing "the threats posed by Iraq and Iran" through isolation and "dual containment."[46]

Clinton struck "decisively and unilaterally" the following month. On June 27, one day after warning the Iraqi government "that its continuing refusal to allow United Nations inspectors to monitor missile test sites could have 'quite serious' consequences," US cruise missiles again rained down on Baghdad. No novice to the manufacture of consent, Clinton's deadly warning to Saddam Hussein was concealed in explanations that the attacks were in retaliation for an assassination plot against former President Bush.[47]

More followed. A month later, Clinton traveled to northeast Asia where he threatened to annihilate North Korea if it attacked South Korea. And, in September, a month before Secretary Aspin formally launched the Nuclear Posture Review, the US Navy forced the *Yin He*, a Chinese cargo ship bound for Iran, to submit to an inspection for chemical weapons components. No munitions were found, but the highly publicized and humiliating search sent a clear message to China and would-be suppliers of weapons and military technologies. At the policy level, Aspin's "Bottom-Up Review" of the Pentagon's post-Cold War priorities reaffirmed that the US must contain "rogue leaders set on regional domination through military aggression while simultaneously pursuing nuclear, biological and chemical weapons capabilities." The US, it declared, must be prepared to fight and win two nearly simultaneous conflicts in "regions important to our interests . . . to defeat hostile regional powers, such as North Korea and Iraq."[48]

During its second year in office, the Clinton administration institutionalized its commitment to "contain" nuclear proliferation by means of a policy termed "counter-proliferation." The Secretary of Defense's Annual Report introduced it as "a broad national strategy . . . analogous to the strategy of containment in the Cold War era" that "focuses on weapons of mass destruction and their delivery."[49]

The policy was described as having two goals: preventing the proliferation of WMD and protecting US military forces who might be threatened by these weapons. "Prevention" included dissuasion, denial of access to technology, arms control diplomacy, international pressure, and agreements to inspect, monitor, or convert nuclear weapons programs. "Protection," Aspen's successor William Perry later explained, was the ability to "bring to bear military, political, economic, and commercial tools by the United States, its allies, and friends in an effort to persuade even the most ardent proliferator that the risks of the threat or use of WMD are not acceptable." As "Operation Merlin," in which the CIA attempted to lead Iranian scientists down a blind alley by providing them with flawed Soviet nuclear weapons blueprints, illustrated, counter-proliferation also includes covert operations.[50]

Counter-proliferation's commitment to "protection" provided new rationales for weapons research, development, and deployment and for armed military interventions. "In future conflicts," Secretary Perry wrote, "commanders will have to assume that US forces are potentially threatened." They must, therefore, be "prepared to seize, disable, or destroy WMD in time of conflict if necessary." Calls for "another Cold War-type effort" provided a new ideological rationale for the military-industrial complex, imperial military interventions, and US nuclear terrorism.[51]

Not so cutting edge was the administration's Nuclear Posture Review issued in October 1993. After months of secret and largely bureaucratic debates over the size and composition of the US nuclear arsenal and related delivery systems, the Pentagon opted for the status quo. As the Review was leaked to the press, those with vested interests in the old order were relieved. The *Washington Post* confirmed that "the Clinton review embraces the Bush policy."[52]

The Review also demonstrated that Orwellian "Newspeak" had survived the end of the Cold War. The Review conceded that the Pentagon understood that the US nuclear arsenal could no longer be justified by a commitment to MAD. Instead, US nuclear weapons would provide "mutual assured safety." The Soviet threat was replaced by a Russian threat. As Perry explained, there was a "real danger that reform in Russia might fail and a new government arise hostile to the United States, still armed with 25,000 nuclear weapons." This necessitated Washington's retention of "a nuclear hedge." And, as in the past, the Review mandated that US nuclear forces be structured "to deal with hostile governments not only in Russia, but in other countries."[53]

The Review, which Clinton used to rationalize his decision not to press for further disarmament negotiations, argued that the US arsenal not be reduced below levels mandated by START I. Trident submarines would continue to be armed with MIRVed missiles; B-52 and B-2 bombers would be retained for nuclear and "conventional" attacks; and 450–500 single-warhead Minuteman III missiles would remain in active "service." In Europe, the US would continue forward deployment of tactical nuclear weapons and the dual-capable aircraft they required. Although the option of launching tactical nuclear weapons from surface ships was removed, reliance on submarine-launched nuclear-armed Tomahawk cruise missiles was not.[54] The "first-use" doctrine also prevailed, as did the nuclear weapons laboratories which were mandated to stockpile and develop new nuclear weapons.

One unidentified "senior official involved in drafting the nuclear weapons policy" put it succinctly: " 'We looked at whether we were content with the dramatic pace of arms reductions' set in motion by the Bush administration and decided that 'the answer was, largely, yes.' "[55]

The *New York Times* editorialized that the Review included one major omission: it failed to propose reductions needed for "securing unlimited extension of the 1968 Nuclear Nonproliferation Treaty . . . and advancing multilateral efforts to curb trade in bomb-making material and technology." Article VI of the Treaty required "good faith" efforts by the nuclear powers to negotiate "cessation of the nuclear arms race at an early date and . . . nuclear disarmament." The Treaty, in which the non-nuclear nations pledged never to develop nuclear weapons in exchange for the elimination of existing nuclear arsenals was due to expire in 1995. As the *New York Times* warned, "non-nuclear states, led by Mexico, [were] trying to get the nuclear powers to keep their end of the bargain . . . . they may have the votes to block extension."[56]

The *New York Times* need not have worried. The Clinton administration, supported by the other declared nuclear powers, was well on the way to ensuring that the Treaty Review Conference ended in failure for Mexico and much of the world. In fact, by late 1994, the "indefinite and unconditional extension" of the Treaty was "a foregone conclusion." The US and the other nuclear powers had enlisted the support of allies, clients, and dependent states to "sign now and talk later." With this diplomatic juggernaut in place, when the Review Conference convened, the US and other nuclear powers easily resisted demands by non-aligned states to link Treaty extension to serious disarmament commitments. They also turned down calls to create more nuclear weapons-free zones and to guarantee that non-nuclear weapons states would not be attacked by nuclear powers.[57]

The declared nuclear powers did bend to demands that they conclude negotiations for a Comprehensive Test Ban Treaty (CTBT) the following year, and they agreed to conduct Review Conferences every five years. At best, these concessions provided grappling holds for future diplomatic struggles, but Mexican Ambassador to the Conference on Disarmament Miguel Marin Bosh was right when he protested that the non-nuclear powers "got almost nothing." Clinton did negotiate a CTBT, but a decade later the US and many key states have yet to ratify it.

Accepting future Review Conferences was no less cynical. Five years on, to prevent the Conference's collapse, the US and other nuclear powers acceded to demands that they commit to 13 significant steps toward disarmament (among them, ratifying the CTBT, strengthening the Anti-Ballistic Missile Treaty, reducing their nuclear arsenals, halting production of weapons-grade nuclear materials,) but the US Ambassador to the Conference correctly stated that the Conference declaration "will have no more impact than it's had in the past." This was not idle talk. John Deutch, Deputy Secretary of Defense and Director of the CIA in the first Clinton administration, explained that "[w]e live in a Trident world . . . The U.S. never intended, nor does it intend now to implement [Article VI]." It is, he said, "just one of those things you have to say to get what you want from a conference."[58] Five years later, at the 2005 Review Conference, the 13 steps remained a dead letter, and the Bush II administration's disregard for its Article VI commitments doomed the Conference to failure.

At roughly the same time, the Clinton administration demanded and won indefinite extension of the Nuclear Non-Proliferation Treaty, declassified sections of the Pentagon's chilling "Essentials of Post-Cold War Deterrence" were published. They re-codified the US commitment to and practice of nuclear terrorism. Deterrence, the "Essentials" instructed, "should create fear in an opponent's mind of extinction." "Non-Russian" nations, it warned, should understand that "the penalty for using Weapons of Mass Destruction . . . should not just be military defeat, but the threat of even worse consequences . . . [W]e must make good on our deterrence statement in such a convincing way that the message to others will be so immediately discernible as to bolster deterrence thereafter." While the US, it promised, was "*not likely* to use nuclear weapons in less than matters of the greatest importance . . . nuclear weapons always cast a shadow over any crisis or conflict in which the US is engaged." Deterrence, "through the threat of use of nuclear weapons," it warned, "will continue to be our top military strategy." The doctrine continued: "Because of the value that comes from what the ambiguity of what the US may do to an adversary . . . . it hurts to portray ourselves as too fully rational and cool-headed . . . . That the US may become irrational and vindictive if its vital interests are attacked should be part of the national persona we project to all adversaries."[59]

Two years later, Clinton's third Secretary of Defense, former Republican Senator William Cohen, went further. After announcing that the B-2 stealth bomber "added substantial new punch to America's nuclear arsenal" and that the Pentagon had deployed a new "bunker-buster" B61-11 nuclear warhead capable of destroying targets buried deep below ground, Cohen explained that "[w]e don't want to engage in a fair fight, a contemporary war of attrition." Instead, "We want to dominate across the full spectrum of conflict so that if we ever have to fight, we win on our terms." Lest anyone misinterpret his message, harkening back to Eisenhower's "massive retaliation," Cohen repeated: "For now . . . and for many years we will be ready to fight Russia or China or a rogue or terrorist in the instant massive Cold War way." US policy was now "full spectrum dominance."[60]

As 1997 drew to an end, under pressure from the Pentagon, Clinton signed the first new Presidential Directive for the use of nuclear weapons since Ronald Reagan in 1981. As part of the Strategic Command's continued preparations, the National Strategic Response Plan replaced the Single Integrated Operational Plan (SIOP). According to the new Directive, the president now had more options when ordering nuclear strikes, "ranging from a demonstration attack with a single weapon to a half-hour launching spasm of more than 600 missiles," many with multiple warheads. While this facilitated possible first-strike nuclear attacks against lesser powers, from China to Iraq, "the core of the new . . . plan" remained the destruction of "Russian nuclear and 'leadership' targets."[61]

CLINTON AND KOREA

Enforcing US hegemony required more than adjusting nuclear war-fighting doctrines, modernizing the nation's nuclear arsenal, or nurturing the dot.com economic boom. Clinton and his senior advisors also believed that "running the world" required threatening nuclear attacks against North Korea, China, Libya, and Iraq.

North Korean leaders have understandably unique perceptions of nuclear weapons and threats. Most Koreans associate the Hiroshima and Nagasaki A-bombings with the end of 35 years of brutal Japanese occupation and colonialism. Soon thereafter North Korea was threatened with nuclear attacks in the early 1950s and again in the 1970s.

The post-Cold War US–North Korean nuclear crisis is best understood in the contexts of Pyongyang's loss of Soviet protection and the economic shocks resulting from the loss of Chinese and Soviet subsidies. These and other insecurities have fueled North Korea's nuclear weapons program. Equally important to understanding the crisis is the US "stick-and-carrot" approach to North Korea, its reliance on coercive threats—economic sanctions and military strikes, and its promises to provide inducements only *after* Pyongyang fulfills all US demands. There is also the problem of successive US administrations refusing to follow through on their commitments.[62]

North Korea's nuclear ambitions can be traced to 1972 when, in secret negotiations with the Park Chung Hee government, and seeking to take advantage of South Korea's incipient nuclear weapons program, Kim Il Sung suggested that the two Koreas develop nuclear weapons together.[63] Few took Pyongyang's ostensible nuclear weapons program seriously until 1991, when IAEA inspections revealed the sophistication of Iraq's nuclear weapons program. As the US "national security" elite transferred its distorted projections of Middle East geopolitical realities to Asia, they concluded that diplomacy would not eliminate the perceived Korean threat to US regional hegemony. North Korea was labeled a "nuclear rogue" state. Before the year was out, Secretary of Defense Cheney canceled scheduled US troop reductions in Korea, and Colin Powell complained that "I'm running out of villains. I'm down to Fidel Castro and Kim Il Sung." Right-wing newspapers like the *Chicago Tribune* followed suit, calling for preemptive US attacks against North Korea's nuclear infrastructure.[64]

Yet, as Leon Sigal and others documented, "evidence of North Korean intentions" was "more ambiguous than the worst-case analyses suggested." Having lost essential support from Moscow and Beijing, North Korean leaders were more exposed to US military threats and "regime change" stratagems. While neighboring economies boomed in the first decades of the "Asia-Pacific Century," North Korea suffered mass famine, calamitous economic contraction, and isolation. For Pyongyang, possession, or apparent possession, of a small deterrent nuclear arsenal was seen as a means to ensure the regime's survival and an invaluable bargaining chip in negotiations to join the Asia-Pacific economy.[65]

Moscow first provided North Korea with a small research reactor in 1962, which operated under IAEA safeguards. A larger reactor built with Soviet assistance at Yongbyon was completed in 1987. First signs of potentially serious nuclear weapons ambitions were given little notice when, in 1989, US spy satellites observed that the Yongbyon reactor had been shut down for the removal and replacement of radioactive fuel rods and confirmed that construction of a larger nuclear plant had begun.

North Korean leaders understood that the collapse of the Soviet Union left the US as the dominant and unchallenged regional force. Contrary to appearances, President Bush's withdrawal of US nuclear weapons from South Korea did not actually reduce the threat confronting Pyongyang. The US retained its ability to launch Tomahawk cruise missiles and other nuclear weapons from its Seventh Fleet armada, and 45,000 US troops remained deployed in nearly 100 US bases and installations across South Korea.

As Bruce Cumings has explained, it was in 1991 (if not earlier) that Pyongyang's leaders "probably decided" to build a small deterrent nuclear force. The country was surrounded by powerful enemies: the US, Japan, and South Korea. By drawing on the Chinese tradition of using appearances to substitute for real military power, North Korea could "display enough activity to make possession of a nuclear device plausible to the outside world." If and when it became a nuclear power, like Israel, it could refuse to publicly declare its nuclear capabilities, thereby providing less incentive for Japan and South Korea (with their advanced technologies and Japan's hundreds of tons of plutonium) to respond in kind. North Korean negotiators could also trade a small nuclear arsenal for US security guarantees and commitments of economic and technological support.[66]

Few, if any, in the US doubted Washington's ability to prevail in a second Korean war, but the staggering human costs of such a war were little known. OpPlan 5007 called for taking the war to the enemy, conquering Pyongyang, replacing the North Korean government, and reunifying the country on US terms. But the human costs of such a "victory" approached the unimaginable. In addition to the cataclysmic consequences of possible US nuclear attacks and sabotage of South Korean reactors by North Korea, there remained the geographic reality of metropolitan Seoul. More than a quarter of the South Korean population then lived in the capital, which lies less than 35 miles from the demilitarized zone (DMZ), where 70 percent of North Korea's military forces, including its heavy artillery, were and remain concentrated. Pentagon planning anticipated that during the first 12 hours of war Seoul would be blasted by 5,000 rounds of artillery. It anticipated that 1 million South Koreans, North Koreans, and Americans would die before the US prevailed.[67]

Within days of his inauguration, President Clinton bowed to Pentagon pressure and announced that, having been suspended for a year, the "Team

Spirit" military exercise targeted against North Korea would resume in March. In February, General Butler announced that post-Cold War retargeting had placed North Korea within the Strategic Command's cross-hairs, and CIA Director Woolsey informed Congress that North Korea was the "most grave current concern." Tensions were further heightened when IAEA Director Hans Blix, armed with US spy satellite photos, called for "special inspections" of two previously unidentified North Korean nuclear installations at Yongbyon. In the wake of revelations about Iraq's pre-war nuclear weapons program, the UN Security Council reinforced the IAEA by making North Korea "the first test of the more vigorous international consensus against nuclear proliferation."[68]

Predictably enough, the threat of economic sanctions against already isolated North Korea did not achieve its desired ends. The threat only "led to North Korean recalcitrance."[69] In mid-March, with tens of thousands of US warriors, B-1 and B-52 bombers, and warships armed with Tomahawk cruise missiles surging toward and around North Korea in the "Team Spirit exercises," Kim Il Sung announced that North Korea would withdraw from the Nuclear Nonproliferation Treaty, implicitly threatening northeast Asian security.

The crisis was thus fully engaged, but as one senior Clinton advisor put it, "[N]obody knows what's going on in North Korea. Nobody knows who decides things there."[70]

Reminiscent of the Cuban Missile Crisis, the Joint Chiefs feared appeasement and warned Clinton, "under no circumstances should [he] engage in negotiations. You should not reward them . . . You should punish them."[71] Unfortunately, Clinton was not as secure, cautious, or as clever as his idol, John Kennedy. But, like Kennedy, he came perilously close to stumbling into a catastrophic war.

As the IAEA's deadline for access to undeclared North Korean nuclear sites approached, State Department officials and members of North Korea's UN delegation met informally in New York, where they framed a set of possible assurances that the US could provide to Pyongyang to scale down the crisis. Ambassador Robert Galluci explained that these assurances could include a pledge not to threaten or use force against North Korea, a continued commitment to a US–DPRK diplomatic dialogue, and North Korea suspending its withdrawal from the NPT.[72]

Serious problems, however, remained. The proposed assurances did not resolve the question of the IAEA's access to the sites and to Yongbyon, and President Kim Young Sam and other conservative South Korean leaders were incensed that the US had signaled its willingness to compromise. They warned that the US seemed to be making important concessions without consulting its long-time ally, that the direct US–North Korean talks indicated US respect for the DPRK's legitimacy, and that Clinton's diplomatic *démarche* was allowing North Korea to buy time to complete its nuclear weapons program.

Anxious to shore up domestic public opinion and the alliance with South Korea, in mid-July Clinton briefly visited Seoul, where he aggravated the crisis. Dressed for a compelling photo-op, Clinton made his way to the DMZ, where he announced that North Korea was "the scariest place on earth" and that it would be "pointless for [North Korea] to try to develop nuclear weapons because if they ever used them, it would be the end of their country as they know it."

While this played well on US television and encouraged South Korean conservatives, it seriously undermined efforts to resolve the crisis by diplomatic means. Deputy Foreign Minister Kang, who was conducting Pyongyang's diplomacy with Galluci, protested that Clinton had violated their recent agreement not to threaten North Korea by "publicly threaten[ing] them with annihilation while standing in military garb on their very border." Kang did more than protest. He pointed the way toward resolution of the crisis by informing Galluci that North Korea was prepared to decommission its graphite nuclear reactors if the US replaced them with light water reactors, which are less amenable to nuclear weapons production.[73]

Galluci supported Kang's proposal, but official Washington was less impressed. It had little regard for the NPT's promise that non-nuclear nations have the right to nuclear technologies for energy production. Nor did the US elite appreciate that many developing nations are driven to emulatc "advanced" nations by accumulating the accoutrements of "development," in this case nuclear reactors for power generation. North Korea's energy needs, Clinton and the Washington establishment insisted, could be met with more traditional energy sources.

The crisis intensified in early November when Blix reported to the General Assembly that the IAEA had made no progress in arranging the mandated special inspections. The General Assembly backed Blix, voting 140–1 that Pyongyang "cooperate immediately" with the IAEA. To underline the gravity of the vote, South Korea's Defense Minister informed the media that a military intervention might be needed to halt North Korea's nuclear program. Les Aspin further aggravated the crisis by sparking a war scare with the false accusation that North Korea was massing forces along the DMZ, and by warning that "We may be entering a kind of danger zone . . . These guys are starving" and may believe that "you can either starve or get killed in a war." Clinton in turn stoked the crisis with his announcement that "North Korea cannot be allowed to develop a nuclear bomb," implying that the US was preparing to take military action.[74]

Pressures for war intensified through the winter. After another series of diplomatic miscues, the IAEA set a late February 1994 final deadline for inspections at Yongbyon, and the Clinton administration pressed the Security Council to support economic sanctions if the inspectors were again denied access to Yongbyon. Reinforcing his military threats, preparations for the "Team Spirit" war games—which could also serve to cover preparations for a US military attack—were accelerated. During a mid-February visit to Washington, the US Ambassador to South Korea, James Laney, warned that Washington's rhetoric and saber-rattling were causing greater fear in South Korea than the North's nuclear weapons program. He feared the administration's escalating militarist rhetoric could lead to an "accidental war."[75]

The IAEA inspection of Yongbyon finally took place in March, but it failed to ease mounting pressures for war. Inspectors were provided access to six sites, but they were refused admission to the plant in which plutonium was reprocessed. Although there was no evidence that the North Koreans were diverting plutonium for weapons production, Blix found it necessary to inform the UN that he could not provide assurances that fissile material was *not* being diverted. One week later North Korea poured rhetorical fuel on the diplomatic fire when a negotiator at the Panmunjom armistice site told his South Korean counterpart that "Seoul is not far from here. If a war breaks out, it will be a sea of fire." President Kim Young Sam's response was to broadcast a video tape of the threat on South Korean television, further alarming the South Koreans.[76]

By spring, Galluci compared the growing crisis to the pressures that triggered World War I, and as General Howell Estes put it, senior US commanders in South Korea "all thought we were going to war." Despite Clinton's pledge to prevent North Korea from becoming a nuclear power, the CIA reported that the odds were "better than even" that Pyongyang already had what it needed to manufacture atom bombs. It was widely assumed that Pyongyang had one or two atomic bombs, and Secretary Perry believed that North Korea's 8,000 fuel rods could be used to make as many as five nuclear warheads.

Kim Il Sung's government was also in a difficult position. If IAEA inspectors were allowed to find that North Korea had not diverted nuclear fuel, its nuclear threat and thus its bargaining power would be severely undermined. On the other hand, if inspectors found that plutonium had been diverted, his government's duplicity could not be denied, and pressure to find the diverted fuel would only increase.[77]

The crisis moved toward a climax in mid-May when, in the absence of IAEA inspectors, North Korea began removing fuel rods from the research reactor, undermining the IAEA's ability to track how individual fuel rods had been used. On June 2, with 60 percent of the fuel rods removed, Blix notified the Security Council, signaling the need for serious international action. Kim Il Sung's response was "sanctions mean war, and there is no mercy in war," and the Clinton administration was equally uncompromising in its active pursuit of sanctions. When, with strong US encouragement, the IAEA Board voted to halt technical assistance to North Korea's nuclear power program, Pyongyang announced its withdrawal from the IAEA and ordered the last of the inspectors to leave. Believing that Kim Il Sung would be true to his word and that sanctions indeed meant war, Clinton, his senior advisors, and the Pentagon made final preparations for a war that polls indicated would be supported by more than half of the US people.[78]

Fortunately, a former president's good intentions and political sleight of hand defused the crisis, winning nearly a decade of respite. Shortly before IAEA inspectors were given final, irreversible orders to leave, North Korea's chief negotiator again pointed the way to a settlement. In exchange for light water reactors, Pyongyang would dismantle its nuclear reprocessing plant. And, in a last, desperate effort to resolve the crisis diplomatically, Kim Il Sung invited former President Carter and a team of NGO advisors to travel to the Hermit Kingdom to explore possible solutions. Committed to prevailing over North Korea, Clinton and his senior advisors were less than pleased by the North Korean *démarche*, fearing where Carter's meddling might lead. There were, however, political costs to denying the former president, and after reiterating the limits of what the US would and would not accept, and winning Carter's agreement that he would travel as a private citizen, Clinton approved the former president's travel plans.

Carter and his entourage found their North Korean hosts unforthcoming. Carter believed that they were serious about going to war if sanctions were imposed, and kowtowing to Washington was not on their agenda. Progress was difficult and incremental, and to find grounds for agreement Carter assumed the roles of negotiator, intermediary, and policymaker. Without Clinton's authorization, he created an opening by promising negotiations for normalization of relations if a diplomatic solution to the crisis could be found. He also offered to recommend that the US arrange construction of light water reactors if Kim Il Sung would permit the IAEA inspectors to remain in North Korea, and if he would freeze his nuclear program until a third round of US–DPRK negotiations. After gaining Kim Il Sung's agreement, Carter circumvented Clinton by announcing to the world on CNN television that an agreement had been reached. He reported its terms and pledged that the Clinton administration would halt its drive for political and economic sanctions.

Clinton and his War Cabinet were furious, denouncing Carter's actions as "near traitorous" and complaining that the former president had made it possible for Kim Il Sung to buy time just as they were about to "pull the trigger."[79] Nonetheless, Carter prevailed, and in the months that followed an "Agreed Framework" was finalized. It committed the US to provide North Korea with two light water reactors, with heavy fuel oil being supplied in the interim. The US also pledged to reduce the level of its sanctions and to improve relations in exchange for North Korea freezing and eventually dismantling its nuclear program. In the years that followed, neither Washington nor Pyongyang fully honored their commitments.

CLINTON AND CHINA

Beyond North Korea lay China. After more than 20 years of relatively peaceful relations, in late 1995 and early 1996 Washington and China found their way back to military confrontation and nuclear threats over Taiwan at a time of major geopolitical transformations and significant political uncertainties in East Asia, China, and the US. A generation into its capitalist revolution, the Chinese economy was booming. In the US, expectations were rising that China's gross domestic product would soon exceed Japan's. Senior Clinton officials, led by Joseph Nye at the Pentagon, saw China as a rising power and worried about the consequences of failing to integrate it into the global order on US and Japanese terms. Twice in the twentieth century, Nye frequently lectured, the world's dominant powers (the US and Britain) failed to integrate rising powers (Germany and Japan) into their systems, resulting in catastrophic world wars. Such miscalculations, he warned, must not be repeated.

Multiplying the challenges posed by China was the political turmoil it produced and the additional uncertainties of generational transition. Deng Xiaoping, who led Communist China's Long March into postmodern capitalism, was on his death bed, and the country's second generation of communist leaders, led by Jiang Zemin, had yet to consolidate or feel secure with their power. Complicating the new leaders' tasks, decentralization of economic power fueled growing provincial demands for greater autonomy. These in turn threatened the central government's traditional powers and thus the country's unity.

As if this were not enough, across the Taiwan Strait, President Lee Teng-hui was pressing Taiwan's campaign for formal independence from China in his reelection campaign. Despite Taiwan's growing economic integration with the mainland, Lee was committed to pursuing Taiwan's full national independence from China and made it the foundation of his reelection campaign. His aggressive approach to pressing Taiwanese independence as part of his election strategy triggered the 1996 crisis. In June 1995, as part of his campaigns, he demonstrated his power and influence by gaining Clinton administration approval for a visa application for an "unofficial" visit to the US, ostensibly to speak at Cornell University graduation exercises.

Mirroring the turbulence and uncertainty of Beijing's and Taiwan's struggles for power, with US presidential and Congressional elections scheduled for November 1996, Clinton, his Republican rivals, and US political classes were engaged in the ostensibly more genteel struggle to lead the world's "indispensable nation." How best to relate to China was among the election year's defining issues.

Then, as now, China's foreign policy priority was regional stability so that the nation's political, economic, and technological resources could focus on growth and development. Chinese leaders maintained that their foreign policy decisions remained based on the "Five Principles of Peaceful Coexistence" articulated in 1954: "mutual respect for sovereignty and territorial integrity, mutual nonaggression, noninterference in each other's internal affairs, equality and mutual benefit, and peaceful coexistence." Respecting China's territorial integrity was a political imperative.[80]

More than a century and a half after having been forced to cede Hong Kong to Britain, the Crown Colony that also served as the motor force for the Chinese economy was scheduled to be repatriated in 1997, with Macao (a Portuguese colony) to follow in 1999. Tibet too was being more firmly integrated into China's economic, political, and social systems through a campaign of Han Chinese colonization. In these contexts, and with 15 years of patient pursuit of "peaceful unification" with Taiwan having borne little fruit, in January 1996 Jiang Zemin addressed the Taiwan question. He put forward his "Eight Point Proposal" and the slogan "Chinese should not fight Chinese." In a speech that some criticized for its "alarmist tone," Jiang warned that forces had "meddled in the issue of Taiwan, interfering in China's international affairs." After 100 years of Japanese colonial occupation and US neocolonialism that had alienated Taiwan from mainland China, it was essential, he lectured, to defend "against the schemes of foreign forces to interfere in China's unification." He went on to remind the world that Beijing had "not renounced the use of force" to ensure that its "renegade province" remained Chinese. As his mentor Deng Xiaoping had warned, "China is capable of blockading Taiwan if we consider it necessary to solve the long term issues to serve the national interest."[81]

Predictably, President Lee's visit to the US was anything but low-key. Coming soon after Washington had eased restrictions on contacts between US and Taiwanese officials, Jiang and his senior advisors understood the visa approval as a "significant change in U.S. policy." Worse, Lee's extravagant speech at Cornell raised Beijing's concerns that he "was moving further and further down the road toward independence."[82]

China's military leaders were not happy and pressed for forceful action, and Jiang and China's new civilian leadership saw no political alternative to supporting the military's demands for a hard-line response. As a first step, the Chinese Ambassador to Washington was recalled, and in mid-July the Peoples' Liberation Army announced that it would conduct three days of missile tests at sea just 90 miles north of Taiwan. In August, the missile "tests" were followed by ten days of live-fire exercises off the Fujian coast. And, in mid-November, shortly before the Taiwanese election, the PLA conducted integrated air, land, and sea maneuvers south of the Taiwan Strait. Beijing's message was clear: this was a taste of what Taiwan could expect if its leaders persisted in pursuing national independence.[83]

Andrew Scobell argues that these military exercises "were undertaken in deadly earnest, but . . . were meant to be strictly limited to a 'show of force' with absolutely no plans to escalate to actual war." They were, he argues, a theatrical production "carefully planned and each move . . . clearly telegraphed well in advance to the other actors . . . . Leaders on both sides of the Strait recognized this was a major theatrical event" designed to limit Taiwanese political discourse and to affect the outcome of Taiwan's election. This may have been a demonstration of China's tradition of avoiding murderous warfare by using "dramatic theatrical displays to overawe the enemy," but, without an invitation, the Clinton administration and the Pentagon opted to join and influence the military drama.[84]

It was the drama's second act in early 1996 that caused its directors grave concern and frightened many of the actors, as well as the global audience.

Beijing set the stage with a warning designed to keep the US at bay. In early January, a "senior PLA official" informed Assistant Secretary of Defense Chas. Freeman that plans for "a missile attack against Taiwan consisting of one conventional missile strike a day for 30 days" had been prepared. Targets, he was told, had been identified, and the PLA was awaiting a "final decision by the Politburo." Freeman was also informed that China could act without fear of retaliation because US leaders "care more about Los Angeles than they do about Taiwan." China, Freeman was warned, "would sacrifice 'millions of men' and 'entire cities' to assure the unity of China," but the US would not risk such sacrifices—an implicit nuclear threat.

In anticipation of the Chinese show of force, or worse, Taiwan urged Washington to send it more missiles, and the Clinton administration developed ideas of its own: the nuclear-capable aircraft carrier *Nimitz* and a supporting fleet were sent through the Taiwan Strait, the first such US naval exercise in 17 years.[85]

As they prepared to send their March missive to the Taiwanese electorate, the Chinese Politburo sent a second message to Washington. Foreign Minister Liu Huaqui was dispatched to the US capital to reassure the US that "China was planning only military exercises and missile tests—not a direct attack on Taiwan." Senior Clinton administration officials responded with what they described as "constructive ambiguity." Both Secretary of Defense Perry and Assistant Secretary of State Lord expressed "concern" about Chinese threats against Taiwan. While Perry expressed confidence that a military confrontation was not imminent, he also signaled that "[w]e don't know what we would do, and you don't because it's going to depend on the circumstances." Meanwhile, an "unnamed official" made it clear that "there's no ambiguity about the seriousness with which we would greet any military action."[86]

On March 5, China formally announced that a second round of "missile tests" and "military exercises" would be held on the eve of Taiwan's election. To demonstrate its ability to close the Strait and thus enforce a devastating blockade, as well as its ability to destroy Taiwan, Beijing warned that missiles would be targeted against sea lanes north *and* south of the Strait, bracketing the province. There would also be aerial bombing and amphibious landing exercises with 40 warships, 260 aircraft, and 150,000 troops mobilized for the "exercises."[87]

Washington's response shocked and frightened China's leadership. Not one, but two, nuclear-capable aircraft carriers and their supporting fleets were sent through the Strait in an intimidating display of US military power and will.[88]

With people in Japan, the South China Sea, and beyond concerned that miscalculations could lead to catastrophe, the confrontation passed with ritual displays of force that illuminated the structure of the unresolved crisis and the hierarchy of terror. In the aftermath of the crisis, President Lee adopted a lower-profile approach to pressing Taiwanese independence, and Washington continued its sticks-and-carrot campaign to integrate China into the US–Japanese-dominated order. The US also deepened its military alliance with Japan through the Clinton–Hashimoto accords to ensure China's containment, while negotiating China's entry into the World Trade Organization.

The 1996 confrontation was little more than the opening act of the US–China post-Cold War drama. Two years later a low-profile meeting of "NGO representatives" from the US, China, and Japan took place in Tokyo to explore a "new security order" for East Asia. The US NGO participants were Joseph Nye and his close collaborator Ezra Vogel, who had served the first Clinton administration as the State Department's National Intelligence Officer for East Asia. Their former student and associate, Kurt Campbell, had succeeded Nye at the Pentagon as point man for US Asia policy.

Shortly before leaving for Asia, Vogel stated privately that his goal for the Tokyo meeting was to negotiate a "grand bargain" with China. How? By pressing US threats to encircle China with theater missile defenses that could "neutralize all of China's missiles." China would then be offered a deal. If it would forgo deployment of more aggressive weapons systems and adopt no more aggressive military doctrines than were already in place, the US would limit its missile defense deployments. When it was pointed out that this would essentially recreate the power relations that followed the Opium War by leaving in place the Seventh Fleet and its nuclear weapons, more than 200 US military bases and installations and 100,000 US troops along China's borders, and the US campaign to deploy arms in space, the former National Intelligence officer had a one word response: "So?"[89]

Not surprisingly, Vogel failed to achieve his "grand bargain." China's leaders resented US plans to create a missile defense shield to reinforce its first-strike nuclear swords and insisted that they would deploy as many missiles as necessary to overwhelm US missile "defenses."[90]

CLINTON'S MIDDLE EAST NUCLEAR THREATS

The Clinton administration's arrogance of power was also reflected in its relations with Libya and Iraq. Careful readers of Clinton's presidential memoirs will find three references to Qadaffi's Libya. Two refer to the 1988 bombing of a passenger plane over Lockerbie, in Scotland, and to Reagan's and Clinton's subsequent bombing attacks to intimidate the Libyan tyrant. The third is an offhand rationalization of Clinton's support for what were then called "theater missile defenses." Lost to the memory hole were Clinton's ambitions for Libya's oil reserves and his responses to Libya's pursuit of chemical and nuclear weapons.[91]

Before assuming office, Clinton signaled the continuity of US commitments to defending "one of the greatest material prizes in world history." One of his first post-election international phone conversations was with Saudi Arabia's King Fahd, during which the King raised concerns about growing dangers from "new hostile powers," including Iran. Clinton used the occasion to reassure Fahd of US commitments to the Saudi monarchy. Weeks later, Clinton returned to the theme, telling the press that Saddam Hussein would be "making a big mistake" if he thought he could exploit openings during the presidential transition period. US resolve, said the president-elect, "is not going to weaken during this period of transition, and certainly not after January 20."[92]

A preoccupation throughout the Clinton years was with what UN Ambassador (later Secretary of State) Madeleine Albright called "Migraine Hussein": ensuring Iraq's full cooperation with the UN inspection regime and the dismantling of its nuclear, biological, and chemical (NBC) weapons infrastructures. Through a combination of UN-authorized and US-enforced sanctions and inspections and non-sanctioned but limited US air strikes, Saddam Hussein's government had been placed "in a box." The Clinton administration was committed to keeping it there. Its principal method was the sanctions regime, which would claim an estimated 1 million Iraqi civilian lives—half of them children's—a cost that Albright told a television audience "was worth the price." Both the Bush I and Clinton administrations were resolved to maintain sanctions until Saddam Hussein's downfall. The US-imposed "no-fly" regime limited Iraqi aircraft to just 40 percent of the country's air space. This protected the Kurds in the north from chemical and other attacks, making possible the emergence of a quasi-independent Kurdish state. When Saddam Hussein's government periodically blocked the work of UN inspectors, demanded the departure of US inspectors, or appeared to threaten Kuwait, Clinton and British Prime Minister Tony Blair responded with bombing and cruise missile attacks, redeployment of aircraft carrier battle groups, and in October 1994 a massive military build-up on the Kuwaiti border.[93]

IAEA inspectors successfully dismantled Iraq's surviving WMD infrastructure after concluding that, had Iraq been left to its own devices, it "might have produced enough highly enriched uranium [HEUR] by 1996 for a small nuclear arsenal." By 1995 UN inspectors reported that Iraq was making no efforts to resurrect its NBC programs. Nonetheless, US leaders worried that as long as Saddam Hussein remained in power, Iraq might resume production of WMD and thus challenge US regional dominance.[94]

It was Libya's WMD program, not Iraq's, that led to the Clinton administration's first Middle East nuclear threats. As William Arkin informed *Bulletin of the Atomic Scientists* readers, "When President Bill Clinton made a short stopover at Aviano Air base . . . in January [1996] nuking Libya was almost surely on his mind. An underground chemical weapons facility at Tarhunah, 50 miles southeast of Tripoli, had just been identified by the CIA." In February, CIA Director Deutch publicly voiced US concerns about Tarhunah, leading senior administration officials to make their nuclear threats.

Ironically, the first threat was made at the April 11 signing of the Pelindaba Treaty, an agreement designed to make Africa nuclear weapons-free. In what would become common features of the second Bush administration—making a commitment then refusing to be bound by it and conflating the very different lethal capabilities of chemical, biological, and nuclear weapons—Robert Bell of the National Security Council publicly stated that the US would not be fully bound by Pelindaba's prohibitions. As he signed the Accord, he said that it "will not limit options available to the United States in response to an attack by an ANFZ [African Nuclear-free Zone] party using weapons of mass destruction." Days later, on April 23, Harold Smith, a member of Secretary of Defense Perry's staff, warned that "if the United States wanted to destroy Tarhunah, it would have to use a nuclear weapon because conventional bombs couldn't penetrate the underground site." Assistant Secretary of Defense Kenneth Bacon underlined the threat, saying a B-61 warhead was the most likely nuclear weapon to be used.[95]

These statements ignited a firestorm within US political circles and internationally, forcing the Clinton administration to reverse course and state that "there is no consideration to using nuclear weapons . . . against this plant preemptively." Nonetheless, these threats, combined with sanctions, ultimately achieved the administration's goals. The classic example of "successful" coercive diplomacy, much of it secret, culminated soon after the Bush II–Cheney invasion of Iraq. Over a six-year period, the Libyan government was positively rewarded, first for acknowledging its role in the bombing of the airliner over Lockerbie, and later for abandoning its chemical and nuclear weapons programs.[96]

There was still Iraq. From the Clinton administration's perspective, the "first major test" of its resolve to keep Saddam Hussein "in a box" came in late October 1997. Anxious to end the crippling sanctions regime, the impact of which was compounded by the costs of his construction of extravagant palaces, Hussein hoped to exploit divisions within the Security Council by blocking UN inspections and demanding that US inspectors be excluded from the UNSCOM inspection teams. Washington responded by reassembling an international coalition to bolster its uncompromising stance at the UN with threats of expanded military attacks. In this first test, assisted by Russian mediation, the Clinton administration prevailed. US inspectors returned to Iraq on an "unconditional basis," backed by the humiliating assurance that "intrusive inspections" of so-called "presidential sites" (Hussein's palaces and other government sites) would be unimpeded.[97]

The 1997 arrangement proved to be a short-term fix. In January, UNSCOM inspectors were prevented from entering "presidential sites." This was followed by Iraqi demands for a three-month moratorium on inspections and a six-month deadline for the UN to give Iraq a "clean bill of health" and to lift sanctions. This displeased the Clinton administration, which again assembled an international coalition to support powerful military attacks against Iraq. Albright claimed that 15 nations would contribute military resources, and that eight were willing to allow their territories or air space to be used in renewed warfare.

The White House and Pentagon campaign to discipline Saddam Hussein was blunted by unexpected interventions. First, in a televised forum at Ohio State University set up by the State Department to mobilize popular US and global support for the planned military strikes, Secretaries Albright and Cohen, and National Security Advisor Sandy Berger were caught offguard and unable to respond to students' challenges. The *coup de grâce* came days later when UN Secretary General Kofi Anan also intervened. To assuage Saddam Hussein's offended honor and to provide him diplomatic cover for backing down in the face of US threats, Anan won his agreement that diplomats of the Secretary General's choosing would accompany UNSCOM inspectors in future visits to "presidential sites." Anan's intervention left Clinton administration officials and other "national security" hawks enraged that this appointed official from Africa had prevented the US from disciplining the furthest reaches of its empire.

Neither Saddam nor Clinton would be denied. In August 1998, against the advice of Russian and French diplomats, Saddam again protested the international community's failure to certify that the Iraqi WMD program no longer existed and to end the sanctions regime. Iraq, he announced, would cease cooperation with the UN inspectors.

Over the next two months, the Clinton administration prepared "Operation Desert Fox," making it known that it "refused to rule out the use of nuclear weapons." In early January, backed by the Sixth Fleet and its implicit nuclear threats, 400 Tomahawk cruise missiles and 650 air strikes devastated Iraq's military command and missile production facilities.[98]

This was at best a dubious achievement. UN inspectors were no longer in position to monitor what, if anything, remained of the Iraqi WMD program. Saddam Hussein remained in power; and the Iraqi people continued to suffer and die under the sanctions regime.[99]

8
"Romance of Ruthlessness"—Seven Minutes to Midnight

When I was young and coming up, it was a dangerous world, and we knew exactly who the "they" were. It was "us" versus "them" and it was clear who the "them" was. Today, we're not so sure who the "they" are, but we know they're there.

George W. Bush
Boston Globe, September 23, 2000[1]

We're an empire now, and when we act, we create our own reality. And while you're studying that reality—judiciously, as you will—we'll act again, creating other new realities, which you can study too, and that's how things will sort out. We're history's actors . . .

Senior advisor to George W. Bush
New York Times,
October 17, 2004[2]

President Truman made the right decision when he used the bomb on Hiroshima . . . . Speculation goes that casualties may have exceeded a million people.

Dick Cheney[3]

In March 2002, one year after George W. Bush assumed the presidency, the *Bulletin of the Atomic Scientists* announced that it was moving the hands on its "Doomsday Clock" forward to "seven minutes to midnight." The reasons given were many: they were concerned about the security of nuclear weapons materials, especially in Russia; there was the continuing crisis between India and Pakistan, which had exchanged nuclear threats in 1999; but primarily, they were alarmed by the Bush administration's "preference for unilateral action rather than cooperative international diplomacy." This was compounded by the "U.S. abandonment of the Anti-Ballistic Missile [ABM] Treaty and U.S. efforts to thwart the enactment of international agreements . . . to constrain proliferation of nuclear, chemical, and biological weapons."[4] Two months later, the *Bulletin* returned to the theme, editorializing that "Not since the resurgence of the Cold War in

Ronald Reagan's first term has U.S. defense strategy placed such an emphasis on nuclear weapons."[5]

During the 2000 presidential campaign, Bush promised voters a "humble" US foreign policy, leading many to expect continuity with his father's administration. Instead, during his first term, he and the neoconservative cabal that rose to power with him engaged in a disastrous "romance of the ruthless." They believed that they could expand and consolidate US global power "if only their ferocity could be unleashed."[6]

As they reminded the world when they assumed power, senior figures in the Bush administration saw themselves as the inheritors of the US imperial traditions of Theodore Roosevelt and Henry Cabot Lodge. As explained here, despite their disdain for what they understood to be the lost opportunities of the Clinton years, their reckless embrace of unilateralism and first-strike nuclear war doctrines was consistent with Clintonian faith and practice. The idealistic neoconservatives were simply more zealous in their disregard for the United Nations and its Charter, in their discriminatory commitments to counter-proliferation, and in precipitously launching disastrous wars.

This chapter begins with a review of the neoconservatives' commitments and ambitions, including those of the ostensible "realist" National Security Advisor and later Secretary of State, Condoleezza Rice. It explains how they disregarded warnings about the all-too-immediate dangers posed by al-Qaeda as they focused obsessively before the 9/11 attacks on abrogating the ABM Treaty. Their goal was to open the way for deployments of first-strike-related "missile defenses" targeted as much against China as against the possibly nuclear North Korea. The chapter roots the criminal tragedies of the Bush II years in the neoconservative Cheney's commitment to impose what he described as "the arrangement for the twenty-first century," to ensure US imperial dominance for decades to come.

After introducing the administration's doctrines of dominance designed to impose "the arrangement" (the *Nuclear Posture Review*, the *National Strategy Statement*, and the *Doctrine for Joint Nuclear Operations*) the chapter explores how they were implemented, why and how the Bush administration sabotaged the Nuclear Nonproliferation Treaty (NPT) and attempted to replace it with the Proliferation Security Initiative, and concludes with the sorry histories of the administration's nuclear threats against North Korea, Iraq, and Iran.

NEOCONSERVATIVES, REALISTS, AND THEIR AMBITIONS

Dick Cheney, Donald Rumsfeld, Lewis Libby (Cheney's Chief of Staff), Deputy Secretary of Defense Paul Wolfowitz, Deputy Secretary of Defense

Zalmay Khalilzad, and the president's brother, Jeb Bush, were all leading figures in the 1990s neoconservative "Project for a New American Century," which protested that "American foreign and defense policy is adrift." Washington, they argued, must "resolve to shape a new century favorable to American principles and interests" and to "make the case and rally support for American global leadership." They envisioned a massive build-up of high-tech weapons and greater reliance on nuclear weapons and military power than on diplomacy. Finally, "regime change" in Iraq, the albatross that eventually scuppered the neoconservative project, was a major neoconservative priority of this group which dominated the first Bush II administration (2001–04).

Somewhat less dogmatic was Condoleezza Rice, who dominated the administration's second term foreign policies. In a major pre-election article published in *Foreign Affairs*, she urged a return to *realpolitik*, arguing that the US should focus on "comprehensive engagements with the big powers," particularly Russia and China. She also made common cause with the neoconservatives, calling for the US to "deal decisively with the threat of rogue regimes and hostile powers." Bridging the neoconservative/realist divide were Zalmay Khalilzad and Richard Armitage, who believed that full spectrum dominance required "reconfiguration" of the country's global infrastructure of 725 foreign military bases and installations. In separate studies, they advocated that bases be "diversified" to better surround and contain what they anticipated to be the primary challenge to US power and global dominance in the twenty-first century: China.

As vice-presidential candidate Cheney, the former Secretary of Defense, boasted, these were leaders who were inspired by the founders of the US overseas empire: Theodore Roosevelt, Henry Cabot Lodge, and Admiral Mahan. There would be imperial continuity, but there would also be imperial change.[7]

Although many were led to believe that the administration's aggressive militarism was a response to the 9/11 terrorist attacks on the World Trade Center and Pentagon, senior administration officials signaled their intentions months earlier. Soon after coming to office Cheney informed an interviewer that there was a primary "organizing event or dynamic at work in the world," and bragged that "the arrangement [for] the twenty-first century is most assuredly being shaped right now." It would, he said, ensure that "the United States will continue to be the dominant political, economic and military power in the world."[8]

Rejecting advice from outgoing Clinton officials and hold-overs like counter-terrorism coordinator Richard Clarke,[9] during most of the first year in office, senior Bush officials devoted little attention to Osama Bin Laden and al-Qaeda. Their primary concerns were winning enormous tax reductions for the wealthy, consolidating US control over the world's energy resources, and containing China. Beijing was seen as Washington's primary "strategic competitor," and, as Armitage and Khalilzad had advised, "realigning" US forces and military doctrine toward Asia and the Pacific and away from Europe was among Rumsfeld's first tasks. Not surprisingly, the administration's first international crisis and test of will resulted from the collision of a US spy plane and the Chinese jet sent to pursue it. China's growing energy demands were also a source of concern, adding incentives for the Bush II administration to address Iraqi and Iranian challenges to US Middle East hegemony. Focusing on Asia and the Middle East were not the only elements of the *Discriminate Deterrence* doctrine, which still applied. Secretary of Defense Rumsfeld made transformation of the military through the "Revolution in Military Affairs"—developing, deploying, and integrating the most advanced war-fighting technologies—the defining institutional commitment of his tenure.

At the top of newly installed Secretary of Defense Rumsfeld's priority list were "missile defenses." In a major speech scheduled for delivery on September 11, 2001, Secretary Rice had prepared to announce that missile defenses were "the new cornerstone of US security policy."[10] They were seen as essential to "the arrangement for the twenty-first century" because of the role they could play in reinforcing US East Asian and Middle East hegemony. They would also provide diplomatic and technological wedges for accelerating US monopoly of the militarization of space. During their first nine months in office, despite repeated "missile defense" test failures, senior administration officials were preoccupied with planning for "missile defense" deployments to ensure the program was irreversible.

During this period, when the administration still maintained the façade of respect for international law and agreements, Bush and his advisors faced a significant obstacle in the form of the Anti-Ballistic Missile (ABM) Treaty. Initial deployment of "missile defenses" in Alaska would not violate the Treaty, but over the longer term follow-on deployments would. As a Heritage Foundation report explained: "We can't get close to deploying missile defense without taking the next step: scrapping the ABM Treaty . . . . As long as the Treaty exists, public debate will center on how to amend it." Abrogating the ABM Treaty thus became a top administration priority. As Richard Clarke has since written, despite his efforts to stress the urgency of addressing threats posed by al-Qaeda, it was not until September 4, 2001—seven days before the attacks on the World Trade Center and the Pentagon—that Bush's senior advisors met to *begin* discussing counter-terrorism strategy. Clarke understood the cause of the delay: for eight months Bush and his Cabinet had been "[d]ebating the fine points of the ABM Treaty."[11]

Few later recalled that the rhetoric used by Bush II in his May 1, 2001 speech to build public support for missile defense deployments and the "vital role" of the US nuclear arsenal included the same slogans that he would repeatedly use to justify his "War on Terror" and invasion of Iraq. Speaking at the National Defense University in May 2001, Bush warned that "Like Saddam Hussein, some of today's tyrants are gripped by an implacable hatred of the United States of America. They hate our friends. They hate our values. They hate democracy and freedom and individual liberty. Many care little for the lives of their own people." Missile defenses, he promised, would "counter the different threats of today's world," but to "do so we must move beyond the constraints of the 30-year-old ABM Treaty."[12]

DOCTRINES OF DOMINANCE

The 9/11 attacks notwithstanding, the administration's Nuclear Posture Review in December 2001 was an extension of the president's National Defense University speech. Its message was unmistakable, and as the *Bulletin of the Atomic Scientists* editorialized, "Not since the resurgence of the Cold War in Ronald Reagan's first term has U.S. defense strategy placed such an emphasis on nuclear weapons." The Review reiterated US commitment to first-strike nuclear war-fighting. For the first time, seven nations were specifically named as primary nuclear targets: Russia, China, Iraq, Iran, Syria, Libya, and North Korea. Consistent with calls by senior administration figures who spoke of their "bias in favor of things that might be usable," the Review urged funding for development of new and more usable nuclear weapons. This included a new "bunker-buster," more powerful than the warhead designed by the Clinton Pentagon to destroy enemy command bunkers and WMD installations sited hundreds of feet beneath the surface. Rumsfeld's weapon was to be 70 times more powerful than the Hiroshima A-bomb.

To ensure that this and other new nuclear weapons could inflict their holocausts, the Review called for accelerating preparations for resumption of nuclear weapons testing at the Nevada test site. It also pressed expansion of the nuclear weapons laboratories to continue modernization of the nuclear arsenal and to train a new generation of nuclear weapons scientists. Among their first projects would be the design of a "reliable replacement warhead" to serve as the military's primary strategic weapon for the first half of the twenty-first century. With a massive infusion of new funds to consolidate and revitalize nuclear research, development, and production facilities, National Nuclear Security Administration Deputy Administrator Tom D'Agistino testified it would "restore us to a level of capability comparable to what we had during the Cold War."[13]

Later, in much the same way that the first Bush administration leaked and then "withdrew" its "Defense Policy Guidance," the Rumsfeld Pentagon published and then ostensibly "rescinded" a non-classified version of its "Doctrine for Joint Nuclear Operations."[14] The Doctrine was revealing, profoundly disturbing, and in the tradition of Clinton's *Essentials of Post-Cold War Deterrence* communicated that the US could all too easily "become irrational and vindictive."

Most striking was the Doctrine's extended discussion of "deterrence." Rather than define deterrence as prevention of nuclear attacks by other nuclear powers, the Doctrine stated that "The focus of US deterrence efforts is . . . *to influence potential adversaries to withhold actions intended to harm US' national interests* . . . based on the adversary's perception of the . . . likelihood and magnitude of the costs or consequences corresponding to these courses of actions." Diplomatically, the Doctrine continued, "the central focus of deterrence is for one nation to exert such influence over a potential adversary's decision process that the potential adversary makes a deliberate choice to refrain from a COA [course of action]." In addition to putting Chinese diplomatic efforts to marginalize US power in Asia on notice or deterring unlikely Russian or French nuclear attacks, the central role of the US nuclear arsenal was global dominance. China, Russia, France, and Germany were reminded of their proper place, and Iran and Venezuela received ample warning not to adopt oil and energy policies—COAs—that would "harm U.S. national interests."[15]

Placing the world on further notice, the Doctrine threatened that "The US does not make positive statements defining the circumstances under which it would use nuclear weapons." Maintaining ambiguity about when the US would use nuclear weapons would help to "create doubt in the minds of potential adversaries." The Doctrine also refused to rule out nuclear attacks against non-nuclear weapons states.

In the tradition of international law "being what those who have the power to impose it say it is,"[16] the Doctrine instructed the US military that "no customary or conventional international law prohibits nations from employing nuclear weapons in armed conflict," and it argued that nuclear wars can be won: "Training," it stated, "can help prepare friendly forces to survive the effects of nuclear weapons and improve the effectiveness of surviving forces."

The Doctrine went on to confirm the bankruptcy of the Moscow Treaty negotiated between the Bush and Putin governments in 2002 to provide political and diplomatic cover for Russia's limited ability to field nuclear weapons and Washington's insistence on abrogating the ABM Treaty. The Doctrine was clear that US nuclear forces would not actually be reduced because "US strategic nuclear weapons remain in storage and serve as an augmentation capability should US strategic nuclear force requirements rise above the levels of the Moscow Treaty."

Increased authority was given to field commanders to propose targets for nuclear attacks and described the circumstances when field commanders could request approval to launch first-strike nuclear attacks:

- "For rapid and favorable war termination on US terms" (the Hiroshima rationale)
- When an enemy uses, or is believed to be planning to use, chemical, biological, or nuclear weapons
- When deep and hardened enemy bunkers contain chemical or biological weapons or WMD command-and-control facilities
- "To counter potentially overwhelming adversary conventional forces"
- "To respond to adversary-supplied WMD use by surrogates" such as al-Qaeda-like cells

The Doctrine also explicitly authorized targeting civilians and cities.

The Bush administration's third major military doctrine was its *National Security Statement*, published on September 20, 2002, in time to reinforce the "marketing campaign" for the invasion of Iraq. At a deeper level, the *Security Statement* codified a new unilateralist approach to empire in which, legitimated by the demand that nations be "for us or against us," there was less concern for the priorities and input of Washington's junior partners. Short-term conceptions of the US national interest would be paramount, and as Richard Hass, Director of Policy Planning at the State Department, had earlier signaled, one of the doctrine's central features was "limits of sovereignty." This was an extension of Clintonian "humanitarian intervention," which was best described during the 1999 US–NATO war against Serbia over Kosovo as the unilateral US abandonment of the UN Charter and its limits on international intervention in favor of a "vague new system that is much more tolerant of military intervention but has few hard-and-fast rules."[17]

Ignoring the 2 million people languishing in US prisons and the precarious economic circumstances of millions in the US, the *Security Statement* began by chauvinistically celebrating that the Cold War ended with "a single model for national success: freedom, democracy, and free enterprise." Wrapped in patriotic human rights rhetoric, the *Security Statement* boasted that the US had become the "ultimate guarantor of international order," and it reprised the 1992 Cheney–Wolfowitz Defense Policy Guidance that had been promulgated in the last days of the Bush I presidency. Preventing the "emergence" of regional or global competitors was once again the explicit first priority of US foreign and military policies. No longer would a rising power need to prepare or threaten to attack the US to warrant "preemptive actions." Instead, they could be devastated and destroyed for the crime of "emerging" as major powers. China and even the European Union were thus implicitly forewarned.[18]

Although much of the *Security Statement* was framed as an aggressive response to al-Qaeda and similar terrorist threats, it also stressed the centrality of US policy toward Asia. In Asia and the Pacific, it announced, the US must "maintain forces . . . that reflect our commitments to our allies, our requirements, our technological advances, and the strategic environment." The US would "look to Japan to continue forging a leading role in regional and global affairs based on our common interests," i.e. the continued deepening of the US–Japanese military alliance. An additional warning was also sent to Beijing:

> China's leaders have not yet made the next series of fundamental choices about the character of their state. In pursuing advanced military capabilities that can threaten its neighbors . . . China is following an outdated path that, in the end, will hamper its own pursuit of national greatness.[19]

The "limits of sovereignty" doctrine did not apply to the US, which refused to accept treaty restrictions that interfered with the imposition of "the arrangement for the twenty-first century." From the beginning, the Bush administration denounced the Kyoto Protocol negotiated to limit global warming, because it limited free enterprise, the "single model for national success." The International Criminal Court was similarly shunned. It would make the US military, the president's senior advisors, and the president himself personally accountable to the laws of war. The Republican-controlled Congress had defeated ratification of the Comprehensive Test Ban Treaty in 1999, and Bush administration commitments to accelerating preparations for renewed nuclear weapons testing trumped the Clinton administration 2000 NPT Review Conference pledge to ratify the CTBT. Similarly, while demanding access to Iraq's chemical and biological warfare plants was seen as an urgent necessity, opening US facilities to inspections was seen as an unconscionable affront. As a result, within months of coming to power, "practically standing alone," the Bush administration brought the seven-year effort to negotiate an inspection regime for the Biological Weapons Convention to an unexpected close. As he walked out of the negotiations, the senior US representative explained that the draft protocol "did not protect sensitive information held by governments or businesses." One year later, "[s]cientists on both sides of the Atlantic warned . . . that the United States [was] developing a new generation of weapons that undermine and possibly violate international treaties on biological and chemical warfare."[20]

UNDERMINING THE NUCLEAR NONPROLIFERATION TREATY

Competing with its illegal invasion of Iraq for the the prize of the most reckless of the Bush–Cheney assaults on the UN system was its campaign against the Nuclear Nonproliferation Treaty (NPT). The administration's goal was simple: to preserve the existing hierarchy of nuclear terrorism, as the *New York Times* reported, by rewriting the NPT "without actually renegotiating it." When the 2005 Review Conference collapsed in failure, there was near-universal agreement with former British Foreign Minister Robin Cook's assessment that "no delegation . . . worked harder to frustrate agreement . . . than the representatives of George Bush."[21]

The Bush administration was anything but subtle in signaling its contempt for the NPT and the Review Conference. For a year, beginning with the 2004 NPT Preparatory Conference and continuing through the first two weeks of the month-long 2005 Review, the Bush administration refused to even agree to an agenda for debate and negotiations. Ambassador-designate John Bolton, notorious for his statement that nothing would be lost if the top ten floors of the UN headquarters simply disappeared, did almost nothing to support the Review Conference. And, although Bush had repeatedly warned that nuclear proliferation posed "the biggest single threat to the United States," as the *New York Times* reported, "the administration decided against sending Secretary of State Condoleezza Rice to the conference, leaving arguments to midlevel diplomats."[22]

The Bush administration's single agenda for the Review Conference was to close the NPT's Article IV loopholes which make it possible for governments to use nuclear power generation as the foundation for developing nuclear weapons programs. However, unlike a 15-year-old IAEA proposal which was backed by many nations, the US did *not* suggest that nuclear energy (including its own) be developed under the IAEA's authority. National Security Adviser Stephen J. Hadley made no secret that Washington's primary concern was to block Iran's nuclear ambitions. As the administration's stated objectives for the Conference made clear, it wanted "[a]ction [to] be taken if warning signs suggest an intent to acquire nuclear weapons, such as the secret pursuit of nuclear fuel cycle facilities."[23]

Most of the world's governments also wanted to close the NPT's loopholes, but as the 110 countries that participated in the Mexican-sponsored Nuclear Weapons-Free Zones conference on the eve of the NPT Review declared, they also wanted movement toward implementation of Article VI. "We are convinced," their final declaration read, "that reaching the objective of permanently eliminating and prohibiting nuclear weapons requires firm political will from all States, particularly those States that possess nuclear weapons." Worse in the eyes of the Bush administration were the demands from the Non-Aligned Movement, led by Malaysia. They demanded "early ratification of the CTBT"; full compliance with "Article VI obligations including the 13 practical steps" accepted at the 2000 Review Conference; implementation of the 1996 International Court of Justice advisory opinion on the illegality of the use and threatened use of nuclear weapons; a fissile material cut-off treaty; application of the NPT to Israel, India, and Pakistan; and establishment of additional nuclear weapons-free zones. Each demand was an abomination to Bush and his cohorts.

After finally accepting a compromise agenda half-way through the Conference, the US continued to paralyze the Conference by refusing to agree to any reference to the 13 agreed steps in the Conference's final declaration. As a result, the Conference was unable to adopt a final resolution and ended in failure. Many wondered if it signaled the end of the NPT order.[24]

The Bush administration did not miss a step in declaring that it was "ready to take over." It asserted that responsibility for nonproliferation lay not in the UN General Assembly but in the Pentagon. Within days of the Conference's collapse, Secretary of State Rice led the administration's public relations diplomacy, boasting that its Proliferation Security Initiative (PSI) "had stopped 11 weapons-related transfers abroad, including two to North Korea and to Iran." As her critics noted, having helped to derail the NPT Review, she had taken "a good little program," the PSI, and "puffed [it] up totally out of proportion."[25]

The quality and legality of PSI remain matters of debate. It is a US-led program, involving just over 15 nations—including Britain, Germany, Holland, Japan, Poland, and Portugal—in seizing shipments of nuclear materials and technologies on land, at sea, and in the air. Consistent with the Bush National Security Statement, PSI operates outside the UN Charter and in violation of the Convention on the Law of the Sea. Perhaps because of the project's secrecy—in part to protect the identities of participating militaries and their operations—Secretary Rice provided few convincing specifics about its successes.[26]

Lest anyone doubt the Bush II administration's disregard for the NPT and its embrace of double standards, they were amply demonstrated in the administration's approaches to Iran's and India's nuclear programs in the year that followed the NPT Review. Despite IAEA Director Mohammed

ElBaradei's testimony that his inspectors had not found evidence that Teheran had a nuclear weapons program and his request for time, patience, and diplomacy to ensure that Iran's primitive uranium enrichment program would be limited to power generation, the US pressed for sanctions. While it encouraged diplomacy by its European allies, it refused to make a non-aggression commitment and insisted that "all options"—including conventional and nuclear attacks—remained on the table. Even as US intelligence reported that Iran would be unable to produce a nuclear weapon on its own for 9–10 years, Bush administration rhetoric, diplomatic maneuvers, and military threats reminded many of his earlier campaign that culminated in the calamitous invasion of Iraq.

Nuclear India, which unlike Iran had consistently refused to sign the NPT and which had been sanctioned by the US and the international community for becoming a nuclear power outside the NPT system, was accorded significantly better treatment. To cement an incipient alliance with India targeted primarily against China and Islamist forces, President Bush offered New Delhi advanced nuclear technologies and nuclear fuel with little asked in return. As Julian Borger wrote in the *Guardian*, "The deal removed the one incentive many countries had to stay in the NPT: the right to buy civilian nuclear technology in return for forgoing the right to build nuclear weapons." Bush made it possible for India to simply circumvent the NPT.[27]

NUKING IRAQ?

Images of two airliners crashing into the World Trade Center, of people plummeting from the upper stories to their deaths, and of the collapse of the twin towers will long be defining icons of the early twenty-first century. Replayed endlessly by sensationalist media and repeatedly exploited by the Bush administration, they became essential to contemporary US identity. The nation's and world's television audiences were not alone in their shock and confusion. Unaware of the source of the attacks, the US military was placed on a Defcon 3 global nuclear alert, and Russia responded with preparations to "exercise all of their strategic nuclear forces." Soviet forces stood down when White House officials finally thought to order the State Department to intercede and explain the US alert.[28]

The 9/11 attacks also provided Bush and Cheney, whose post-election popularity was flagging, the political cover needed to promote war and new domestic policies that the US people would not otherwise have supported. Bush became a self-described "war president" and ruled by magnifying and manipulating people's fears. In speech after speech he described the attacks as an act of war instead of framing them as crimes that could be addressed through domestic and international law, court systems, intelligence, and diplomacy. When, on 9/11, Rumsfeld advised the president that international law forbade retribution and would permit a military attack only to prevent future attacks, Bush responded angrily, "I don't care what the international lawyers say, we are going to kick some ass."[29] The leaders of the world's sole surviving superpower then turned to debate whose "ass" to kick.

Despite the CIA's evidence of al-Qaeda's responsibility for the terrorist attacks, when the administration's senior officials met on September 12, Wolfowitz framed much of the debate by insisting that "there was no greater menace in the world than Iraqi President Hussein." Iraq, he urged, should be at the head of the target list. Wolfowitz did not win these initial debates because Vice-President Cheney did not want to "lose momentum" by attacking Iraq first. Cheney did, however, promise that Iraq could be targeted "at some point."[30]

Within days of the 9/11 attacks, world leaders, including representatives of the European Union, were informed that they could either be for or against the US, and there was no room for equivocation. Governments would have to choose. This was quickly illustrated in Central Asia where, instead of pursuing diplomacy with the Taliban despite indications that it might be willing to deliver al-Qaeda's leaders to the US, the Bush administration opted for war. Among the signals Rumsfeld sent to both the Taliban and the world was an oblique nuclear threat in which he refused to "rule out" the use of tactical nuclear weapons against caves in which Osama Bin Laden was believed to be hiding. Pakistan's military, whose intelligence services had supported the Taliban's rise to, and exercise of, power, was informed that it could assist the US in ousting the Taliban or become a primary target for US military power. General Musharraf, Pakistan's dictatorial leader, opted to join Washington in replacing Afghanistan's brutal theocratic government with provincial warlords and the CIA's long-term asset, Hamid Karzai.[31]

As the US air war and its special forces on the ground opened the way for the Afghan Northern Alliance to march on Kabul, Bush and his neoconservatives felt increasingly free to focus on Iraq. In late November Bush gave Rumsfeld the green light to begin preparations for an invasion to overthrow Saddam Hussein, and in late December, after the defeat of the Taliban, Chairman of the Joint Chiefs General Tommy Franks turned fully to the task.

Despite the administration's rhetoric, its numerous rationales, and the benefits its client state Israel expected to accrue from the removal of Saddam Hussein, like "Desert Storm," Bush's invasion would be a war for oil. After the US invasion, when asked why the US had invaded Iraq but not North Korea, Wolfowitz urged his audience to "look at it simply. The most important difference" between the two countries was that "economically, we just had no choice in Iraq. The country swims on a sea of oil." He would later explain that his intent had been to explain why economic sanctions against Iraq would not suffice, but the priority US occupation troops gave to protecting Iraq's oil ministry while allowing nearly every other governmental installation—including military bases—to be looted testified otherwise. Elsewhere Wolfowitz explained that "for bureaucratic reasons, we settled on one issue—weapons of mass destruction—because it was the one reason everyone could agree on."[32]

President Bush used his January 2002 State of the Union speech to begin building domestic and international support for the planned invasion. Using a shocking slogan that brought to mind the Nazi-led Axis alliance, he warned that an "axis of evil" threatened the US and the rest of the civilized world. This was perhaps the administration's most audacious effort to "create reality." As many understood, if there was an "axis of evil," it was not Iraq, Iran, and North Korea. Baghdad and Teheran were such bitter rivals that when US and British forces launched their invasion, Saddam Hussein's military strategy continued to be based on his belief that the greatest threat to his regime was an Iraqi Shi'ite uprising backed by Iran. Iraq's military was deployed accordingly, hastening Hussein's defeat. Nor was there an alliance between Baghdad and distant Pyongyang. Saddam Hussein had indeed made a $10 million down-payment for North Korean missile manufacturing equipment, but Kim Jong Il sent nothing in return.[33]

The war proved to be "one of the greatest strategic blunders in U.S. history." Orchestrated by the administration's neoconservatives, US and international public opinion were mobilized through a campaign of lies, cherry-picked "intelligence," and catastrophic miscalculations. As Sir Richard Dearlove, head of British MI6 intelligence reported to Tony Blair and his Cabinet in the summer of 2002, "Bush wanted to remove Saddam, through military action" and the "intelligence and facts were being fixed around the policy." Bush claimed that Iraq was seeking to purchase African uranium, and that if it developed or received fissile materials, it "would be able to build a nuclear weapon within a year." Cheney warned that "[m]any of us are convinced that Saddam will acquire nuclear weapons fairly soon." Rumsfeld threatened that Saddam might use pilotless drones or his alliance with al-Qaeda "as a means of delivering chemical and biological weapons." And Secretary Rice joined the campaign, testifying that it would be foolhardy to wait to see a "mushroom cloud" to take Hussein's nuclear weapons program seriously. Yet, many knew that Iraq had no nuclear, chemical, or biological weapons. There was no

African uranium, no mobile weapons plants, and no military program designed to attack the US.[34] Nor was there a "sinister nexus between Iraq and the al-Qaeda terrorist network." Saddam Hussein, in fact, feared al-Qaeda and had not collaborated with its terrorists.

When the first wave of invading US forces moved quickly to seize and protect the country's oil ministry in Baghdad, but not its hospitals, libraries, or priceless historical treasures, it became crystal-clear that the invasion had been a war for oil. The Bush administration had conquered Iraq to reconsolidate its hold on "the prize" as an essential step in imposing "the arrangement for the twenty-first century."[35]

Threatened use of the US nuclear arsenal played an important, if not necessary, role in Washington's pyrrhic victory. Before the war, in testimony to the UN Security Council, Mohamed ElBaradei reassured the world that there was "no evidence of ongoing prohibited nuclear or nuclear-related activities in Iraq." There were, however, questions about the fate of Iraq's once vast chemical and biological weapons stores. US war planners feared that if Saddam still had such weapons, he might rely on them as a last resort in defending himself and his regime.

On December 10, 2002, as US forces continued to move into position for the invasion, the Bush administration took steps to ensure that Saddam Hussein remained locked in the "box" inherited from the Clinton administration. It published an unclassified six-page "strategy" that warned "The United States will continue to make clear that it reserves the right to respond with overwhelming force—including through resort to all our options—to the use of W.M.D. against the United States, our forces abroad, and friends and allies." To ensure that this nuclear threat was not missed, administration "officials" told the press that the "strategy" bore "considerable resemblance to a private warning that Secretary of State James A. Baker III sent to Saddam Hussein . . . before the Persian Gulf War in 1991."[36]

Iraq had no weapons of mass destruction, and its military was seriously decayed as of result of the Iraq–Iran and "Desert Storm" wars, the decade of sanctions, and the corruptions of dictatorship. Saddam Hussein's regime was quickly overcome by a combination of Rumsfeld's *blitzkrieg* and Iraqi military incompetence. Bush prematurely declared "MISSION ACCOMPLISHED," and a little more than a year later the US National Intelligence Estimate advised that Iraq faced three possible futures: it could collapse into the chaos of a failed state with forces like al-Qaeda finding sanctuaries there and having relative freedom of action; it could descend into the paroxysms of civil war; or, more hopefully, it could endure a period of the tenuous stability of a militarized and increasingly fundamentalist (and Iranian influenced) Shi'a society.[37]

THREATENING NORTH KOREA

Having suffered a humiliating and potentially calamitous defeat in its six-year game of nuclear chicken with North Korea, at this writing it remains to be seen whether the Bush–Cheney government has the vision, will, or integrity to address and to overcome failures resulting from neoconservative arrogance toward Pyongyang. Unable to resolve internal divisions over whether US imperial interests were best served by attempting to overthrow North Korea's unique brand of Stalinism or to negotiate an accommodation with it, the Bush administration had careened between making nuclear threats, participating half-heartedly in negotiations, and seeking to economically strangle the Pyongyang dictatorship. Along the way, it failed to seriously pursue diplomatic openings that might have prevented the October 9, 2006 test that demonstrated North Korea's limited nuclear weapons capabilities.

Beginning in March 2001, it was clear that the newly installed Bush–Cheney government had not learned the lessons of its predecessors' early arrogance toward North Korea. Two months after coming to office, it derailed diplomacy and a nearly completed comprehensive agreement with the Hermit Kingdom which had been negotiated in the last days of the Clinton administration. Compounding this self-inflicted wound, during his first meeting with an Asian head of state, President Bush humiliated South Korean President Kim Dae Jung and undermined Secretary of State Powell.

The invitation extended to President Kim had indicated that the Bush administration would build on Clinton's Korean diplomacy and support the South Korean leader's "Sunshine" policy toward North Korea which was designed to facilitate a "soft landing" for North Korea. South Korea's elite had concluded that military defeat of North Korea or the sudden implosion of the dictatorial regime would result in disaster for the nation as a whole. Seoul lacked the economic and political resources needed to peacefully integrate North Korea's 21 million people without massive long-term disruptions. Beijing's leaders agreed with those around Kim Dae Jung that the sudden collapse of Pyongyang's communist monarchy would unleash a destabilizing deluge of North Koreans desperate for security and a better life into China and South Korea. Kim's "Sunshine" policy was proactive, encouraging investment in North Korea to improve its economic infrastructure, and it relied on long-term multilayered engagements to harmonize what had become related but increasingly different Korean societies.

Rather than receiving the anticipated support from President Bush, South Korea's heroic president was greeted with the news that North

Korea's leader could not be trusted—implying that there was no legitimate foundation for "Sunshine" diplomacy. With their visceral antipathy to Clinton's approach to the world and their neoconservative resolve never to "appease" US enemies, Bush and his most trusted advisors had opted to reverse course. Instead of building on the lessons of 1994, fulfilling US commitments under the Agreed Framework, and concluding the comprehensive negotiations with North Korea, the president announced that he had ordered a complete review of US–North Korean relations.

In fact, since the signing of the Agreed Framework, Pyongyang's violations of the agreement were less egregious than Washington's. The US failed to follow through on progress toward normalizing diplomatic relations. Delivery of heavy fuel oil often lagged. So too did construction of the light water nuclear reactors, ending economic sanctions, and reducing the military threat to North Korea. In retaliation for US delays, the DPRK delayed IAEA inspections. It had also sought leverage in negotiations with the US by initially resisting demands to inspect what the Clinton administration mistakenly believed was a nuclear site at Kunchang-ni. While offering little evidence to confirm their accusations, conservative Republicans had also charged that although North Korea had abided by the letter of the Agreed Framework, it was seeking "a second path to nuclear weapons" by enriching uranium.[38]

With the nuclear reactors at Yongbyon frozen by the Agreed Framework, missiles, not nuclear weapons, became the focus of US–North Korean tensions during the later Clinton years. In early 1998, the US ratcheted up tensions by imposing additional economic sanctions to punish Pyongyang for selling missile technologies and components to Pakistan. Tensions increased again when, to mark Kim Jong Il's birthday, North Korea launched a three-stage Taepodong-1 rocket that passed over Japan. Japanese political culture and the US "national security" elite were shaken. Although the rocket failed to place its communications satellite into orbit, it demonstrated North Korea's ability to attack Japan. This was exploited by Japanese conservatives in their campaign to scrap the peace constitution and to rationalize Japanese participation in the US missile defense program. It was in this context that Secretary of Defense Perry had developed the comprehensive approach to North Korea and Secretary of State Albright all but finalized negotiations with the Hermit Kingdom on the eve of the 2000 presidential election.

Despite having been demeaned by President Bush as a "pygmy" to be "loathed," and having his government named a member of the "axis of evil" and target of US nuclear weapons, Kim Jong Il was not without means to seriously engage the US diplomatically. In what has since been called the "Kelly moment," North Korea's leaders sent a double-edged message to Washington to deter possible US attacks and to indicate its openness to "cooperative engagement."[39]

In June 2002, after a small but deadly North–South Korean naval skirmish over fishing rights and the demarcation of their respective territorial waters, diplomacy seemed to promise better times. Mid-level US and North Korean diplomats exchanged visits. Pyongyang announced economic reforms, including the creation of a "Special Economic Zone" similar to the one used to launch China's capitalist revolution. Japanese Prime Minister Koizumi traveled to North Korea for a summit in which Kim Jong Il apologized for Cold War-era kidnappings of Japanese nationals and signaled his intention to pursue normalization of relations with Tokyo. Koizumi returned with a message for President Bush and his Special Envoy, Assistant Secretary of State James Kelly, who was scheduled to visit Pyongyang in October: North Korea hoped for "a comprehensive advancement in resolving security and other issues, including missiles and the problem of nuclear development."[40]

Unfortunately, Assistant Secretary Kelly was sent to North Korea to deliver a self-defeating ultimatum. After divisive battles within the Bush administration over the direction of its Korean policies, hardliners had prevailed. Kelly's message was framed to ensure its rejection: North Korea must "dramatically alter its behavior across a range of issues, including its WMD programs, development and export of ballistic missiles, threats to its neighbors, support for terrorism, and the deplorable treatment of the North Korean people." Failure to do so would lead to "dire consequences from the international community." Kelly also charged that the US had evidence that Pyongyang was producing highly enriched uranium for atom bombs, a charge that Kelly's hosts initially denied, insisting they were "fabrications."[41] But following overnight consultations, the North Koreans responded with diplomatic jujitsu. First, Vice-Foreign Minister Kang Sok-ju, who had negotiated the Agreed Framework with the Clinton administration, informed Kelly that "of course, we have a nuclear program and more." North Korea, he continued, "was justified to pursue such capabilities and . . . it considered the agreed framework nullified." North Korea, he warned, had "stronger weapons" that it could wield if Washington insisted on threatening the DPRK.

There was more. Harkening back to the unconsummated 2000 negotiations with the Clinton administration. Kang reiterated that North Korea wanted a "comprehensive solution" for all "matters of concern" between it and the US. Few in the US were as perceptive as the scholar Leon Sigal, who understood that "By acknowledging its covert nuclear program . . . Pyongyang [was] putting it on the negotiating table."[42]

Having opted for confrontation, the Bush administration chose to ignore the North Korean offer to negotiate and interpreted Kang's statement as a confession. Kang's nuclear claim was widely publicized to justify the US campaign to further isolate the DPRK and possible future military action. Others, including some members of South Korea's Parliament and US scholars, were not convinced that North Korea actually had a high enriched uranium program (HEUP). With no hard evidence from either the Bush administration or North Korea, they stressed that the "alleged HEUP . . . ha[d] not been proven to actually exist." Statements about the existence of the program served the interests of both Washington and Pyongyang.[43]

The crisis deepened and became far more complex in the months that followed. In January 2003, Colin Powell once again spoke for the administration, announcing, "We cannot suddenly say 'Gee, we're so scared. Let's have negotiations because we want to appease your misbehavior.' This kind of action cannot be rewarded." Powell's spokesman added, "We have no intention of sitting down and bargaining again." Instead, ignoring Kim Dae Jung's warnings that halting oil shipments would cause Pyongyang to restart its Yongbyon nuclear reprocessing plant, Washington cut off the shipments. As Kim Dae Jung warned, the reactors were fired up.[44]

Soon the confrontation reached the point that leading members of the Korean parliament, academia, and civil society saw it as potentially cataclysmic. One delegation that traveled to the US to prevent a second—potentially nuclear—Korean War warned of the "possibility of extreme action on the part of North Korea and the Bush administration." In meetings with members of Congress and their staff, scholars, the media, and the public, they explained that like the "First World War . . . the situation" threatened to "spin out of control," and they advised that the intensifying nuclear crisis could be resolved diplomatically. They urged that the US share whatever evidence it had that Pyongyang was actually producing highly enriched uranium for nuclear weapons, and that Washington offer Pyongyang a "*de facto* non-aggression treaty" in exchange for "North Korean abandonment of nuclear weapons."[45]

More unsettling news soon reached Washington. In South Korea administration leaders were counting on old hardline Korean conservatives to replace what they saw as Kim Dae Jung's appeasement-prone government in a sharply contested presidential election.

Instead, a military accident involving US soldiers once again transformed South Korean politics, driving a wedge into the increasingly tenuous US–South Korean alliance and seriously complicating the Bush administrations strategic calculations. Two schoolgirls walking down a narrow street to a friend's birthday party were killed when they were run over by a massive US tank. Adding US insult to Korean injury, the US Army refused to hold anyone accountable. The unequal treaty, called a Status of Forces Agreement, between Seoul and Washington left South Koreans powerless to do more than protest publicly and, spurred by ever more massive candle-lit vigils, to elect as president the human rights lawyer and Kim Dae Jung protégé, Roh Moo-hyun. Unlike his conservative opponent, and more than Kim Dae Jung, Roh spoke for a generation with little or no memory of the Korean War, for young people who had risked imprisonment and otherwise sacrificed to overcome U.S.-sponsored military dictatorships, and for others who resented the almost five decades of "abuses and usurpations"[46] caused by the tens of thousands of US troops based in their country. Roh came to office having called for withdrawal of US forces from South Korea and deeply committed to Kim Dae Jung's "Sunshine" policy.

Amidst these political and geostrategic cross-currents, Pyongyang proceeded cautiously, not crossing the "red line" of actually reprocessing plutonium. It did, however, in shows of force, "test-fire" short-range missiles, challenge a US spy plane, and issue its customary bloodcurdling threats.

Bush administration hardliners responded by upping the ante: 24 nuclear-capable long-range bombers were dispatched to Guam; and an aircraft carrier, F-117 stealth fighters, and an Aegis destroyer and its cruise missiles were very publicly redeployed to South Korea. The Pentagon also let it be known that if it acted quickly, it could "take out North Korea's nuclear reactor without contaminating the region with radiation." A "second, more comprehensive and devastating nuclear strike," it warned, "would then deter North Korea from retaliation with missile attacks on Seoul or Tokyo."[47]

The Bush administration faced little domestic opposition to its campaign of military confrontation and nuclear threats against North Korea. Even if they had wanted to challenge them, leading Democrats had hamstrung themselves. During the political struggle leading up to the invasion of Iraq, many had protested that Bush was attacking the wrong country. North Korea, they argued, posed the more immediate threat.[48]

Fortunately, Bush, Cheney, and Rumsfeld were not well positioned to follow through on their threats. The unexpected quagmire in Iraq, as well as the anticipated staggering consequences of a second Korean War, imposed chastening realities and limits on their actions. The Chinese government, anxious to maintain regional peace, exercised diplomatic leadership and intervened by bringing the US, Russia, North and South Korea, and eventually Japan together for what became known as the "six-party" negotiations. While North Korea continued to express its willingness to freeze its nuclear program in exchange for energy assistance, US non-aggression commitments, and movement toward normalization of relations, it also threatened and eventually resumed enrichment of its fuel rods. To strengthen its negotiating hand, it invited US scientists to examine it nuclear weapons program and tested short- and long-range missiles.

The Bush administration was not alone in applying pressure to North Korea. Using sticks and carrots, Beijing briefly closed an oil pipeline to forcefully encourage North Korea to rejoin the six-party talks. It encouraged Kim Jong Il to be more forthcoming in negotiations by welcoming him to Shenzhen to show him the awesome economic advances made possible by opening to the West and capitalism. There was also pressure from the IAEA, with ElBaradei describing North Korea as "the most serious threat" to the nonproliferation regime.

Meanwhile, neither Beijing nor Seoul kowtowed to the world's sole superpower. China exercised what leverage it could over the Bush administration, at one point chastising it for becoming the principal "obstacle" in the six-party talks. It also blocked a US-backed Security Council resolution which would have legitimized military action to reinforce sanctions against North Korea.[49] Seoul also pursued a somewhat independent policy by distancing itself from repeated US threats, resuming Cabinet-level meetings with Kim Jong Il's government, and providing North Korea with food and fuel shipments despite Washington's objections.[50]

Much like the 1994 Agreed Framework, the first three years of six-party talks served as a face-saving means to avoid war. In September 2005, Chinese diplomacy won what initially appeared to be an agreement in principle that North Korea would dismantle its nuclear program in exchange for improved US ties and economic assistance. However, Pyongyang seemed to back away from the agreement the following day and the US "undercut its own offer" by reverting to a policy of regime change. It placed still more crippling financial sanctions, "ostensibly to punish the North for selling counterfeit dollars."[51]

On the Korean Peninsula, Secretary Rumsfeld's reconfiguration of US military bases was used to pacify the South Korean public by "reducing the size of the U.S. footprint" on their country while simultaneously increasing its war-fighting capacities. Plans were announced to redeploy US bases and military concentrations away from the DMZ and out of Seoul and to relocate them in more isolated communities further south. Politically, this strategy was less than fully successful. Many South Koreans feared that the redeployments made war more, not less, likely, with US forces being moved to comparative safety beyond the range of North Korean artillery.[52]

Meanwhile, across the Sea of Japan, Washington and Tokyo continued to deepen their military alliance, including pressing the campaign to eliminate Japan's peace constitution. Despite constitutional restrictions, leading figures in the Japanese government warned of possible first-strike Japanese attacks against North Korea. The US and Japan worked together in the United Nations to back sanctions with threats of military force.

Three years after the "Kelly moment" the intense confrontation continued unabated. In its second *National Security Statement*, issued in March 2006, the Bush administration reiterated its commitments to "preempt emerging threats" through "*proactive counter-proliferation efforts*" and "resort to force." The *Security Statement* warned of the "serious nuclear proliferation challenge" posed by North Korea, which was charged with "a long and bleak record of duplicity and bad-faith negotiations" designed "to split the United States from its allies." North Korea was again warned that it "must give up all of its existing nuclear weapons programs." Signaling the Bush administration's orientation toward "regime change," the *Security Statement* also warned that the "United States has broader concerns regarding the DPRK," and Pyongyang was charged with counterfeiting US currency, trafficking narcotics, threatening South Korea "with its army and its neighbors with its missiles," and brutalizing and starving its own people. The *Security Statement* insisted that until the "*DPRK regime*" opened its political system, the US would take "*all necessary measures to protect . . . against the adverse effects of their bad conduct*."[53]

"Senior officials" speaking to the press were more direct. The administration, they reported, had decided "to move toward more confrontational measures." They repeated that the administration had concluded that "the six-nation nuclear disarmament talks were a waste of time and that direct action was the only tactic that might force North Korea to give up its nuclear weapons program." While maintaining military and diplomatic pressure on Pyongyang, the US continued its campaign to isolate the DPRK monetarily by freezing its assets in banks around the world. The administration's plan, one "senior official" explained, was to "squeeze them" economically and militarily, "but keep the negotiations going." Their hope was that the six-party diplomacy would eventually "serve as little more than a vehicle for accepting North Korea's capitulation."[54]

The military option remained. In a sentence that National Security Advisor Stephen Hadley said applied equally "to both Iran and North Korea," the revised *Security Statement* warned that diplomatic efforts "must succeed if confrontation is to be avoided."[55]

In September 2006—one month before the Korean nuclear test—the US conducted the largest US-led naval exercises held in the Pacific since the Vietnam War. The "exercise" was designed to send a message to both Pyongyang and Beijing: Even if the US was tied down in the Iraqi quagmire, it still had the power to annihilate both East Asian nations.[56]

The morning of October 9, 2006 brought first reports of a partially successful North Korean nuclear weapons test and the near-complete failure of Bush administration nuclear threats and arrogance directed against Pyongyang.

In the weeks that followed, the Bush administration won limited UN sanctions against North Korea, which continued to insist that its nuclear weapons program was defensive and designed only to deter a US attack. The UN resolution provided for limited economic sanctions and for the interdiction of nuclear weapons-related equipment bound for and from North Korea. This was an important show of unity made possible in part by Beijing's anger that North Korea had failed to heed its warnings not to conduct a nuclear weapons test. However, Washington's and Tokyo's commitments to the sanctions regime appeared to be far greater than those in Beijing and Seoul, where the prospect of North Korean implosion remained more threatening than Pyongyang's limited nuclear capabilities. While endorsing the sanctions, President Roh's government was clear that South Korean investments in the North's economy would continue, and Beijing took no apparent steps to inspect North Korean shipments coming into and across China.

The North Korean "test" and the Security Council resolution did not mark the diplomatic end-game. Outgoing UN Secretary General Kofi Anan and former US President Jimmy Carter pointed the way for future diplomacy by reiterating that the North Korean nuclear test was "unacceptable," but pressed bilateral negotiations between Washington and Pyongyang. Carter was clear that "What must be avoided is to leave a beleaguered nuclear nation convinced that it is permanently excluded from the international community, its existence threatened." North Korea signaled openness to substantive negotiations by reiterating its commitment to a nuclear weapons-free Korean Peninsula in exchange for successful bilateral negotiations with the US. And China won an agreement from all six parties to resume their negotiations.

The dangers, however, had hardly passed. Before the six-party talks reconvened, the senior US general in Korea was warning that additional North Korean nuclear tests were likely. The US accelerated deployments of missile defenses to Japan, and Clinton-era Secretary of Defense Perry warned that if China and South Korea did not coerce North Korea by threatening its food and oil supplies to prevent completion of a large nuclear reactor, the US "might take the only meaningful coercive action available to it—destroying the reactor before it could come on line."[57]

In Japan there were "noises about the possibility . . . of starting its own nuclear program," while Prime Minister Abe reiterated his commitment to revise Japan's war-renouncing constitution before leaving office.

Half-way around the world, US forces led war games in the Persian Gulf designed to interdict shipments of unconventional weapons bound for . . . Iran![58]

At the deepest level the failed diplomacy and nuclear dangers involving the US, North Korea, and Iran all flowed from the hypocritical conceit that the US and other nuclear powers were entitled to possess and wield nuclear weapons while others were to kowtow to their threats. In fact, counter-proliferation campaigns backed by nuclear threats were at best stop-gap measures. Humanity faced the choice of nuclear weapons abolition or their global proliferation and the nuclear wars that would inevitably follow.

9
Abolition or Annihilation

Humans cannot coexist with nuclear weapons.

Japan Confederation of A- and H-Bomb Sufferers' Organizations[1]

[C]ompliance with the NPT obligations is not a question of *à la carte* . . . Each article of the NPT is legally binding, at all times and in all circumstances.

Miguel Ruiz-Cabanas Izquierdo, Mexican Ambassador to Japan[2]

Never doubt that a small group of thoughtful, committed citizens can change the world. Indeed, it is the only thing that has.

Margaret Mead[3]

Speaking on the eve of the 2005 Nuclear Nonproliferation Review Conference, Christopher Weeramantry, then the recently retired Vice-President of the International Court of Justice, warned that humanity was approaching "the point of no return." He warned that unless the nuclear weapons states honored the World Court's 1999 advisory opinion on the illegality of the use and threatened use of nuclear weapons and fulfilled their NPT commitments, catastrophic nuclear war would inevitably follow.[4]

Our existential plight has changed little in the 50 years since Bertrand Russell and Albert Einstein sounded the alarm that "All, equally, are in peril, and if the peril is understood, there is hope that they may collectively avert it."[5] The danger of a US–Soviet (now Russian) thermonuclear exchange carrying the possibility of nuclear winter no longer haunts us as it once did, but as Daniel Ellsberg and others have warned, the probability of nuclear war has actually increased. Yet initiatives taken by governments, elected officials, NGOs, and popular movements provide hope that the unthinkable is not inevitable. Nuclear weapons abolition is not an impossible dream. Model treaties put forward by the Australian and Malaysian governments and by international lawyers and physicians provide road maps to a world without nuclear weapons. What is most needed is popular will: the people's power rooted in individual efforts and sacrifices that can shake governments and transform national policies.

This chapter is written with the understanding that individual people and the political movements that we create, support, and in which we participate affect the human condition. It is written in the hope that some readers will join nuclear weapons abolition movements or find other ways to build on the courageous efforts of those who have preceded us. I begin with a reality check because successful strategies require identifying vested interests and forces that must be overcome. The United States' and other nations' reliance on nuclear weapons, and those nations and non-state forces which seek to rectify the imbalance of terror by obtaining them, have deep historical, cultural, and economic roots. These powerful forces should not be underestimated.

People can change things for the better. Because it is difficult to find histories of the now six decade-old nuclear weapons abolition movement, as a small corrective, I have provided an impressionistic introduction to these movements. I have also highlighted the efforts of Nobel laureates and other statesmen who have not only called for nuclear weapons abolition, but who have played important roles in preventing nuclear war, in limiting nuclear weapons proliferation, and in creating the tough proposals and the diplomatic pressures needed to move the nuclear powers.

Since Manhattan Project scientists made appeals for nuclear weapons abolition that were codified in the UN General Assembly's first resolution, efforts to contain and eliminate the dangers of nuclear war have been rooted in international law and the imperatives of legal and treaty obligations being fulfilled. The chapter reviews the nuclear powers' legal obligations to eliminate their genocidal arsenals, first and foremost in Article VI of the Nuclear Nonproliferation Treaty and in the advisory opinion of International Court of Justice. After clarifying the differences between arms control and arms abolition, I review the history and limitations of arms control agreements. I conclude by describing the post-Cold War transformation of the nuclear disarmament movement as it turned away from arms control and back to its abolitionist roots. I describe some of the most creative campaigns and include a summary of the most essential elements of a nuclear weapons abolition treaty that have been identified in arms control negotiations, in a succession of UN proposals, and in model treaties developed by the Australian and Malaysian governments.

REALITY CHECK

Because we are confronted by a challenge with deep historical roots and enduring force, it would be foolish to underestimate the existential nuclear challenges. Some argue that with the 1945 Trinity test in the New Mexico desert the nuclear genie was released from its bottle, never to be recaptured. Others use the metaphor of Adam and Eve: humanity has tasted the forbidden fruit and must now learn to live with its lost innocence or perish. And, like the men and women in Plato's allegorical cave, whose limited life experiences led them to believe that reality was limited to shadows on the wall, most people have been born since the atomic bombings of Hiroshima and Nagasaki and accept nuclear weapons as part of the natural order. For them, the inherent but distant dangers of nuclear war are not unlike earthquakes, volcanoes, tsunamis—"things happen." Only in times of great crisis have vast numbers of people confronted the man-made threat that is now woven so deeply into the fabric of modern civilization: cataclysmic thermonuclear war.

It may have become a cliché, but Einstein was right when he said that everything has changed except the way humans think. *Hibakusha* who had this truth branded into their bones and psyches have long warned that "humans and nuclear weapons cannot coexist," providing the lens through which to envision new thinking and life-affirming paradigms. However, from the first censorship of news reports, photographs, and film footage from Hiroshima and Nagasaki, through the secrecy surrounding continuing US nuclear threats, the US people have been blinkered lest they freely consider the human condition and make their way to freedom.

Today, instead of seeing nuclear weapons as "a hammer over" the Soviets, US leaders have embraced nuclear weapons as the "cornerstone" of the nation's foreign and military policy. Thermonuclear weapons are the postmodern version of Theodore Roosevelt's "big stick" and the ultimate enforcer of "full spectrum dominance." In the first decade of the twenty-first century, US presidents have relied more frequently on nuclear threats than most of their Cold War predecessors. Although somewhat chastened by its uncertain victory in Afghanistan and its military quagmire in Iraq, the Bush II administration "refined," but did not move to change, its commitments to unilateralism and first-strike nuclear warfare. Its second *National Security Statement* reaffirmed the commitment to take "anticipatory action" and to "act preemptively" in exercising its "inherent right of self defense." Even as power over US foreign and military policy appeared to pass from Vice-President Cheney and Secretary of Defense Rumsfeld to Secretary of State Rice and other administration "realists," the Bush administration continued to press Congress to fund development, production, and preparations for testing a new generation of genocidal nuclear weapons while expanding its first-strike "missile defense" deployments.[6]

While the Bush II administration derided those who are "reality-based," neither the long-cherished belief in US exceptionalism nor the steady transformation of the US political system from liberal democracy and republic to authoritarian plutocracy and empire have eliminated the law of cause and effect. There are costs involved in ignoring Cassandra's persistent warnings. For six decades Manhattan Project scientists, *Hibakusha*, directors of the International Atomic Energy Agency, Nobel laureates, religious leaders, renowned writers, government officials, and concerned citizens have raised the alarm that the US and other nuclear powers are threatening human survival.

They understand that because no nation will long tolerate what it perceives to be an unjust and oppressive imbalance of power, possession of nuclear weapons is the driving force of their proliferation. And, as illustrated by the Indian and Pakistani nuclear weapons programs, reliance on nuclear arsenals and threats to use them breed proliferation. With North Korea having declared itself and demonstrated that it is a nuclear weapons state, there are growing concerns that Japan and South Korea will follow. For more than three decades senior Japanese officials have contended that the country's "peace constitution" gives it the right to possess "tactical" nuclear weapons. They assert that they have simply "not chosen to exercise this right."[7]

With nuclear weapons technology six decades old, it is increasingly accessible. Today, more than 400 nuclear reactors provide energy for 32 national economies, and more reactors are likely to come on line as governments recklessly seek alternatives to dependence on oil and gas, as well as to slow global warming. As the Indian, Iranian, and North Korean nuclear programs remind us, these power plants can all too easily be used to develop the expertise and fissile materials needed for nuclear weapons. That 39 specified nations are required to sign and ratify the Comprehensive Test Ban Treaty before it can go into force illustrates that dozens of nations are widely recognized as having the potential to become nuclear powers. And, as long as industrialized nations depend on nuclear power for energy generation, many non-nuclear nations will see them as essential to prosperity and will insist on their right to construct them. We thus face both immediate and long-term nuclear dangers.

There have been other costs and dangers. The nuclear fuel cycle and the production and testing of US nuclear weapons have claimed the lives of tens of thousands of uranium miners, down-winders, and "atomic" veterans. They have contaminated the environment and hundreds of thousands of people at a distance, as winds and rivers carried radioactive fallout.

As other nations became nuclear powers, their peoples have been similarly victimized. Poorly monitored, low-level medical and industrial radioactive wastes, including those looted from Soviet and Iraqi sites, also increase the possibility of "dirty bombs" being used by non-state terrorists. Dirty bombs do not cause massive fission or fusion explosions. Instead, deadly low-level radioactive particles are spread over a comparatively small area—for example, Wall Street, Fleet Street, The Ginza or Midan Tahrir in Cairo. The number of people murdered would be limited, but the resulting fear and economic damage would be enormous.[8]

And, as in 1995 when Russian military technicians mistook a Norwegian weather rocket for a US missile armed with multiple warheads, the danger of accidental nuclear war remains, especially as nuclear weapons proliferate.[9]

ARMS CONTROL

Campaigns for arms control and nuclear weapons abolition have at times complemented and reinforced one another. Their goals are, however, different. Because abolition can only be achieved through verifiable arms control agreements, the two are often confused. Arms control advocates seek to limit, but not completely remove, nuclear dangers. Over three decades (1961–91) US and Soviet diplomats used arms control negotiations to gain or reinforce strategic advantages and to co-opt popular movements demanding greater nuclear disarmament or abolition.

Calls for abolition began two months before Hiroshima and Nagasaki were ravaged, when Manhattan Project scientists in Chicago prepared the Franck Report, warning of the dangers of a nuclear arms race. They raised the possibility of halting the production of fissile material, and they called for creation of a supranational organization that could protect the postwar world from nuclear weapons. After the Hiroshima and Nagasaki A-bombings, the first UN General Assembly resolution mandated establishment of the International Atomic Energy Commission to "make specific proposals . . . for the elimination from national armaments of atomic weapons and of all other major weapons adaptable to mass destruction."[10]

Disarmament movements reflecting nations' unique historical experiences and their political realities developed in the 1950s. The World Peace Council (WPC), founded in 1950, was largely controlled by the Soviet Foreign Ministry, but its Stockholm Appeal, which was launched in March 1950, urged "the unconditional prohibition of the atomic weapons" with "strict international control" to enforce their elimination. The Appeal also demanded that the first government to use nuclear weapons be branded "a war criminal." The declaration was signed by millions of people in Communist nations and by more than 30 million people in France and Italy.[11] Many believed that the petition helped to prevent the US from using nuclear weapons during the Korean War.

In 1955, following the "Bravo" H-bomb test on Bikini Atoll, the first World Conference against Atomic and Hydrogen Bombs was held in Tokyo and Hiroshima and led to the creation of the Japan Council against A- and H-bombs. In the US, the pediatrician Benjamin Spock, *Saturday Review* editor Norman Cousins, and the American Friends Service Committee's General Secretary Clarence Pickett responded to Albert Schweitzer's "Call to Conscience" by founding SANE, the Committee for a Sane Nuclear Policy. Its goal was to "develop public support for a boldly conceived and executed policy which will lead mankind away from war and toward peace and justice." And, in 1958, after nuclear tests on Christmas Island and the Labour Party's reaffirmation of its commitment to a nuclear-armed Britain, Bertrand Russell, Kingsley Martin, Canon John L. Collins, Peggy Duff, and others launched the Campaign for Nuclear Disarmament (CND).[12]

One response to growing demands for an end to nuclear weapons testing and for nuclear disarmament were the McCloy–Zorin Accords in 1961. This US–Soviet agreement demonstrated that arms control negotiations could succeed and identified principles for "future multilateral negotiations" to achieve "general and complete disarmament." The principles included "elimination of all stockpiles of nuclear, chemical, bacteriological, and other weapons of mass destruction and cessation of the production of such weapons," elimination of "all means of delivery of weapons of mass destruction," and implementation of disarmament in "an agreed sequence, by stages until it is completed, with each measure and stage carried out within specified time-limits." Future arms control agreements were to be "balanced" so that no "State or group of States [can] gain military advantage and that security [be] ensured for all."

These Accords served as the diplomatic foundation for the Limited Test Ban Treaty in 1963, and its vision of "general and complete disarmament" was enshrined in Article VI of the NPT.[13]

As the Soviet Union approached parity with the US in the 1970s, the pace of arms control negotiations accelerated. Although it ostensibly committed the nuclear powers to "good faith" negotiations to eliminate their nuclear arsenals, the 1968 NPT was primarily designed to consolidate the hierarchy of terror by preventing other nations from joining the nuclear "club." Contrary to the McCloy–Zorin Accords, the 1971 SALT I Treaty was calculated to lock in US strategic advantages by limiting the number of US and Soviet land-based ICBMs and legitimating the continued presence of US bombers in Western Europe. The Treaty's subtext was its acceleration of the arms race on two fronts. Although each power agreed to limit its nuclear-armed ICBMs to just over 1,000, no limits were placed on the number of warheads each missile could carry. This led to a race to deploy MIRVs (multiple independent reentry vehicles—multiple thermonuclear warheads), multiplying the genocidal power of each missile. The Treaty also hastened the nuclear arms race at sea where the US had a larger fleet and enormous technological advantages.[14]

The Anti-Ballistic Missile (ABM) Treaty, signed at the same time as SALT I, limited the number of ABM batteries Washington and Moscow could each possess to two in order to prevent a defensive missile arms race. The Treaty was widely seen as an effort to preserve MAD by outlawing the creation of missile shields that could reinforce first-strike arsenals. Each nation was to remain vulnerable to nuclear attacks by the other, rendering a thermonuclear exchange unthinkable. The right-wing US Committee on the Present Danger, many of whose members later occupied senior positions in the Reagan administration, believed that even with the ABM Treaty, MAD could be circumvented by deploying Pershing II and Tomahawk cruise missiles in Europe. With their eight-minute flight time and pinpoint accuracy, the Pershing IIs were designed to "decapitate" the Soviet leadership before it could order a retaliatory strike. The slower cruise missiles would eliminate most of Moscow's second-strike capabilities, and "Star Wars" missile defense shields were to be the last line of defense. Even if the system were not infallible, its advocates believed it would render Soviet leaders more malleable.

SALT II, concluded in 1979, limited missile launchers to 2,250 on each side, of which 1,250 could carry multiple warheads. This, too, reinforced the right-wing campaign to deploy the Euromissiles and the nuclear arms race at sea. Ultimately, the US deployed 14 Trident submarines, each capable of launching 24 missiles armed with a total of approximately 2,000 thermonuclear warheads.[15]

This was called "arms control."

A global movement to prevent the deployment of the Euromissiles and Soviet SS-20s, and to "freeze" the nuclear arms race forced the Reagan administration to reverse course and negotiate the Intermediate-Range Nuclear Forces Treaty with Mikhail Gorbachev in 1987. With the START treaties and its limited unilateral disarmament, the first Bush administration reinforced US nuclear dominance while simultaneously reducing the dangers of accidental or unintended nuclear war. Negotiations for the Comprehensive Test Ban Treaty were completed by the Clinton administration in 2000, but the US has yet to ratify it, and may never do so.

Other nuclear arms control agreements, some designed to advance nuclear weapons abolition, have been initiated by Third World, Non-Aligned, and "Middle Powers" nations. They negotiated five nuclear weapons-free zone treaties: Pelindaba for Africa, Tlatelolco for Latin America, Rarotonga for the South Pacific, Bangkok for Southeast Asia, and Semipalatinsk for Central Asia. (Antartica is the sixth NWFZ.) Although these nations lack the resources to fully enforce their nuclear-free zones from intrusions by the US and other nuclear powers, especially at sea, they have limited nuclear weapons proliferation and have somewhat insulated these nations from the nuclear powers. The zones also helped to establish a climate of moral suasion and have provided Arab states with a model to press for Israeli nuclear disarmament and to contain possible Iranian nuclear ambitions. Calls for a nuclear weapons-free zone are also seen as a way to reduce the dangers of nuclear war in northeast Asia.

On the eve of the 1995 NPT Extension Conference, Non-Aligned nations pressed for the adoption of five measures: 1) a commitment to negotiate the CTBT; 2) negotiation of a fissile material cut-off treaty and phasing out of nuclear and non-nuclear powers' stockpiles; 3) "full security assurances to non-nuclear-weapon states"; 4) continued access to nuclear technologies for peaceful purposes; and 5) extending the NPT to include Israel, India, and Pakistan.[16]

Although the Clinton administration, with the assistance of other nuclear powers, forced NPT extension through the UN Conference disregarding these demands, they resurfaced five years later in the platform of the New Agenda Coalition (Brazil, Egypt, Ireland, Mexico, Slovenia, South Africa, and Sweden). Through steadfast and creative diplomacy, they won an "irrevocable commitment" from the US and other declared nuclear powers to fulfill their Article VI Treaty obligations and to take 13 critical steps in that direction. The world awaits the implementation of those steps.

A major breakthrough in Track II diplomacy (collaboration between governments and NGOs) grew out of the World Court Project. Three NGOs, including two Nobel prize recipients, formed the Project, which was joined by more than 700 other organizations who pressed their governments to support a UN General Assembly resolution requesting that the International Court of Justice provide an advisory opinion on the legality of the use and threatened use of nuclear weapons.[17] The World Court ruled that the use or threatened use of nuclear weapons is "the ultimate evil." Citing the Nuremberg Principles under which Nazi war criminals were tried, the World Court concluded that "a threat or use of nuclear weapons would generally be contrary to the rules of international law applicable in armed conflict, and in particular their principles and rules of humanitarian law." One disturbing caveat, which was a function of ICJ judges being nominated by their governments, was its inability to "conclude definitively" whether the use of nuclear weapons would be legal "in an extreme circumstance of self-defence, in which the very survival of a State would be at stake." However, the judges were unanimous that the nuclear powers are bound by Article VI of the NPT, and it reminded the world that "there exists an obligation to pursue in good faith and bring a conclusion to negotiations leading to nuclear disarmament in all of its aspects . . ."[18]

The decision has had an enormous impact, inspiring abolitionists around the world and providing non-nuclear governments with a new foundation for their continued struggle to enforce Article VI compliance. Foremost among governmental campaigns has been Malaysia's. Unnoticed by the US media, since the ICJ ruling Malaysia's UN Ambassador has introduced a General Assembly resolution every year calling for an international conference to negotiate a nuclear weapons convention providing for "the complete elimination of nuclear weapons with a specified framework of time to eliminate all nuclear weapons . . . ." The General Assembly has repeatedly endorsed Malaysia's resolution by overwhelming margins, with China and some US allies voting for it. To reinforce its campaign, Malaysia, supported by 20 or more co-sponsors, regularly submits a draft treaty to demonstrate that abolition is possible and to provide a model for achieving it.[19]

REVITALIZED ABOLITION MOVEMENTS

Like all popular movements, support for nuclear weapons abolition has peaked and declined, surged and ebbed like ocean waves and tides.[20] The initial shock and horror at what the US inflicted on the people of Hiroshima and Nagasaki was reflected in journalists' notes and photographs and in film footage seized by the Pentagon. For the US public, the first meaningful descriptions of the A-bombs' destruction and their impacts on people's lives came in John Hersey's 1946 articles published in the *New Yorker* and later as a book. Unfortunately, the original version of the 1955 Japanese film *Godzilla*, which communicates the existential dread that was born with atomic and hydrogen bombs and points to the sacrifices that will be needed to achieve their abolition, has long been denied to US audiences.

The combination of *Hibakusha* testimonies, scientists' warnings, and fears instilled by the Cuban Missile Crisis fueled a popular movement that culminated in negotiation of the 1963 Limited Test Ban Treaty between the US and the USSR. With the end of the Vietnam War, and reports of US plans to base Pershing II and cruise missiles in Europe, a second disarmament wave was generated in the mid- and late 1970s. By the early 1980s, millions of people thronged onto the streets of New York and Western European capitals. Smaller demonstrations were held in cities and town squares. Religious leaders and congregational activists educated and mobilized their communities and denominations. Statewide referendums were organized, and legislative and electoral campaigning transformed the power of the streets into national policy. Together, the popular movements in the US and Europe, with elite forces including sectors of the CIA, and Gorbachev's disarmament diplomacy, defeated Reagan's brinkmanship, won the "nuclear weapons freeze," and contributed mightily to the end of the Cold War.[21]

The Japanese movement, which grew out of the nuclear furnaces of Hiroshima, Nagasaki, and Bikini Atoll, has been central to the global abolition movement. The larger wing of the Japan Council against A- and H-bombs—*Gensuikyo*—today comprises 60 national organizations, including women's, labor, religious, youth, and *Hibakusha* organizations with a combined membership of 2.5 million. *Gensuikyo* and its sibling *Gensuikin* grew out of the nationwide outrage that followed the 1954 "Bravo" H-bomb test on Bikini Atoll in the Marshall Islands. Two years after the end of the formal US military occupation and its censorship, the Japanese were learning what the people of Hiroshima and Nagasaki had suffered when the *Fifth Lucky Dragon*, a small fishing vessel, returned to port outside of Tokyo. Its crew members, sick from the H-bomb's radioactive fallout, described what had seemed to them to be the sun rising in the west and their experience of a bomb 1,000 times more powerful than the Hiroshima A-bomb. Others were victimized by the "Bravo" test. Marshall Islanders were deliberately exposed to the H-bomb's radiation, and an estimated 856 Japanese fishing boats, their 10,000 crewmen, and their catches were also exposed to radioactive fallout. A third nuclear weapon had claimed Japanese victims and threatened the nation's food supply.[22]

Physicians, housewives, civic, religious, and labor leaders, and the Socialist and Communist parties launched a nationwide petition calling for the abolition of A- and H-bombs. Within a year they garnered 34 million signatures—more than half of Japan's registered voters. On the tenth anniversary of the first A-bombings, 25,000 participants traveled to Hiroshima for the first World Conference against A- and H-bombs. So broad was the conference's appeal and moral mandate that Japan's right-wing Prime Minister Hatoyama thought it wise to send personal greetings.

Delegates were moved by the words and courage of some of the first *Hibakusha* willing to speak publicly. Emerging from their seclusion and private agonies, these A-bomb victims "exposed" themselves and what they thought of as their "ugly features." They described what they had seen, lost, and survived; appealed for assistance; and urged "no more Hiroshimas." The words of Suzu Kuboyama, the wife of the *Fifth Lucky Dragon*'s radio operator who died soon after the ship returned to harbor, fueled popular resistance to both nuclear weapons and to the US–Japan Mutual Security Treaty (AMPO) imposed by Washington as the price for ending its formal military occupation. Conference participants learned that Aikichi Kuboyama's last words were said to have been "Let me be the last victim of the atomic and hydrogen bombs," and Mrs Kuboyama vented her anger, protesting that "Atomic artillery and rockets are brought into Japan though everyone opposes this." She appealed to her audience to prevent the US from bringing such weapons to Japan, to oppose the use of nuclear weapons, and for an end to the production, testing, and use of the hated weapons. As it closed, the World Conference issued a declaration calling for "prevention of nuclear war, abolition of all nuclear weapons, and relief and solidarity for the *Hibakusha*." This became the foundation for *Gensuikyo* and helped to fuel the powerful AMPO movement which nearly defeated extension of the military alliance in 1960.[23]

The following year *Hibakusha*, including Chieko Watanabe, Senji Yamaguchi, and others, encouraged by the support they had received and the roles they had played at the World Conference, joined by A-bomb victims from ten prefectures established *Nihon Hidankyo*, the Japan Confederation of A- and H- Bomb Sufferers' Organizations. *Hidankyo* provided a platform for their abolition demands and a vehicle for mutual support and to mobilize political pressure for essential medical and other benefits denied by the conservative US client state.[24]

The Japan Council against Atomic and Hydrogen Bombs and *Nihon Hidankyo* have since played major roles in Japanese political life, in keeping the global disarmament movement focused on the most essential lessons of Hiroshima and Nagasaki, and in inspiring and weaving together abolitionists from many nations. Despite divisions in the Japanese movement, the World Conference serves as a forum where disparate and sometimes competing agendas, international perspectives, and political forces have been informed and challenged by one another, usually finding ways to make common cause. Fifty years after its founding, the World Conference continues to function at three levels: helping to build and support popular movements; pursuing Track II diplomacy; and supporting *Hibakusha*.

Gensuikyo's work with *Hibakusha* "inform[s] the public in Japan and internationally of the damage of the atomic bombing, of the current situation of the *Hibakusha* . . . and to demand compensation" for them. This has included providing forums for *Hibakusha* and sending them abroad to teach the lessons of Hiroshima and Nagasaki while they still can. With the American Friends Service Committee, "global *Hibakusha*" delegations have been organized to help build the abolition movement in forums that include the Hague Appeal for Peace, the UN NGO Millennium Forum, and the World Social Forum.

The British have also provided important leadership in the abolition struggle. One of Einstein's last acts was to sign an appeal written by Bertrand Russell and Joseph Rotblat known as the Russell–Einstein Manifesto.[25] In addition to influencing public opinion, the Manifesto served as the inspiration for the founding of the international Pugwash Conference of scientists and for the Campaign for Nuclear Disarmament (CND). As Rotblat recalled, he and Russell decided on a division of labor: Rotblat took the lead in organizing Pugwash, while Russell played a leading role in CND. In the early 1960s, Russell with younger activists, including Michael Randle and Pat Arrowsmith, launched the Committee of 100 for Civil Disobedience against Nuclear Warfare, which challenged Britain's nuclear weapons program with sit-ins outside the Ministry of Defence, Parliament, and on London streets. Being universalist in their commitments, they condemned the US nuclear arsenal and carried abolition banners and leaflets into the Kremlin.[26]

In the US, as evidence grew that strontium-90 from atmospheric nuclear weapons tests was poisoning milk (including breast milk), SANE was organized, while others upped the ante with civil disobedience. Courageous pacifists, including A. J. Muste of the Fellowship of Reconciliation and Dorothy Day of the Catholic Worker, were jailed for publicly refusing to participate in mandatory "civil defense" drills designed to frighten the public into accepting preparations for nuclear war. Others were jailed for attempting to sail boats into the Pacific Ocean's "forbidden zone" where the US continued H-bomb tests or to block access to US harbors.[27] As would be the case for decades, this movement's demands ranged across a spectrum from strict abolition, to nuclear war prevention, to more limited calls for a test ban treaty. It was to contain this movement as well as to symbolically pull back from the abyss that opened with the Cuban Missile Crisis, that Kennedy and Khrushchev concluded the Limited Test Ban Treaty.

The second wave of the US abolition movement was launched in 1976, following the end of the Vietnam War, when activists stepped off on the Continental Walk for Disarmament and Human Needs. During the walk from San Francisco to Washington, DC, activists—including Buddhist priests from Japan—stopped in communities along the way to awaken a nation long preoccupied by the Vietnam War's daily death toll to the continuing dangers of nuclear war. Two years later, thousands of US activists, joined by *Hibakusha* and Japanese and European delegations, held a "die-in" outside the United Nations to press the urgency of real progress at the UN Special Session on Disarmament.

In Europe and the US, in response to the growing power and influence of the Committee on the Present Danger in Congress, a small core of organizers developed strategies that soon brought millions out to demonstrate their opposition to Euromissile deployments, increased nuclearization of the seas, and the sharp escalation in US–Soviet tensions. Veterans of the Vietnam era peace movement and environmentalists working to halt construction of nuclear power plants became national and community-based leaders of the US and European movements. In Britain, E. P. Thompson and Diane Kaldor launched END (European Nuclear Disarmament) with their *Protest & Survive* manifesto which demanded a halt to new US and Soviet missile deployments and greater democracy in Eastern Europe. CND's membership swelled to 250,000 activists, who participated in local educational meetings, vigils, street demonstrations, and militantly nonviolent women's encampments on Greenham Common and outside other military bases which were being prepared as launching sites for the Pershing II and cruise missiles. Across the English Channel, the German activist Petra Kelly's impassioned speeches and willingness to commit civil disobedience made her the Joan of Arc of the continental movement and had millions marching from Amsterdam to Milan.

In the US, the *Call to Halt the Nuclear Arms Race*, authored by the scholar Randall Forsberg and initially launched by the American Friends Service Committee (AFSC), the Fellowship of Reconcilation (FOR), and the War Resisters League (WRL) ignited a political prairie fire when organizers, including Randy Kehler and David McCauley, placed the call on local referendum ballots and on New England town meeting warrants. Within three years, moved by their fears of Reagan's nuclear threats and encouraged by the European demonstrations, in June 1982, one million people were marching in the streets of New York. Five months later, voters in eight states cast their ballots for a freeze.[28]

After it forced the Reagan administration to negotiate the INF Treaty, the Freeze/Euromissile movement waned. The nuclear consciousness, think-tanks, and networks that it spawned remained and served as the foundation for the post-Cold War abolition movement. With the threat of a US–Soviet (now Russian) thermonuclear exchange diminished, this new wave has focused less on arms control and nuclear war prevention, rooting itself more deeply in original abolitionist visions. Its calls have been for the complete elimination of nuclear weapons.

POST-COLD WAR ABOLITIONISTS

The turn to abolition, at both elite and community-based levels, came with the 1995 NPT Review and Extension Conference and its failure to do more than reinforce the existing nuclear hierarchy. The Cold War was over, but the nuclear danger remained. Thousands of abolitionists from Europe, across the US, Japan, and other countries converged on New York in the spring of 1995 to reinforce the demands of Non-Aligned and other nations for meaningful implementation of Article VI in exchange for the Treaty's extension. The activists lobbied national delegations to the UN, provided NGO testimonies, held vigils, marched, met with the press, and conducted public educational meetings. To underline the moral imperative of abolition, Daniel Ellsberg, who had helped to design Presidents Kennedy's and Johnson's nuclear war plans, fasted publicly throughout the four-week UN Conference. As he began his fast, he correctly predicted that with "an engineered, bribed and coerced, reluctant majority," the US would extend the NPT in ways that "will weaken rather than strengthen the non-proliferation regime." Instead of moving the world toward abolition and security, he predicted that the US-dominated conference would "raise the probability of more Hiroshimas." Ellsberg appealed to world religious and political leaders to join him in his fast "to demand recommitment by the Treaty members, particularly the nuclear weapons states, to the abolition of nuclear weapons and to concrete steps toward that goal."[29]

The relative failure of the NPT Extension Conference—indefinite continuation of the Treaty with no meaningful commitments from the nuclear powers to do more than to negotiate the Test Ban Treaty—had at least four enduring outcomes, at least one that was particularly dangerous. The blatant hypocrisy of the US and other nuclear powers spurred Hindu Nationalists in their drive to demonstrate India's nuclear capabilities and its refusal to be intimidated by China. In 1998, India, followed almost immediately by Pakistan, challenged the NPT order with a succession of A- and H-bomb "tests."

On the positive side of the 1995 Review and Extension Conference ledger, an unintended consequence was the establishment of the New Agenda Coalition (NAC) that worked with non-aligned nations to continue pressing for abolition at the UN and in other forums. President Nelson Mandela, of South Africa, whose life-long commitment demonstrated that greater justice and fundamental political change are possible, placed his moral authority behind the Coalition's campaign. Speaking at the opening session of the 1998 General Assembly, he urged the nuclear weapons states "to make a firm commitment to eliminating nuclear weapons." Mandela charged that "no rational answer can be advanced to explain in a satisfactory manner" why the nuclear powers continued to refuse to implement Article VI. The unacceptable answer, he explained, was "Cold War inertia and an attachment to the use of the threat of brute force to assert the primacy of some states over others." Mandela announced that with other Coalition members, South Africa was introducing a resolution titled "Towards a Nuclear Weapons Free World: The Need for a New Agenda."[30]

Two years later, the NAC's determination bore fruit. In the final days of the 2000 NPT Review Conference, as the diplomatic confab approached collapse in the face of US and other nuclear powers' intransigence, the Coalition extracted an "unequivocal commitment" from the nuclear powers to implement Article VI and to take 13 significant steps toward abolition.

Another initiative resulting from the failed 1995 NPT Conference was the Canberra Commission created by Australia's Labor government. Among its members was the recently retired former head of the US Strategic Command General Lee Butler who, stricken with what the psychologist Robert J. Lifton describes as the "retirement syndrome," warned that the "highly discriminatory" nuclear hierarchy was inherently "unstable," and that "possession of nuclear weapons by any state is a constant stimulus to other states to acquire them." The Commission's report included "practical steps toward a nuclear weapon-free world" in the form of a road map to abolition. In quick succession, the Commission's report was backed by the ICJ's advisory opinion and a model nuclear weapons abolition treaty developed by leading international jurists, physicians, engineers, and scientists.[31]

Within the US, other former nuclear warriors joined Butler in a short-lived abolition offensive. A Henry L. Stimson Center panel report, chaired by former NATO Commander General Andrew Goodpaster, which included former Assistant Secretary of Defense Paul Nitze and former Secretary of Defense Robert McNamara, urged abolition. Their report warned that "[i]n the long term, only a policy aimed at steadily curbing global reliance on nuclear weapons—including our own—is likely to progressively eliminate nuclear dangers."[32]

The next round in the elite campaign came with the "Statement on Nuclear Weapons by International Generals and Admirals" from 17 countries, including the US, Russia, France, Japan, India, and Pakistan. Their statement warned that "the continuing existence of nuclear weapons in the armories of nuclear powers, and the ever present threat of acquisition of these weapons by others, constitute a peril to global peace and security and to the safety and survival of the people we are dedicated to protect . . ." The generals and admirals warned that there is "no alternative" to nuclear weapons abolition, and they urged massive reductions in nuclear weapons stockpiles, standing down of nuclear weapons, and negotiations to achieve "continuous, complete and irrevocable elimination of nuclear weapons." Once the US and Russian arsenals were reduced to between 1,000 and 1,500 nuclear warheads or fewer, "[t]he other three nuclear states and the three threshold states should be drawn into the reduction process as still deeper reductions are negotiated down to the level of hundreds."[33] President Clinton's response was that nuclear weapons remained "the cornerstone of our policy."

Backed by the generals and admirals, by retired Senator Alan Cranston, Senator Doug Roche of Canada, and others, Butler became the poster boy for this elite movement at press conferences, in media interviews, and well-staged public forums. Uncompromising in his statements that the US military had "served the world supremely well" in the twentieth century, he nonetheless called US nuclear weapons and nuclear war policies "irrational," and confessed that "much of what I took on faith was either wrong, enormously simplistic, extraordinarily fragile, or simply morally intolerable."[34]

Butler was wary of popular movements, and he alienated potential allies by advising audiences that "traditional marches, demonstrations, ban the bomb symbols, and calculated confrontations . . . are more hurtful than helpful" to the goal of abolition. We may never know if he was correct. After his 15 minutes of fame, he passed into history and comfortable retirement.

Fortunately, other elite figures have been more steadfast. Paul Nitze, who in Reykjavik negotiated the short-lived agreement with Soviet leaders to eliminate nuclear weapons over a 15-year period—an agreement that was scuttled as soon as President Reagan's most senior advisors realized what Nitze had done—has continued to affirm that there is "no compelling reason why we should not unilaterally get rid of our nuclear weapons."

Confident of Washington's non-nuclear arsenal, he has been consistently clear that maintaining nuclear weapons "is costly and adds nothing to our security."[35]

Following the Bush administration's sabotage of the 2005 NPT Review Conference, former President Carter used the *Washington Post* to warn that "The United States is the major culprit in this erosion of the NPT." During his 1976 election campaign, Carter had decried the hypocrisy of US nuclear weapons and war policies, saying that "by enjoining sovereign nations to forgo nuclear weapons, we are asking for a form of self-denial that we have not been able to accept ourselves. I believe," he added, that "we have little right to ask others to deny themselves such weapons . . . unless we demonstrate meaningful progress towards the goal of control, then reduction and ultimately, the elimination of nuclear arsenals." During his presidency, he was unable to practice this "self-denial," and he promoted research for a neutron bomb, deployment of nuclear-armed cruise missiles in Europe, and launched nation-killing Trident submarines. In retirement there was less reason to compromise his beliefs.[36]

More inspiring have been the courageous and enduring efforts of two Nobel laureates and the surviving *Hibakusha* of *Nihon Hidankyo* who have repeatedly been nominated for the Nobel Peace Prize. In his nineties, Joseph Rotblat continued to travel the world, speaking at conferences, meeting with government officials, encouraging community-based activists, and chastising scientists complicit in preparing a nuclear Armageddon. By honoring him with its Peace Prize in 1995 following the failure of the NPT Review and Extension Conference, the Nobel Committee sent a message to the world, and Rotblat made the most of the opportunity. He used his acceptance speech to urge world leaders and scientists to "*[r]emember your humanity and forget the rest*," and he reminded the world that the General Assembly's "very first" resolution "called for the elimination of nuclear weapons." He appealed that "for the sake of humanity—we must get rid of *all* nuclear weapons." Speaking as a scientist, realist, and Gandhian strategist, Rotblat explained that "We have the technical means to create a nuclear-weapon-free world in about a decade," but "*[w]hen it comes to nuclear weapons . . . . [it is] . . . the technician, not the commander in the field, who is at the heart of the arms race*." In a call to conscientious mutiny, Rotblat appealed to "*all scientists in all countries to cease and desist from work creating, developing, improving and manufacturing further nuclear weapons—and . . . other weapons of potential mass destruction such as chemical and biological weapons*." Because knowledge and thus the ability to create nuclear weapons persist, Rotblat went further, warning that "The only way to prevent [nuclear war] is to abolish war altogether." Not a utopian, he provided reasons to believe war could share the same fate as cannibalism and slavery. Ten years later, on the eve of the 60th anniversary of the Hiroshima and Nagasaki A-bombings, Rotblat renewed his call, again pressing scientists to stop making nuclear weapons and urged "the nuclear powers [to] honor their obligations under the Non-Proliferation Treaty."[37]

The Nobel Committee sent another message in 2005 after the collapse of the 2005 NPT Review Conference. Although compromised by his support for nuclear power generation, Mohamed ElBaradei, Director General of the International Atomic Energy Agency, was honored with the Peace Prize. During the Bush administration's campaign of lies about nuclear and other weapons of mass destruction in Iraq, ElBaradei had persisted in reporting the unwelcome truth that his investigators had found no evidence that Iraq had resumed its nuclear weapons program. As the 2005 NPT Review Conference approached, he was similarly candid and balanced. He advised that if proliferation was to be prevented, "the right of countries to enrich uranium or reprocess plutonium as part of their civilian program[s]" had to be limited, but he also insisted that the nuclear powers that still possessed nearly 30,000 nuclear warheads must "move toward total disarmament." Speaking in Washington, DC and elsewhere, he had been clear that the nuclear powers' "double standard" was a major obstacle to nonproliferation. It was time, he said, to "abandon the unworkable notion that it is morally reprehensible for some countries to pursue nuclear weapons but morally acceptable for others to rely on them." For these transgressions, the Bush II administration sought, but failed, to oust ElBaradei from the IAEA. The Nobel Peace Prize bolstered his position and added to his power.[38]

Many abolitionists were disappointed by the Nobel Committee's choice of ElBaradei. Some, whose work addressed the linkage between nuclear power generation and nuclear weapons production, were outraged. Others mourned a lost opportunity. *Nihon Hidankyo* had again been nominated for the prize, and in the days leading up to the announcement of the recipient, *Hidankyo* was tipped in the European press to receive its overdue recognition.[39]

Like Nazi death camp survivors, the politically engaged *Hibakusha* were steadfast as they endured physical and psychic pain while speaking essential and challenging truths. Over the course of six decades, they had not only recreated their lives, but—sometimes rising from their hospital beds—journeyed across Japan and around the world to describe what they had seen, lost, and suffered. They had cared for one another, helped to create three generations of abolitionists, and played a central role in building the global abolition movement. *Hidankyo*'s members had testified at the United Nations, marched and held vigils in Tokyo and other world capitals, and testified at the International Court of Justice. With wisdom and generous spirits, they had made common cause with "Global *Hibakusha*," working in solidarity with Koreans who shared the agonies of Hiroshima and Nagasaki and still worse discrimination, and with nuclear weapons test and production victims from the Marshall Islands, Kazakhstan, Russia, the US, Polynesia, and other nations.

Awarding *Nihon Hidankyo* the Peace Prize would have provided another global platform for the world's most articulate and dedicated abolitionists. It would also have sent the message that the world condemned six decades of US nuclear imperialism.

ABOLITION 2000

Further down the hierarchy of honored abolitionists are those who straddle the demands of international diplomacy, movement building, grassroots organizing, and developing critical policy analyses. As it became clear that the 1995 NPT Review and Extension Conference would fail to hold the US and other nuclear powers accountable to Article VI, representatives of hundreds of NGOs from across the world met in New York to create a new network: Abolition 2000. Within months, nearly 1,000 NGOs from 75 countries signed onto the network's declaration. Looking ahead to the NPT Review Conference five years later, the network's eleven-point founding statement called for negotiation of a "nuclear weapons abolition convention that requires the phased elimination of all nuclear weapons within a time-bound framework, with provisions for verification and enforcement" by the time the Review Conference convened. Abolition 2000 member organizations agreed to work for "an unconditional pledge" by the nuclear powers "not to use or threaten to use nuclear weapons," for negotiation of the CTBT, a halt to production and deployment of "new and additional nuclear weapons systems," strict accounting and safeguards for all weapons-grade fissile material, and for the creation of more nuclear weapons-free zones. Meeting two years later in French-Occupied Polynesia, Abolition 2000 adopted its Moorea Declaration which embraced long-marginalized nuclear weapons victims/resisters. As the Declaration read, "Colonized and indigenous peoples have, in the large part, borne the brunt of this nuclear devastation—from the mining of uranium and the testing of nuclear weapons on indigenous peoples' land, to the dumping, storage and transport of plutonium and nuclear wastes, and the theft of land for nuclear infrastructure." The ultimate human sacrifice had been inflicted on their families and communities. Their "lands, air and waters were taken for the nuclear build-up, from the very start of the nuclear era."[40]

Unable to generate the mass response of the early 1980s, and lacking that era's financial and organizational resources, Abolition 2000's core organizers have struggled to develop an inspiring strategy and the appropriate balance between community-based education, organizing, and Track II diplomacy. They have organized *Hibakusha* speaking tours; a peace walk from the Oak Ridge nuclear laboratory to the United Nations; won the support of more than 1,000 mayors from Hooglede (in Belgium) and Honolulu to Hue for an Emergency Campaign initiated by the mayors of Hiroshima and Nagasaki; organized conferences; conducted citizens' "inspection tours" of US military bases; engaged in civil disobedience actions outside nuclear weapons labs; and built alliances with the larger post-9/11 peace and anti-war movements. Lest the movement lose its way, *Hibakusha*, Japanese activists and mayors, and some in the US peace movement—particularly Catholic "plowshares" activists who have risked long prison sentences for hammering missile nose cones and pouring their own blood into the controls of nuclear submarines—have been uncompromising.[41]

Despite Abolition 2000, the new millennium was not welcomed by a nuclear weapons abolition treaty. Abolition 2000's success was helping to keep the vision of a nuclear weapons-free world alive for a more fertile time. They worked with New Agenda Coalition members and other governments to maintain steady pressure on the US and other nuclear weapons states. They also did what they could to limit nuclear atrocities—from the development and deployment of new nuclear weapons to preventing potential nuclear wars against Iraq, Iran, and North Korea. Throughout, Abolition 2000 served its primary function of providing abolitionists with a means to exchange information, developing common or complementary strategies, issuing joint statements, and coordinating popular education and mobilization, especially during the NPT Review conferences.

Among the most impressive campaigns initiated by Abolition 2000 member groups was one inspired by Terumi Tanaka, *Nihon Hidankyo*'s General Secretary, which in 1999 demonstrated the accuracy of polls reporting that up to 80 percent of US Americans support nuclear weapons abolition.[42] Moved by Dr Tanaka's compelling testimony in the course of a speaking tour across New England, AFSC staff and other Vermont activists returned to the town meeting strategy used to launch the Nuclear Weapons Freeze movement in 1980/81. New England town meetings, at which community members come together once a year to discuss and vote on community issues from the need for new roads to the purchase of fire trucks, pre-date the US revolution and remain the mythic essence of US democracy.

The Vermont campaign began with a peace walk across the state, during which marchers stopped in communities to engage local citizens, identify people who could do follow-up organizing, and win local press attention. Later, petitions were circulated to place abolition on "town warrants" (the town meeting agendas). Educational literature was produced, and more meetings were organized, including a speaking tour by retired Admiral James Carroll who had signed the Generals and Admirals statement, and still more press conferences were held to build public support for the campaign. On election day with margins of 3:1 and more, 55 Vermont towns and cities voted that the US should negotiate a treaty to eliminate all nuclear weapons. Building on this victory, Vermont campaign organizers took abolition to the state legislature, where the Senate voted unanimously and the House of Representatives voted overwhelmingly that the first priority of US foreign policy should be to negotiate an abolition treaty. Vermont thus became the first US state to formally call for nuclear weapons abolition.

Elsewhere in the US Abolition 2000 member organizations and activists have worked with religious leaders to create the National Religious

Partnership on the Nuclear Weapons Danger to build nuclear consciousness and engage the religious community in day-to-day abolition efforts. The Nuclear Age Peace Foundation initiated trainings for the next generation of abolition organizers, and the Western States Legal Foundation produced valuable analytical studies and won the support of United for Peace and Justice (UFPJ), the country's principal post-9/11 national peace coalition, for abolition. With assistance from 1,000 Japanese peace activists who traveled to New York for the 2005 NPT Review Conference, UFPJ took the lead in organizing the largest US nuclear disarmament demonstration since a million people rallied for the Freeze in 1982. Other organizations have taken the lead in lobbying Congress, supporting US nuclear victims, engaging in nonviolent civil disobedience, and working with city councils, mayors, and the Massachusetts state legislature to win endorsements of the Mayors for Peace Emergency Campaign.

In Europe, Abolition 2000 member organizations arranged public forums, circulated petitions, lobbied, and played lead roles in the Global Campaign Against Weapons and Nuclear Power in Space. In addition to supporting the Mayors for Peace campaign, activists in Britain, Belgium, France, and Sweden have organized "Citizens Weapons Inspection" teams, venturing legally or trespassing on US military bases in a campaign to force the withdrawal of US military bases and the nuclear weapons that are deployed in Europe. Like *Gensuikyo*, which made developing the next generation of abolitionists a priority, the Mouvement de la Paix in France was particularly imaginative in engaging, training, and mobilizing young activists. They came to New York during the 2005 NPT Review Conference to lobby and learn in UN hallways and offices and to demonstrate on the streets of New York. Months later, nearly 100 traveled to Hiroshima and Nagasaki for life-changing meetings with *Hibakusha*, participation in peace walks, commemorative events, youth rallies and conferences to mark the 60th anniversary of the first A-bombings.

At this writing, Britain's CND "No Trident Replacement" campaign has raised the albeit still distant possibility that London could be the first of the original nuclear powers to dismantle its arsenal. Even Foreign Secretary Margaret Beckett has been forced to concede the need for a "public debate on whether the country still needs Trident missiles."[43] And, as the US, Britain, and Israel threatened to attack Iran to prevent it from developing nuclear weapons, CND's leadership courageously provided Iran's Ambassador a platform at their annual conference to explain his government's policies and to respond to challenging questions from British abolitionists and the national media. CND was committed to providing a comprehensive understanding of the issues and dangers involved in the crisis.[44] Norwegian and English abolitionists provided consistent support for Mordechai Vanunu, the Israeli nuclear technician imprisoned for 18 years—much spent in solitary confinement—for taking proof of Israeli's nuclear weapons program to the international press.

Popular resistance to nuclear weapons has not, of course, been limited to Europe and the US. Immediately following the 1998 Indian nuclear weapons "tests," the former Indian Navy chief, Admiral L. Ramdas, provided leadership and inspiration as that country's peace movement mobilized to challenge the government's nuclear ambitions. The filmmaker Anand Patwardan made an important contribution to help Indians—many mired in poverty—understand the dangers of nuclear weapons by quickly producing a devastating five-minute film that was broadcast on August 6, the anniversary of the Hiroshima A-bombing. Patwardan's film focused on the human suffering caused by the first A-bombs and urged the nation to turn back on the nuclear road. Journalists, including Praful Bidwai and Achin Vanaik, used the press to explain why India's nuclear arsenal and the chauvinist celebrations organized by the Hindu Nationalist ruling party were extremely dangerous. With teachers; religious, women's and labor leaders; students; Gandhians; and left-wing political parties, they helped to build the Coalition for Disarmament and Peace, which demanded Indian and universal nuclear disarmament. Vanaik and Bidwai also traveled round the world to rally expatriate Indians and to deepen cooperation with other disarmament movements.[45]

When Pakistan responded to the Indian nuclear "tests" with bombs of its own, dissenting physicists there, including Pervez Hoodboy, A. H. Nyar, and Zia Mian, along with journalists like Beena Sarwar, condemned the country's nuclear weapons program. To reinforce and help build the growing South Asian disarmament movement, Focus on Global South (an NGO based in Bangkok) organized a conference in neutral Bangladesh where Indian and Pakistani disarmament leaders could meet safely, strategize, engage, and be supported by South Asian elites and popular movements. The presence of Japanese, Philippine, Thai, and US abolitionists encouraged the process and provided links to the global movement. The conference's Dhaka Declaration warned that "India's and Pakistan's nuclearization has made the entire South Asian region hostage to their mutual rivalry and compromised its security." It "deplored" the hardening nuclear doctrines of the two nuclear powers and declared that "it is imperative that India and Pakistan cease all activity pertaining to the development, manufacture, introduction or deployment of nuclear weapons and ballistic missiles." While the conference's primary concern was South Asia, its participants understood that the failure of the declared nuclear powers to fulfill their NPT obligations was a primary cause of the nuclear danger they faced. This, too, was addressed in the Declaration, which demanded that the nuclear powers "honor their disarmament obligations under Article VI of the Nuclear Non-Proliferation Treaty as reemphasized by the 1996 World Court Judgment."[46]

A REAL BARRIER

Since the end of the Cold War, the US media and the nation's political discourse have focused on the dangers of "horizontal proliferation," the danger that "rogue" states with nuclear power plants and nuclear weapons programs could "go nuclear," and that leakage from nuclear stockpiles could find its way to "rogue" states or to non-state terrorist groups like al-Qaeda. One nightmare scenario envisions the overthrow of the military regime in Pakistan, with its nuclear arsenal falling into the hands of radical Islamists. Others focus on leakage from Russia's nuclear stockpiles. It doesn't take a genius to understand that under-funded initiatives like the Congressional Nunn–Lugar Nuclear Threat Initiative, which was designed to secure the world's nuclear weapons, fissile materials, and nuclear wastes, need to be supported.

However, these efforts can be no more than stop-gap measures as long as the US threatens nuclear war, insists on maintaining the terrorizing imbalance of power, and continues to threaten other nations with nuclear attacks. Rotblat put it simply when he warned that the NPT is at best "an interim arrangement . . . one cannot imagine an international law that permanently discriminates between nations. If some states are allowed to keep nuclear weapons, because they claim they are needed for their security, one cannot deny the acquisition of these weapons to other states."[47]

It is not surprising that US elite figures, ranging from Republicans such as UN Ambassador John Bolton and Secretary of State Condoleezza Rice and Democrats including former CIA Directors Stansfield Turner and John Deutch, have little regard for the country's Article VI obligations. Decades ago, the theologian Reinhold Niebuhr put it well when he wrote that "the moral attitudes of dominant and privileged groups are characterized by universal self-deception and hypocrisy. The unconscious and conscious identification of their special interests with general interest and universal values . . . . is equally valued." In an observation that applies to the US Empire as well as to its repeated use of nuclear weapons to enforce it, Niebuhr explained that these privileged classes are "only partly conscious of the violence and coercion by which they and their privileges are preserved . . . . The force they use is either the covert force of economic power or it is the police [read military] power of the state."[48] In this context, what Washington and many in the US term "peace" is simply

resigned acceptance of the inequities imposed by US threats and its use of murderous force—including nuclear war.

Resistance is often conceived in heroic terms. Certainly, courage is sometimes needed to publicly counter what passes for received wisdom. This applies to *Hibakusha*, who speak from the experience of immense psychic and physical pain. It is also present in acts of civil disobedience, both small and large, in Daniel Ellsberg's 1995 fast, and in Mordechai Vanunu's 18 years' incarceration.

We need, however, to look beyond "courage." In his novel *The Plague*, which universalized lessons to be taken from the Nazi era, the French philosopher Albert Camus explained that our task is "to set up a real barrier against the disease, otherwise we might just as well do nothing." In raising this "real barrier," Camus understood that "[t]here's no question of heroism . . . . It's a matter of common decency . . . the only means of fighting a plague is—common decency."[49]

How, then, do we practice "common decency" in our time?

As in medicine, identifying and naming the source of what threatens us is essential to developing a successful antidote. Empires do not rise or fall in the course of a single presidency, or even a generation. They are vast, integrated, and extremely powerful social structures. After two centuries of militarized expansionism, creating a continental and then a global empire, the US has created a postmodern imperium. It was Senator Patrick Moynihan who, in 1991, pleaded for patience rather than war when he reminded his colleagues and the nation that maintaining a "foreign legion" in Europe for 45 years and the dispatching of 500,000 troops to the Persian Gulf recalled the Roman Empire. Battered and increasingly isolated though it may be by US and global resistance to the Bush II war presidency, the US remains the seat of an empire that preserves itself and expands by relying on all of its resources: political, economic, military, social, intellectual, and spiritual. To be successful, strategies for abolition and survival need to struggle in each of these dimensions.

In the late 1990s, during the trial of Phil Berrigan and other Plowshare activists, an appeal circulated through cyberspace. Its message was that "Like most [of] us, President Clinton is both an idealist and a pragmatist." Readers were told that in his second inaugural address Clinton had shared his dream of a land of new promise in which "our children will sleep free from the threat of nuclear, chemical, or biological weapons." Oblivious to the purposes of Clinton's rhetoric, the cyberspace appeal urged people to back the idealist in Clinton by sending him a message each month encouraging him to honor his inaugural vision.

Petitioning Caesar is not a "real barrier" to the dangers of nuclear holocaust. What impresses elected officials? Lacking financial resources to finance expensive election campaigns, peace and justice movements must look elsewhere—to bodies and ballots. Congressman Ed Markey provided part of the answer when he remarked that the only way to budge members of Congress is to threaten them with electoral failure. Recall that John F. Kennedy did not visit Martin Luther King, Jr. or move to protect civil rights organizers in the South until he understood that doing so would help him gain, and then hold on to, power as president. Two decades of US aggression in Indochina ended only after waves of popular protest across the US and a highly focused national campaign taught most Congressmen and women that they needed to vote to halt funding for the war if they were to be reelected. The Reagan administration was forced to turn away from the rhetoric of "winning nuclear wars" and engage in arms control negotiations only after the Nuclear Freeze Movement educated and organized millions of voters, attracting Congressional allies—including Markey—along the way.

Gandhi provided other models of "common decency." One of his great contributions was to demonstrate that imperial power could be overcome through nonviolent *civil* disobedience. The cornerstone of the Indian struggle for liberation from British colonial rule was what Gandhi called *satyagraha* (truth force), including the understanding that oppressors can be moved to change as well as be changed and moved. Through actions as small as spinning cotton and as large and self-sacrificing as the "Salt March," the power of the British Empire was brought to its knees.[50]

Each struggle for freedom is unique, but consistent to each is the truth told by the slavery abolitionist Frederick Douglass that power concedes nothing without a struggle.

Just as empire is based on multiple, interrelated foundations, so too must be successful struggles for fundamental cultural and political change. Change necessarily takes place across a wide spectrum of individual and collective actions. In addition to people willing to labor with elected officials or to organize election campaigns to oust them, a successful movement needs people who can research and write, preach, hand out leaflets on street corners and in university halls, fund-raise, lead guerrilla theater, make eye-catching banners, and organize conferences and international networks. Just as much as a successful movement needs the organizers who can attend to the logistics of a mass demonstration and charismatic leaders who can lead people on the streets, it also needs scholars, teachers, childcare providers, those who like to organize pot-luck dinners, and people willing to risk imprisonment. Today we would also be lost without committed computer technicians and web-page designers!

We can take lessons from other movements and struggles in the past. During the Nazi occupation of the Netherlands, school teachers used picture books to instruct children about how to protect themselves against menacing foreign intruders, and railworkers went on strike to slow the transport of German troops and munitions. In Denmark, resistance flyers were translated into Braille, which could not have been done without skilled translators and printers.

The Dutch artist Rob Wout, known as Opland, gave heart to millions of Europeans by playfully illustrating resistance to the Euromissiles. His cartoon of a no-nonsense woman dispatching a nuclear missile with a swift kick became the logo of Europe's anti-nuclear movement in the 1970s and 1980s. In the US, Bob Dylan's *Masters of War* bitterly denounced those who have "thrown the worst fear that can ever be hurled." In the troubadour's tradition of popular education, Dylan's lyrics exposed some of the ways that society and "the war machine" work. Joan Baez's rendition of *What Have They Done to the Rain?* intimately illuminated what the masters of war were doing to the planet. The movement hymns *We Shall Overcome* and *Ain't Gonna Let Nobody Turn Me 'Round* helped two generations of labor and civil rights activists to find the courage to carry on in the face of beatings, arrests, and even murder. And to this day Boston commuters can marvel at the silhouetted portrait of Ho Chi Minh, painted by a Catholic nun, hidden in an abstract painting that decorates a commercial gas storage tank on a major highway.

The power of an empire is great, but change is the constant of the universe. Empires fall as well as rise. Each decays or is quietly transformed from within while being challenged by external forces. At enormous cost to both the US Empire and the US people, the Bush II–Cheney government refused to accept that the era of classical colonialism cannot be restored. Neither invasions nor nuclear threats could recreate a twenty-first-century version of that era. With its titanic national and trade deficits, and its growing dependence on foreign investments, the US Empire is increasingly susceptible to the demands of others—including the demands for nuclear disarmament. If horizontal proliferation can be contained, and if the New Agenda Coalition and Non-Aligned nations persist, in time the US will have little choice but to honor its Article VI obligations.

The political and technical proposals needed for the elimination of nuclear weapons have long been known. The first policy step is a clear reaffirmation of the US obligation to *implement* Article VI of the Nuclear Nonproliferation Treaty. Second is renunciation of its "first-strike" nuclear war-fighting doctrines. If the US begins, other nuclear powers will follow.

Other essential steps have been identified and recalibrated since the McCloy–Zorin Agreement of 1961. A nuclear weapons abolition treaty would require intense negotiation, but its elements would certainly include:

- Verified and irreversible dismantling of nuclear weapons and nuclear weapons installations. To increase confidence, as weapons are destroyed, they should be placed under international control, beyond the reach of national governments.
- Halting production of weapons-grade fissile material, as well as verifying and securely containing existing stockpiles.
- Verification, including societal verification, in which citizens are expected to notify international authorities of any violations of the nuclear weapons abolition treaty and are protected for doing so.
- Intrusive inspection systems in which no installations or buildings are off-limit at any time, including those of the declared nuclear weapons nations.
- Investing in a supranational authority, possibly an expanded Security Council, with the authority to isolate, contain, or remove threats to the nuclear weapons-free order, including governments that refuse to participate in, or attempt to break out of, the nuclear weapons-free regime.[51]

What would be more secure than "mutual assured safety" reinforced by unilateralist US counter-proliferation policies and wars? The answer was given 60 years ago in the UN Charter and a generation ago in the Palme Commission's *Common Security* report. Essential principles are that each nation has the right to security, that military force is not a legitimate instrument for resolving conflicts, and that policies that seek the advantage of one nation over others only generate greater insecurity. Real security cannot be attained through military superiority.[52]

In 2004, during the official commemorations of the Hiroshima and Nagasaki A-bombings, the mayors of those cities spoke for their communities and for much of the world. Mayor Akiba of Hiroshima warned that "the egocentric worldview of the US government is reaching extremes," and that other nations "buying into the worthless policy of 'nuclear insurance' are salient symbols of our times." We must pledge, he declared, "to do everything in our power . . . for the total abolition of nuclear power." Mayor Itoh of Nagasaki was equally critical of the US stockpile of nearly 10,000 nuclear weapons, its subcritical nuclear weapons tests, and its preparations to develop and use "mini-nuclear weapons" with the destructive power of the Nagasaki A-bomb. He also addressed the US people saying, "The path leading to the eventual survival of the human race unequivocally requires the elimination of nuclear arms. The time has come to join hands and embark on this path."[53]

Decades earlier, the theologian Martin Buber asked, "What must be done?" His answer was elementary and revolutionary: "[Do] not withhold yourself."[54]

We have road maps to a nuclear weapons-free world. We can reach the destination of nuclear weapons abolition only if we find within ourselves the moral and political will that has been lacking for far too long, if we "do not withhold ourselves," and if we have the courage to do "everything in our power." Hope, imagination, and resolute will can be contagious. They are also essential for human survival.

Notes

INTRODUCTION

1. Larry A. Niksch, "North Korea's Nuclear Weapons Program," Congressional Research Service, The Library of Congress, May 25, 2006, http://fpc.state.gov/documents/organization/67840.pdf (September 8, 2006).
2. Federation of American Scientists, *Weapons of Mass Destruction around the World*, http://fas.org/nuke/guide/summary.htm (August 29, 2006).
3. Jodi Wilgoren, "Kerry Promises Speedier Efforts to Secure Nuclear Arms," *New York Times*, June 2, 2004; David Krieger, "Kerry Pledges to Give Nuclear Terrorism His Top Priority," June 10, 2004, www.wagingpeace.org (September 9, 2006); *The National Security Strategy of the United States of America*, The White House, March 16, 2006, pp. 18 and 21.
4. John Deutch, "Loose Nukes," a forum held at the Massachusetts Institute of Technology, October 14, 1997, audiotape provided to author.
5. Zbigniew Brzezinski, *The Grand Chessboard: American Primacy and its Geostrategic Imperatives*, New York: Basic Books, 1997, p. 8.
6. Cited by Noam Chomsky in *The Last Empire*, Cambridge Documentary Films, 1994.
7. Department of Defense, *Doctrine for Joint Nuclear Operations*, Joint Publication 3–12, March 15, 2005.
8. Seymour M. Hersh, "The Iran Plans," *The New Yorker*, April 17, 2006; Eric Schmitt, "U.S. Hurries Plan to Hit Iran, Article Says," *The New York Times*, April 9, 2006.
9. Ibid.; *The National Security Strategy of the United States of America*, p. 20; David E. Sanger, "Report Backs Iraq Strike and Cites Iran Peril," *New York Times*, March 16, 2006; David Ruppe, "U.S. Test to Model Low-yield Nuclear Bomb Effects," *Global Security Newswire*, April 4, 2006, http://www.nt.org/d%5Fnewswire/issues/2006/4/4/34757f44%D51cd%2D4998%Daf51%2D137b84f37a66.html (August 29, 2006).
10. Author's notes of Professor Ello's lectures.
11. Noam Chomsky, *The Chomsky Reader*, edited by James Peck, New York: Pantheon, 1987, p. 318; Elie Abel, *The Missile Crisis*, Philadelphia: J. B. Lippincott, 1966, p. 182; President George H. W. Bush, February 1, 1991, quoted in Robert Perry, *The Nation*, April 15, 1991; and Anthony Lewis, *New York Times*, March 15, 1991.
12. Cited by Daniel Ellsberg in *The Last Empire*, Cambridge Documentary Films, 1994.

1 DEADLY CONNECTIONS: EMPIRE AND NUCLEAR WEAPONS

1. William Appleman Williams, *The Tragedy of American Diplomacy*, New York: Delta Books, 1962, p. 17.
2. Johan Galtung and Dietrich Fischer, "Towards a Nuclear Weapons Free World," circulated on the Internet by South Asians against Nukes, September 9, 1998.
3. Daniel Ellsberg, in *The Last Empire*, Cambridge Documentary Films, 1994.

4. Gar Alperovitz "The Hiroshima Decision: A Moral Reassessment," *Christianity and Crisis*, February 1, 1992.
5. See, among others, Gar Alperovitz, "Enola Gay: Was Using the Bomb Necessary?" *Miami Herald*, December 14, 2006. Martin J. Sherwin, *A World Destroyed: The Atomic Bomb and the Grand Alliance*, New York: Vintage Books, 1975, p. 203.
6. Sherwin, ibid.
7. McGeorge Bundy, *Danger and Survival: Choices about the Bomb in the First Fifty Years*, New York: Random House, 1988, p. 96.
8. Gar Alperovitz, "Hiroshima: Historians Reassess," *Foreign Policy*, Summer 1996, p. 26.
9. Tsuyoshi Hasegawa, *Racing the Enemy: Stalin, Truman, and the Surrender of Japan*, Cambridge, MA: The Belknap Press of Harvard University Press, 2005, p. 222.
10. It should be noted that others were killed as the US raced to build the atomic bombs. These people included uranium miners who were not warned about, or protected from, the deadly radiation. Technicians working with Ernest Lawrence's cyclotrons in California and at Oak Ridge were also exposed to radiation which resulted in cancers.
11. *The Last Empire*, Cambridge Documentary Films, 1985.
12. Chandra Muzzafar, "Bandung: 50 Years After," *JUST Commentary*, Selangor Darul Ehsan, Malaysia, May 2005.
13. A recent example was the sudden and unexplained cancellation of planning for a Social Science Resources Council conference on US global network of foreign military bases in June 2005, which resulted from fears that Congressional Republicans might challenge or cut SSRC funding.
14. Howard Zinn, *Declarations of Independence: Cross-Examining American Ideology*, New York: HarperCollins, 1990, p. 73.
15. Donald Kagan, *The Peloponnesian War*, New York: Viking, 2003.
16. Noam Chomsky, *The Chomsky Reader*, edited by James Peck, New York: Pantheon, 1987, pp. 317–18.
17. Zbigniew Brzezinski, "America's New Geostrategy," *Foreign Affairs*, Spring 1988.
18. See, among others, Ronald Steel, "Totem and Taboo," *The Nation*, September 20, 2004; Niall Ferguson, *Empire: The Rise and Demise of the British World Order and the Lessons for Global Power*, New York: Basic Books, 2002; Niall Ferguson, *Colossus: The Rise of America's Empire*, New York: Penguin, 2004; Robert Kagan, *Of Paradise and Power*, New York: Alfred A. Knopf, 2003; Ivo H. Daalder and James M. Lindsay, "American Empire, Not 'If' but 'What Kind,' " *New York Times*, May 10, 2003.
19. Walter Russell Mead, *Mortal Splendor: The American Empire in Transition*, Boston, MA: Houghton Mifflin, 1987, p. 4.
20. Ibid., p. 9; Walter LaFeber, "An Inclination to Intervene," *Boston Globe*, May 16, 1993; and "Somalia Leads Where?" *Boston Globe*, December 13, 1992.
21. William Appleman Williams, *Empire as a Way of Life*, New York: Oxford, 1980, p. viii. See also Richard J. Barnet, *Intervention and Revolution: The United States in the Third World*, New York: World Publishing, 1968.
22. Author's 1974 conversation with a British truck driver who had served in the British Army for 18 years and fought in many of Britain's last colonial wars.
23. Mead, *Mortal Splendor*, p. 5.
24. Ibid., pp. 19–22.
25. President Dwight D. Eisenhower's Farewell Address, January 17, 1961. Quoted in Kevin Phillips, *American Dynasty: Aristocracy, Fortune, and the Politics of Deceit in the House of Bush*, New York: Viking Press, 2004.
26. "If I Ruled the World" was recorded by Robert Goulet, Tony Bennet, and Frank Sinatra.

27. See, among others, Jonathan Schell, *The Time of Illusion*, New York: Vintage, 1975.
28. Chomsky, *The Chomsky Reader*, p. 6.
29. "Remarks by the President to the AFL-CIO Biennial Convention," Pittsburgh, PA, September 24, 1997.
30. E. J. Dionne, Jr., "War Politics: Bush looks to McKinley—George W. Bush and William McKinley," *Commonweal*, April 19, 2002, http://www.findarticles.com/p/articles/mi_m1252/is_8_129/ai_86140134 (September 5, 2006); Strobe Talbot, *The Russia Hand: A Memoir of Presidential Diplomacy*, New York: Random House, 2002; Richard Bernstein, " Threats and Responses: A Heritage of Protest; the Germans Who Toppled Communism Resent the U.S.," *New York Times*, February 22, 2003.
31. Edna St. Vincent Millay 1931.
32. *Discriminate Deterrence, Report of the Commission on Integrated Long-Term Strategy*, Washington, DC: The Department of Defense, January 11, 1988.
33. Ezra F. Vogel, *Japan as Number 1*, Boston, MA: Harvard University Press, 1980.
34. *Discriminate Deterrence.* See also Clinton's responses to military-related questions during his televised debates with President George H. Bush; and Bill Clinton and Al Gore, *Putting People First: How We Can All Change America*, New York: Times Books, 1992, pp. 131–2.
35. "U.S. Strategy Plan Calls for Insuring No Rivals Develop," *New York Times*, March 8, 1992.
36. This quotation from Dick Cheney first appeared in Nicholas LeMann, "The Quiet Man," *The New Yorker*, May 2, 2001.
37. Background briefing, Institute for Defense and Disarmament Studies, Spring 1992.
38. *The Daily Star* (London), August 10, 1990, cited in Milan Rai and Declan McHugh, "Nuclear Targeting of the Third World," London: Campaign for Nuclear Disarmament, 1992; *Bulletin of the Atomic Scientists*, November 1990; *Guardian*, December 24, 1990; *Boston Sunday Globe*, January 20, 1991; McGeorge Bundy, "Nuclear Weapons and the Gulf," *Foreign Affairs*, Fall 1991, p. 83; World Conference against Atomic and Hydrogen Bombs, Tokyo, 1991; *The Financial Times*, February 4, 1991, cited in Rai and McHugh, "Nuclear Targeting of the Third World"; *Boston Globe*, February 2, 1991.
39. Rick Atkinson, *Crusade: The Untold Story of the Persian Gulf War*, Boston, MA: Houghton Mifflin, 1993, pp. 86 and 89.
40. "U.S. Nuclear Weapons Stockpile," *Bulletin of the Atomic Scientists*, July/August 1994.
41. David E. Sanger, "Bush Warns Foes not to Use Weapons of Mass Destruction on U.S. Troops," *New York Times*, December 11, 2002; Deborah Orin, "U.S. Warns: We'll Nuke You—Bush: Use WMD at Your Peril," *New York Post*, December 11, 2002; Reuters, "Rumsfeld Won't Rule out Nuclear Bomb against Iraq," *New York Times*, February 13, 2003.
42. John Prados, *Hoodwinked: The Documents That Reveal how Bush Sold Us a War*, New York: The New Press, 2004, pp. 21–22, 29, and 32.
43. Among others see "Confronting Iraq Threat 'Is Crucial' to Winning War on Terror," transcript of a speech by President Bush, *New York Times*, October 8, 2002; Michael R. Gordon and Judith Miller, "U.S. Says Hussein Intensifies Quest for A-Bomb Parts," *New York Times*, September 8, 2002; Condoleezza Rice, "Why We Know Iraq is Lying," *New York Times*, January 23, 2003; "Excerpts From Kerry Speech," *New York Times*, May 28, 2004.
44. Editorial, "America as Nuclear Rogue," *New York Times*, March 12, 2002; Natural Resources Defense Council, "Faking Nuclear Restraint: The Bush Administration's Secret Plan for Strengthening U.S. Nuclear Forces," February 2002, http://www.nrdc.org/media/pressreleases/020213a.asp (August 29, 2006).

45. Natural Resources Defense Council, "Faking Nuclear Restraint"; David Krieger, "Kerry Pledges to Give Nuclear Terrorism His Top Priority," http://www.wagingpeace.org/ articles/2004/06/10_krieger_kerry-pledges.htm.
46. "Abolition 2000: A Survey on Nuclear Weapons," prepared by Lake Sosin Snell & Associates, April 1997.
47. The phrase is taken from Noam Chomsky, *American Power and the New Mandarins: Historical and Political Essays*, New York: Vintage, 1967.
48. See, among others, Gar Alperovitz, *The Decision to Use the Atomic Bomb and the Architecture of an American Myth*, New York: Alfred A. Knopf, 1995; Barton Bernstein, "The Atomic Bombings Reconsidered," *Foreign Affairs*, January/February 1995; Hasegawa, *Racing the Enemy*; Robert Jay Lifton and Greg Mitchell, *Hiroshima in America: Fifty Years of Denial*, New York: G. P. Putnam's Sons, 1995; Sherwin, *A World Destroyed*.
49. Hasegawa, *Racing the Enemy*, p. 159.
50. Ibid., p. 202.
51. Ibid., p. 170.
52. Gar Alperovitz, "The Hiroshima Decision: A Moral Reassessment," *Christianity and Crisis*, February 3, 1992.
53. Gareth Porter, *Perils of Dominance: Imbalance of Power and the Road to War in Vietnam*, Berkeley, CA: University of California Press, 2005, pp. 1–31.
54. Graham T. Allison, Albert Carnesale, and Joseph S. Nye, Jr., *Hawks, Doves & Owls: An Agenda for Avoiding Nuclear War*, New York: W. W. Norton, 1985; McGeorge Bundy, William J. Crowe, Jr., and Sidney D. Drell, *Reducing Nuclear Danger: The Road away from the Brink*, New York: Council on Foreign Relations, 1993; The Harvard Nuclear Study Group, *Living with Nuclear Weapons*, Cambridge, MA: Harvard University Press, 1983; Herman Kahn, *Thinking about the Unthinkable*, New York: Avon Books, 1962; Henry A. Kissinger, *Nuclear Weapons and Foreign Policy*, New York: Doubleday Anchor Books, 1958; Glenn T. Seaborg with Benjamin S. Loeb, *Stemming the Tide: Arms Control in the Johnson Years*, Lexington, MA: Lexington Books, 1972.
55. Department of Defense, *Doctrine for Joint Nuclear Operations*, Joint Publication 3–12, March 15, 2005.
56. Porter, *Perils of Dominance*, p. vii.
57. Department of Defense, *Doctrine for Joint Nuclear Operations*, p. I-6; Porter, *Perils of Dominance*, pp. 12–18 and 13; Marc Trachtenberg, "A 'Wasting Asset': American Strategy and the Shifting Nuclear Balance," *International Security* 13 (Winter 1988–89); Melvyn P. Leffler, *A Preponderance of Power: National Security, the Truman Administration and the Cold War*, Stanford, CA: Stanford University Press, 1992, and others; cited in Robert C. Aldridge, *First Strike: The Pentagon's Strategy for Nuclear War*, Boston, MA: South End Press, 1983, p. 25.
58. Barry M. Blechman and Stephen S. Kaplan, *Force without War: Writing on the Denial of History and the Smithsonian Controversy*, Stony Creek, CT: The Pamphleteer's Press, 1997, p. 420.
59. Porter, *Perils of Dominance*, p. 15.
60. From an unpublished interview with Noam Chomsky conducted by the author for the film *The Last Empire*, produced by Cambridge Documentary Films, 1984.
61. See, among others, Bruce G. Blair, "Keeping Presidents in the Nuclear Dark: The SIOP Option that Wasn't," *The Defense Monitor*, Washington, DC: Center for Defense Information, Volume XXXIII, No. 2, March/April 2004.
62. "Take Nuclear Weapons off Alert Status: A Plea by Nobel Laureates, Parliamentarians, the Europarliament, and NGOs around the World," April 2005,

http://www.wagingpeace.org/articles/2005/04/00_take-nuclear-weapons-off-alert-status.htm (August 29, 2006).

63. Dwight D. Eisenhower, *Mandate for Change*, New York: Doubleday, 1963, p. 181.
64. Military Implications of the Treaty on the Limitation of Strategic Offensive Arms and Protocol Thereto (Salt II Treaty). Hearings before the Senate Armed Service Committee, July 24, 1979, Part 1, pp. 169–70, cited in Aldridge, *First Strike*.
65. Cambridge Documentary Films, *The Last Empire*, 1994.
66. Board of Directors, "It's Seven Minutes to Midnight," *Bulletin of the Atomic Scientists*, March/April 2002, pp. 4–7.
67. In his April 8, 2003 testimony before the Senate Armed Services Strategic Subcommittee, Linton Brooks, the Administrator of the National Nuclear Security Administration, testified that the Bush administration had a "bias in favor of things that might be usable," and the administration's repeated demands for funding research and development of "bunker-buster" nuclear weapons 70 times more powerful than the Hiroshima A-bomb revealed the depth of this "bias."
68. Daniel Ellsberg, "A Call to Mutiny," in Joseph Gerson, *The Deadly Connection: Nuclear War and U.S. Intervention*, Philadelphia: New Society Publishers, 1986, pp. 62–4.
69. E. L. Doctorow, " The State of Mind of the Union," *The Nation*, March 22, 2003.
70. US military forces in the two world wars were, in fact, segregated. It was the need to mobilize society as a whole for the war effort in the name of democracy that unleashed social and political forces that contributed mightily to the postwar Civil Rights movement of the 1950s and 1960s.
71. Gerard J. DeGroot, *The Bomb: A Life*, Cambridge, MA: Harvard University Press, 2005, p. 2; Jonathan Schell, *The Unconquerable World: Power, Nonviolence, and the Will of the People*, New York: Metropolitan Books, 2003, p. 43.
72. Hermann Hesse, *If the War Goes On . . .*, New York: Farrar, Straus & Giroux, 1971 (English translation).
73. Cited in Zia Mian, "Lingering Shadows of World War II," *Foreign Policy in Focus*, June 14, 2005.
74. DeGroot, *The Bomb*, p. 28.
75. "On 6 August a US officer requested 'to have the following towns obliterated' by the air force: Chongsong, Chinbo and Kusu-dong . . ." National Archives, RG338, KMAG file, box 5418, cited in Bruce Cumings, "Korea: Forgotten Nuclear Threats," http://www.nautilus.org/fora/security/053A_Cumings.html (August 29, 2006); Paul Shannon, "The ABC's of the Vietnam War," *Indochina Newsletter*, Spring–Summer 2000; "Impact of the Vietnam War," prepared for the use of the Committee on Foreign Relations, United States Senate by the Foreign Affairs Division, Congressional Research Service, Library of Congress, June 30, 1971; "Relief and Rehabilitation of War Victims in Indochina: One Year after the Ceasefire," a study mission report prepared for the use of the Subcommittee to Investigate Problems Connected with Refugees and Escapees of the Committee on the Judiciary, United States Senate, 93rd Congress, second session, January 27, 1974; "A Time to Heal," a publication of the *Indochina Resource Center*, Berkeley, December 1976; "Civilian Casualties," *Indochina Chronicle*, Nos. 6 & 7, October 15, 1971, *Indochina Resource Center*, Washington, DC; "Six Million Victims," Project Air War, Washington, DC.
76. Hans Bethe, cited in DeGroot, *The Bomb*, p. 162.
77. Richard Falk's introduction to Aldridge, *First Strike*, p. 11; Hannah Arendt, *Eichman in Jerusalem: A Report on the Banality of Evil*, New York: Viking Press, 1963.
78. Mian, *Foreign Policy in Focus*.
79. US News and World Report, August 15, 1960, pp. 68–71, cited in DeGroot, *The Bomb*.

80. Ibid.; Gregg Herken, *Brotherhood of the Bomb: The Tangled Lives and Loyalties of Robert Oppenheimer, Ernest Lawrence, and Edward Teller*, New York: Henry Holt and Co., 2002, pp. 208–9.
81. Mian, *Foreign Policy in Focus*.
82. John Burroughs, *The (Il)legality of Threat or Use of Nuclear Weapons: A Guide to the Historic Opinion of the International Court of Justice*, Munster: Die Deutsche Bibliothek—CIP Einheitsaufnahme, 1997.
83. http://nautilus.org/archives/nukestrat/USA/Advisory/essentials95.txt; Noam Chomsky, "Nuclear Terror at Home," International Relations Center, February 26, 2005. Circulated on the Internet by the Institute for Cooperation in Space, February 27, 2005, emphasis added; David Krieger, "Nuclear Weapons: A Call for Public Protest," Nuclear Age Peace Foundation, www.wagingpeace@napf.org.
84. Author's notes from the meeting. Participants in the meeting included Professor Shoji Sawada, Junko Kayashige, Rev. Sanai Hashimoto, Claudia Peterson, James Matlack, and the author.
85. "Japan, U.S. Withheld Findings on Bikini Test Health Problems," *Japan Times*, March 1, 2005; "Remarks by the Honorable Abacca Anjain, Senator, Rongelap Atoll, Republic of the Marshall Islands," Vancouver World Peace Forum, June 24, 2006; and *Proving Grounds*, Produced by Primordial Soup Productions.
86. See, among others, Mian, *Foreign Policy in Focus*.
87. Richard Falk's introduction to Aldridge, *First Strike*, p. 11.
88. Cited in Paul C. Light, "Filibusters Are Only Half the Problem," *New York Times*, June 3, 2005.
89. Steward Udall, *The Myths of August*, cited in "Hiroshima's Elusive Lessons," *East Valley Tribune*, Mesa, Arizona, August 6, 2004.
90. These incidents are documented throughout the volume.

2 FIRST NUCLEAR TERRORISM—HIROSHIMA AND NAGASAKI

1. Yuki Tanaka, "Firebombing and Atom Bombing: An Historical Perspective on Indiscriminate Bombing," *Foreign Policy in Focus Policy Report*, May 2005, http://www.fpif.org/papers/0505bomb_body.html (August 30, 2006).
2. Cited in Tsuyoshi Hasegawa, *Racing the Enemy: Stalin, Truman, and the Surrender of Japan*, Cambridge, MA: Belknap Press of Harvard University Press, 2005, p. 164.
3. Howard Zinn, *Declarations of Independence: Cross-Examining American Ideology*, New York: HarperCollins, 1990, p. 95.
4. See, among others, *New York Times*, February 1, 1958, cited in Robert Jay Lifton, *Death in Life: Survivors of Hiroshima*, New York: Random House, 1967, p. 333; Gar Alperovitz, "The Hiroshima Decision: A Moral Reassessment," *Christianity and Crisis*, February 3, 1992; Bernard E. Trainor, ". . . And Why We Should Remember the Men in the Pacific, Too," *Boston Globe*, June 5, 1994.
5. See, among others, Wilfred Burchett, *Shadows of Hiroshima*, London: Verso, 1983; Hiroshi Iwadare, "Media Report on Hiroshima and Nagasaki," International Citizens' Conference for No More Hiroshimas and No More Nagasakis, Tokyo, July 2005; Peter Kuznick, "The Criminality of Nuclear Weapons: Apocalypse Then, Apocalypse Now," International Citizens' Conference for No More Hiroshimas and No More Nagasakis, Tokyo, July 2005; Hiroka Takashi (former mayor of Hiroshima), speech at International Citizens' Conference for No More Hiroshimas and No More Nagasakis, Tokyo, July 2005.

6. McGeorge Bundy, *Danger and Survival: Choices about the Bomb in the First Fifty Years*, New York: Random House, 1988, p. 96.
7. Kuznick, "The Criminality of Nuclear Weapons."
8. Gar Alperovitz, "Enola Gay: Was Using the Bomb Necessary?" *Miami Herald*, December 14, 2003.
9. William Appleman Williams, *The Tragedy of American Diplomacy*, New York: Delta Books, 1962, p. 254.
10. Martin J. Sherwin, *A World Destroyed: The Atomic Bomb and the Grand Alliance*, New York: Vintage Books, 1975, pp. 190–4.
11. Harry Truman, Letter to Samuel McCrea Cavert, General Secretary, Federal Council of Churches of Christ in America, August 11, 1945, Harry S. Truman Library.
12. Ibid., p. 27.
13. Albert Einstein was quoted as saying, "If I had known that the Germans would not succeed in constructing the atom bomb, I would never have lifted a finger," Gerard J. DeGroot, *The Bomb: A Life*, Cambridge, MA: Harvard University Press, 2005, p. 22.
14. See, among others, Thomas Powers, *Heisenberg's War: The Secret History of the German Bomb*, New York: Alfred A. Knopf, 1993; and Michael Frayn, *Copenhagen*, New York: Anchor Books, 1998.
15. Nicholas Dawidoff has written the best accounts of the decisive moment in the US determination that the German A-bomb project would not be a factor in the war. In his book *The Catcher Was A Spy*, he describes the dispatch of OSS agent Moe Berg to Zurich, where he was ordered to listen to a speech given by Heisenberg and either to kidnap or, if he concluded that Germany was on the verge of creating an A-bomb, to kill the German physicist. Hiding behind the curtains in the lecture hall, Berg concluded that Heisenberg's project posed no danger to the US. Heisenberg went on to survive the war and to play a major role in German postwar science. Nicholas Dawidoff, *The Catcher Was A Spy: The Mysterious Life of Moe Berg*, New York: Pantheon Books, 1994, pp. 191–4.
16. Sherwin, *A World Destroyed*, p. 145.
17. Ibid., p. 5.
18. Leslie R. Groves, *In The Matter of J. Robert Oppenheimer*, Washington: US Atomic Energy Commission, US Government Printing Office, 1954, p. 173; see also Joseph Rotblat's preface to *Hiroshima's Shadow*, edited by Kai Bird and Lawrence Lifschultz, Stony Creek, CT: The Pamphleteer's Press, 1997, p. xvii.
19. "Americans Support Hiroshima Bombing," *Daily Yomiuri*, August 7, 2005.
20. Williams, *The Tragedy of American Diplomacy*, p. 254.
21. Alperovitz, *Christianity and Crisis*.
22. Dwight D. Eisenhower, *Mandate for Change*, cited in Gar Alperovitz, "Hiroshima: Historians Reassess," *Foreign Policy*, Summer 1995.
23. Ibid.
24. Williams, *The Tragedy of American Diplomacy*, p. 254.
25. DeGroot, *The Bomb*, p. 153. While the March 9–10 fire bombing of Tokyo claimed the most victims of any single military attack (100,000–140,000 people, mostly civilians), Peter Kuznick reports that 99.5 percent of the city of Toyama was burned to the ground. See Kuznick, "The Criminality of Nuclear Weapons."
26. Alperovitz, *Christianity and Crisis*.
27. See, among others, Gar Alperovitz, *The Decision to Use the Atomic Bomb and the Architecture of an American Myth*, New York: Alfred A. Knopf, 1995; Walter LaFeber, *The Clash: U.S.–Japanese Relations throughout History*, New York: W. W. Norton 1997; John W. Dower, *Empire and Aftermath: Yoshida Shigeru and the Japanese Experience*,

1878–1954, Cambridge, MA: Harvard University Press, 1979. Joseph Gerson and Bruce Birchard, eds., *The Sun Never Sets . . . Confronting the Network of U.S. Foreign Military Bases*, Cambridge, MA: South End Press, 1991, pp. 123–48 and 167–98.

28. Saburo Ienaga, *The Pacific War, 1931–1945*, New York: Pantheon, 1978, p. 58.
29. Ibid., p. 9.
30. Ibid., pp. 9–10; Dower, *Empire and Aftermath*, p. 167; Edward Behr, *Hirohito: Behind the Myth*, New York: Vintage Books, 1989, pp. 228 and 258.
31. Ienga, *The Pacific War*, pp. 133–45; Behr, *Hirohito*, pp. 174–5.
32. Behr, *Hirohito*, pp. 228 and 258; Yoshitaka Oka, *Konoe Fumimaro: A Political Biography*, New York: Madison Books, 1992, pp. 173 and 187.
33. Michael Blow, *The History of the Atomic Bomb*, New York: American Heritage Publishing Co., 1968.
34. Editors of *TIME. V-J Day: America's World War II Triumph in the Pacific*, New York: TIME Books, 2005, pp. 106–8.
35. Sherwin, *A World Destroyed*, pp. 167–8; Gar Alperovitz, *Atomic Diplomacy: Hiroshima and Potsdam*, New York: Vintage, 1965, pp. 98–100.
36. Gar Alperovitz, "Why The United States Dropped the Bomb," *Technology Review*, August / September 1990.
37. Cited in Hasegawa, *Racing the Enemy*, p. 53.
38. Alperovitz, *Technology Review*.
39. Barton Bernstein, "A Postwar Myth: 500,000 U.S. Lives Saved," *The Bulletin of the Atomic Scientists*, cited in full in Bird and Lifshultz, eds., *Hiroshima's Shadow*.
40. Ibid., pp. 104–5.
41. Hasegawa, *Racing the Enemy*, pp. 52, 110, and 117–18; and DeGroot, *The Bomb*, p. 78.
42. Alperovitz, *Technology Review*, emphasis added.
43. See, among others, William Johnston in the introduction to Takashi Nagai, *The Bells of Nagasaki*, Tokyo: Kodansha, 1949, 1984 edition.
44. Sherwin, *A World Destroyed*, p. 203.
45. "How to Tell Japs from the Chinese," *LIFE Magazine*, December 15, 1941.
46. John Dower, *Japan at War & Peace*, New York: New Press, 1993, p. 264.
47. Ibid., p. 39.
48. Letter from President Truman to Samuel McCrea Cavert, General Secretary, Federal Council of Churches of Christ in America, August 11, 1945, Truman Library.
49. Sherwin, *A World Destroyed*, p. 200.
50. Ibid., pp. 67–8.
51. Ibid., p. 84 (emphasis added), pp. 88 and 89.
52. Ibid., p. 83.
53. Ibid., pp. 88–9, 96–7, and 118.
54. Ibid., pp. 131, 104–5, and 111; Bernstein, *Foreign Affairs*.
55. Sherwin, *A World Destroyed*, p. 144; Kuznick, "The Criminality of Nuclear Weapons."
56. Sherwin, *A World Destroyed*, pp. 8–9, and 148.
57. Alperovitz, *Atomic Diplomacy*, pp. 11–12; Sherwin, *A World Destroyed*, pp. 157–8.
58. Daniel Yeregin, *Shattered Peace: The Origins of the Cold War and the National Security State*, Boston, MA: Houghton Mifflin, 1978: pp. 78–9; Sherwin, *A World Destroyed*, pp. 157 and 159; Hasegawa, *Racing the Enemy*, pp. 65–6.
59. Alperovitz, *Technology Review*.
60. Hasegawa, *Racing the Enemy*, p. 25.
61. Ibid., p. 35.
62. Ibid., p. 32.
63. DeGroot, *The Bomb*, p. 74.

64. Alperovitz, *Technology Review*.
65. Hasegawa, *Racing the Enemy*, pp. 25–6.
66. Alperovitz, *Atomic Diplomacy*; Carl Oglesby and Richard Shaull, *Containment and Change*, New York: Macmillan, 1967.
67. Alperovitz, *Technology Review*.
68. Sherwin, *A World Destroyed*, pp. 189–90.
69. Hasegawa, *Racing the Enemy*, pp. 28 and 9.
70. Ibid., p. 37.
71. Sherwin, *A World Destroyed*, p. 190; Alperovitz, *Technology Review*.
72. Behr, *Hirohito*, p. 292; Hasegawa, *Racing the Enemy*, p. 123.
73. Alperovitz, *Technology Review*.
74. Ibid., pp. 26 and 56–7.
75. Ibid., pp. 72–3.
76. Ibid., p. 95.
77. Hasegawa, *Racing the Enemy*, p. 78; Alperovitz, *Technology Review*, pp. 98–9.
78. Cited in Hasegawa, *Racing the Enemy*, p. 124.
79. Ibid., p. 134; Alperovitz, *Technology Review*.
80. Bernstein, "A Postwar Myth."
81. Sherwin, "A World Destroyed," p. 235; Alperovitz, *Technology Review*; DeGroot, *The Bomb*, p. 77.
82. Hasegawa, *Racing the Enemy*, p. 158.
83. Cited in Sherwin, *A World Destroyed*, p. 223.
84. Kai Bird and Martin J. Sherwin, *American Prometheus: The Triumph and Tragedy of J. Robert Oppenheimer*, New York: Alfred A. Knopf, p. 309.
85. Ibid., p. 209; Hasegawa, *Racing the Enemy*, p. 141.
86. Hasegawa, *Racing the Enemy*, p. 135.
87. Ibid., p. 142.
88. Sherwin, *A World Destroyed*, p. 227.
89. Hasegawa, *Racing the Enemy*, pp. 166, 169, and 182.
90. Ibid., p. 169.
91. Ibid., pp. 164, 166, 179, and 182.
92. Robert Jay Lifton, *Death in Life: Survivors of Hiroshima*, New York: Random House, 1967, p. 16.
93. Ibid., p. 18.
94. Hiroshima Peace Memorial Museum: Hiroshima, Japan.
95. Masae Shima, unpublished translation, of "A-bomb Crime?"
96. Johnston, Introduction to Nagai, *The Bells of Nagasaki*, p. xiii.
97. David Rubin, "Remembering Normand Brissett," *Boston Globe*, August 20, 2005.
98. Naomi Shohno, *The Legacy of Hiroshima: Its Past, Our Future*, Tokyo: Kosei Publishing Co., 1986, pp. 15 and 56 (emphasis in original).
99. Masao Nakazawa, "A-bomb's Psychological Effect and PTSD," talk given at the International Citizens' Conference for No More Hiroshimas and No More Nagasakis, July 30, 2005.
100. John W. Dower, *Japan in War & Peace: Selected Essays*, New York: New Press, 1993, pp. 244–5.
101. Sankichi Toge, cited in Shima, "A-bomb Crime?"
102. Shuntaro Hida, *The Day Hiroshima Disappeared*, Stony Creek, CT: The Pamphleteer's Press, 1997. Extended excerpt with permission of Dr Hida.
103. Junko Kayashige, "I Cannot Keep Silent During Summer," Hiroshima. A 1994 revision of a speech first given in 1970.

104. Wilfred Burchett, *Shadows of Hiroshima*, London: Verso, 1983, pp. 35–6.
105. Hasegawa, *Racing the Enemy*, p. 184.
106. Ibid., pp. 184–5.
107. Ibid., p. 186.
108. Ibid., p. 185.
109. A Citizens' Group to Convey Testimonies of Hiroshima and Nagasaki, *Give Me Water: Testimonies of Hiroshima and Nagasaki*, Tokyo, 1973, p. 52.
110. "New Contexts, New Dangers: Preventing Nuclear War in the Post-Cold War Age," Transcripts from the October 29–31 Conference, Cambridge: American Friends Service Committee, 1993, p. 12. See also Senji Yamaguchi, *Burnt Yet Undaunted: Verbatim Account of Senji Yamaguchi*, Tokyo: Japan Confederation of A- and H-Bomb Sufferers' Organizations (Nihon Hidankyo), 2002.
111. Shima, "A-bomb Crime?"
112. Ibid.
113. http://mainichi.co.jp/specials/0506/06/0617weller.html (September 8, 2006); see also, "Hiroshima Cover Up," Common Dreams, http://www.commondreams.org/views05/0805-20.htm (September 8, 2006).
114. Behr, *Hirohito*, p. 299.
115. Hasegawa, *Racing the Enemy*, p. 212.
116. Ibid., pp. 300–1 and 219–21.
117. Ibid.; Burchett, *Shadows of Hiroshima*, p. 105.
118. Hasegawa, *Racing the Enemy*, pp. 235–5.
119. Burchett, *Shadows of Hiroshima*, p. 104.
120. *Guardian*, July 16, 2005, www.guardian.co.uk; Shima, "A-bomb Crime?"
121. Kenzubaro Oe, *Hiroshima Notes*, Tokyo: YMCA Press, 1981, p. 60.
122. Lawrence S. Wittner, *One World or None: A History of the World Nuclear Disarmament Movement through 1953*, Stanford, CA: Stanford University Press, 1993, p. 48.
123. Cited in DeGroot, *The Bomb*, p. 277.
124. Declaration of The International Citizens' Conference for No More Hiroshimas and No More Nagasakis, held in Tokyo July 29–31, 2005 and organized by *Nihon Hidankyo*, the Japan Confederation of A- and H-Bomb Sufferers' Organizations.
125. Notes and receipt from author's visit to the National Atomic Museum July 3, 2006.

3 POSTWAR ASIA—TARGETING KOREA AND CHINA

1. Gerard J. DeGroot, *The Bomb: A Life*, Cambridge, MA: Harvard University Press, 2005, p. 274.
2. Donald Greenlees, "How North Korea Fulfilled its Nuclear Dream," *International Herald Tribune*, October 23, 2006; Walter Pincus, "The Deep Roots of a Conflict," *Washington Post National Weekly Edition*, October 23–29, 2006.
3. During an interview with Adam Weiss, Speaker of the House Tip O'Neill's senior foreign policy advisor, that the author was reminded that thinking in terms of two years into the future—the term of a member of the US House of Representatives—constitutes the long term for the majority of elected US officials.
4. Cited in Gareth Porter, *Perils of Dominance: Imbalance of Power and the Road to War in Vietnam*, Berkeley: University of California Press, 2005.
5. *Webster's New World Dictionary*, Cleveland and New York: The World Publishing Co., 1966, p. 293.
6. Porter, *Perils of Dominance*, p. 6.

7. Tony Palomba, "First Strike: Shield for Intervention," in *The Deadly Connection: Nuclear War and U.S. Intervention*, edited by Joseph Gerson, Philadelphia: New Society Publishers, 1984, p. 80.
8. Dwight D. Eisenhower, *Mandate for Change*, Volume 1, New York: Doubleday, 1963, pp. 178–81.
9. Ibid., p. 20.
10. Porter, *Perils of Dominance*, p. 25.
11. Eisenhower, *Mandate for Change*, p. 35.
12. Porter, *Perils of Dominance*, pp. 25–6.
13. Leon Sigal, *Disarming Strangers*, Princeton, NJ: Princeton University Press, 1998, p. 20; Bruce Cumings, *The Origins of the Korean War: Liberation and the Emergence of Separate Regimes 1945–1947*, Princeton, NJ: Princeton University Press, 1981, p. 483.
14. Cumings, ibid.; Bruce Cumings, *The Origins of the Korean War: The Roaring of the Cataract 1947–1950*, Princeton, NJ: Princeton University Press, 1990.
15. Chung Kyungmo, "Korea Today, Korea Tomorrow: A Korean Perspective," in John Sullivan and Roberta Foss, *Two Koreas—One Future?* Lanham, MD: University Press of America, 1987, pp. 137–9.
16. Bruce Cumings, *Korea's Place in the Sun: A Modern History*, New York: W. W. Norton, 1997, pp. 193–5, and 247–9.
17. Ibid., p. 272.
18. Bruce Cumings, "Korea: Forgotten Nuclear Threats," Nautilus Institute, Policy Forum Online, January 11, 2005, http://www.nautilus.org/fora/security/0503A_Cumings.html (August 31, 2006).
19. Scott Shane, "U.S. Reclassified Many Documents in Secret Review," *New York Times*, February 21, 2006; Cumings, *Korea's Place in the Sun*, pp. 277–9.
20. Cumings, ibid.; Don Oberdorfer, *The Two Koreas: A Contemporary History*, Reading, MA: Addison-Wesley, 1997, p. 252; Cumings, *Korea's Place in the Sun*, pp. 288–91.
21. Cumings, *Korea's Place in the Sun*, p. 291.
22. Ibid., pp. 291–2.
23. Ibid., p. 292; Bruce Cumings, "Spring Thaw for Korea's Cold War?" *Bulletin of the Atomic Scientists*, April 1992; DeGroot, *The Bomb*, pp. 187 and 190.
24. Nuclear Information Project, http://www.nukestrat.com / korea / koreahistory.htm; Cumings, *Korea's Place in the Sun*.
25. Ibid., pp. 480–1. John H. Kim, "Timeline of Nuclear Threats on the Korean Peninsula," unpublished manuscript, 2005.
26. Author's 2003–05 conversations with Leo Chang, son of John Chang, South Korea's wartime Ambassador to the United Nations and prime minister in 1960.
27. Andrew Scobell, *China's Use of Military Force: Beyond the Great Wall and the Long March*, Cambridge: Cambridge University Press, 2003, p. 174.
28. Gordon H. Chang, *Friends and Enemies: The United States, China, and the Soviet Union, 1948–1972*, Stanford, CA: Stanford University Press, 1990, pp. 116–18.
29. Ibid., pp. 120–1.
30. Ibid., p. 171.
31. Porter, *Perils of Dominance*, p. 13.
32. Chang, *Friends and Enemies*, pp. 126–33; Porter, *Perils of Dominance,* p. 28.
33. Porter, ibid., p. 27.
34. Ibid.
35. Ibid.
36. Ibid., p. 28; Chang, *Friends and Enemies*, pp. 183–6.
37. Chang, ibid., pp. 185–6.

38. Ibid., pp. 188–9.
39. Ibid., pp. 186–91; Porter, *Perils of Dominance*, p. 28.
40. Porter, ibid., p. 238.
41. Ibid., pp. 229–47.
42. Ibid., pp. 59–60.
43. Cited in Chang, *Friends and Enemies*, p. 250.
44. Author's notes of Ellsberg's speech to International Physicians for Prevention of Nuclear Weapons, Cambridge, MA, October 1, 2005.
45. Ibid., pp. 228 and 250; Anand Girdhardas, "63 Tapes Reveal Kennedy and Aides Discussed Using Nuclear Arms in a China–India Clash," *New York Times*, August 26, 2005.
46. Harrison Salisbury, *War between Russia and China*, New York: Bantam Books, 1970, p. 152.

4 THE CUBAN MISSILE CRISIS—PRESTIGE, CREDIBILITY, AND POWER

1. Cited in Anatoly I. Gribkov and William Y. Smith, *Operation ANADYR: U.S. and Soviet Generals Recount the Cuban Missile Crisis*, Chicago: edition q, inc., 1994, p. 5.
2. Elie Abel, *The Missile Crisis*, Philadelphia: J. B. Lippincott, 1966, p. 182.
3. "When Kennedy Faced Armageddon, And His Own Scornful Generals," *New York Times*, October 5, 1997.
4. "Radio–TV Address of the President to the Nation from the White House," October 22, 1961, cited in Laurence Chang and Peter Kornbluh, eds., *The Cuban Missile Crisis, 1962*, New York: The New Press, 1998, pp. 160–4.
5. Theodore C. Sorenson, "The Leader Who Led," *New York Times*, October 18, 1997.
6. Cited in Max Frankel, *High Noon in the Cold War: Kennedy, Khrushchev, and the Cuban Missile Crisis*, New York: Ballantine Books, 2004, p. 177.
7. Theodore Sorensen, *Kennedy*, New York: Harper & Row, 1965.
8. *Boston Globe*, July, 29, 1994.
9. Edmundo Desnoes, cited in James G. Blight, Bruce J. Allyn, and David A. Welch, *Cuba on the Brink: Castro, The Missile Crisis, and the Soviet Collapse*, New York: Pantheon Books, 1993, p. 15.
10. See, Frankel, *High Noon in the Cold War*, p. 174; and Gareth Porter, *Perils of Dominance: Imbalance of Power and the Road to War in Vietnam*, Berkeley: University of California Press, 2005, pp. 7–31.
11. Robert McNamara, cited in Richard E. Neustadt and Graham T. Allison's afterword to Robert F. Kennedy, *Thirteen Days: A Memoir of the Cuban Missile Crisis*, New York: W. W. Norton & Co., 1969.
12. Interview with Noam Chomsky by the author for the film *The Last Empire*, Cambridge Documentary Films, 1985.
13. Maurice Zeitlin and Robert Sheer, *Cuba: Tragedy in Our Hemisphere*, New York: Grove Press, 1963, p. 30.
14. Tad Szulc, *New York Times*, April 24, 1960 cited in Zeitlin and Sheer, *Cuba*, p. 31.
15. Blight et al., *Cuba on the Brink*, pp. 324–5.
16. Ibid., p. 324.
17. C. Wright Mills, *Listen Yankee: The Revolution in Cuba*, New York: Ballantine Books, 1960, p. 20.
18. Blight et al., *Cuba on the Brink*, p. 327.
19. Edward P. Carpol and Howard Schonberger, "The Shift to Global Expansion 1865–1900," in William Appleman Williams, ed., *From Colony to Empire: Essays in the*

History of American Foreign Relations, New York: John Wiley & Sons, 1972, pp. 135–202.
20. See Zeitlin and Sheer, *Cuba*, p. 34; and James Petras and Maurice Zeitlin, *Latin America: Reform or Revolution*, New York: Fawcett Library, 1968, p. 270.
21. Zeitlin and Sheer, *Cuba*, p. 22.
22. Ibid., pp. 38–9.
23. Blight et al., *Cuba on the Brink*, p. 322.
24. Zeitlin and Sheer, *Cuba*, p. 34.
25. Blight et al., *Cuba on the Brink*, p. 322.
26. Zeitlin and Sheer, *Cuba*, p. 50.
27. Ibid., p. 52.
28. John Gerassi, *The Great Fear in Latin America*, New York: Collier Books, 1967, p. 394.
29. Blight et al., *Cuba on the Brink*, pp. 335–6.
30. Porter, *Perils of Dominance*.
31. Ibid., pp. 1, 2 and 5.
32. Paul Kennedy, *The Rise and Fall of Great Powers*, New York: Random House, 1987; and Karen A. Rasler and William R. Thompson, *The Great Powers and Global Struggle 1490–1993*, Seattle: University of Washington Press, 1987, cited in Porter, *Perils of Dominance*.
33. Ibid., pp. 12–13.
34. Frankel, *High Noon in the Cold War*, p. 56; Porter, *Perils of Dominance*, pp. 5–7.
35. Porter, ibid., pp. 21–4.
36. Frankel, *High Noon in the Cold War*, p. 44.
37. Arthur M. Schlesinger, Jr., *A Thousand Days: John F. Kennedy in the White House*, Boston, MA: Houghton Mifflin, 1965, p. 3.
38. David Halberstam, *The Best and the Brightest*, Greenwich, CT: Fawcett Publications, 1973.
39. Seymour Hersh, *The Dark Side of Camelot*, Boston, MA: Little, Brown, 1997, pp. 234–6.
40. Michael R. Beschloss, "Foreign Policy's Big Moment," *New York Times*, April 11, 1999.
41. McGeorge Bundy, *Danger and Survival: Choices about the Bomb in the First Fifty Years*, New York: Random House, 1988, p. 381.
42. Gribkov and Smith, *Operation ANADYR*, p. 86; Heather A. Purcell, and James K. Galbraith, "Did The U.S. Military Plan a Nuclear First Strike for 1963?" *The American Prospect*, Fall 1994; Daniel Ellsberg, "Call to Mutiny," in Joseph Gerson, *The Deadly Connection: Nuclear War & U.S. Intervention*, Philadelphia: New Society Publishers, 1986, pp. 41–2.
43. Frankel, *High Noon in the Cold War*, p. 50.
44. Halberstam, *The Best and the Brightest*, pp. 19–65; Tetsuya Kataoka, *The Price of a Constitution: The Origin of Japan's Postwar Politics*, New York: Crane Russak, 1991, pp. 1 and 110.
45. Porter, *Perils of Dominance*, p. 18.
46. Gribkov and Smith, *Operation ANADYR*, pp. 79–80.
47. Roy Medvedev, *Khrushchev*, Garden City, NY: Doubleday, 1983, p. 177.
48. James Reston, *New York Times Magazine*, November 15, 1964, cited in Abel, *The Missile Crisis*, p. 37.
49. Nikita Khrushchev, *Khruschev Remembers: The Glasnost Tapes*, Boston, MA: Little, Brown, 1990, p. 495.
50. Anastas Mikoyan advised Khrushchev that he had misread Kennedy at the Vienna summit—neither Kennedy nor US "ruling circles" would tolerate the deployment of Soviet missiles in Cuba. Frankel, *High Noon in the Cold War*, p. 11.
51. Daniel Ellsberg, "Call to Mutiny," in Gerson, *The Deadly Connection*, p. 41.

52. Notes of July 20, 1961 National Security Council Meeting, declassified June 4, 1991, cited in "Forecast and Solution: Grappling with the Nuclear."
53. Porter, *Perils of Dominance*, p. 15.
54. Sorensen, *Kennedy*, p. 512.
55. Ibid., p. 17.
56. Daniel Ellsberg, Notes from keynote speech at IPPNW's 25th anniversary commemoration. October 1, 2005.
57. Gerson, *The Deadly Connection*, pp. 81–2; cited in Porter, *Perils of Dominance*, p. 7.
58. Frankel, *High Noon in the Cold War*, pp. 44–52. Frankel was the *New York Times* correspondent in Moscow during Khrushchev's first years in power.
59. See Debora Shapley, *Promise and Power: The Life and Times of Robert McNamara*, Boston, MA: Little, Brown, 1993, p. 168; and Khrushchev, *Khrushchev Remembers*, pp. 492–3.
60. Khrushchev, ibid., p. 57.
61. Gribkov and Smith, *Operation ANADYR*, p. 81.
62. Blight et al., *Cuba on the Brink,* p. 18.
63. See Sorensen, *Kennedy*, pp. 534–5 and Gerassi, *The Great Fear in Latin America*, pp. 251–2.
64. Sorensen, *Kennedy*, p. 535.
65. CIA Assistant Director Ray Cline, cited in Gribkov and Smith, *Operation ANADYR*, p. 90.
66. Frankel, *High Noon in the Cold War*, p. 68.
67. Tim Weiner, "Declassified Papers Show anti-Castro Ideas Proposed to Kennedy," *New York Times,* November 19, 1997; George Lardner Jr. and Walter Pincus, "Stranger than Fiction: X-files on Cuba Declassified," *Washington Post*, reprinted in the *Boston Globe*, November 19, 1997.
68. Marion Lloyd, "Soviets Close to Using A-bomb in 1962 Crisis, Forum is Told," *Boston Sunday Globe*, October 13, 2002.
69. Chang and Kornbluth, cited in Gribkov and Smith, *Operation ANADYR*, pp. 90–2.
70. See Bundy, *Danger and Survival*, p. 416; and Pierre Salinger, "Gaps in the Cuban Missile Crisis Story," *New York Times*, February 5, 1989.
71. "Memorandum of MONGOOSE Meeting Held on Thursday, October 4, 1962," in Graham Allison, *Nuclear Terrorism: The Ultimate Preventable Catastophe*, New York: Henry Holt & Co., 2004, pp. 111–12.
72. Khrushchev, *Khrushchev Remembers*, p. 493, Gribkov and Smith, *Operation ANADYR*, p. 167, and Shapley, *Promise and Power*, p. 167.
73. Kennedy, *Thirteen Days*, p. 41.
74. Ibid., p. 125, emphasis added; Frankel, *High Noon in the Cold War*, p. 7.
75. Kennedy, *Thirteen Days*, pp. 112–13.
76. Excom members included Secretary of State Dean Rusk, Secretary of Defense Robert McNamara, Director of the CIA John McCone, Secretary of the Treasury Douglas Dillon, National Security Advisor McGeorge Bundy, Presidential Counsel Theodore Sorensen, Under-Secretary of State George Ball, Deputy Under-Secretary of State U. Alexis Johnson, Chairman of the Joint Chiefs of Staff Maxwell Taylor, Assistant Secretary of State for Latin America Edward Martin. Others who participated in Excom meetings included Chip Bohlen, who left to become Ambassador to France after the first day of the crisis and was replaced by former Ambassador to the Soviet Union Llewellyn Thompson, Deputy Secretary of Defense Roswel Gilpatric, Assistant Secretary of Defense Paul Nitze, Vice-President Lyndon B. Johnson, Ambassador to the United Nations Adlai Stevenson; Special Assistant to the President Kenneth O'Donnell, Deputy Director of the USIA Don Wilson, and the former Secretary of State Dean Acheson.
77. Sorensen, *Kennedy*, p. 680.

78. Kennedy, *Thirteen Days*, p. 74.
79. Ibid., pp. 113–14.
80. Ibid., pp. 14, 36, and 117. It should be recalled that Le May led the fire bombing of Tokyo and later ordered unauthorized flights over the Soviet Union during the Eisenhower administration, possibly to provide the *casus belli* for a preemptive war against the Soviet Union. Paul Lashmar, "Stranger than 'Strangelove,' " *Washington Post National Weekly Edition*, July 11–17, 1994.
81. Porter, *Perils of Dominance*, pp. x and 17; Frankel, *High Noon in the Cold War*, pp. 79 and 98, "Word for Word/The Cuban Missile Crisis: When Kennedy Faced Armageddon, And His Own Scornful Generals," *New York Times*, October 5, 1997.
82. Abel, *The Missile Crisis*, p. 173.
83. Khrushchev, *Khrushchev Remembers*, pp. 170–3, Cited in Porter, *Perils of Dominance*, p. 25.
84. Ibid., pp. 493–4.
85. J. A. M. [McCone] Memorandum, "Proposed Plan of Action for Cuba," 21 August 1962, in Allison, *Nuclear Terrorism*, pp. 31–2; August 23 memo of McCone discussion with John F. Kennedy, Allison, *Nuclear Terrorism*, p. 29.
86. September 2, 1962 memo from Ray S. Cline "Recent Soviet Military Activities in Cuba" in Allison, *Nuclear Terrorism*, p. 35.
87. September 10, McCone to Carter and Elder, in Allison, *Nuclear Terrorism*, p. 59.
88. Frankel, *High Noon in the Cold War*, p. 29.
89. Ibid., pp. 34–5.
90. Ernest R. May and Philip D. Zelikow, eds., *The Kennedy Tapes: Inside the White House During the Cuban Missile Crisis*, Cambridge, MA: The Belknap Press of Harvard University Press, 1997, p. 91.
91. Cited in "Word for Word: The Cuban Missile Crisis," *New York Times*, October 5, 1998; May and Zelikow, *The Kennedy Tapes*, p. 79.
92. Ibid., p. 156.
93. Ibid., p. 91.
94. Special National Intelligence Estimate—19 October, Allison, *Nuclear Terrorism*, p. 214.
95. Shapley, *Promise and Power*, p. 167; Kennedy, *Thirteen Days*, p. 27; Frankel, *High Noon in the Cold War*, p. 85.
96. Theodore Sorensen, "Summary of Agreed Facts and Premises, Possible Courses of Action and Unanswered Questions," October 17, 1962, in Laurence Chang and Peter Kornbluh, eds., *The Cuban Missile Crisis, 1962: A National Security Archive Documents Reader*, New York: The New Press, p. 124.
97. Chang and Kornbluh, cited in Gribkov and Smith, *Operation ANADYR*, p. 157; and Kennedy, *Thirteen Days*, p. 124.
98. Sorensen, "Summary of Agreed Facts and Premises," p. 683.
99. Abel, *The Missile Crisis*, p. 60; Chang and Kornbluh, *The Cuban Missile Crisis, 1962*, p. 157.
100. Frankel, *High Noon in the Cold War*, p. 77.
101. Kennedy, *Thirteen Days*, p. 45.
102. Ibid., p. 12. See also Shapley, *Promise and Power*, p. 173.
103. Frankel, *High Noon in the Cold War*, p. 92.
104. Ibid., p. 173. See also Kennedy, *Thirteen Days*, p. 13; Sorensen, "Summary of Agreed Facts and Premises," p. 687.
105. Abel, *The Missile Crisis*, pp. 64–5.

106. McCone, Memorandum for the File, "Conversation with General Eisenhower—Wednesday, 17 October, 1962," Allison, *Nuclear Terrorism*, pp. 167–8.
107. Porter, *Perils of Dominance*, p. 17.
108. Gribkov and Smith, *Operation ANADYR*, p. 121; Kennedy, *Thirteen Days*, p. 85.
109. Porter, *Perils of Dominance*, p. 6.
110. These figures were given to Ellsberg, then a senior administration nuclear war planner, in response to questions he posed to the Pentagon officials responsible for developing the SIOP. He regrets that he did not make this highly secret report public at the time. Daniel Ellsberg, 25th Anniversary Celebration of the Founding of International Physicians for the Prevention of Nuclear War, Cambridge, MA, October 1, 2005.
111. Khrushchev, *Khrushchev Remembers*, p. 493.
112. Fred Kaplan, "Detailing JFK's Stance during Missile Crisis," *New York Times*, October 21, 1987.
113. May and Zelikow, *The Kennedy Tapes*, p. 151.
114. Cited in Frankel, *High Noon in the Cold War*, p. 81.
115. Abel, *The Missile Crisis*, p. 190.
116. Frankel, *High Noon in the Cold War*, p. 104.
117. "Cable received from U.S. Ambassador to Turkey Raymond Hare to State Department, regarding Turkish Missiles, October 27, 1962" in Chang and Kornbluh, *The Cuban Missile Crisis, 1962*, p. 231.
118. Frankel, *High Noon in the Cold War*, p. 128.
119. Ibid., pp. 157–8.
120. Kennedy, *Thirteen Days*, p. 72.
121. Kaplan, "Detailing JFK's Stance"; and Kennedy, *Thirteen Days*, p. 74.
122. Blight et al., *Cuba on the Brink*, p. 353; Kennedy, *Thirteen Days*, pp. 165–6; Abel, *The Missile Crisis*, pp. 197–8.
123. Ibid., pp. 72–3; Shapley, *Promise and Power*, p. 180.
124. Kaplan, "Detailing JFK's Stance."
125. Kennedy, *Thirteen Days*, p. 168.
126. Gribkov and Smith, *Operation ANADYR*, p. 144.
127. Transcripts from Kennedy's secret tape recordings. "When Kennedy Faced Armageddon, And His Own Scornful Generals," *New York Times*, October 5, 1997; Frankel, *High Noon in the Cold War*, p. 105.
128. Ibid., pp. 117–18.
129. J. Anthony Lukas, "Class Reunion: Kennedy's Men Relive the Cuban Missile Crisis," *New York Times Magazine*, August 30, 1987. See also Shapley, *Promise and Power*, p. 178.
130. Ibid., p. 178.
131. Lukas, "Class Reunion."
132. Abel, *The Missile Crisis*, p. 155.
133. Shapley, *Promise and Power*, pp. 176–7.
134. Gribkov and Smith, *Operation ANADYR*, p. 144.
135. Ibid., p. 128; Abel, *The Missile Crisis*, p. 194.
136. Kevin Sullivan, "Nuclear Conflict was One Word away in Cuba Missile Crisis," *Guardian Weekly*, October 17–23, 2002.
137. Marion Lloyd, "Soviets Close to Using A-bomb in 1962 Crisis, Forum is Told," *Boston Sunday Globe*, October 13, 2002; Sullivan, "Nuclear Conflict was One Word away."
138. Gribkov and Smith, *Operation ANADYR*, p. 63.
139. Ibid., p. 63.
140. Ibid., pp. 43 and 63, emphasis added.
141. Ibid., pp. 6, 7, and 53.

142. "CINCLANT's Request to Have Tactical Nuclear Weapons Available for U.S. Invasion Force," Chang and Kornbluh, *The Cuban Missile Crisis, 1962*, p. 186.
143. Blight et al., *Cuba on the Brink*, pp. 251–2, emphasis added.
144. Khrushchev, *Khrushchev Remembers*, p. 177; Blight et al., *Cuba on the Brink*, p. 481, emphasis added.
145. Ibid., pp. 357–8.
146. See, among others, Eric Alterman, "Profile in Courage?" *The Nation*, November 10, 1997.
147. It should be noted that Kennedy's commitment to ensure that Cuba was not invaded was not formally implemented because Castro prevented UN oversight of the missiles' withdrawal, as provided for in Kennedy's proposal. To overcome this diplomatic difficulty, Soviet forces suffered the further humiliation of having to submit to US aerial surveillance of their ships as the missiles were withdrawn. President Johnson and Secretary of State Kissinger later gave equivalent assurances that Cuba would not be invaded.
148. See, among others, Allison, *Nuclear Terrorism*, p. 245; Frankel, *High Noon in the Cold War*, p. 105; May and Zelikow, *The Kennedy Tapes*, p. 271.

5 VIETNAM: FAILURES OF NUCLEAR DIPLOMACY

1. Gareth Porter, *Perils of Dominance: Imbalance of Power and the Road to War in Vietnam*, Berkeley: University of California Press, 2005, p. 220.
2. H. R. Haldeman, *The Ends of Power*, New York: Times Books, 1978, p. 83.
3. Seymour Hersh, *The Price of Power: Kissinger in the White House*, New York: Summit Books, 1983, p. 126.
4. "No More Hiroshimas," Tokyo, October–November, 1970.
5. Hersh, *The Price of Power*, p. 124.
6. "The Pentagon Papers" is the name given to "The Defense Department History of United States Decisionmaking on Vietnam." They were secretly researched and assembled at the request of Secretary of Defense McNamara and made public through the courageous efforts of Daniel Ellsberg in 1971. Excerpts were first published in June 1971 in *The Washington Post* and *The New York Times*. A collection of excerpts was edited by Neil Sheehan, Hedrick Smith, E. W. Kenworthy, and Fox Butterfield, and published as *The Pentagon Papers* in New York by Bantam Books in 1971. The complete study was published as *The Senator Gravel Edition, The Pentagon Papers: The Defense Department History of United States Decisionmaking on Vietnam*, Boston, MA: Beacon Press, 1971.
7. Len Ackland, ed., *Credibility Gap: A Digest of the Pentagon Papers*, Philadelphia: American Friends Service Committee, 1972.
8. Sheehan, *Pentagon Papers*, p. 278; Assistant Secretary of Defense John McNaughton, January 1966, cited in Ackland, *Credibility Gap*, p. 111.
9. Hersh, *The Price of Power*, p. 119.
10. Ngo Vinh Long, "Vietnam: Conventional War and the Use of Nuclear Threats," in *The Deadly Connection: Nuclear War and U.S. Intervention*, edited by Joseph Gerson, Philadelphia: New Society Publishers, 1984, p. 214.
11. Daniel Ellsberg, *Papers on the War*, New York: Simon & Schuster, 1972, p. 9.
12. These statistics are taken from *Indochina Newsletter*, November–December 1982. They are drawn from studies by the Committee on Foreign Relations of the US Senate, the Congressional Research Service, *The Boston Globe*, the Committee on the Judiciary of

the US Senate, the International Institute for Strategic Studies, the Indochina Resource Center, the American Friends Service Committee, Project Air War, the Center for International Studies of Cornell University, the Coalition to Stop Funding the War, the Department of Defense, and Amnesty International.

13. Ibid.
14. Sheehan et al., *Pentagon Papers*, p. 9.
15. Michio Kaku and Daniel Axelrod, *To Win a Nuclear War: The Pentagon's Secret War Plans*, Boston, MA: South End Press, 1987, p. 88.
16. Porter, *Perils of Dominance*, pp. 11, 32–40.
17. Fawn M. Brodie, *Richard Nixon: The Shaping of His Character*, Cambridge, MA: Harvard University Press, 1983, p. 20.
18. David Halberstam, *The Best and The Brightest*, Greenwich, CT: Fawcett Publications, 1972, pp. 170–1.
19. Ibid., p. 73.
20. Kaku and Axelrod, *To Win a Nuclear War*, p. 89; Brodie, *Richard Nixon*, p. 322.
21. Prados, *The Sky Would Fall*, p. 92, cited in Kaku and Axelrod, *To Win a Nuclear War*, p. 90.
22. Brodie, *Richard Nixon*, p. 322; Porter, *Perils of Dominance*, p. 232.
23. Daniel Ellsberg, "A Call to Mutiny," in Gerson, *The Deadly Connection*, p. 55; and Kaku and Axelrod, *To Win a Nuclear War*, p. 92.
24. Kaku and Axelrod, ibid., p. 91.
25. "Remembering Dien Bien Phu," *Boston Globe*, May 7, 1994; Porter, *Perils of Dominance*, pp. 32–41.
26. Porter, ibid., p. 35.
27. Charles Fourniau, *Le Vietnam Face à la Guerre*, Paris: Editions Sociales, 1966, p. 45; Porter, *Perils of Dominance*, pp. 35, 72–86 and 232.
28. Dwight D. Eisenhower, *Mandate for Change*, cited in John Gerassi, *North Vietnam: A Documentary*, Indianapolis: Bobbs-Merril, 1968, p. 23.
29. George McTurnan Kahin and John W. Lewis, *The United States in Vietnam*, New York: Delta Books, 1967, p. 77.
30. Porter, *Perils of Dominance*, p. 113.
31. Ibid., p. 114.
32. Noam Chomsky, *The Indochina Newsletter* 18, November–December 1982, http://www.chss.montclair.edu/english/furr/chomskyin1282.html.
33. Ibid., pp. 166–78; Hugh Higgins, *Vietnam*, London: Heinemann, 1982, p. 51.
34. Porter, *Perils of Dominance*, p. 142.
35. Paul Joseph, *Cracks in the Empire: State Politics in the Vietnam War*, New York: Columbia University Press, 1987, p. 140.
36. Ibid., p. 139.
37. Porter, *Perils of Dominance*, p. 187.
38. Ibid., p. 152.
39. Ibid., pp. 51–5.
40. Ibid., pp. 53–4.
41. Ibid., pp. 139–40; Porter, *Perils of Dominance*, pp. 2–107.
42. Ibid., pp. 56–8.
43. Ibid., p. 66.
44. Ibid., pp. 122–7.
45. Ibid., p. 172.

46. Theodore C. Sorensen and Arthur Schlesinger Jr., "What Would J.F.K. Have Done?" *New York Times*, December 4, 2005; Porter, *Perils of Dominance*, pp. 166–8.
47. Ibid., pp. 170 and 174–6.
48. Ibid., pp. 172–8.
49. Ibid., p. 182.
50. Hugh Higgins, *Vietnam*, London: Heinemann, 1982, p. 66; Sheehan, *Pentagon Papers*, p. 233.
51. Ibid., p. 181.
52. Ibid., p. 183.
53. Higgins, *Vietnam*, p. 68.
54. Ibid., pp. 185–7.
55. Ibid., pp. 187–9.
56. Sheehan et al., *Pentagon Papers*, pp. 279 and 282.
57. Chomsky, *Indochina Newsletter*; Higgins, *Vietnam*, p. 68.
58. Ibid., p. 190.
59. Ellsberg, *Papers on the War*, pp. 62–4.
60. Ibid., p. 63.
61. Sheehan et al., *Pentagon Papers*, p. 256.
62. Porter, *Perils of Dominance*, pp. 193–7.
63. Ibid., p. 200, emphasis added.
64. Higgins, *Vietnam*, pp. 71–4.
65. Cited in Porter, *Perils of Dominance*, p. 193. See also Melvin R. Laird, "Iraq: Learning the Lessons of Vietnam," *Foreign Affairs*, November/December 2005.
66. Edward Herman, *Atrocities in Vietnam: Myths and Realities*, Philadelphia: Pilgrim Press, 1970, pp. 50–6 and 63.
67. Ellsberg, *Papers on the War*, p. 234.
68. Herman, *Atrocities in Vietnam*, p. 51.
69. Kaku and Axelrod, *To Win a Nuclear War*, p. 155.
70. Ibid., p. 165.
71. Ackland, *Credibility Gap*, p. 83.
72. Noam Chomsky, *At War With Asia*, cited in Higgins, *Vietnam*, p. 78.
73. Frank Harvey, *Air War-Vietnam*, New York: Bantam Books, 1968, pp. 139–40.
74. Harrison Salisbury, cited in Gerassi, *North Vietnam*, p. 46–7.
75. Ngo Vinh Long, "Vietnam," p. 210.
76. Truong Nhu Tang, with David Chanoff and Doan Van Toai, *A Viet Cong Memoir: An Inside Account of the Vietnam War and Its Aftermath*, New York: Vintage Books, 1986, pp. 167–8.
77. Ibid., p. 78.
78. Buttinger, *Vietnam: A Political History*, cited in Higgins, *Vietnam*, p. 92.
79. Porter, *Perils of Dominance*, p. 221.
80. Ibid., p. 220.
81. Peter Hays and Nina Tannenwald, "Nixing Nukes in Vietnam," *Bulletin of the Atomic Scientists*, May/June 2003. The JASONS' report was titled "Tactical Nuclear Weapons in South-East Asia."
82. John Prados and Ray W. Stubbe, *Valley of Decision: The Siege of Khe Sanh*, Boston, MA: Houghton Mifflin, 1991, p. 289.
83. Malcome Browne, "Battlefields of Khe Sanh: Still One Casualty a Day," *New York Times*, May 13, 1994.

84. Peter Brush, "The Battle of Khe Sanh 1968," http://www.library.vanderbilt.edu/central/brush/BattleKheSanh1968.htm (September 1, 2006).
85. Ibid.
86. Sheehan et al., *The Pentagon Papers*, pp. 616–17.
87. Target selection officer Major Baig, quoted in Brush, "Battle of Khe Sanh."
88. Prados and Stubbe, *Valley of Decision*, p. 289.
89. Brush, "Battle of Khe Sanh"; Chaplain Ray William Stubbe, "A Desperate Place: How Did We Ever Make It Out Alive?" http://www.geocities.com/ksvredclay/issue-52-special-feature.htm?20055 (September 1, 2006).
90. Ibid., p. 297.
91. Ibid., p. 412.
92. Ibid., p. 291.
93. Ibid.
94. General William C. Westmoreland, *A Soldier Reports*, Garden City, NY: Doubleday, and 1976, p. 228.
95. Prados and Stubbe, *Valley of Decision*, p. 292.
96. Ellsberg, *Papers on the War*, p. 201.
97. Ibid., p. 292.
98. Prados and Stubbe, *Valley of Decision*, p. 413.
99. Brush, "Battle of Khe Sanh."
100. *Washington Post*, National Weekly Edition, May 23–29, 1994.
101. The NLF estimated it lost 5,000 dead, 10,000 wounded, and 7,000 taken prisoner in the Tet Offensive's assault on Saigon alone. *Washington Post*, National Weekly Edition, May 23–29, 1994; http://en.wikipedia.org/wiki/Tet_offensive; Forrest, "Tet Offensive: A Turning Point in the Vietnam War," http://www.marxist.com/1968/vietnam.html.
102. Chomsky, in *Indochina Newsletter*.
103. Higgins, *Vietnam*, p. 81.
104. Brush, "Battle of Khe Sanh."
105. United Press International, "Nixon Reveals Four Times He Pondered Nuclear Bomb," *New York Times*, June 22, 1985.
106. William Burr and Jeffrey Kimball, "Nixon's Nuclear Ploy," *Bulletin of the Atomic Scientists*, January/February 2003; Harrison E. Salisbury, *War between Russia and China*, New York: W. W. Norton, 1969.
107. Hung and Schecter, *The Palace File*, New York: Harper & Row, 1978, p. 21.
108. "Many Nixons," *The Nation*, May 16, 1994.
109. Haldeman, *The Ends of Power*, p. 82.
110. Brodie, *Richard Nixon*, p. 323.
111. Leonard Mosley, *Dulles: A Biography of Eleanor, Allen and John Foster*, p. 342, cited in Brodie, *Richard Nixon*, p. 320.
112. *New York Times*, cited in Brodie, ibid., p. 321.
113. Ibid., p. 108.
114. Kaku and Axelrod, *To Win a Nuclear War*, p. 163.
115. Hersh, *The Price of Power*, p. 24; see also Hung and Schecter, *The Palace File*, p. 21.
116. Hersh, *The Price of Power*, pp. 16–20; Haldeman, *The Ends of Power*, p. 84; Kaku and Axelrod, *To Win a Nuclear War*, p. 163.
117. Neil Sheehan, "The Graces of Indochina," *New York Times*, April 28, 1994; Burr, *The Kissinger Transcripts: Top Secret Talks with Beijing and Moscow,* New York, 1999.
118. Hersh, *The Price of Power*; Burr and Kimball, "Nixon's Nuclear Ploy."
119. Haldeman, *The Ends of Power*, p. 83. Emphasis in the original.

120. Hersh, *The Price of Power*, p. 52.
121. Ibid., p. 48.
122. Ibid., pp. 49–50.
123. Ibid., p. 51.
124. Burr and Kimball, "Nixon's Nuclear Ploy."
125. Kaku and Axelrod, *To Win a Nuclear War*, p. 164.
126. Hersh, *The Price of Power*, p. 121.
127. Ibid., pp. 120 and 123–4; Richard Nixon, *R.N.: The Memoirs of Richard Nixon*, New York: Grosset & Dunlap, 1978, cited in Kaku and Axelrod, *To Win a Nuclear War*, p. 165; Burr and Kimball, "Nixon's Nuclear Ploy."
128. William Burr and Jeffrey Kimball, "Nixon White House Considered Nuclear Options against North Vietnam," *National Security Archive Electronic Briefing Book* No. 195, July 31, 2006, http://www.gwu.edu/~nsarchive/NSAEBB195/ index.htm.#4 (September 4, 2006).
129. Ellsberg, *Papers on the War*, p. 48.
130. Hersh, *The Price of Power*, p. 127.
131. Ibid., p. 124.
132. Ibid., pp. 124–5; Kaku and Axelrod, *To Win a Nuclear War*, p. 165.
133. Burr and Kimball, "Nixon's Nuclear Ploy."
134. Ibid. The quotation is from Kissinger's preparation of Nixon for his meeting with Ambassador Dobrynin.
135. Burr and Kimball, "Nixon's Nuclear Ploy."
136. Ibid.
137. Hersh, *The Price of Power*, p. 128.
138. Ibid., p. 127.
139. Ibid., p. 128.
140. Ibid., p. 127.
141. Ibid., p. 129.
142. Hersh, *The Price of Power*, p. 134.
143. Nixon, *R.N.*, pp. 497–9.
144. Hersh, *The Price of Power*, pp. 129–31.
145. To protect the secret of the bombing of Cambodia, Nixon created a secret unit within the White House, "the plumbers." He later used the plumbers to illegally break into the office of Daniel Ellsberg's psychiatrist and during the 1972 election, into the Watergate offices of the Democratic Party. Revelations of the latter crime led to his impeachment. See, among others, Jonathan Schell, *The Time of Illusion*, New York: Vintage Books, 1975.
146. Norodom Sihanouk and Wilfred Burchett, *My War with the C.I.A.: Cambodia's Fight for Survival*, Harmondsworth: Penguin Books, 1973; Jonathan S. Grant, Laurence A. G. Moss, and Jonathan Unger, eds., *Cambodia: The Widening War in Indochina*, New York: Washington Square Press, 1971.
147. Paul Shannon, "The ABC's of the Vietnam War," *Indochina Newsletter*, Spring–Summer 2000; "Impact of the Vietnam War," prepared for the use of the Committee on Foreign Relations, United States Senate by the Foreign Affairs Division, Congressional Research Service, Library of Congress, June 30, 1971; "Relief and Rehabilitation of War Victims in Indochina: One Year after the Ceasefire," a study mission report prepared for the use of the Subcommittee to Investigate Problems Connected with Refugees and Escapees of the Committee on the Judiciary, United States Senate, 93rd Congress, second session, January 27, 1974; "A Time to Heal," a publication of the

Indochina Resource Center, Berkeley, December 1976; "Civilian Casualties," *Indochina Chronicle*, Nos 6 and 7, October 15, 1971, *Indochina Resource Center*, Washington, DC; "Six Million Victims," Project Air War, Washington, DC 1972; "The Legacy of the War," Philadelphia: American Friends Service Committee; Carolyn Eisenberg, "Peace in Our Time," *The Nation*, November 5, 2001.

148. Associated Press, " 'I'd Rather Use the Nuclear Bomb,' Nixon States on Tape," *The Japan Times*, March 2, 2002; Deb Riechmann, "Nixon Discussed Nuclear Strike in Vietnam," *Boston Globe*, March 1, 2002.
149. Letter from President Nixon to President Thieu, January 5, 1972, cited in Hung and Schecter, *The Palace File*, pp. 62–82.
150. Hung and Schecter, ibid., p. 144; emphasis added.
151. Ibid., p. 209. See, also, Frank Snepp, *Decent Interval: An Insider's Account of Saigon's Indecent End Told by the CIA's Chief Strategy Analyst in Vietnam*, New York: Vintage Books, 1978.
152. Henry Kissinger, *Years of Upheaval*, Boston, MA: Little, Brown, p. 326.
153. Hung and Schecter, *The Palace File*, p. 275.

6 THE MIDDLE EAST: MONOPOLIZING "THE PRIZE"

1. Noam Chomsky, "The Drift Towards War and the Alternatives," in Peggy Duff, ed., *War or Peace in the Middle East?*, London: Spokesman Books, 1978, p. 27.
2. The term "geopolitical center of the struggle for world power" is taken from a lecture given by Eqbal Ahmad at the AFSC conference "The U.S. in the Middle East: Arms, Oil, and the Multinationals," Harvard University, January 28, 1977; Maxwell Taylor, *Christian Science Monitor*, June 16, 1978.
3. Cited in Joe Stork, *Middle East Oil and the Energy Crisis*, New York: Monthly Review Press, 1975, p. 34.
4. See Albert Hourani, *A History of the Arab Peoples*, Cambridge, MA: Harvard University Press, 1991, pp. 279–332; A. J. P. Taylor, *The Struggle for Mastery in Europe 1848–1918*, London: Oxford University Press, 1971, pp. 509–32; Daniel Yergin, *The Prize*, New York: Simon & Schuster, 1991, pp. 165–83.
5. Avi Shlaim, *War and Peace in the Middle East: A Critique of American Policy*, New York: Viking, 1994, p. 3; Stork, *Middle East Oil,* p. 34.
6. Cited in Irene Gendzier, *Notes from the Minefield: United States Intervention in Lebanon and the Middle East, 1945–1958*, New York: Columbia University Press, 1997, pp. 30–1. The report was prepared by Loy Henderson, Director of the State Department's Office of Near Eastern and Africa Affairs.
7. Shlaim, *War and Peace in the Middle East*, pp. 39–40; William B. Quandt, *Decade of Decisions: American Policy toward the Arab–Israeli Conflict 1967–1976*, Washington, DC: The Brookings Institution, 1977, p. 9.
8. Chomsky, "The Drift Towards War and the Alternatives," p. 27.
9. Noam Chomsky, "The Gulf Crisis: How We Got Here," an interview with Noam Chomsky and Eqbal Ahmad, in Greg Bates, ed., *Mobilizing Democracy*, Monroe, ME: Common Courage Press, 1991, p. 7.
10. Stork, *Middle East Oil*, p. 35.
11. Ibid., p. 293.
12. Walter Pincus, "The Long and Secret U.S.–Saudi Affair," *Washington Post National Weekly Edition*, February 17–23, 1992.
13. Gendzier, *Notes from the Minefield*, p. 31.

14. See, among others, ibid., p. 41.
15. Of these seven oil conglomerates, five were US-based (Standard Oil of New Jersey, Standard Oil of California, Standard Oil of New York (later Mobil), The Texas Oil Company (Texaco), and Gulf Oil Company. Shell was Dutch-controlled, and British Petroleum (formerly the Anglo-Persian Oil Company), UK-controlled.
16. Noam Chomsky, "Patterns of Intervention," in Joseph Gerson, *The Deadly Connection: Nuclear War and U.S. Intervention*, Philadelphia: New Society Publishers, 1986, p. 64.
17. Ibid., p. 64.
18. Seth P. Tillman, *The United States in the Middle East: Interests and Obstacles*, Bloomington: Indiana University Press, 1982, p. 265.
19. Daniel Ellsberg, "Call to Mutiny," in Gerson, *The Deadly Connection*, p. 37.
20. Chomsky, "Patterns of Intervention," p. 64.
21. Wilbur Crane Eveland, *Ropes of Sand: America's Failure in the Middle East*, New York: W. W. Norton, 1980; Denis F. Doyon, "Middle East Bases: Model for the Future," in Joseph Gerson and Bruce Burckhard, eds., *The Sun Never Sets . . . Confronting the Network of Foreign U.S. Military Bases*, Boston, MA: South End Press, 1991; Seymour M. Hersh, *The Price of Power: Kissinger in the Nixon White House*, New York: Summit Books, 1983; Donald Neff, *Warriors at Suez: Eisenhower Takes America into the Middle East*, New York: Linden Press, 1981.
22. Shlaim, *War and Peace in the Middle East*, p. 39.
23. Stephen Green, *Taking Sides: America's Secret Relations with a Militant Israel*, New York: William Morrow and Co., 1984, pp. 193–9, 204, and 244.
24. Shlaim, *War and Peace in the Middle East*, pp. 41–2.
25. John J. Mearsheimer and Stephen M. Walt, "The Israel Lobby and U.S. Foreign Policy," John F. Kennedy School of Government, Harvard University, 2006, http://papers.ssrn.com/so13/papers.cfm?abstract_id891198 (September 2, 2006).
26. Andrey and George McT. Kahin, "Subversion as Foreign Policy," cited in Gendzier, *Notes from the Minefield*, p. 151.
27. Neff, *Warriors at Suez*, pp. 226–7.
28. Gendzier, *Notes from the Minefield*, p. 154.
29. Neff, *Warriors at Suez*, p. 87.
30. Green, *Taking Sides*, p. 116; Neff, *Warriors at Suez*, pp. 112–16.
31. Neff, ibid., p. 227.
32. Hersh, *The Price of Power*, pp. 33–46.
33. Neff, *Warriors at Suez*, pp. 281 and 290.
34. Green, *Taking Sides*, p. 100.
35. Michael B. Oren, *Six Days of War: June 1967 and the Making of the Modern Middle East*, New York: Ballantine Books, 2003, p. 9; Hersh, *The Price of Power*, p. 35.
36. Neff, *Warriors at Suez*, p. 253.
37. Ibid., p. 258.
38. Ibid., pp. 258 and 262.
39. Green, *Taking Sides*, pp. 132–3.
40. Neff, *Warriors at Suez*, p. 280.
41. Hersh, *The Price of Power*, p. 40.
42. Green, *Taking Sides*, p. 130.
43. Hersh, *The Price of Power*, p. 42, Neff, *Warriors at Suez*, pp. 360 and 267.
44. Green, *Taking Sides*, p. 142; Shlaim, *War and Peace in the Middle East*, p. 30.
45. Neff, *Warriors at Suez*, p. 403.
46. Ibid., pp. 404 and 412–13.
47. Ibid., pp. 406 and 412–13.

48. *Time Magazine*, July 29, 1985, cited in Michio Kaku and Daniel Axelrod, *To Win a Nuclear War: The Pentagon's Secret War Plans*, Boston, MA: South End Press, 1987, p. 168.
49. David C. Gordon, *Lebanon: The Fragmented Nation*, Stanford, CA: Hoover Institution Press, 1980, p. 42.
50. SWNCC Country Study on Long-Range Assistance to Lebanon, June 8, 1948, cited in Gendzier, *Notes from the Minefield*, p. 115.
51. Gendzier, *Notes from the Minefield*, pp. 172, 189, and 207.
52. Ibid., pp. 145–6.
53. Ibid., pp. 181, 190–2, and 202.
54. Ibid., pp. 204–5 and 215–21.
55. Ibid., p. 219.
56. Ibid., p. 241.
57. Ibid., pp. 246–9.
58. Eveland, *Ropes of Sand*, p. 296.
59. Gendzier, *Notes from the Minefield*, pp. 272 and 367.
60. Cited in ibid., p. 306.
61. Richard K. Betts, *Nuclear Blackmail and Nuclear Balance*, Washington, DC: The Brookings Institution, 1987, p. 66.
62. Mohamed Heikal, *The Cairo Documents*, pp. 133–4, cited in Betts, ibid., p. 67; Gareth Porter, *The Perils of Dominance: Imbalance of Power and the Road to War in Vietnam*, Berkeley: University of California Press, 2005, pp. 22–3, and Gendzier, *Notes from the Minefield*, p. 320.
63. Ibid., p. 320.
64. Interview with William M. Arkin, September 14, 1994; William M. Arkin and Richard W. Fieldhouse, *Nuclear Battlefields: Global Links in the Arms Race*, Cambridge, MA: Ballinger, 1985, p. 102.
65. Richard Nixon, *R.N.: The Memoirs of Richard Nixon*, New York: Grosset & Dunlap, 1978, p. 483.
66. Yuval Ne'eman, "Israel in the Nuclear Weapons Age," cited in Avner Cohen, *Israel and the Bomb*, New York, Columbia University Press, 1998, p. 1.
67. Oren, *Six Days of War*, p. 19.
68. Ibid., pp. 28, 43, and 54–5.
69. Ibid., p. 15.
70. Cohen, *Israel and the Bomb*, pp. 99–120; Oren, *Six Days of War*, p. 16.
71. Cohen, ibid., pp. 21–2.
72. Green, *Taking Sides*, pp. 180 and 193.
73. Cohen, *Israel and the Bomb*, pp. 33–5.
74. Ibid., pp. 36–7.
75. Ibid., pp. 38–42.
76. Green, *Taking Sides*, pp. 180 and 193; Oren, *Six Days of War*, pp. 43–7.
77. Ibid., pp. 56, 58, and 66–7.
78. Ibid., pp. 158–9.
79. Ibid., pp. 63, 75–6, and 83.
80. Green, *Taking Sides*, p. 199.
81. Oren, *Six Days of War*, pp. 77–8.
82. Ibid., p. 86.
83. Ibid., pp. 133–4; conversations with the author, February 10, 1977.
84. Oren, *Six Days of War*, pp. 86–90.
85. Ibid., pp. 94–6 and 117.

86. Ibid., pp. 101–16.
87. Ibid., pp. 123–4.
88. Ibid., pp. 133–4.
89. Ibid., pp. 153–69.
90. Ibid., pp. 159 and 166–7.
91. Ibid., pp. 175–82.
92. Ibid., pp. 184–92.
93. Ibid., pp. 162–3 and 195.
94. Ibid., pp. 196–210.
95. Cited in ibid., p. 210.
96. Ibid., pp. 214, 217 and 224–5.
97. Ibid., pp. 214, 217 and 224–5.
98. Ibid., pp. 236–43.
99. Ibid., pp. 234–5.
100. Ibid., p. 262.
101. Neff, *Warriors at Suez*, p. 280; Oren, *Six Days of War*, p. 29.
102. Neff, *Warriors at Suez*, p. 281; Oren, *Six Days of War*, p. 298.
103. Oren, ibid., p. 299.
104. Hersh, *The Price of Power*, p. 234.
105. Neff, *Warriors at Suez*, p. 317.
106. Quandt, *Decade of Decisions*, p. 81.
107. Hersh, *The Price of Power*, p. 238.
108. Ibid., p. 238.
109. Walter Isaacson, *Kissinger: A Biography*, New York: Simon & Schuster, 1992, p. 294.
110. Kaku and Axelrod, *To Win a Nuclear War*, p. 169; Barry M. Blechman and Stephen S. Kaplan, *Force without War: U.S. Armed Forces as a Political Instrument*, Washington, DC: The Brookings Institution, 1978, pp. 47–9.
111. Hersh, *The Price of Power*, p. 241.
112. Shlaim, *War and Peace in the Middle East*, p. 43.
113. Mohamed Abdel El-Gamasy, *The October War: Memoirs of Field Marshal El-Gamasy of Egypt*, Cairo: American University of Cairo Press, 1993, p. 204.
114. Shlaim, *War and Peace in the Middle East*, p. 47.
115. El-Gamasy, *The October War*, p. 198. When the author first traveled in Egypt, in 1975, he was struck by the number of times members of the Egyptian elite, newspaper editors, politicians, etc., expressed their humiliation and anger about Israeli references to Egypt as a "dead body"; Shlaim, *War and Peace in the Middle East*, p. 43.
116. Ibid., pp. 46–7.
117. El-Gamasy, *The October War*, p. 144.
118. Ibid., pp. 185–6; Hourani, *A History of the Arab Peoples*, p. 419.
119. Isaacson, *Kissinger*, pp. 514 and 528.
120. Ibid., pp. 514 and 516.
121. Seymour M. Hersh, *The Sampson Option: Israel's Nuclear Arsenal and American Foreign Policy*, New York: Random House, 1991; Raymond L. Garthoff, *Detente and Confrontation: American–Soviet Relations from Nixon to Reagan*, Washington, DC; The Brookings Institution, 1985; Isaacson, *Kissinger*; Henry Kissinger, *Years of Upheaval*, Boston: Little, Brown, 1982; Quandt, *Decade of Decisions*; Nadav Safran, *Israel: the Embattled Ally*, Cambridge, MA: Harvard University Press, 1978.
122. Hersh, *The Sampson Option*, pp. 225–7.
123. Ibid., p. 229.
124. Safran, *Israel*, pp. 482–3, emphasis added.

125. William B. Quandt, "How Far Will Israel Go?" *Washington Post Book World*, November 24, 1991; Hersh, *The Sampson Option*, pp. 230–1.
126. Isaacson, *Kissinger*, pp. 52–3.
127. Ibid., p. 528.
128. El-Gamasy, *The October War*, p. 297; Isaacson, *Kissinger*, p. 528.
129. Kissinger, *Years of Upheaval*, p. 571; Garthoff, *Detente and Confrontation*, p. 374.
130. Isaacson, *Kissinger*, p. 530.
131. Kissinger, *Years of Upheaval*, pp. 579–84.
132. Ibid., p. 591; Isaacson, *Kissinger*, p. 532.
133. Garthoff, *Detente and Confrontation*, p. 379.
134. Ibid., p. 380.
135. Isaacson, *Kissinger*, pp. 536–7.
136. James Carroll, "Richard Nixon and 'the Jews,' " *Boston Globe*, January 7, 1997. Also notes from conversation between the anonymous Rand analyst and the author.
137. Initiated in 1973 by David Rockefeller, and led by Zbigniew Brzezinski, the Trilateral Commission brought together US, Japanese, and Western European elites. Concerned that competing capitalist interests had resulted in two world wars during the twentieth century, it sought to integrate and better harmonize the policies, agendas, and elites of the "trilateral" nations. See, among others, Holly Sklar, ed., *Trilateralism: The Trilateral Commission and Elite Planning for World Management*, Boston, MA: South End Press, 1980.
138. Gerard DeGroot, *The Bomb: A Life*, Cambridge, MA: Harvard University Press, 2005, p. 306.
139. Denis Doyon, "Middle East Bases: Model for the Future," in Joseph Gerson, *The Sun Never Sets . . . Confronting the Networks of US Foreign Military Bases*, Boston, MA: South End Press, 1991, pp. 280–1.
140. Robert Tucker, "The Purposes of American Power," *Foreign Affairs*, Winter 1980/81.
141. Joseph Gerson, *With Hiroshima Eyes: Atomic War, Nuclear Extortion and Moral Imagination*, Philadelphia: New Society Publishers, 1995, p. 155, pp. 177–8.
142. Doyon, "Middle East Bases," p. 286.
143. Shlaim, *War and Peace in the Middle East*, p. 78.
144. Ibid., p. 116.
145. From a conversation between a recently released US Army lieutenant, formerly based in Kansas, and the author during a conference organized by Physicians for Social Responsibility at the Harvard School of Public Health in the early 1980s.

7 NUKES AND THE NEW WORLD ORDER—WHAT WE SAY GOES

1. NBC Nightly News, February 2, 1991 cited in Mitchel Cohen, " 'What We Say Goes!' " *Counter Punch*, December 28, 2002; and Noam Chomsky. " 'What We Say Goes': The Middle East in the New World Order," http://zmag.org/Chomsky/ articles/z9105-what-we-say.htm (September 3, 2006).
2. James Baker, *The Politics of Diplomacy*, cited in David E. Sanger, "Bush Warns Foes Not to Use Weapons of Mass Destruction on U.S. Troops," *New York Times*, December 11, 2006.
3. Cited in "Nuclear Posture Review," Washington, DC: Department of Defense, September 20, 1994.
4. NBC News, February 2, 1991.

5. Jürgen Habermas. *The Past as Future*, Lincoln, NB: University of Nebraska Press, 1994, p. 6; Dilip Hiro, *Desert Shield to Desert Storm: The Second Gulf War*, New York: Routledge, 1992, p. 250; see also the report of the Harvard Study Team Report: Public Health in Iraq After the Gulf War, Boston, May 1991.
6. Maxwell Taylor, *Christian Science Monitor*, June 16, 1978.
7. McGeorge Bundy, "Nuclear Weapons and the Gulf," *Foreign Affairs*, Fall 1991, p. 83.
8. *New York Times*, June 17, 1991; McGeorge Bundy, William J. Crowe, Jr., and Sidney D. Dress, *Reducing Nuclear Danger: the Road Away From the Brink*, New York: Council on Foreign Relations Press, 1993, p. 25.
9. *New York Times*, October 1, 1991.
10. *New York Times*, October 6, 1991.
11. The number of post-Soviet nations depends on the frame of reference being used. Included here are Tajikistan, Kyrgyzstan, Uzbekistan, Turkmenistan, Kazakhstan, Azerbaijan, Armenia, Georgia, Moldova, Ukraine, Belarus, Lithuania, Latvia, Estonia, and Russia.
12. *Manchester Guardian Weekly Edition*, October 2, 1994; *New York Times*, February 17, 1992.
13. *New Contexts, New Dangers: Preventing Nuclear War in the Post-Cold War Era*, American Friends Service Committee, Cambridge: 1993.
14. Joseph Gerson, "Legacies of the Storm: Desert Shield, Desert Storm and the Diplomacy of the Israeli–Palestinian–Arab Conflict," *Scandinavian Journal of Development Alternatives*, June–September 1993; "The Gulf War and the New Order," in Robert Elias and Jennifer Turpin, eds., *Rethinking Peace*, Boulder, CO: Lynne Rienner Publishers, 1994.
15. Avi Shlaim, *War and Peace in the Middle East: A Critique of American Policy*, New York: Viking, 1994, p. 130.
16. Ellen Knickmeyer, "Ghosts of Iraq's Birth," *Washington Post National Weekly Edition*, March 13–19, 2006.
17. Ibid., pp. 71 and 86–90. "CIA Said to Suspect Iraq Bomb Bid in 1989," *Boston Globe*, August 6, 1992.
18. Ibid., p. 92; Bob Woodward, *The Commanders*, New York: Simon & Schuster, 1991, p. 252; Gerson, "Legacies of the Storm."
19. Shlaim, *War and Peace in the Middle East*, p. 92.
20. Ibid., pp. 92–4.
21. Noam Chomsky, " 'What We Say Goes': The Middle East in the New World Order," in Cynthia Peters, ed., *Collateral Damage: The 'New World Order' At Home & Abroad*, Boston, MA: South End Press, 1992, p. 65.
22. Woodward, *The Commanders*, pp. 258–9; Chomsky, " 'What We Say Goes,' " pp. 64–6; Gerson, "Legacies of the Storm."
23. See, among others, Zbigniew Brzezinski, *The Grand Failure: The Birth and Death of Communism in the Twentieth Century*, New York: Charles Scribner's Sons, 1987.
24. Joint Economic Committee of the US Congress, cited in *Japan Times*, August 11, 1987.
25. Cited in Michele A. Flournoy, "Implications for U.S. Military Strategy," in Robert D. Blackwill and Albert Carnesale, eds., *New Nuclear Nations: Consequences for U.S. Policy*, New York: Council on Foreign Relations, 1993, p. 137.
26. Hiro, *Desert Shield to Desert Storm*, p. 250.
27. See note 5; The order reads: "Attack Iraqi political-military leadership and command-and-control; gain and maintain air superiority; sever Iraqi supply lines; destroy chemical, biological and nuclear capability; destroy Republican Guard forces in the Kuwaiti Theater; liberate Kuwait."

28. See the 2002 US Nuclear Posture Review and National Security Statement.
29. See BASIC Report 90.6, "Environmental Dangers of the Gulf," British American Security Information Council, Washington, DC. The American Friends Service Committee received credible reports of shipments of nuclear weapons through Westover Air Force Base in Chicopee, Massachusetts in November 1990.
30. Woodward, *The Commanders*, p. 260; *International Herald Tribune*, August, 9, 1990, cited in Milan Rai and Declan McHugh, "Nuclear Targeting of the Third World," London: CND, 1992; *The Daily Star*, August 10, 1990, cited in Rai and McHugh, "Nuclear Targeting of the Third World."
31. *Bulletin of the Atomic Scientists*, November 1990; *The Guardian*, December 24, 1990; *The Boston Sunday Globe*, January 20, 1991.
32. Bundy, "Nuclear Weapons and the Gulf."
33. World Conference against Atomic and Hydrogen Bombs, Tokyo, 1991; *The Financial Times*, February 4, 1991, cited in Rai and McHugh, "Nuclear Targeting of the Third World"; *Boston Globe*, February 2, 1991.
34. Rick Atkinson, *Crusade: The Untold Story of the Persian Gulf War*, Boston, MA: Houghton Mifflin, 1993, pp. 86 and 89.
35. Thomas D. Williams, "Weapons Dust Worries Iraqis: Provisional Government Seeks Cleanup; U.S. Downplays Risks," *Hartford Courant*, November 1, 2004.
36. "Kosovo Depleted Uranium," *New Scientist*, 5 June, 1999; Kathleen Sullivan, "Pentagon to Add Uranium to 'Smart Book,' " *San Francisco Examiner*, September 20, 1998; Eric Hoskins, "Making the Desert Glow," *New York Times*, January 21, 1993; Laura Flanders, "Mal de guerre," *The Nation*, March 7, 1994; David Grown, "An Invisible Enemy: The Cause of 'Gulf War Syndrome' is as Elusive as its Treatment," *Washington Post Weekly Edition*, August 15–21, 1994.
37. Jawad Al-Ali, "Effects and the Use of Depleted Uranium on Iraq," speech given at the Japan Peace Conference, Naha, Okinawa, January 29, 2004, http://webarchive.afsc.org/newengland/pesp/dr-al-ali.htm (September 8, 2006).
38. The author was a classmate of Bill Clinton's at Georgetown University's School of Foreign Service, where he observed the early stages of this pattern and followed them through Clinton's rise to Governor of Arkansas and from that base to a major force in the Democratic Party. See also David Maraniss, *First in His Class: A Biography of Bill Clinton*, New York: Simon & Schuster, 1996.
39. *New York Times*, March 19, 1999.
40. Brian Hall, "Overkill is not Dead," *New York Times Magazine,* March 15, 1998; Senior Staff Member, Armed Services Committee, US House of Representatives, in a conversation with the author, August 31, 1994; Department of Defense, Washington, DC, October 29, 1993; William J. Perry, Department of Defense, Washington, DC, September 22, 1994; Ambassador Linton Brooks, "The New Nuclear Threat," *Proceedings*, May 1994; *Discriminate Deterrence*, Washington DC: Department of Defense, January 11, 1988.
41. Gill Bates and James Mulvenon, "China's Nuclear Agenda," *New York Times*, September 7, 2001; James R. Woolsey, Testimony before Senate Committee on Governmental Affairs, "Proliferation Threats of the 1990s," February 24, 1993; *Boston Globe*, June 12, 1994.
42. *New Contexts, New Dangers*; Alexei Arbatov, "Start II, Red Ink, and Boris Yeltsin," *Bulletin of the Atomic Scientists*, April 1993.
43. *New York Times*, February 25, 1993; Lewis A. Dunn, "New Nuclear Threats to U.S. Security," in Robert D. Blackwill and Albert Carnesale, eds., *New Nuclear Nations: Consequences for U.S. Policy*, New York: Council on Foreign Relations Press, 1993, p. 41; Thomas F. Ramos, "The Future of Theater Nuclear Weapons," *Strategic Review*, Fall 1991, pp. 41–7.

44. *Boston Globe*, July 12, 1993; *New York Times*, March 24, 1994; William M. Arkin and Robert S. Norris. "Tiny-Nukes for Mini Minds," *Bulletin of the Atomic Scientists*, April 1992.
45. Statement before the Senate Foreign Relations Committee, Washington, DC, January 13, 1993, Washington, DC: Department of State, January 25, 1993, p. 47; Anthony Lake, "Confronting Backlash States," *Foreign Affairs*, March/April 1994, pp. 45–55, emphasis added.
46. Martin Indyk, Address to the Soref Symposium, The Washington Institute, May 18, 1993, provided by the White House.
47. *New York Times*, June 26, 1993.
48. *New York Times*, September 6, 1993; Les Aspin, *Bottom-Up Review, Force Structure Excerpts*, Washington: Department of Defense, September 1, 1993.
49. William J. Perry, *Annual Report to the President and the Congress*, Washington: Department of Defense, 1994; "Path to Counterproliferation Acquisition Strategy," Washington, DC: Department of Defense, May 1, 1994.
50. Ibid.; James Risen, *State of War: The Secret History of the CIA and the Bush Administration*, New York: Free Press, 2006, pp. 193–213.
51. Perry, *Annual Report*.
52. *Washington Post National Weekly Edition*, October 3–9, 1994; *New York Times*, September 23, 1994.
53. William J. Perry, "Remarks Prepared for Delivery by the Secretary of Defense William J. Perry to the Henry L. Stimson Center," Washington, DC: Department of Defense, September 20, 1994; "Press Conference with Secretary of Defense William J. Perry . . .," News Release, Department of Defense, September 22, 1994.
54. "Dod Review Recommends Reduction in Nuclear Force," News Release, Department of Defense, September 22, 1994.
55. *New York Times*, September 22, 1994; *Janes Defense Weekly*, July 30, 1994.
56. *New York Times*, September 26, 1994.
57. "Nuclear States, Non-Aligned Press NPT Agendas at PrepCom," *Disarmament Times*, 29 September 1994; Ambassador Miguel Marin Bosch, "The Road to the Elimination of Nuclear Weapons—the Guarantee for Human Survival," Transcript of the International Symposium: Fifty Years since the Atomic Bombing of Hiroshima and Nagasaki, Hiroshima, July 30–August 2, 1995.
58. John Deutch, "Loose Nukes," a forum held at the Massachusetts Institute of Technology, October 14, 1997, audiotape provided to author.
59. The Policy Committee, Department of Defense, "Essentials of Post-Cold War Deterrence [1995]," http://nautilus.org/archives/nukestrat/USA/Advisory/essentials.95.txt (September 2, 2006).
60. Jonathan S. Landay, "US Quietly Adds a Bunker-Buster to Nuclear Arsenal," *Christian Science Monitor*, April 8, 1997; Associated Press, "Defense Chief Urges Modernization of Arms," *New York Times*, April 29, 1997; Gerard J. DeGroot, *The Bomb: A Life*, Cambridge, MA: Harvard University Press, 2005, p. 344.
61. William M. Arkin, "Nuclear Misdirective," *The Nation*, December 29, 1997.
62. Leon V. Sigal, *Disarming Strangers: Nuclear Diplomacy with North Korea*, Princeton, NJ: Princeton University Press, 1998, pp. 5–9.
63. Bruce Cumings, *Korea's Place in the Sun: A Modern History*, New York: W. W. Norton, 1997, p. 467.
64. Cited in Jim Wolffe, "Powell Sees Opportunity for US to Reduce Military Strength," *Defense News*, April 8, 1991.
65. Ibid., p. 6.

66. Cumings, *Korea's Place in the Sun*, pp. 467–9.
67. William M. Arkin, "Inside U.S. War Plans," http://blogs.washingtonpost.com/earlywarning/2005/11/inside_uswar_plans.html (September 2, 2006); Don Oberdorfer, *The Two Koreas: A Contemporary History*, Reading, MA: Addison-Wesley, 1998, pp. 312 and 324.
68. Oberdorfer, *The Two Koreas*, pp. 276–7.
69. Sigal, *Disarming Strangers*, p. 9.
70. Statement of an anonymous Defense Department official, February 5, 1996, from an interview with Leon V. Sigal, *Disarming Strangers*, p. 10.
71. Oberdorfer, *The Two Koreas*, p. 282.
72. Ibid., p. 285.
73. Ibid., pp. 288–9.
74. Ibid., pp. 294–5.
75. Ibid., pp. 301–2.
76. Ibid., pp. 301–6.
77. Ibid., pp. 306–8.
78. Ibid., pp. 310 and 323.
79. Ibid., pp. 311–21.
80. Andrew J. Nathan and Rober S. Ross, *The Great Wall and the Empty Fortress: China's Search for Security*, New York: W. W. Norton, 1997, p. 4.
81. Andrew Scobell, *China's Use of Military Force: Beyond the Great Wall and the Long March*, Cambridge: Cambridge University Press, 2003, pp. 173–6.
82. Ibid., p. 180.
83. Ibid., p. 176.
84. Ibid., p. 177.
85. Patrick E. Tyler, "China Threatens Taiwan, it Makes Sure U.S. Listens," *New York Times*, January 24, 1996.
86. Paul Quinn-Judge, "US Signals Concern on China's Attitude toward Taiwan," *Boston Globe*, February 7, 1996.
87. Scobell, *China's Use of Military Force*, pp. 176–82.
88. The author's interviews with a broad range of Chinese scholars and officials in Beijing and Shanghai, July 1998; Scobell, ibid., p. 182.
89. Interview with Ezra Vogel, Fairbanks Center, Harvard University, April 16, 1996.
90. This perspective was repeated in a series of interviews conducted by the author in Beijing and Shanghai in July 1998, among them with Xia Liping and Chen Dong Zia of the Shanghai Institute for International Studies; author's notes.
91. Bill Clinton, *My Life*, New York: Alfred A. Knopf, 2004, pp. 717, 751, and 852.
92. *Los Angeles Times*, "Clinton, Saudi Discuss Iran," reprinted in the *Boston Globe*, November 11, 1992; *New York Times*, "Clinton Warns Iraqi's Leader against Testing U.S. Resolve," December 31, 1992.
93. Madeleine Albright, *Madam Secretary*, New York: Miramax Books, 2003, pp. 272–6.
94. See, among others, David Albright and Robert Kelley, "Has Iraq Come Clean at Last?" *Bulletin of the Atomic Scientists*, November/December 1995; "U.N. Says Iraqi Atom Arms Industry is Gone," *New York Times*, September 4, 1992; Paul Lewis, "Bowing to U.N. Iraq Will Permit Arms Monitors," *New York Times*, November 27, 1993; "U.N. Says Monitors for Iraq are in Place," *New York Times*, October 7, 1994.
95. William M. Arkin, "Nuking Libya," *Bulletin of the Atomic Scientists*, July 1996; Michael T. Klare, "Nuking Libya," *The Nation*, July 8, 1996.
96. Flynt Leverett, "More than Threats Led to Qaddafi's Reversal," *International Herald Tribune*, January 24–25, 2004.

97. Albright, *Madam Secretary*, pp. 276–80.
98. Hall, "Overkill is not Dead."
99. Clinton, *My Life*, p. 832; Albright, *Madam Secretary*, p. 286.

8 "ROMANCE OF RUTHLESSNESS"—SEVEN MINUTES TO MIDNIGHT

1. Robert Kagan, *Of Paradise and Power: America and Europe in the New World Order*, New York: Alfred A. Knopf, 2003.
2. Ron Suskind, "Without a Doubt," *New York Times Magazine*, October 17, 2004.
3. ABC News, February 3, 1991, cited in "Open Letter to the President of the United States of America," July 31, 1991, Tokyo, *Nihon Hidankyo*.
4. Board of Directors, *Bulletin of the Atomic Scientists*, March/April 2002; Anwar Iqbal, "N-Missiles Had Been Readied for Launch: Kargil crisis," *Dawn Magazine*, http://www.dawn.com/2005/06/20/top4.htm.
5. *Bulletin of the Atomic Scientists*, May/June 2002.
6. Paul Berman, "Neo No More," *The New York Times Book Review*, March 26, 2006.
7. E. J. Dionne, Jr., "War Politics: Bush looks to McKinley—George W. Bush and William McKinley," *Commonweal*, April 19, 2002; Ivo H. Daalder and James M. Lindsay, "American Empire, Not 'If' but 'What Kind,' " *New York Times*, May 10, 2003; Zia Mian, "A New American Century?" *Foreign Policy in Focus*, May 4, 2005, http://www.presentdanger.org/commentary/2005/0505amcent_body.html (September 6, 2006); Condoleezza Rice, "The National Interest," *Foreign Affairs*, January/February 2000, Vol. 79, No. 1.
8. Nicholas Lemann, " The Quiet Man," *The New Yorker*, May 2, 2001.
9. Richard A. Clarke, *Against All Enemies: Inside America's War on Terror*, New York: The Free Press, 2004. Clarke was Deputy Assistant Secretary of State for Intelligence under Reagan, Assistant Secretary of State for Politico-Military Affairs under President George H. W. Bush, and National Coordinator for Security, Infrastructure, Protection, and Counterterrorism for President Clinton and during President George W. Bush's first year in office.
10. Tom Regan, "Out of Focus: Missile Defense, not al-Qaeda, was at Top of White House Agenda pre-9-11," *Christian Science Monitor*, April 1, 2004.
11. Joseph Gerson, "The Politics and Geopolitics of 'Missile Defenses,' " American Friends Service Committee, July 1992; Jerry Elmer, "Missile Defense in Perspective: U.S. Counterforce Nuclear Doctrine," American Friends Service Committee, July 2001; Richard Clarke, *Against All Enemies: Inside America's War on Terror*, New York: Free Press, 2004, p. 26.
12. David E. Sanger and Steven Lee Myers, "Bush's Missile Plan: The Overview; Missile Shield Along with Nuclear Cuts; Calls '72 Treaty Outdated," *New York Times*, May 2, 2001; George W. Bush, "Bush's Missile Plan: In Bush's Words: 'Substantial Advantages of Intercepting Missiles Early,' " *New York Times*, May 2, 2001.
13. "Nuclear Posture Review" [Excerpts], Global Security.org, 8, January 2002, http://www.globalsecurity.org/wmd/library/policy/dod/npr.htm (September 6, 2005); "U.S. Nuclear Forces, 2002," *Bulletin of the Atomic Scientists*, May/June 2002; Linton Brooks' testimony before the April 8, 2003 Senate Armed Services Strategic Subcommittee; Joseph Gerson, "U.S. Elections, The NPT, and the Continuing Centrality of the Japanese Peace Movement," http://webarchive.afsc.org/newengland/pesp/Nonnucleartalk1104.htm (Sepember 6, 2006); David Clup, "Bush Administration Unveils Plans to Produce 125 New Nuclear Weapons a Year: Seeks Return to Cold War

Nuclear Weapons Capabilities," Washington, DC, Friends Committee on National Legislation, April 6, 2006.

14. Department of Defense, *Doctrine for Joint Nuclear Operations*, Joint Publication 3–12, 15 March, 2005.
15. Ibid., emphasis added.
16. This was the fundamental lesson that Professor William O'Brien taught his students, including the author, at Georgetown University's School of Foreign Service in the 1960s.
17. Nicholas Lemann, "The Next World Order," *The New Yorker*, April 1, 2002; Michael J. Glennon, "The New Interventionism: The Search for a Just International Law," *Foreign Affairs*, May/June 1999.
18. Eliot Cohen, cited in Richard Falk, "The New Bush Doctrine," *The Nation*, July 15, 2002; United States National Security Statement, http://www.whitehouse.gov/nsc/nss/2002/nssintro.html (September 6, 2006).
19. Ibid.
20. Friends Committee on National Legislation, "Treaty Overview: A Summary of U.S. Compliance to Five Arms Control Treaties," January 16, 2003, http://www.fcnl.org/issues/arm/test-ban_1031-02.htm; Alexander G. Higgins, "US Opts out of Germ-War Talks," *The Boston Globe*, July 26, 2001; Julian Borger, "US 'Has Secret Bio-Weapons Programme,' " *The Guardian Weekly*, October 31–November 6, 2002.
21. David E. Sanger, "Reshaping Nuclear Rules," *New York Times*, March 15, 2005; Robin Cook, "America's Broken Nuclear Promises Endanger Us All," *Guardian*, May 27, 2005.
22. Michael Hirsh and Eve Conant, "A Nuclear Blunder?" *Newsweek*, May 11, 2005, http://www.msnbc.msn.com/id/7817986/site/newsweek; David E. Sanger, "Month of Talks Fails to Bolster Nuclear Treaty," *New York Times*, May 28, 2005.
23. US State Department, Bureau of Arms Control, "2005 Non-Proliferation Treaty (NPT) Review Conference: U.S. Objectives," April 21, 2005, http://www.state.gov/t/ac/rls/or/44994.htm (September 6, 2006).
24. Ibid.; US Department of State, Bureau of Arms Control, "2005 Non-Proliferation Treaty (NPT) Review Conference: U.S. Objectives," April 21, 2005, http://www.state.gov/t/ac/rls/or/44994.htm; John Hallam, "Drifting toward the Apocalypse—A Postmortem on the Nuclear Nonproliferation Treaty Review Conference May 2–27, 2005," Friends of the Earth Australia.
25. Reuters, "U.S. Hails Nonproliferation Push," May 31, 2005, http://www.nytimes.com/reuters/politics/politics-security-proliferation-usa.html (June 9, 2005).
26. "U.S. Ready to Take over Where NPT Confab Failed," *Daily Yomiuri* (Tokyo), June 27, 2005; Reuters, "U.S. Hails Nonproliferation Push," *New York Times*, May 31, 2005; Reuters, "U.S. and Allies Pursue a Plan To Block Ships Carrying Arms," *New York Times*, September 5, 2003; David E. Sanger, "Rice to Discuss Antiproliferation Program," *New York Times*, May 30, 2005; Lawrence J. Korb, "Bush Failing at Nuclear Security," *Boston Sunday Globe*, January 2, 2005.
27. Julian Borger, "Bush Gamble Risks Nuclear Arms Race," *Guardian Weekly*, March 10–16, 2006. See also Z. Mian, A. H. Nayyar, R. Rajaraman, and M. V. Ramana, "Fissile Materials in South Asia and the implications of the U.S.–India Deal," draft report for the International Panel on Fissile Materials, July 11, 2006.
28. Clarke, *Against All Enemies*, pp. 15–16.
29. Ibid., p. 24.
30. Ibid., p. 30; Bob Woodward, *Bush at War*, New York, Simon & Schuster, 2002, pp. 60 and 91.
31. See, among others, Praful Bidwai, "South Asia on the Nuclear Brink?" *Inter Press Service*, November 2, 2001; John F. Burns, "U.S. Demands Air and Land Access to

Pakistan," *New York Times*, September 15, 2001; Douglas Frantz with Todd S. Purdum, "Pakistan Faces Increased U.S. Pressure to Curb Militants," *New York Times*, December 16, 2001; Barry Bearak, "Pakistan Is," *The New York Times Magazine*, December 7, 2003; Douglas Frantz, "Pakistan Ended Aid to Taliban Only Hesitantly," *New York Times*, December 8, 2001; Caroline Frost, "Hamid Karzai: Profile," *Documentaries*, BBC Four, http://www.bbc.co.uk/bbcfour/documentaries/profile/hamid-karzai.shtml (September 6, 2005).

32. Bob Woodward, *Plan of Attack*, New York: Simon & Schuster, 2004, pp. 52–64. This quote appeared in the German newspapers *Der Tagesspiegel* and *Die Welt*, June 4, 2003; Deputy Secretary Wolfowitz interview with Karen DeYoung, *News Transcript*, Washington, DC: United States Department of Defense, May 28, 2003, http://www.defenselink.mil/transcripts/2003/tr20030528-depsecdef0222.html.
33. David E. Sanger and Thom Shanker, "Pyongyang Reneged on Missiles for Saddam," *International Herald Tribune*, December 2, 2003; Michael R. Gordon and Bernard E. Trainor, " Dash to Baghdad Left Top U.S. Generals Divided," *New York Times*, March 13, 2006.
34. Quotations cited in John Prados, *Hoodwinked: The Documents that Reveal How Bush Sold Us a War*, New York: New Press, 2004, pp. 21–31.
35. See, among others, " The Downing Street Memorandum," http://downingstreetmemo.com. (August 29, 2006); Don Van Natta Jr., "Bush Was Set on Path to War, British Memo Says," *New York Times*, March 27, 2006; Woodward, *Plan of Attack*; Secretary of State Colin Powell, speech to the UN Security Council, February 5, 2003, cited in Lewis H. Lapham, "The Case for Impeachment: Why We Can no Longer Afford George W. Bush," *Harper's Magazine*, March 2006.
36. David E. Sanger, "Bush Warns Foes Not to Use Weapons of Mass Destruction on U.S. Troops," *New York Times*, December 11, 2002.
37. Douglas Jehl, "The Conflict in Iraq: Intelligence; "C.I.A. Reports Offer Warnings on Iraq's Path," *New York Times*, December 7, 2004, http://select.nytimes.com/search/restricted/article?res=F70815FB3E550C748CDDAB0994DC404482 (September 6, 2006).
38. Tim Beal, *North Korea: The Struggle against American Power*, London: Pluto Press, 2005, pp. 258–9.
39. Victor D. Cha and David C. Kang, *Nuclear North Korea: A Debate on Engagement Strategies*, New York: Columbia University Press, 2003, p. 130; Timothy Savage, "Pyongyang's Dangerous Game," Nautilus of America/The Nautilus Institute, 2002.
40. *Associated Press/Wall Street Journal*, "South Korea Navy Fires Shots at Northern Boats," June 3, 2003, provided by *Korea Economic Reader*, June 3, 2003; ibid, p. 131; Alexandre Y. Mansourov, "The Kelly Process, Kim Jong Il's Grand Strategy, and the Dawn of a Post-Agreed Framework Era on the Korean Peninsula!" Nautilus Institute, October 22, 2002, http://nautilus.org/fora/security/0206A_Anexandre.html (September 6, 2006).
41. Cha and Kang, *Nuclear North Korea*, p. 132.
42. National Council for Peace on the Korean Peninsula; Mansourov, " The Kelly Process"; Leon V. Sigal, "A Bombshell That's Actually an Olive Branch," Nautilus of America/The Nautilus Institute, October 23, 2002.
43. Sigal, ibid., p. 132; Mansourov, " The Kelly Process."
44. Cha and Kang, *Nuclear North Korea*, p. 142, Table B.
45. "Recommendations for Peace on the Korean Peninsula by the National Council for Peace on the Korean Peninsula," June 2, 2003. Available from the American Friends Service Committee.

46. One of the justifications contained in the US Declaration of Independence for the rupture and Revolutionary War against Britain in 1776 was that George III had "Kept among us, in times of peace, Standing Armies," which committed intolerable "abuses and usurpations."
47. John Feffer, "Is North Korea Next?," *Foreign Policy in Focus*, March 24, 2003, http://www.fpif.org/commentary/2003/0303nknext_body.html (September 6, 2006).
48. Ibid.
49. Warren Hoge, "U.N. Council, in Weakened Resolution, Demands End to North Korean Missile Program," *New York Times*, July 16, 2006.
50. Norimitsu Onishi, "In Rare Talks, the 2 Koreas Agree to Talk again Next Month," *New York Times*, May 20, 2003; Anthony Failoa. "Despite U.S.' Attempts, N. Korea Anything but Isolated," *Washington Post*, May 12, 2005; Chris Buckley, "Seoul Tries to Break Deadlock in Talks," *International Herald Tribune*, July 28, 2005.
51. Editorial, "Testing North Korea," *New York Times*, November 5, 2006.
52. See, among others, Steven R. Weisman, "U.S. to Send Signal to North Koreans in Naval Exercise," *New York Times*, August 18, 2003; David E. Sanger and Thom Shanker, "U.S. Aides Remain Divided as They Weigh Korea Risks," *New York Times*, May 1, 2003; Howard W. French, "G.I's Will Gradually Leave Korea DMZ to Cut War Risk," *New York Times*, June 16, 2003; "Argument over U.S. Base," *Korea Herald*, November 26, 2003; Jeong Taeksang, "Transformation of the South Korea–U.S. Alliance and a Stolen Future," speech to the World Conference against Atomic and Hydrogen Bombs, Hiroshima, August 3, 2006.
53. *The National Security Strategy of the United States of America*, The White House, March 16, 2006, pp. 18 and 21. Emphasis in the original.
54. Joel Brinkley, "U.S. Squeezes North Korea's Money Flow," *New York Times*, March 10, 2006.
55. Sanger, "Report Backs Iraq Strike and Cites Iran Peril."
56. Jung Sung-Ki, "Washington, Tokyo Near Unified Command," *Korea Times*, September 5, 2006, http://search.hankookicom/times_view.php?term=washington%2c+tokyo+near+unified+command++&path=hankooki3/times/1page/200609/Kt2006090518090668040.htm&media=Kt (September 7, 2006). "DESCRIPTION: 060617-N-7130B-291 USS RONALD REAGAN," http://www.reagan.navy.mil/photos_for_page/june_2006/2_reagan_valiant_shield/pages/060617-N-7130B-291.html (September 7, 2006); US Department of Defense "Exercise Valiant Shield 2006 Kicks off," http://www.defenselink.mil/home/photoessays/2006-06/p20060619al.html (September 7, 2006).
57. "Perry: US Might Use Force on DPRK," *The Yomiuri Shimbun*, November 5, 2006; http://www.yomiuri.co.jp/dy/world/20061105DY01005.html (November 5, 2006).
58. Hassan M. Fattah, "US-led Exercise in Persian Gulf Sets Sights on Deadliest Weapons," *New York Times*, October 31, 2006.

9 ABOLITION OR ANNIHILATION

1. Transcripts. 2004 World Conference against A- & H-Bombs, Hiroshima and Nagasaki, August 2–9, 2004, Tokyo: Japan Council against Atomic and Hydrogen Bombs (*Gensuikyo*), p. 1.
2. Miguel Ruiz-Cabanas Izquierdo, Statement of the Ambassador to Japan from the United Mexican States, 2005 World Conference against A- & H-Bombs, Tokyo: Japan Council against A- & H-Bombs (*Gensuikyo*), 2005, emphasis in original.
3. http://www.knowprose.com/node/12808 (November 4, 2006).

4. From tape-recording of speech given by Judge Weeramantry at the Spring 2005 meeting of the American Bar Association Section of International Law, Washington, DC, April 13, 2005.
5. http://www.pugwash.org/about/manifesto.htm (September 5, 2006).
6. White House, "National Security Strategy of the United States," March 2006, p. 18.
7. Author's notes, interview with Mr. Takamizawa, Japan Defense Agency, March 12, 1996. See also, among others, " 'Use of Nuclear Weapons by Japan Would be Constitutional': Cabinet Legislative Bureau Director General," *Japan Press Service*, June 22, 1998; "Japan Hints at Reversal of Bar on Nuclear Arms," *Boston Globe*, July 9, 1993.
8. See, among others, *Exposure: Victims of Radiation Speak Out*, *The Chogoku Newspaper*, Tokyo: Kodansha International, 1992; Peter H. Eichstaedt, *If You Poison Us: Uranium and Native Americans*, Santa Fe: Red Crane Books, 1994; John G. Fuller, *The Day We Bombed Utah*, New York: New American Library, 1984; Zhores A. Medvedev, *Nuclear Disaster in the Urals*, New York: Vintage Books, 1980; Michael Uhl and Tod Ensign, *GI Guinea Pigs: How the Pentagon Exposed Our Troops to Dangers More Deadly than War: Agent Orange and Atomic Radiation*, US: Playboy Press, 1980. People of Christmas Island, Tahiti and Kazakhstan were exposed, respectively, to fallout from British, French, Soviet, and possibly Chinese nuclear weapons tests.
9. Bruce G. Blair, Harold A. Feiveson, and Frank N. von Hippel, "Taking Nuclear Weapons off Hair-Trigger Alert," *Scientific American*, November, 1997.
10. Joseph Rotblat, Jack Steinberger, and Bhalchandra Udagaonkar, eds., *A Nuclear-Weapon-Free World: Desirable? Feasible?*, Boulder, CO: Westview Press, 1993, p. 20.
11. Lawrence Wittner, *One World or None: A History of the World Nuclear Disarmament Movement Through 1953*, Stanford, CA: Stanford University Press, 1993, pp. 182–4.
12. Lawrence Wittner, *Resisting the Bomb: A History of the World Nuclear Disarmament Movement Through 1954–1970*, Stanford, CA: Stanford University Press, 1997, pp. 52–4. Peggy Duff, *Left, Left, Left: A Personal Account of Six Protest Campaigns 1945–65*, London: Allison & Busby, 1971, pp. 118–21; Kate Hudson, *CND—Now More Than Ever: The Story of a Peace Movement*, London: Vision Paperbacks, 2005, pp. 42–5.
13. http://www.nuclearfiles.org/menu/key issues/nuclear-weapons/issues/arms-control-disarmament/mccloy-zorin-accords_1961-09-20.htm (September 4, 2006).
14. Seymour Hersh, *The Price of Power: Kissinger in the Nixon White House*, New York: Summit Books, p. 229.
15. Jimmy Carter, *Keeping Faith*, New York: Bantam Books, 1982, p. 221; Robert S. Norris and Hans M. Kristensen, "NRDC: Nuclear Notebook—U.S. Nuclear Forces, 2006," *The Bulletin of the Atomic Scientists*, January/February 2006.
16. *Disarmament Times*, NGO Committee on Disarmament, Inc, Vol. XVII, No. 4, New York: September 29, 1994.
17. Founding members of the World Court Project were the International Association of Lawyers Against Nuclear Arms (IALANA), the International Peace Bureau (IPB), and the International Physicians for the Prevention of Nuclear War (IPPNW).
18. Reuters, "World Court Condemns Use of Nuclear Weapons," *New York Times*, July 9, 1996; http://www.un.org/law/icjsum/9623.htm (September 4, 2006).
19. Ambassador Hussein Haniff, "Perspective for Abolition of Nuclear Weapons," Transcript, World Conference against Atomic and Hydrogen Bombs; "Facts Faxed," NGO Committee on Disarmament, New York, October 1997; *Disarmament Times*, "Action Alert," NGO Committee on Disarmament, New York, 31 October, 1996; Lawyers Committee on Nuclear Disarmament, "Follow-up to the International Court of Justice Advisory Opinion on the Legality of the Threat or Use of Nuclear Weapons:

Legal, Technical and Political Elements Required for the Establishment and Maintenance of a Nuclear Weapons-free World," Draft working paper for the 2005 NPT Review Conference, http://www.lcnp.org/disarmament/npt/2005nPTmalaysia-wp.htm.

20. See, among others, Wittner, *One World or None*; Wittner, *Resisting the Bomb*; Lawrence S. Wittner, *Toward Nuclear Abolition: A History of the World Nuclear Disarmament Movement 1971 to the Present*, Stanford, CA: Stanford University Press, 2003; Hudson, *CND*; Duff, *Left, Left, Left*; Simeon A. Sahaydachny, *Nuclear Trojan Horse*, New York: Riverside Church Disarmament Program and the Lawyers Committee on Nuclear Policy, 1985; John Burroughs, *The (Il)legality of Threat or Use of Nuclear Weapons: A Guide to the Historic Opinion of the International Court of Justice*, Munster: Die Deutsche Bibliothek—CIP-Einheitsaufnahme, 1997; Robert Kleidman, *Organizing for Peace: Neutrality, the Test Bank, and the Freeze*, Syracuse, NY: Syracuse University Press, 1993; Pam Solo, *From Protest to Policy: Beyond the Freeze to Common Security*, Cambridge, MA: Ballinger, 1988.
21. Among the leading advocates of the "Freeze" was the recently retired CIA Director William Colby. The author has reason to believe, but cannot prove, additional CIA involvement. See, among others, Wittner, *Toward Nuclear Abolition*, Hudson, *CND*, Duff, *Left, Left, Left*; World Conference against A- and H-Bombs.
22. "Introducing the Japan Council against Atomic and Hydrogen Bombs (Japan *Gensuikyo*," http://www10.plala.or.jp/antiatom/html/e/description_gensuikyo.htm (September 4, 2006); Bernard J. O'Keefe, *Nuclear Hostages*, Boston, MA: Houghton Mifflin, pp. 158–208.
23. The *Hibakusha* who are quoted are Misako Yamaguchi and Akimoto Takahashi. See "Japan Council against Atomic and Hydrogen Bombs, 'Happiness will Come Back to Us,' " *No More Hiroshimas*, Tokyo, 1955. Other materials, including correspondence and the unpublished biographical manuscript of Matashichi Oishi, and materials provided the Japan Council against Atomic and Hydrogen Bombs (*Gensuikyo*).
24. Senji Yamaguchi, *Burnt Yet Undaunted*, Tokyo: Japan Confederation of A- and H-Bomb Sufferers' Organizations, 2002, pp. 60–1.
25. In a conversation with the author, Joseph Rotblat said that in 1955 as Lord Russell was returning to London from Paris by plane, he was devastated to hear an announcement made by the pilot that Albert Einstein had died. Prior to leaving for Paris, Russell had not yet received Einstein's signature on the appeal. Besides losing a valued associate, he believed that the joint manifesto had died with the esteemed physicist. On returning home, Russell sorted through his mail and to his enormous relief found that Einstein had signed and mailed the statement as one of his last acts.
26. Conversation between the author and Rotblat, October 24, 1998; Hudson, *CND*; Duff, *Left, Left, Left*, pp. 179 and 239.
27. Wittner, *Resisting the Bomb*; Barbara Reynolds, *The Phoenix and the Dove*, Nagasaki: Nagasaki Appeal Committee, undated.
28. The author was an organizer for the Continental Walk and was intimately involved in helping to launch the Nuclear Weapons Freeze movement.
29. Daniel Ellsberg, "The Way to Bet: On US Policy, the Outcome of the NPT Conference, and The Future of Proliferation if We Don't Try to Change it, This Month," April 6, 1995, faxed to the author, April 16, 1995; Daniel Ellsberg, "Call to a Fast for the Abolition of Nuclear Weapons," April 16, 1995, faxed to the author April 16, 1995.
30. Nelson Mandela, United Nations General Assembly, 21 September, 1998. Circulated by the Lawyers Committee on Nuclear Policy.
31. James Carroll, "Rumsfeld and the Big Picture," *The Boston Globe*, March 27, 2006; The Canberra Commission on the Elimination of Nuclear Weapons, http://www.dfat.gov.au/

cc/cchome.html (September 4, 2006); International Association of Lawyers Against Nuclear Arms, International Network of Engineers and Scientists Against Proliferation; International Physicians for the Prevention of Nuclear War, "Security and Survival: The Case for a Nuclear Weapons Convention," Cambridge, MA: IPPNW, 1999.

32. "Statement on Nuclear Weapons by International Generals and Admirals," December 4, 1996, circulated by Disarmament Clearing House and Greenpeace in Washington, DC; "Generals Speak out for Nuclear Disarmament," *Peacework*, January 1997.
33. James Brooke, "Former Cold Warrior Has a New Mission: Nuclear Cuts," *New York Times*, January 8, 1997; Gar Alperovitz, Alex Campbell, and Thad Williamson, "Down & Out: A Nuclear Path," *The Nation*, December 30, 1996; "Statement on Nuclear Weapons by International Generals and Admirals," December 4, 1996, circulated by Disarmament Clearing House and Greenpeace in Washington, DC.
34. General George Lee Butler, "Ending the Nuclear Madness," Waging Peace Series, Booklet 10, Santa Barbara: Nuclear Age Peace Foundation, September, 1999; R. Jeffrey Smith, "Retired Nuclear Warrior Sounds Alarm on Weapons," *Washington Post*, December 4, 1996.
35. Paul H. Nitze, "A Threat Mostly to Ourselves," *New York Times*, October 28, 1999.
36. Strobe Talbott, *The Master of the Game: Paul Nitze and the Nuclear Peace*, New York: Alfred A. Knopf, 1988; Nitze, "A Threat Mostly to Ourselves"; Jimmy Carter, "Saving Nonproliferation," *Washington Post*, March 28, 2005; Gerard J. DeGroot, *The Bomb: A Life*, Cambridge, MA: Harvard University Press, 2005, p. 302.
37. Joseph Rotblat, "Remember Your Humanity," 10 December, 1995, Oslo, Norway, http://www.pugwash.org/award/Rotblatnobel.htm (September 4, 2006), emphasis in the original; Joseph Rotblat, "Message to the Inheritors of the Manhattan Project from Professor Sir Joseph Rotblat FRS," July 16, 2005, distributed by Pamela Meidell, Atomic Mirror, emphasis in the original.
38. Interview with Mohamed ElBaradei, "U.S. Nuke Update Scheme Undermines Disarmament," *The Daily Yomiuri*, January 28, 2004; Bryan Bender, "World's Nuclear Powers Decried as Hypocrites," *The Boston Globe*, June 22, 2004; Walter Gibbs, "Accepting Nobel, ElBaradei Urges a Rethinking of Nuclear Strategy," *New York Times*, December 11, 2005.
39. Bjoern Lindahl, "Nobel Prize Tipped to go to Anti-Nuclear Weapons Efforts," *Mail & Guardian* online, http://www.mg.co/za/articledirect.aspx?area=breaking_news_international_news/&articleid=252348 (September 4, 2006). See also reports by Agence France Presse.
40. "Abolition 2000 Global Network to Eliminate Nuclear Weapons: Background and History," Santa Barbara; "Abolition 2000 Statement," 25 April 1995; "Moorea Declaration," 25 January 1997; undated letter to Abolition 2000 Partner organizations signed by Alice Slater and Jacqueline Cabasso.
41. World Conference against A- & H-Bomb Transcripts; Mayors for Peace, http://www.mayorsforpeace.org/english/membercity/northamerica.html (September 4, 2006); Charles A. Radin, "Warriors for Peace," *The Boston Globe Magazine*, July 27, 1997.
42. Lake Sosin Snell & Associates, "Abolition 2000: A Survey on Nuclear Weapons," April 1997.
43. David Cracknell, "Beckett: We May not Need Nuclear Missiles," *Sunday Times*, November 1, 2006, http://www.timesonline.co.uk/article/0,2087-2426973.html (November 3, 2006).
44. Author's notes. CND Annual Conference, London, October 15, 2005.
45. Praful Bidwai and Achin Vanaik, *New Nukes: India, Pakistan and Global Nuclear Disarmament*, New York: Olive Branch Press, 2000.
46. Author's notes; Focus on Global South, *Focus-on-Security* 19, Vol. 3, No. 1, Bangkok, March 13, 2000.

47. Transcript, World Conference against Atomic and Hydrogen Bombs, Tokyo, 1993.
48. Reinhold Niebuhr, *Moral Man and Immoral Society*, New York: Charles Scribners & Sons, 1932, p. 117.
49. Albert Camus, *The Plague*, New York: Modern Library, 1948, pp. 57 and 150.
50. See, among others, Geoffrey Ashe, *Gandhi*, New York, Stein and Day, 1969; Mohandas K. Gandhi, *An Autobiography: The Story of My Experiments with Truth*, Boston, MA: Beacon Press, 1965.
51. Transcript, World Conference; Rotblat, Steinberger, and Udgaonkar, *A Nuclear Weapon-free World*, pp. 6–15 and 48–51.
52. Independent Commission on Disarmament and Security Issues. *Common Security: A Blueprint for Survival*, New York: Simon & Schuster, 1982, pp. 8–10.
53. The City of Hiroshima, Peace Declaration, August 6, 2004; Nagasaki Peace Declaration, August 9, 2004.
54. Martin Buber, *Pointing the Way*, New York: Harper & Row, 1957, p. 110.

Selected Bibliography

Elie Abel. *The Missile Crisis*, New York: J. B. Lippincott, 1966.

Madeleine Albright. *Madam Secretary*, New York: Miramax Books, 2003.

Robert C. Aldridge. *First Strike!: The Pentagon's Strategy for Nuclear War*, Boston, MA: South End Press, 1983.

Graham Allison. *Nuclear Terrorism: The Ultimate Preventable Catastrophe*, New York: Henry Holt & Co., 2004.

Graham T. Allison, Albert Carnesale, and Joseph S. Nye, Jr., eds. *Hawks, Doves, & Owls: An Agenda for Avoiding Nuclear War*, New York: W. W. Norton, 1985.

Gar Alperovitz. *The Decision to Use the Atomic Bomb and the Architecture of an American Myth*, New York, Alfred A. Knopf, 1995.

American Friends Service Committee. *Search for Peace in the Middle East*, New York: Hill and Wang, 1970.

Jacques Attali. *Millennium: Winners and Losers in the Coming World Order*, New York: Times Books, 1991.

Richard J. Barnet. *Intervention and Revolution: America's Confrontation with Insurgent Movements around the World*, New York: The New American Library 1968.

Richard J. Barnet. *The Alliance: America-Europe-Japan Makers of the Postwar World*, New York: Simon & Schuster, 1983.

Richard Baum. *Burying Mao: Chinese Politics in the Age of Deng Xiaoping*, Princeton, NJ: Princeton University Press, 1994.

Tim Beal. *North Korea: The Struggle against American Power*, London: Pluto Press, 2005.

Michael R. Beschloss and Strobe Talbot. *At the Highest Levels: The Inside Story of the End of the Cold War*, Boston: Little, Brown, 1993.

Richard K. Betts. *Nuclear Blackmail and Nuclear Balance*, Washington, DC: Brookings Institution, 1987.

Praful Bidwai and Achin Vanaik. *New Nukes: India, Pakistan and Global Nuclear Disarmament*, New York: Olive Branch Press, 2000.

Kai Bird and Lawrence Lifschultz. *Hiroshima's Shadow: Writings on the Denial of History and the Smithsonian Controversy*, Stony Creek, CT: The Pamphleteer's Press, 1997.

Kai Bird and Martin J. Sherwin. *American Prometheus: The Triumph and Tragedy of J. Robert Oppenheimer*, New York: Alfred A. Knopf, 2005.

Barry M. Blechman and Stephen S. Kaplan. *Force Without War: U.S. Armed Forces as a Political Instrument*, Washington, DC: The Brookings Institution, 1978.

James G. Blight, Bruce J. Allyn, and David A. Welch. *Cuba on the Brink: Castro, the Missile Crisis, and the Soviet Collapse*, New York: Pantheon Books, 1993.

Hans Blix. *Disarming Iraq*, New York: Pantheon Books, 2004.

Fawn M. Brodie. *Richard Nixon: The Shaping of His Character*, Cambridge, MA: Harvard University Press, 1983.

Dino A. Brugioni. *Eyeball to Eyeball: The Inside Story of the Cuban Missile Crisis*, New York: Random House, 1990.

McGeorge Bundy. *Danger and Survival: Choices about the Bomb in the First Fifty Years*, New York: Random House, 1988.

McGeorge Bundy, William J. Crowe, Jr., and Sidney D. Drell. *Reducing Nuclear Danger: The Road away from the Brink*, New York: Council on Foreign Relations, 1993.

Wilfred Burchett, *Shadows of Hiroshima*, London: Verso, 1983.

William Burr, ed., *The Kissinger Transcripts: The Top-Secret Talks with Beijing & Moscow*, New York: The New York Review of Books, 1999.

Richard Butler. *Fatal Choice: Nuclear Weapons and the Illusion of Missile Defense*, Boulder, CO: Westview Press, 2001.

Zbigniew Brzezinski. *The Grand Chessboard: American Primacy and its Geostrategic Imperatives*, New York: Basic Books, 1998.

Albert Camus. *The Plague*, New York: Modern Library, 1948.

Albert Carnesale, Paul Doty, Stanley Hoffman, Samuel Huntington, Joseph S. Nye, Jr. and Scott D. Sagan. *Living with Nuclear Weapons: The Harvard Nuclear Study Group*, Cambridge, MA: Harvard University Press, 1983.

Jimmy Carter. *Keeping Faith*, New York: Bantam Books, 1982.

Central Intelligence Agency. *The Secret Cuban Missile Crisis Documents*, New York: Brassey's U.S., 1994.

Victor D. Cha and David C. Kang. *Nuclear North Korea: A Debate on Engagement Strategies*, New York: Columbia University Press, 2003.

Gordon H. Chang. *Friends and Enemies: The United States, China, and the Soviet Union, 1948–1972*, Stanford, CA: Stanford University Press, 1990.

Laurence Chang and Peter Kornbluh, eds. *The Cuban Missile Crisis, 1962: A National Security Archive Documents Reader*, New York: The New Press, 1998.

Noam Chomsky. *American Power and the New Mandarins: Historical and Political Essays*, New York: Vintage, 1967.

Noam Chomsky. *Peace in the Middle East? Reflections on Justice and Nationhood*, New York: Viking, 1969.

Noam Chomsky. *On Power and Ideology*. The Managua Lectures. Boston, MA: South End Press, 1987.

Noam Chomsky. *World Orders Old and New*, New York: Columbia University Press, 1994.

Noam Chomsky. *Fateful Triangle: The United States, Israel & The Palestinians*, Boston, MA: South End Press, 1999.

Noam Chomsky. *Hegemony or Survival: America's Quest for Global Dominance*, New York: Metropolitan Books, 2003.

Richard A. Clarke. *Against All Enemies: Inside America's War on Terror*, New York: The Free Press, 2004.

Bill Clinton. *My Life*, New York: Alfred A. Knopf, 2004.

Avner Cohen. *Israel and the Bomb*, New York: Columbia University Press, 1998.

Haruko Taya Cook and Theodore F. Cook, eds. *Japan at War: An Oral History*, New York: The New Press, 1992.

Bruce Cumings: *Korea's Place in the Sun: A Modern History*, New York: W. W. Norton, 1997.

Nicholas Dawidoff. The *Catcher was a Spy: The Mysterious Life of Moe Berg*, New York: Pantheon Books, 1994.

Gerard J. DeGroot. *The Bomb: A Life*, Cambridge, MA: Harvard University Press, 2005.

Department of Defense. *Doctrine for Joint Nuclear Operations*, Washington, DC, March 15, 2005.

Anatoly Dobrynin. *In Confidence: Moscow's Ambassador to America's Six Cold War Presidents (1962–1986)*, New York: Times Books, 1995.

John W. Dower. *Empire and Aftermath: Yoshida Shigeru and the Japanese Experience, 1878–1954*, Cambridge, MA: Harvard University Press, 1979.

John W. Dower. *Japan in War & Peace: Selected Essays*, New York: The New Press, 1993.

Peggy Duff. *Left, Left, Left: A Personal Account of Six Protest Campaigns 1945–1965*, London: Allison & Busby, 1971.

Peggy Duff, ed. *War or Peace in the Middle East*, London: Spokesman, 1978.
Mohamed Abdel Ghani El-Gamasy. *The October War: Memoirs of Field Marshal El-Gamasy of Egypt*, Cairo: American University in Cairo Press, 1993.
Daniel Ellsberg. *Papers on the War*, New York: Simon & Schuster, 1972.
Daniel Ellsberg. *Secrets: A Memoir of Vietnam and the Pentagon Papers*, New York: Viking, 2002.
Wilbur Crane Eveland. *Ropes of Sand: America's Failure in the Middle East*, New York: W. W. Norton, 1980.
Ismail Fahmy. *Negotiating for Peace in the Middle East*, Baltimore, MD: The Johns Hopkins University Press, 1983.
John Feffer. *North Korea, South Korea: U.S. Policy at a Time of Crisis*, New York: Seven Stories Press, 2003.
Niall Ferguson. *Empire: The Rise and Demise of the British World Order and the Lessons for Global Power*, New York: Basic Books, 2002.
Niall Ferguson. *Colossus: The Price of America's Empire*, New York: Penguin Books, 2004.
Frances Fitzgerald. *Way Out There in the Blue: Reagan, Star Wars and the End of the Cold War*, New York: Simon & Schuster, 2000.
Max Frankel. *High Noon in the Cold War: Kennedy, Khrushchev, and the Cuban Missile Crisis*, New York: Ballantine Books, 2004.
Michael Frayn. *Copenhagen*, New York: Anchor Books, 1998.
Aleksander Fursenko and Timothy Naftalk. *One Hell of a Gamble: Khrushchev, Castro & Kennedy 1958–1964*, New York: W. W. Norton, 1997.
Jeffrey E. Garten. *A Cold Peace: America, Japan, Germany and the Struggle for Supremacy*, New York: Times Books, 1992.
Raymond L. Garthoff. *Détente and Confrontation: American–Soviet Relations from Nixon to Reagan*, Washington, DC: Brookings Institution, 1985.
Irene L. Gendzier. *Notes From the Minefield: United States Intervention in Lebanon and the Middle East 1945–1958*. Boulder, CO: Westview Press, 1999.
Joseph Gerson, ed. *The Deadly Connection: Nuclear War & US Intervention*, Philadelphia: New Society Publishers, 1986.
Joseph Gerson. *With Hiroshima Eyes: Atomic War, Nuclear Extortion, and Moral Imagination*, Philadelphia: New Society Publishers, 1995.
Joseph Gerson. *The Politics and Geopolitics of "Missile Defenses,"* Cambridge, MA: American Friends Service Committee, 2001.
Joseph Gerson and Bruce Birchard, eds. *The Sun Never Sets: Confronting the Network of Foreign U.S. Military Bases*, Boston, MA: South End Press, 1991.
Bruce Gilley. *Tiger on the Brink: Jiang Zemin and China's New Elite*, Berkeley: University of California Press, 1998.
David C. Gordon. *Lebanon: The Fragmented Nation*, London: Croom Helm, 1980.
Stephen Green. *Taking Sides: America's Secret Relations with a Militant Israel*, New York: William Morrow and Co., 1984.
General Anatoli I. Gribkov and General William Y. Smith. *Operation ANDAYR: U.S. and Soviet Generals Recount the Cuban Missile Crisis*, Chicago: edition q inc., 1994.
David Halberstam. *The Best and the Brightest*, Greenwich, CT: Fawcett Books, 1973.
H. R. Halderman. *The Ends of Power*. New York: Times Books, 1978.
Morton H. Halperin. *China and the Bomb*, New York: Fredrick A. Praeger, 1967.
Tsuyoshi Hasegawa. *Racing the Enemy: Stalin, Truman, and the Surrender of Japan*, Cambridge, MA: Harvard University Press, 2005.
Gregg Herken. *Brotherhood of the Bomb: The Tangled Lives and Loyalties of Robert Oppenheimer, Ernest Lawrence, and Edward Teller*, New York: Henry Hold & Co., 2002.

Seymour Hersh. *Kissinger in the Nixon White House*. New York: Summit Books, 1983.
Seymour Hersh. *The Sampson Option: Israel's Nuclear Arsenal and American Foreign Policy*, New York: Random House, 1991.
Seymour Hersh. *The Dark Side of Camelot*. New York: Little, Brown, 1997.
Dilip Hiro. *Iran under the Ayatollahs*. London: Routledge & Kegan Paul, 1985.
David Holloway. *Stalin & the Bomb: The Soviet Union and Atomic Energy 1939–1956*, New Haven, CT: Yale University Press, 1994.
Kate Hudson. *CND—Now More Than Ever: The Story of a Peace Movement*, London: Vision Paperbacks, 2005.
Nguyen Tien Hung and Jerrold L. Schecter. *The Palace File*, New York: Harper & Row, 1978.
Saburo Ienaga. *The Pacific War 1931–1945*, New York: Pantheon Books, 1978.
Independent Commission on Disarmament and Security Issues. *Common Security: A Blueprint for Survival*, New York: Simon & Schuster, 1982.
Chalmers Johnson. *The Sorrows of Empire: Militarism, Secrecy and the End of the Republic*. New York: Metropolitan Books, 2004.
Paul Joseph. *Cracks in the Empire: State Politics in the Vietnam War*, New York: Columbia University Press, 1987.
Robert Kagan. *Of Paradise and Power: America and Europe in the New World Order*, New York: Alfred A. Knopf, 2003.
Herman Kahn. *Thinking about the Unthinkable*, New York: Avon Library Books, 1962.
Michio Kaku and Daniel Axelrod. *To Win a Nuclear War: The Pentagon's Secret War Plans*, Boston, MA: South End Press, 1987.
Paul Kennedy. *The Rise and Fall of the Great Powers: Economic Change and Military Conflict from 1500 to 2000*, New York: Random House, 1987.
Robert F. Kennedy. *Thirteen Days: A Memoir of the Cuban Missile Crisis*, New York: W. W. Norton, 1969.
Rashid Khalidi. *Resurrecting Empire: Western Footprints and America's Perilous Path in the Middle East*, Boston, MA: Beacon Press, 2005.
Stephen Kinzer. *All the Shah's Men: An American Coup and the Roots of Middle East Terror*, Hoboken, NJ: John Wiley & Sons, 2003.
Henry A. Kissinger. *Nuclear Weapons and Foreign Policy*, New York: Doubleday Anchor Books, 1958.
Robert Lacey. *The Kingdom: Arabia & The House of Sa'ud*, New York: Harcourt Brace Jovanovich, 1981.
Walter LaFeber. *The Clash: U.S.–Japanese Relations throughout History*, New York: W. W. Norton, 1997.
Lansing Lamont. *Day of Trinity*, New York: Athenaeum, 1985.
Robert Jay Lifton. *Death in Life: Survivors of Hiroshima*, New York: Random House, 1967.
Robert S. McNamara. *Blundering into Disaster: Surviving the First Century of the Nuclear Age*, New York: Pantheon Books, 1986.
George McTurnan Kahin and John W. Lewis, *The United States in Vietnam*, New York: Delta Books, 1967.
James Mann. *About Face: A History of America's Curious Relationship with China from Nixon to Clinton*, New York: Alfred A. Knopf, 1999.
James Mann. *Rise of the Vulcans: The History of Bush's War Cabinet*, New York: Viking, 2004.
Ernest R. May and Philip D. Zelikow, eds. *The Kennedy Tapes: Inside the White House During the Cuban Missile Crisis*, Cambridge, MA: Harvard University Press, 1997.
Walter Russell Mead. *Mortal Splendor: American Empire in Transition*, Boston, MA: Houghton, Mifflin, 1987.

Lewis Mumford. *The Myth of the Machine: The Pentagon of Power*, New York: Harcourt, Brace, Jovanovich, 1964.

Lewis Mumford. *The Myth of the Machine: Technics and Human Development*, New York: Harcourt, Brace Jovanovich, 1966.

Andrew J. Nathan and Robert S. Ross. *The Great Wall and the Empty Fortress: China's Search for Security*, New York: W. W. Norton, 1997.

National Security Strategy of the United States of America, Washington, DC: The White House, September 20, 2002.

National Security Strategy of the United States of America, Washington, DC: The White House, March 2006.

Donald Neff. *Warriors at Suez: Eisenhower Takes America into the Middle East*, New York: The Linden Press, 1981.

Donald Neff. *Warriors for Jerusalem: The Six Days that Changed the Middle East*, New York: The Linden Press, 1984.

Reinhold Niebuhr. *Moral Man and Immoral Society*, New York: Charles Scribners Sons, 1932.

Don Oberdorfer. *The Two Koreas: A Contemporary History*, Reading, MA: Addison-Wesley, 1998.

Kenzaburo Oe. *Hiroshima Notes*, Tokyo: YMCA Press, 1981.

Michael B. Oren. *Six Days of War: June 1967 and the Making of the Modern Middle East*, New York: Ballantine Books, 2002.

Michael A. Palmer. *Guardians of the Gulf: A History of America's Expanding Role in the Persian Gulf, 1833–1992*, New York: The Free Press, 1992.

Han S. Park. *North Korea: The Politics of Unconventional Wisdom*, Boulder, CO: Lynne Rienner, 2002.

Chris Patten. *Not Quite the Diplomat: Home Truths about World Affairs*, London: Penguin Books, 2005.

Kevin Phillips. *American Dynasty: Aristocracy, Fortune, and the Politics of Deceit in the House of Bush*, New York: Viking, 2004.

William R. Polk. *The United States and the Arab World,* Cambridge, MA: Harvard University Press, 1975.

Gareth Porter. *Perils of Dominance: Imbalance of Power and the Road to War in Vietnam*, Berkeley: University of California Press, 2005.

Thomas Powers. *Heisenberg's War: The Secret History of the German Bomb*, New York: Alfred A. Knopf, 1993.

John Prados. *Hoodwinked: The Documents That Reveal How Bush Sold Us a War*, New York: The New Press, 2004.

Martin S. Quigley. *Peace without Hiroshima: Secret Action at the Vatican in the Spring of 1945*, New York: Madison Books, 1991.

Barbara Reynolds. *The Phoenix and the Dove*, Nagasaki: Nagasaki Appeal Committee, undated.

Richard Rhodes. *Dark Sun: The Making of the Hydrogen Bomb*, New York: Simon & Schuster, 1995.

James Risen. *State of War: The Secret History of the CIA and the Bush Administration*, New York: The Free Press, 2006.

Joseph Rotblat, Jack Steinberger, and Bhalchandra Udgaonkar, eds. *A Nuclear-Weapon Free World: Desirable? Feasible?*, Boulder, CO: Westview Press, 1993.

Murray A. Rubinstein, ed. *Taiwan: A New History*, Armonk, NY: M. E. Sharpe, 1999.

Greg Ruggerio and Stuart Sahulka, eds. *Critical Mass: Voices for a Nuclear-Free Future*, Westfield, NJ: Open Media and Campaign for Peace and Democracy, 1996.

Harrison E. Salisbury. *War Between Russia and China*, New York: Bantam Books, 1970.

Michael Schaller. *The United States and China in the Twentieth Century*, New York: Oxford University Press, 1979.

Jonathan Schell. *The Fate of the Earth*, New York: Alfred A. Knopf, 1982.

Jonathan Schell. *The Gift of Time: The Case for Abolishing Nuclear Weapons Now*, New York: Metropolitan Books, 1998.

Andrew Scobell. *China's Use of Military Force: Beyond the Great Wall and the Long March*, New York: Cambridge University Press, 2003.

Deborah Shapley. *Promise and Power: The Life and Times of Robert McNamara*. Boston: Little, Brown, 1993.

Neil Sheehan, Hedrick Smith, E. W. Kenworthy, and Fox Butterfield. *The Pentagon Papers, The New York Times*, New York: Bantam Books, 1971.

Martin J. Sherwin. *A World Destroyed: The Atomic Bomb and the Grand Alliance*, New York: Vintage Books, 1977.

Avi Shlaim. *War and Peace in the Middle East: A Critique of American Policy*, New York: Viking, 1994.

Leon V. Sigal. *Disarming Strategies: Nuclear Diplomacy with North Korea*, Princeton, NJ: Princeton University Press, 1998.

Holly Sklar, ed. *Trilateralism: The Trilateral Commission and Elite Planning for World Management*, Boston, MA: South End Press, 1980.

Frank Snepp. *Decent Interval: An Insider's Account of Saigon's Indecent End Told by the CIA's Chief Strategy Analyst in Vietnam*, New York: Vintage Books, 1978.

Scott Snyder. *Negotiating on the Edge: North Korean Negotiating Behavior*, Washington, DC: United States Institute of Peace Press, 1999.

Ralph Stavins, Richard J. Barnet, and Marcus G. Raskin. *Washington Plans an Aggressive War*, New York: Vintage Books, 1967.

Joe Stork. *Middle East Oil and the Energy Crisis*, New York: Monthly Review Press, 1975.

John M. Swomley, Jr. *American Empire: The Political Ethics of Twentieth-Century Conquest*, New York: Macmillan, 1970.

Strobe Talbott. *Deadly Gambits: The Reagan Administration and the Stalemate in Nuclear Arms Control*, New York: Alfred A. Knopf, 1984.

Strobe Talbott. *The Russia Hand: A Memoir of Presidential Diplomacy*, New York: Random House, 2002.

Truong Nhu Tang. *A Viet Cong Memoir*, New York: Vintage Books, 1985.

E. P. Thompson and Dan Smith, eds. *Protest and Survive*, New York: Monthly Review Press, 1981.

Lester Thurow. *HEAD to HEAD: The Coming Economic Battle Among Japan, Europe, and America*, New York: William Morrow & Co., 1992.

Harry S. Truman. *Year of Decisions*. Garden City, NY: Doubleday, 1955.

Harry S. Truman. *Years of Trial and Hope: 1946–1952*, Garden City, NY: Doubleday 1956.

Patrick Tyler. *A Great Wall: Six Presidents and China*, New York: A Century Foundation Book, 1999.

Arthur Waley. *The Opium War through Chinese Eyes*, Stanford, CA: Stanford University Press, 1958.

Weapons of Mass Destruction Commission. *Weapons of Terror: Freeing the World of Nuclear, Biological and Chemical Arms*, Stockholm, 2006.

C. G. Weeramantry. *Nuclear Weapons and Scientific Responsibility*, Wolfboro, NH: Longwood Academic, 1977.

Weeramantry International Center for Peace Education and Research. *Illegality of Nuclear Weapons, Proceedings of a Seminar held on 24th October, 2003*, Colombo, Sri Lanka, 2003.

Craig R. Whitney. *The WMD Mirage: Iraq's Decade of Deception and America's False Premises for War*, New York: Public Affairs, 2005.

Lawrence S. Wittner. *Resisting the Bomb: A History of the World Nuclear Disarmament Movement 1954–1970*, Stanford, CA: Stanford University Press, 1977.

Lawrence S. Wittner. *One World or None: A History of the World Nuclear Disarmament Movement through 1953*, Stanford, CA: Stanford University Press, 1993.

Lawrence S. Wittner. *Toward Nuclear Abolition: A History of the World Nuclear Disarmament Movement 1971 to the Present*. Stanford, CA: Stanford University Press, 2003.

William Appleman Williams. *The Tragedy of American Diplomacy*. New York: Dell, 1962.

William Appleman Williams, ed. *From Colony to Empire: Essays in the History of American Foreign Relation*s, New York: John Wiley & Sons, 1972.

William Appleman Williams. *Empire as a Way of Life: An Essay on the Causes and Character of America's Present Predicament along with a Few Thoughts about an Alternative*, New York: Oxford University Press, 1980.

Bob Woodward. *Bush at War*, New York: Simon & Schuster, 2002.

Bob Woodward. *Plan of Attack*, New York: Simon & Schuster, 2004.

World Conference against Atomic and Hydrogen Bombs, transcripts, 1983–2005, Japan Council against Atomic and Hydrogen Bombs (*Gensuikyo*), Tokyo.

Senji Yamaguchi. *Burnt Yet Undaunted: Verbatim Account of Senji Yamaguchi*, Tokyo: Japan Confederation of A- & H- Bomb Sufferers' Organizations (*Hidankyo*), 2002.

Daniel Yergin. *Shattered Peace: The Origins of the Cold War and the National Security State*, Boston, MA: Houghton Mifflin, 1978.

Daniel Yergin. *The Prize: The Epic Quest for Oil, Money & Power*, New York; Simon & Schuster, 1991.

Herbert York. *Making Weapons, Talking Peace: A Physicist's Odyssey from Hiroshima to Geneva*, New York: Basic Books, 1987.

Oka Yoshitake. *Konoe Fumimaro: A Political Biography*, New York: Madison Books, 1992.

Suisheng Zhao, ed. *Across the Taiwan Strait: Mainland China, Taiwan, and the 1995–1996 Crisis*, New York: Routledge, 1999.

Index

Compiled by Susan Tricklebank